MANAGEMENT

Third Edition

Editor

Dr. Fred H. Maidment
Kean College of New Jersey

Dr. Fred Maidment is associate professor of management at
Kean College of New Jersey. He received his bachelor's
degree from New York University in 1970 and his master's
degree from Bernard M. Baruch College of the City
University of New York. In 1983 he received his doctorate
from the University of South Carolina. His research
concerns training and development in industry. He resides in
Lebanon, Pennsylvania, with his wife and four children.

A Library of Information from the Public Press

The Dushkin Publishing Group, Inc.
Sluice Dock, Guilford, Connecticut 06437

Cover illustration by Mike Eagle

The Annual Editions Series

Annual Editions is a series of over 60 volumes designed to provide the reader with convenient, low-cost access to a wide range of current, carefully selected articles from some of the most important magazines, newspapers, and journals published today. Annual Editions are updated on an annual basis through a continuous monitoring of over 300 periodical sources. All Annual Editions have a number of features designed to make them particularly useful, including topic guides, annotated tables of contents, unit overviews, and indexes. For the teacher using Annual Editions in the classroom, an Instructor's Resource Guide with test questions is available for each volume.

VOLUMES AVAILABLE

Africa
Aging
American Foreign Policy
American Government
American History, Pre-Civil War
American History, Post-Civil War
Anthropology
Biology
Business Ethics
Canadian Politics
Child Growth and Development
China
Comparative Politics
Computers in Education
Computers in Business
Computers in Society
Criminal Justice
Drugs, Society, and Behavior
Dying, Death, and Bereavement
Early Childhood Education
Economics
Educating Exceptional Children
Education
Educational Psychology
Environment
Geography
Global Issues
Health
Human Development
Human Resources
Human Sexuality
India and South Asia
International Business
Japan and the Pacific Rim

Latin America
Life Management
Macroeconomics
Management
Marketing
Marriage and Family
Mass Media
Microeconomics
Middle East and the Islamic World
Money and Banking
Multicultural Education
Nutrition
Personal Growth and Behavior
Physical Anthropology
Psychology
Public Administration
Race and Ethnic Relations
Russia, Eurasia, and Central/Eastern Europe
Social Problems
Sociology
State and Local Government
Third World
Urban Society
Violence and Terrorism
Western Civilization, Pre-Reformation
Western Civilization, Post-Reformation
Western Europe
World History, Pre-Modern
World History, Modern
World Politics

Library of Congress Cataloging in Publication Data
Main entry under title: Annual Editions: Management. 3/E.
    1. Management—Periodicals. I. Maidment, Fred, comp. II. Title: Management.
ISBN 1–56134–281–5   658'.05

Third Edition

Manufactured by The Banta Company, Harrisonburg, Virginia 22801

Printed on Recycled Paper

To the Reader

In publishing ANNUAL EDITIONS we recognize the enormous role played by the magazines, newspapers, and journals of the *public press* in providing current, first-rate educational information in a broad spectrum of interest areas. Within the articles, the best scientists, practitioners, researchers, and commentators draw issues into new perspective as accepted theories and viewpoints are called into account by new events, recent discoveries change old facts, and fresh debate breaks out over important controversies.

Many of the articles resulting from this enormous editorial effort are appropriate for students, researchers, and professionals seeking accurate, current material to help bridge the gap between principles and theories and the real world. These articles, however, become more useful for study when those of lasting value are carefully *collected, organized, indexed,* and *reproduced* in a *low-cost format,* which provides easy and permanent access when the material is needed. That is the role played by *Annual Editions.* Under the direction of each volume's *Editor,* who is an expert in the subject area, and with the guidance of an *Advisory Board,* we seek each year to provide in each ANNUAL EDITION a current, well-balanced, carefully selected collection of the best of the public press for your study and enjoyment. We think you'll find this volume useful, and we hope you'll take a moment to let us know what you think.

Management is evolving into a highly exciting and diverse profession. Managers are the people charged with getting things done in today's society—a society that has been molded by the success of the management profession. The world faces many new challenges, and those challenges will be met, at least in part, by managers.

Managers must respond to a changing society by keeping informed on the developments in the field. The articles that have been chosen for the third edition of *Annual Editions: Management* comprise a cross-section of the current, and a selected few classic, articles on the subject. This collection addresses the various components of management, with emphasis on the functions of planning, organizing, directing, controlling, and staffing. Articles have been chosen from a wide variety of publications, including *The Harvard Business Review, The Executive,* and *Business Week.*

This publication contains a number of features designed to make it useful for people interested in management. These include a *topic guide* for locating articles on specific subjects, a *table of contents* with abstracts that summarize each article with key ideas in bold italics. This volume is organized into seven units, each dealing with specific interrelated topics in management. Each section begins with an overview that provides the necessary background information, allowing the reader to place the selections in the context of the book. Important topics are emphasized, and challenge questions address major themes. Also, at the end of each section are short classic cases and exercises that are designed to easily and effectively implement and expand on the general topic of the section.

This is the third edition of *Annual Editions: Management,* and I hope that it will be one of a long line of books addressing the evolution of management. This collection, I believe, provides the reader with the most complete and current selection of readings available on the subject. We would like to know what you think. Please take a few minutes to complete the article rating form in the back of the volume. Anything can be improved, and we need your help to improve *Annual Editions: Management.*

Fred Maidment

Fred Maidment
Editor

Contents

Unit 1

Managers, Performance, and the Environment

The seven articles in this section examine some of the dynamics of management in today's business environment.

The concepts in bold italics are developed in the article. For further expansion please refer to the Topic Guide and the Index.

Planning

The five articles in this section discuss the elements of planning, decision making, support systems, and strategic analysis.

Organizing

The five selections in this section examine how organization impacts on the job of managing. Topics discussed include elements of organization, job design, and what is needed to fundamentally change a business.

Unit 4

Directing

The five selections in this section examine how the elements of communication, leadership, motivation, and performance contribute to the art of directing a business organization.

Controlling

The five articles in this section consider what makes up effective control of the business organization.

Unit 6

Staffing and Human Resources

The five selections in this section examine the elements necessarily considered when a workforce is developed.

The concepts in bold italics are developed in the article. For further expansion please refer to the Topic Guide and the Index.

Unit 7

Perspectives and Trends

The eight articles in this section examine some of the current and future challenges faced by business. Topics include the multinational enterprise, small business management, social responsibility, and the future of a career in management.

The concepts in bold italics are developed in the article. For further expansion please refer to the Topic Guide and the Index.

Topic Guide

This topic guide suggests how the selections in this book relate to topics of traditional concern to students and professionals involved with the study of management. It is useful for locating articles that relate to each other for reading and research. The guide is arranged alphabetically according to topic. Articles may, of course, treat topics that do not appear in the topic guide. In turn, entries in the topic guide do not necessarily constitute a comprehensive listing of all the contents of each selection.

TOPIC AREA	TREATED IN:	TOPIC AREA	TREATED IN:
Business Ethics	3. How to Spot Unsuccessful Executives 4. Managing in the Midst of Chaos 6. Business in the 21st Century 12. How Corporate Culture Drives Strategy 13. Coming of the New Organization 19. 21st Century Communication Tool 23. Criteria of Organizational Effectiveness 24. Principles of the New or Prospective Front-Line Supervisor 29. Rethinking Diversity 30. Plight of the Seasoned Worker 32. Leasing Workers 33. Social Responsibility in Future Worlds 36. Human Rights 37. How I Made—and Agonized Over—My Choices at NBC 39. White Collar Wasteland 40. Corporate Image, Recruitment Image	**Corporate Strategy/ Organization**	2. Management's New Gurus 4. Managing in the Midst of Chaos 5. Can You Manage in the New Economy? 6. Business in the 21st Century 7. How We Will Work in the Year 2000 9. Implement Entrepreneurial Thinking 10. Bible for Benchmarking 11. Planning Deming Management 12. How Corporate Culture Drives Strategy 13. Coming of the New Organization 14. Can GM Remodel Itself? 17. Decisive Response to Crisis 20. Developing Effective Leadership 22. Incentive Plan Pushes Production 23. Criteria of Organizational Effectiveness 26. Competing with Crayolas® 27. Keys to Starting a TQM Program 29. Rethinking Diversity 32. Leasing Workers 35. Entrepreneurial Start-Up and Growth 36. Human Rights 38. Organizing the Voluntary Association
Communication	1. Manager's Job 2. Management's New Gurus 4. Managing in the Midst of Chaos 7. How We Will Work in the Year 2000 8. New Look at Managerial Decision Making 9. Implement Entrepreneurial Thinking 11. Planning Deming Management 12. How Corporate Culture Drives Strategy 13. Coming of the New Organization 14. Can GM Remodel Itself? 17. Decisive Response to Crisis 19. 21st Century Communication Tool 20. Developing Effective Leadership 21. What Do Workers Want? 24. Principles for the New or Prospective Front-Line Supervisor 26. Competing with Crayolas® 27. Keys to Starting a TQM Program 31. Future of Labor-Management Relations 40. Corporate Image, Recruitment Image	**Decision Making**	1. Manager's Job 3. How to Spot Unsuccessful Executives 4. Managing in the Midst of Chaos 5. Can You Manage in the New Economy? 7. How We Will Work in the Year 2000 8. New Look at Managerial Decision Making 10. Bible for Benchmarking 11. Planning Deming Management 13. Coming of the New Organization 17. Decisive Response to Crisis 37. How I Made—and Agonized Over—My Choices at NBC 40. Corporate Image, Recruitment Image
Corporate Credibility	4. Managing in the Midst of Chaos 6. Business in the 21st Century 11. Planning Deming Management 12. How Corporate Culture Drives Strategy 13. Coming of the New Organization 14. Can GM Remodel Itself? 17. Decisive Response to Crisis 19. 21st Century Communication Tool 20. Developing Effective Leadership 21. What Do Workers Want? 22. Incentive Plan Pushes Production 23. Criteria of Organizational Effectiveness 24. Principles for the New or Prospective Front-Line Supervisor 27. Keys to Starting a TQM Program 29. Rethinking Diversity 30. Plight of the Seasoned Worker 31. Future of Labor-Management Relations 33. Social Responsibility in Future Worlds 36. Human Rights 37. How I Made—and Agonized Over—My Choices at NBC 39. White Collar Wasteland 40. Corporate Image, Recruitment Image	**Employee Benefits**	15. High Skills under the Hood 16. Golden Employees 22. Incentive Plan Pushes Production 29. Rethinking Diversity 30. Plight of the Seasoned Worker 32. Leasing Workers
		Financing	25. Trick to Managing Cash? 32. Leasing Workers 35. Entrepreneurial Start-Up and Growth
		Human Resources	13. Coming of the New Organization 15. High Skills under the Hood 16. Golden Employees 28. Human Side of Enterprise 29. Rethinking Diversity 30. Plight of the Seasoned Worker 31. Future of Labor-Management Relations 32. Leasing Workers 39. White Collar Wasteland 40. Corporate Image, Recruitment Image
		International Trade	5. Can You Manage in the New Economy? 6. Business in the 21st Century

TOPIC AREA	TREATED IN:	TOPIC AREA	TREATED IN:
International Trade (cont'd)	14. Can GM Remodel Itself? 17. Decisive Response to Crisis 36. Human Rights	**Motivation (cont'd)**	20. Developing Effective Leadership 21. What Do Workers Want? 22. Incentive Plan Pushes Production 27. Keys to Starting a TQM Program 28. Human Side of Enterprise 29. Rethinking Diversity 30. Plight of the Seasoned Worker 38. Organizing the Voluntary Association 40. Corporate Image, Recruitment Image
Labor Relations	11. Planning Deming Management 12. How Corporate Culture Drives Strategy 14. Can GM Remodel Itself? 15. High Skills under the Hood 16. Golden Employees 17. Decisive Response to Crisis 21. What Do Workers Want? 22. Incentive Plan Pushes Production 24. Principles for the New or Prospective Front-Line Supervisor 26. Competing with Crayolas® 29. Rethinking Diversity 30. Plight of the Seasoned Worker 31. The Future of Labor-Management Relations 32. Leasing Workers 39. White Collar Wasteland 40. Corporate Image, Recruitment Image	**Not-for-Profit Organizations**	6. Business in the 21st Century 11. Planning Deming Management 20. Developing Effective Leadership 33. Social Responsibility in Future Worlds 38. Organizing the Voluntary Association
		Organized Labor	13. Coming of the New Organization 14. Can GM Remodel Itself? 15. High Skills under the Hood 17. Decisive Response to Crisis 24. Principles for the New or Prospective Front-Line Supervisor 29. Rethinking Diversity 31. Future of Labor-Management Relations 32. Leasing Workers
Management Accountability	1. Manager's Job 3. How to Spot Unsuccessful Executives 5. Can You Manage in the New Economy? 10. Bible for Benchmarking 11. Planning Deming Management 13. Coming of the New Organization 14. Can GM Remodel Itself? 17. Decisive Response to Crisis 20. Developing Effective Leadership 23. Criteria of Organizational Effectiveness 24. Principles for the New or Prospective Front-Line Supervisor 27. Keys to Starting a TQM Program 29. Rethinking Diversity 33. Social Responsibility in Future Worlds 36. Human Rights 37. How I Made—and Agonized Over—My Choices at NBC	**Organizing**	1. Manager's Job 4. Managing in the Midst of Chaos 7. How We Will Work in the Year 2000 11. Planning Deming Management 12. How Corporate Culture Drives Strategy 13. Coming of the New Organization 14. Can GM Remodel Itself? 17. Decisive Response to Crisis 22. Incentive Plan Pushes Production 26. Competing with Crayolas® 27. Keys to Starting a TQM Program 32. Leasing Workers 38. Organizing the Voluntary Association
Managers/ Management	1. Manager's Job 2. Management's New Gurus 3. How to Spot Unsuccessful Executives 4. Managing in the Midst of Chaos 5. Can You Manage in the New Economy? 8. New Look at Managerial Decision Making 9. Implement Entrepreneurial Thinking 11. Planning Deming Management 13. Coming of the New Organization 20. Developing Effective Leadership 24. Principles for the New or Prospective Front-Line Supervisor 37. How I Made—and Agonized Over—My Choices at NBC 39. White Collar Wasteland	**Productivity/ Performance**	3. How to Spot Unsuccessful Executives 9. Implement Entrepreneurial Thinking 10. Bible for Benchmarking 11. Planning Deming Management 14. Can GM Remodel Itself? 15. High Skills under the Hood 16. Golden Employees 17. Decisive Response to Crisis 18. Theory of Human Motivation 21. What Do Workers Want? 22. Incentive Plan Pushes Production 26. Competing with Crayolas® 27. Keys to Starting a TQM Program 28. Human Side of Enterprise 30. Plight of the Seasoned Worker 32. Leasing Workers
		Shareholders	14. Can GM Remodel Itself? 36. Human Rights
		Small Business	9. Implement Entrepreneurial Thinking 16. Golden Employees 32. Leasing Workers 35. Entrepreneurial Start-Up and Growth 38. Organizing the Voluntary Association
Motivation	1. Manager's Job 8. New Look at Managerial Decision Making 9. Implement Entrepreneurial Thinking 10. Bible for Benchmarking 11. Planning Deming Management 12. How Corporate Culture Drives Strategy 16. Golden Employees 17. Decisive Response to Crisis 18. Theory of Human Motivation	**World Economy**	5. Can You Manage in the New Economy? 6. Business in the 21st Century 14. Can GM Remodel Itself? 36. Human Rights

Managers, Performance, and the Environment

- **Management Classic (Article 1)**
- **Managers and Management (Articles 2–3)**
- **Management: Skills, Roles, and Performance (Articles 4 and 5)**
- **The Environment (Articles 6 and 7)**
- **Case I: Robin Hood**
- **Exercise I: Managerial Development**

The need for management has been recognized since the early days of civilization. The concepts of leadership, administration, and management have existed since at least before the time of Plato. Some of the early modern writers in management included Frederick W. Taylor, Elton Mayo, and Mary Parker Follett. These people helped to establish the basis of modern management theory during the first part of the twentieth century.

Management has come a long way since the days of Taylor, Mayo, and Follett. The techniques and theories that they and their successors helped to develop have contributed to the establishment of industrialized countries as major forces in the world. These ideas have helped American culture dominate the better part of this century, and the success of Western concepts is even now being seen in Eastern Europe and the republics of the former Soviet Union. Management—the way people arrange their lives and businesses—is a major part of the success that capitalism is currently enjoying. The failure that the communist system experienced in the former Soviet bloc was not a failure of industrialism; rather, it was a failure of a system that attempted to use that industrial base unsuccessfully. This was not a failure of the machines or the workers that comprised the system, but of the way the system operated and managed its equipment and people. It was a situation that the people of those countries would no longer tolerate as they rushed to embrace capitalism, democracy, pluralism, and, finally, management as a key to their future in the twenty-first century.

As a discipline, management faces new challenges. These challenges are mostly the result of management's success. They include the transformation of the American economy from one based upon industrialization to one based upon knowledge, and the challenge of other economies, in particular the Japanese and the other "tigers" of the Pacific Rim, as well as the new integrated Europe. Another challenge is the new role of managers and management, with more women, African Americans, and other minorities, as well as a more demanding group of workers with different expectations, entering the workforce.

Management is responding to these challenges in various ways. Many new ideas are constantly being projected in the midst of the chaos that is the legacy of the post–cold war world. Times have, indeed, changed, and the tools necessary to meet those changes are only now being developed, as may be seen in the articles "Managing in the Midst of Chaos" and "Management's New Gurus."

The new economy and the firms it will support will be very different from the environment of the past. The dominating strength of corporations will be based upon brains, not brawn; the economic system will be international, not national, in scope; and competition will be even more fierce, while an organization's competitive advantages in the marketplace will be more fleeting. This is a result of the dependance upon ideas and creativity that is necessary to build and sustain organizations. Future organizations that think, create, and adapt to the changing conditions of an increasingly fluid environment are the ones that will survive and be successful, as "Business in the 21st Century" points out.

America's new economy, and the managers who plan, direct, organize, control, and staff its businesses, must provide new, different, and creative approaches to meet the new, competitive, global environment. This will require better products and services, produced and marketed with improved, more efficient methods. Organizations no longer compete only domestically, as they did in the 1950s, when General Motors, Ford, and Chrysler dominated an American auto industry that included such names as Studebaker, Packard, Hudson, DeSoto, and Nash. Today, these firms compete on an international basis with names like Nissan, Toyota, Honda, Volkswagen, and B.M.W. Corporations the world over must meet these new conditions or accept the fate of past organizations and follow Studebaker in its drive to oblivion.

Looking Ahead: Challenge Questions

Management, as a discipline, has evolved significantly during the twentieth century. What do you think will happen in the future?

Managers are learning that different situations require different skills and different approaches. How do you think this will change the job of manager in the future?

Managers cannot change the external environment in which they must operate. In what ways do you think this environment will change during your life?

The Manager's Job:
Folklore and Fact

———

The classical view says that the manager organizes, coordinates, plans, and controls; the facts suggest otherwise.

Henry Mintzberg

Henry Mintzberg is the Bronfman Professor of Management at McGill University. His latest book is Mintzberg on Management: Inside Our Strange World of Organizations *(Free Press, 1989). This article appeared originally in HBR July-August 1975. It won the McKinsey Award for excellence.*

If you ask managers what they do, they will most likely tell you that they plan, organize, coordinate, and control. Then watch what they do. Don't be surprised if you can't relate what you see to these words.

When a manager is told that a factory has just burned down and then advises the caller to see whether temporary arrangements can be made to supply customers through a foreign subsidiary, is that manager planning, organizing, coordinating, or controlling? How about when he or she presents a gold watch to a retiring employee? Or attends a conference to meet people in the trade and returns with an interesting new product idea for employees to consider?

These four words, which have dominated management vocabulary since the French industrialist Henri Fayol first introduced them in 1916, tell us little about what managers actually do. At best, they indicate some vague objectives managers have when they work.

The field of management, so devoted to progress and change, has for more than half a century not seriously addressed *the* basic question: What do managers do? Without a proper answer, how can we teach management? How can we design planning or information systems for managers? How can we improve the practice of management at all?

What do managers do? Even managers themselves don't always know.

Our ignorance of the nature of managerial work shows up in various ways in the modern organization—in boasts by successful managers who never spent a single day in a management training program; in the turnover of corporate planners who never quite understood what it was the manager wanted; in the computer consoles gathering dust in the back room because the managers never used the fancy on-line MIS some analyst thought they needed. Perhaps most important, our ignorance shows up in the inability of our large public organizations to come to grips with some of their most serious policy problems.

Somehow, in the rush to automate production, to use management science in the functional areas of marketing and finance, and to apply the skills of the behavioral scientist to the problem of worker motivation, the manager–the person in charge of the organization or one of its subunits–has been forgotten.

I intend to break the reader away from Fayol's words and introduce a more supportable and useful description of managerial work. This description derives from my review and synthesis of research on how various managers have spent their time.

In some studies, managers were observed intensively; in a number of others, they kept detailed diaries; in a few studies, their records were analyzed. All kinds of managers were studied–foremen, factory supervisors, staff managers, field sales managers, hospital administrators, presidents of companies and nations, and even street gang leaders. These "managers" worked in the United States, Canada, Sweden, and Great Britain.

A synthesis of these findings paints an interesting picture, one as different from Fayol's classical view as a cubist abstract is from a Renaissance painting. In a sense, this picture will be obvious to anyone who has ever spent a day in a manager's office, either in front of the desk or behind it. Yet, at the same time, this picture throws into doubt much of the folklore that we have accepted about the manager's work.

Folklore and Facts About Managerial Work

There are four myths about the manager's job that do not bear up under careful scrutiny of the facts.

Folklore: The manager is a reflective, systematic planner. The evidence on this issue is overwhelming, but not a shred of it supports this statement.

Fact: Study after study has shown that managers work at an unrelenting pace, that their activities are characterized by brevity, variety, and discontinuity, and that they are strongly oriented to action and dislike reflective activities. Consider this evidence:

Half the activities engaged in by the five chief executives of my study lasted less than nine minutes, and only 10% exceeded one hour.[1] A study of 56 U.S. foremen found that they averaged 583 activities per eight-hour shift, an average of 1 every 48 seconds.[2]

How often can you work for a half an hour without interruption?

The work pace for both chief executives and foremen was unrelenting. The chief executives met a steady stream of callers and mail from the moment they arrived in the morning until they left in the evening. Coffee breaks and lunches were inevitably work re-

lated, and ever-present subordinates seemed to usurp any free moment.

A diary study of 160 British middle and top managers found that they worked without interruption for a half hour or more only about once every two days.[3]

Of the verbal contacts the chief executives in my study engaged in, 93% were arranged on an ad hoc basis. Only 1% of the executives' time was spent in open-ended observational tours. Only 1 out of 368 verbal contacts was unrelated to a specific issue and could therefore be called general planning. Another researcher found that "in *not one single case* did a manager report obtaining important external information from a general conversation or other undirected personal communication."[4]

Is this the planner that the classical view describes? Hardly. The manager is simply responding to the pressures of the job. I found that my chief executives terminated many of their own activities, often leaving meetings before the end, and interrupted their desk work to call in subordinates. One president not only placed his desk so that he could look down a long hallway but also left his door open when he was alone–an invitation for subordinates to come in and interrupt him.

Clearly, these managers wanted to encourage the flow of current information. But more significantly, they seemed to be conditioned by their own work loads. They appreciated the opportunity cost of their own time, and they were continually aware of their ever-present obligations–mail to be answered, callers to attend to, and so on. It seems that a manager is always plagued by the possibilities of what might be done and what must be done.

When managers must plan, they seem to do so implicitly in the context of daily actions, not in some abstract process reserved for two weeks in the organization's mountain retreat. The plans of the chief executives I studied seemed to exist only in their heads–as flexible, but often specific, intentions. The traditional literature notwithstanding, the job of managing does not breed reflective planners; managers respond to stimuli, they are conditioned by their jobs to prefer live to delayed action.

Folklore: The effective manager has no regular duties to perform. Managers are constantly being told to spend more time planning and delegating and less time seeing customers and engaging in negotiations. These are not, after all, the true tasks of the manager. To use the popular analogy, the good manager, like the good conductor, carefully orchestrates everything in advance, then sits back, responding occasionally to an unforeseeable exception. But here again the pleasant abstraction just does not seem to hold up.

Fact: Managerial work involves performing a number of regular duties, including ritual and cere-

mony, negotiations, and processing of soft information that links the organization with its environment. Consider some evidence from the research:

A study of the work of the presidents of small companies found that they engaged in routine activities because their companies could not afford staff specialists and were so thin on operating personnel that a single absence often required the president to substitute.[5]

One study of field sales managers and another of chief executives suggest that it is a natural part of both jobs to see important customers, assuming the managers wish to keep those customers.[6]

Someone, only half in jest, once described the manager as the person who sees visitors so that other people can get their work done. In my study, I found that certain ceremonial duties – meeting visiting dignitaries, giving out gold watches, presiding at Christmas dinners – were an intrinsic part of the chief executive's job.

Studies of managers' information flow suggest that managers play a key role in securing "soft" external information (much of it available only to them because of their status) and in passing it along to their subordinates.

Folklore: The senior manager needs aggregated information, which a formal management information system best provides. Not too long ago, the words *total information system* were everywhere in the management literature. In keeping with the classical view of the manager as that individual perched on the apex of a regulated, hierarchical system, the literature's manager was to receive all important information from a giant, comprehensive MIS.

But lately, these giant MIS systems are not working – managers are simply not using them. The enthusiasm has waned. A look at how managers actually process information makes it clear why.

Fact: Managers strongly favor verbal media, telephone calls and meetings, over documents. Consider the following:

In two British studies, managers spent an average of 66% and 80% of their time in verbal (oral) commu-

> # Today's gossip may be tomorrow's fact — that's why managers cherish hearsay.

nication.[7] In my study of five American chief executives, the figure was 78%.

These five chief executives treated mail processing as a burden to be dispensed with. One came in Saturday morning to process 142 pieces of mail in just over three hours, to "get rid of all the stuff." This same manager looked at the first piece of "hard" mail he had received all week, a standard cost report, and put it aside with the comment, "I never look at this."

These same five chief executives responded immediately to 2 of the 40 routine reports they received during the five weeks of my study and to 4 items in the 104 periodicals. They skimmed most of these periodicals in seconds, almost ritualistically. In all, these chief executives of good-sized organizations initiated on their own – that is, not in response to something else – a grand total of 25 pieces of mail during the 25 days I observed them.

An analysis of the mail the executives received reveals an interesting picture – only 13% was of specific and immediate use. So now we have another piece in the puzzle: not much of the mail provides live, current information – the action of a competitor, the mood of a government legislator, or the rating of last night's television show. Yet this is the information that drove the managers, interrupting their meetings and rescheduling their workdays.

Consider another interesting finding. Managers seem to cherish "soft" information, especially gossip, hearsay, and speculation. Why? The reason is its timeliness; today's gossip may be tomorrow's fact. The manager who misses the telephone call revealing that the company's biggest customer was seen golfing with a main competitor may read about a dramatic drop in sales in the next quarterly report. But then it's too late.

To assess the value of historical, aggregated, "hard" MIS information, consider two of the manager's prime uses for information – to identify problems and opportunities[8] and to build mental models (e.g., how the organization's budget system works, how customers buy products, how changes in the economy affect the organization). The evidence suggests that the manager identifies decision situations and builds models not with the aggregated abstractions an MIS provides but with specific tidbits of data.

Consider the words of Richard Neustadt, who studied the information-collecting habits of Presidents Roosevelt, Truman, and Eisenhower: "It is not information of a general sort that helps a President see personal stakes; not summaries, not surveys, not the *bland amalgams.* Rather...it is the odds and ends of *tangible detail* that pieced together in his mind illuminate the underside of issues put before him. To help himself he must reach out as widely as he can for every scrap of fact, opinion, gossip, bearing on his interests and relationships as President. He must become his own director of his own central intelligence."[9]

The manager's emphasis on this verbal media raises two important points. First, verbal information is stored in the brains of people. Only when people write this information down can it be stored in the files of the organization – whether in metal cabinets or on magnetic tape – and managers apparently do not write down much of what they hear. Thus the strategic data bank of the organization is not in the memory of its computers but in the minds of its managers.

Second, managers' extensive use of verbal media helps to explain why they are reluctant to delegate tasks. It is not as if they can hand a dossier over to subordinates; they must take the time to "dump memory" – to tell subordinates all about the subject. But this could take so long that managers may find it easier to do the task themselves. Thus they are damned by their own information system to a "dilemma of delegation" – to do too much or to delegate to subordinates with inadequate briefing.

Folklore: Management is, or at least is quickly becoming, a science and a profession. By almost any definition of *science* and *profession*, this statement is false. Brief observation of any manager will quickly lay to rest the notion that managers practice a science. A science involves the enaction of systematic, analytically determined procedures or programs. If we do not even know what procedures managers use, how can we prescribe them by scientific analysis? And how can we call management a profession if we cannot specify what managers are to learn? For after all, a profession involves "knowledge of some department of learning or science" *(Random House Dictionary).*[10]

Fact: The managers' programs – to schedule time, process information, make decisions, and so on – remain locked deep inside their brains. Thus, to describe these programs, we rely on words like *judgment* and *intuition*, seldom stopping to realize that they are merely labels for our ignorance.

I was struck during my study by the fact that the

Research on Managerial Work

In seeking to describe managerial work, I conducted my own research and also scanned the literature to integrate the findings of studies from many diverse sources with my own. These studies focused on two different aspects of managerial work. Some were concerned with the characteristics of work – how long managers work, where, at what pace, with what interruptions, with whom they work, and through what media they communicate. Other studies were concerned with the content of work – what activities the managers actually carry out, and why. Thus, after a meeting, one researcher might note that the manager spent 45 minutes with three government officials in their Washington office, while another might record that the manager presented the company's stand on some proposed legislation in order to change a regulation.

A few of the studies of managerial work are widely known, but most have remained buried as single journal articles or isolated books. Among the more important ones I cite are:

☐ Sune Carlson developed the diary method to study the work characteristics of nine Swedish managing directors. Each kept a detailed log of his activities. Carlson's results are reported in his book *Executive Behaviour.* A number of British researchers, notably Rosemary Stewart, have subsequently used Carlson's method. In *Managers and Their Jobs,* she describes the study of 160 top and middle managers of British companies.

☐ Leonard Sayles's book *Managerial Behavior* is another important reference. Using a method he refers to as "anthropological," Sayles studied the work content of middle and lower level managers in a large U.S. corporation. Sayles moved freely in the company, collecting whatever information struck him as important.

☐ Perhaps the best-known source is *Presidential Power,* in which Richard Neustadt analyzes the power and managerial behavior of Presidents Roosevelt, Truman, and Eisenhower. Neustadt used secondary sources – documents and interviews with other parties.

☐ Robert H. Guest, in *Personnel,* reports on a study of the foreman's working day. Fifty-six U.S. foremen were observed and each of their activities recorded during one eight-hour shift.

☐ Richard C. Hodgson, Daniel J. Levinson, and Abraham Zaleznik studied a team of three top executives of a U.S. hospital. From that study they wrote *The Executive Role Constellation.* They addressed the way in which work and socioemotional roles were divided among the three managers.

☐ William F. Whyte, from his study of a street gang during the Depression, wrote *Street Corner Society.* His findings about the gang's workings and leadership, which George C. Homans analyzed in *The Human Group,* suggest interesting similarities of job content between street gang leaders and corporate managers.

My own study involved five American CEOs of middle- to large-sized organizations – a consulting firm, a technology company, a hospital, a consumer goods company, and a school system. Using a method called "structural observation," during one intensive week of observation for each executive, I recorded various aspects of every piece of mail and every verbal contact. In all, I analyzed 890 pieces of incoming and outgoing mail and 368 verbal contacts.

executives I was observing – all very competent – are fundamentally indistinguishable from their counterparts of a hundred years ago (or a thousand years ago). The information they need differs, but they seek it in the same way – by word of mouth. Their decisions concern modern technology, but the procedures they use to make those decisions are the same as the procedures used by nineteenth century managers. Even the computer, so important for the specialized work of the organization, has apparently had no influence on the work procedures of general managers. In fact, the manager is in a kind of loop, with increasingly heavy work pressures but no aid forthcoming from management science.

Considering the facts about managerial work, we can see that the manager's job is enormously complicated and difficult. Managers are overburdened with obligations yet cannot easily delegate their tasks. As a result, they are driven to overwork and forced to do many tasks superficially. Brevity, fragmentation, and verbal communication characterize their work. Yet these are the very characteristics of managerial work that have impeded scientific attempts to improve it. As a result, management scientists have concentrated on the specialized functions of the organization, where it is easier to analyze the procedures and quantify the relevant information.[11]

But the pressures of a manager's job are becoming worse. Where before managers needed to respond only to owners and directors, now they find that subordinates with democratic norms continually reduce their freedom to issue unexplained orders, and a growing number of outside influences (consumer groups, government agencies, and so on) demand attention. Managers have had nowhere to turn for help. The first step in providing such help is to find out what the manager's job really is.

Back to a Basic Description of Managerial Work

Earlier, I defined the manager as that person in charge of an organization or subunit. Besides CEOs, this definition would include vice presidents, bishops, foremen, hockey coaches, and prime ministers. All these "managers" are vested with formal authority over an organizational unit. From formal authority comes status, which leads to various interpersonal relations, and from these comes access to information. Information, in turn, enables the manager to make decisions and strategies for the unit.

The manager's job can be described in terms of various "roles," or organized sets of behaviors identified with a position. My description, shown in "The Manager's Roles," comprises ten roles. As we shall see, formal authority gives rise to the three interpersonal roles, which in turn give rise to the three informa-

The Manager's Roles

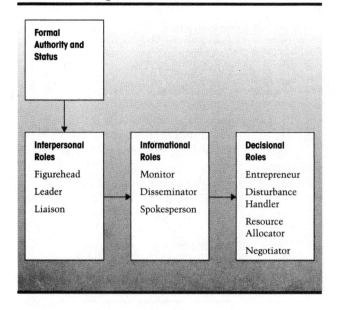

tional roles; these two sets of roles enable the manager to play the four decisional roles.

Interpersonal Roles

Three of the manager's roles arise directly from formal authority and involve basic interpersonal relationships. First is the *figurehead* role. As the head of an organizational unit, every manager must perform some ceremonial duties. The president greets the touring dignitaries. The foreman attends the wedding of a lathe operator. The sales manager takes an important customer to lunch.

The chief executives of my study spent 12% of their contact time on ceremonial duties; 17% of their incoming mail dealt with acknowledgments and requests related to their status. For example, a letter to a company president requested free merchandise for a crippled schoolchild; diplomas that needed to be signed were put on the desk of the school superintendent.

Duties that involve interpersonal roles may sometimes be routine, involving little serious communication and no important decision making. Nevertheless, they are important to the smooth functioning of an organization and cannot be ignored.

Managers are responsible for the work of the people of their unit. Their actions in this regard constitute the *leader* role. Some of these actions involve leadership directly – for example, in most organizations the managers are normally responsible for hiring and training their own staff.

In addition, there is the indirect exercise of the leader role. For example, every manager must moti-

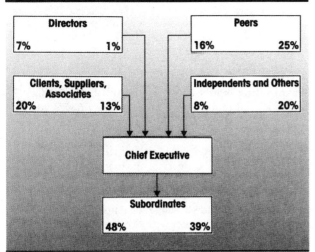

The Chief Executive's Contacts

Directors		Peers	
7%	1%	16%	25%

Clients, Suppliers, Associates		Independents and Others	
20%	13%	8%	20%

Chief Executive

Subordinates

48%	39%

Note: The first figure indicates the proportion of total contact time spent with each group and the second figure, the proportion of mail from each group.

vate and encourage employees, somehow reconciling their individual needs with the goals of the organization. In virtually every contact with the manager, subordinates seeking leadership clues ask: "Does she approve?" "How would she like the report to turn out?" "Is she more interested in market share than high profits?"

The influence of managers is most clearly seen in the leader role. Formal authority vests them with great potential power; leadership determines in large part how much of it they will realize.

The literature of management has always recognized the leader role, particularly those aspects of it related to motivation. In comparison, until recently it has hardly mentioned the *liaison* role, in which the manager makes contacts outside the vertical chain of command. This is remarkable in light of the finding of virtually every study of managerial work that managers spend as much time with peers and other people outside their units as they do with their own subordinates—and, surprisingly, very little time with their own superiors.

In Rosemary Stewart's diary study, the 160 British middle and top managers spent 47% of their time with peers, 41% of their time with people inside their unit, and only 12% of their time with their superiors. For Robert H. Guest's study of U.S. foremen, the figures were 44%, 46%, and 10%. The chief executives of my study averaged 44% of their contact time with people outside their organizations, 48% with subordinates, and 7% with directors and trustees.

The contacts the five CEOs made were with an incredibly wide range of people: subordinates; clients, business associates, and suppliers; and peers—managers of similar organizations, government and

trade organization officials, fellow directors on outside boards, and independents with no relevant organizational affiliations. The chief executives' time with and mail from these groups is shown in "The Chief Executive's Contacts." Guest's study of foremen shows, likewise, that their contacts were numerous and wide-ranging, seldom involving fewer than 25 individuals, and often more than 50.

Informational Roles

By virtue of interpersonal contacts, both with subordinates and with a network of contacts, the manager emerges as the nerve center of the organizational unit. The manager may not know everything but typically knows more than subordinates do.

Studies have shown this relationship to hold for all managers, from street gang leaders to U.S. presidents. In *The Human Group*, George C. Homans explains how, because they were at the center of the information flow in their own gangs and were also in close touch with other gang leaders, street gang leaders were better informed than any of their followers.[12] As for presidents, Richard Neustadt observes: "The essence of [Franklin] Roosevelt's technique for information-gathering was competition. 'He would call you in,' one of his aides once told me, 'and he'd ask you to get the story on some complicated business, and you'd come back after a couple of days of hard labor and present the juicy morsel you'd uncovered under a stone somewhere, and *then* you'd find out he knew all about it, along with something else you *didn't* know. Where he got this information from he wouldn't mention, usually, but after he had done this to you once or twice you got damn careful about *your* information.'"[13]

We can see where Roosevelt "got this information" when we consider the relationship between the interpersonal and informational roles. As leader, the manager has formal and easy access to every staff member. In addition, liaison contacts expose the manager to external information to which subordinates often lack access. Many of these contacts are with other managers of equal status, who are themselves nerve centers in their own organization. In this way, the manager develops a powerful database of information.

Processing information is a key part of the manager's job. In my study, the CEOs spent 40% of their contact time on activities devoted exclusively to the transmission of information; 70% of their incoming mail was purely informational (as opposed to requests for action). Managers don't leave meetings or hang up the telephone to get back to work. In large part, communication *is* their work. Three roles describe these informational aspects of managerial work.

As *monitor*, the manager is perpetually scanning

Retrospective Commentary

Henry Mintzberg

Over the years, one reaction has dominated the comments I have received from managers who read "The Manager's Job: Folklore and Fact": "You make me feel so good. I thought all those other managers were planning, organizing, coordinating, and controlling, while I was busy being interrupted, jumping from one issue to another, and trying to keep the lid on the chaos." Yet everything in this article must have been patently obvious to these people. Why such a reaction to reading what they already knew?

Conversely, how to explain the very different reaction of two media people who called to line up interviews after an article based on this one appeared in the *New York Times.* "Are we glad someone finally let managers have it," both said in passing, a comment that still takes me aback. True, they had read only the account in the *Times,* but that no more let managers have it than did this article. Why that reaction?

One explanation grows out of the way I now see this article—as proposing not so much another view of management as another face of it. I like to call it the insightful face, in contrast to the long-dominant professional or cerebral face. One stresses commitment, the other calculation; one sees the world with integrated perspective, the other figures it as the components of a portfolio. The cerebral face operates with the words and numbers of rationality; the insightful face is rooted in the images and feel of a manager's integrity.

Each of these faces implies a different kind of "knowing," and that, I believe, explains many managers' reaction to this article. Rationally, they "knew" what managers did—planned, organized, coordinated, and controlled. But deep down that did not feel quite right. The description in this article may have come closer to what they really "knew." As for those media people, they weren't railing against management as such but against the cerebral form of management, so pervasive, that they saw impersonalizing the world around them.

In practice, management has to be two-faced—there has to be a balance between the cerebral and the insightful. So, for example, I realized originally that managerial communication was largely oral and that the advent of the computer had not changed anything fundamental in the executive suite—a conclusion I continue to hold. (The greatest threat the personal computer poses is that managers will take it seriously and come to believe that they can manage by remaining in their offices and looking at displays of digital characters.) But I also thought that the dilemma of delegating could be dealt with by periodic debriefings—

disseminating words. Now, however, I believe that managers need more ways to convey the images and impressions they carry inside of them. This explains the renewed interest in strategic vision, in culture, and in the roles of intuition and insight in management.

The ten roles I used to describe the manager's job also reflect management's cerebral face, in that they decompose the job more than capture the integration. Indeed, my effort to show a sequence among these roles now seems more consistent with the traditional face of management work than an insightful one. Might we not just as well say that people throughout the organization take actions that inform managers who, by making sense of those actions, develop images and visions that inspire people to subsequent efforts?

Perhaps my greatest disappointment about the research reported here is that it did not stimulate new efforts. In a world so concerned with management, much of the popular literature is superficial and the academic research pedestrian. Certainly, many studies have been carried out over the last 15 years, but the vast majority sought to replicate earlier research. In particular, we remain grossly ignorant about the fundamental content of the manager's job and have barely addressed the major issues and dilemmas in its practice.

But superficiality is not only a problem of the literature. It is also an occupational hazard of the manager's job. Originally, I believed this problem could be dealt with; now I see it as inherent in the job. This is because managing insightfully depends on the direct experience and personal knowledge that come from intimate contact. But in organizations grown larger and more diversified, that becomes difficult to achieve. And so managers turn increasingly to the cerebral face, and the delicate balance between the two faces is lost.

Certainly, some organizations manage to sustain their humanity despite their large size—as Tom Peters and Robert Waterman show in their book *In Search of Excellence.* But that book attained its outstanding success precisely because it is about the exceptions, about the organizations so many of us long to be a part of—not the organizations in which we actually work.

Fifteen years ago, I stated that "No job is more vital to our society than that of the manager. It is the manager who determines whether our social institutions serve us well or whether they squander our talents and resources." Now, more than ever, we must strip away the folklore of the manager's job and begin to face its difficult facts.

the environment for information, interrogating liaison contacts and subordinates, and receiving unsolicited information, much of it as a result of the network of personal contacts. Remember that a good part of the information the manager collects in the monitor role arrives in verbal form, often as gossip, hearsay, and speculation.

In the *disseminator* role, the manager passes some privileged information directly to subordinates, who would otherwise have no access to it. When subordinates lack easy contact with one another, the manager may pass information from one to another.

In the *spokesperson* role, the manager sends some information to people outside the unit—a president makes a speech to lobby for an organization cause, or a foreman suggests a product modification to a supplier. In addition, as a spokesperson, every manager must inform and satisfy the influential people who control the organizational unit. For the foreman, this may simply involve keeping the plant manager informed about the flow of work through the shop.

The president of a large corporation, however, may spend a great amount of time dealing with a host of influences. Directors and shareholders must be advised about finances; consumer groups must be assured that the organization is fulfilling its social responsibilities; and government officials must be satisfied that the organization is abiding by the law.

Decisional Roles

Information is not, of course, an end in itself; it is the basic input to decision making. One thing is clear in the study of managerial work: the manager plays the major role in the unit's decision-making system. As its formal authority, only the manager can commit the unit to important new courses of action; and as its nerve center, only the manager has full and current information to make the set of decisions that determines the unit's strategy. Four roles describe the manager as decision maker.

As *entrepreneur,* the manager seeks to improve the unit, to adapt it to changing conditions in the environment. In the monitor role, a president is constantly on the lookout for new ideas. When a good one appears, he initiates a development project that he may supervise himself or delegate to an employee (perhaps with the stipulation that he must approve the final proposal).

There are two interesting features about these development projects at the CEO level. First, these projects do not involve single decisions or even unified clusters of decisions. Rather, they emerge as a series of small decisions and actions sequenced over time. Apparently, chief executives prolong each project both to fit it into a busy, disjointed schedule, and so that they can comprehend complex issues gradually.

Second, the chief executives I studied supervised as many as 50 of these projects at the same time. Some projects entailed new products or processes; others involved public relations campaigns, improvement of the cash position, reorganization of a weak department, resolution of a morale problem in a foreign division, integration of computer operations, various acquisitions at different stages of development, and so on.

Chief executives appear to maintain a kind of inventory of the development projects in various stages of development. Like jugglers, they keep a number of projects in the air; periodically, one comes down, is given a new burst of energy, and sent back into orbit. At various intervals, they put new projects on-stream and discard old ones.

The scarcest resource managers have to allocate is their own time.

While the entrepreneur role describes the manager as the voluntary initiator of change, the *disturbance handler* role depicts the manager involuntarily responding to pressures. Here change is beyond the manager's control. The pressures of a situation are too severe to be ignored—a strike looms, a major customer has gone bankrupt, or a supplier reneges on a contract—so the manager must act.

Leonard R. Sayles, who has carried out appropriate research on the manager's job, likens the manager to a symphony orchestra conductor who must "maintain a melodious performance,"[14] while handling musicians' problems and other external disturbances. Indeed, every manager must spend a considerable amount of time responding to high-pressure disturbances. No organization can be so well run, so standardized, that it has considered every contingency in the uncertain environment in advance. Disturbances arise not only because poor managers ignore situations until they reach crisis proportions but also because good managers cannot possibly anticipate all the consequences of the actions they take.

The third decisional role is that of *resource allocator.* The manager is responsible for deciding who will get what. Perhaps the most important resource the manager allocates is his or her own time. Access to the manager constitutes exposure to the unit's nerve center and decision maker. The manager is also charged with designing the unit's structure, that pattern of formal relationships that determines how work is to be divided and coordinated.

Also, as resource allocator, the manager authorizes the important decisions of the unit before they are implemented. By retaining this power, the manager can ensure that decisions are interrelated. To fragment this power encourages discontinuous decision making and a disjointed strategy.

There are a number of interesting features about the manager's authorization of others' decisions. First, despite the widespread use of capital budgeting procedures—a means of authorizing various capital expenditures at one time—executives in my study made a great many authorization decisions on an ad hoc basis. Apparently, many projects cannot wait or simply do not have the quantifiable costs and benefits that capital budgeting requires.

Second, I found that the chief executives faced incredibly complex choices. They had to consider the impact of each decision on other decisions and on the organization's strategy. They had to ensure that the decision would be acceptable to those who influence the organization, as well as ensure that resources would not be overextended. They had to understand the various costs and benefits as well as the feasibility of the proposal. They also had to consider questions of timing. All this was necessary for the simple approval of someone else's proposal. At the same time, however, the delay could lose time, while quick approval could be ill-considered and quick rejection might discourage the subordinate who had spent months developing a pet project.

One common solution to approving projects is to pick the person instead of the proposal. That is, the manager authorizes those projects presented by people whose judgment he or she trusts. But the manager cannot always use this simple dodge.

The final decisional role is that of *negotiator*. Managers spend considerable time in negotiations: the president of the football team works out a contract with the holdout superstar; the corporation president leads the company's contingent to negotiate a new strike issue; the foreman argues a grievance problem to its conclusion with the shop steward.

These negotiations are an integral part of the manager's job, for only he or she has the authority to commit organizational resources in "real time" and the nerve-center information that important negotiations require.

The Integrated Job

It should be clear by now that these ten roles are not easily separable. In the terminology of the psychologist, they form a gestalt, an integrated whole. No role can be pulled out of the framework and the job be left intact. For example, a manager without liaison contacts lacks external information. As a result, that manager can neither disseminate the information that employees need nor make decisions that adequately reflect external conditions. (This is a problem for the new person in a managerial position, since he or she has to build up a network of contacts before making effective decisions.)

Here lies a clue to the problems of team management.[15] Two or three people cannot share a single managerial position unless they can act as one entity. This means that they cannot divide up the ten roles unless they can very carefully reintegrate them. The real difficulty lies with the informational roles. Unless there can be full sharing of managerial information—and, as I pointed out earlier, it is primarily verbal—team management breaks down. A single managerial job cannot be arbitrarily split, for example, into internal and external roles, for information from both sources must be brought to bear on the same decisions.

To say that the ten roles form a gestalt is not to say that all managers give equal attention to each role. In fact, I found in my review of the various research studies that sales managers seem to spend relatively more of their time in the interpersonal roles, presumably a reflection of the extrovert nature of the marketing activity. Production managers, on the other hand, give relatively more attention to the decisional roles, presumably a reflection of their concern with efficient work flow. And staff managers spend the most time in the informational roles, since they are experts who manage departments that advise other parts of the organization. Nevertheless, in all cases, the interpersonal, informational, and decisional roles remain inseparable.

Toward More Effective Management

This description of managerial work should prove more important to managers than any prescription they might derive from it. That is to say, *the managers' effectiveness is significantly influenced by their insight into their own work.* Performance depends on how well a manager understands and responds to the pressures and dilemmas of the job. Thus managers who can be introspective about their work are likely to be effective at their jobs. The questions in "Self-Study Questions for Managers" may sound rhetorical; none is meant to be. Even though the questions cannot be answered simply, the manager should address them.

Let us take a look at three specific areas of concern. For the most part, the managerial logjams—the dilemma of delegation, the database centralized in one brain, the problems of working with the management scientist—revolve around the verbal nature of the manager's information. There are great dangers in centralizing the organization's data bank in the minds of its managers. When they leave, they take their memory with them. And when subordinates are out of convenient verbal reach of the manager, they are at an informational disadvantage.

The manager is challenged to find systematic ways to share privileged information. A regular debriefing session with key subordinates, a weekly memory dump on the dictating machine, maintaining a diary for limited circulation, or other similar methods may ease the logjam of work considerably. The time spent disseminating this information will be more than regained when decisions must be made. Of course, some will undoubtedly raise the question of confidentiality. But managers would be well advised to weigh the risks of exposing privileged information against having subordinates who can make effective decisions.

If there is a single theme that runs through this article, it is that the pressures of the job drive the manager to take on too much work, encourage interruption, respond quickly to every stimulus, seek the tangible and avoid the abstract, make decisions in small increments, and do everything abruptly.

Here again, the manager is challenged to deal consciously with the presures of superficiality by giving serious attention to the issues that require it, by stepping back in order to see a broad picture, and by making use of analytical inputs. Although effective managers have to be adept at responding quickly to numerous and varying problems, the danger in managerial work is that they will respond to every issue equally (and that means abruptly) and that they will

Self-Study Questions for Managers

1. Where do I get my information, and how? Can I make greater use of my contacts? Can other people do some of my scanning? In what areas is my knowledge weakest, and how can I get others to provide me with the information I need? Do I have sufficiently powerful mental models of those things I must understand within the organization and in its environment?

2. What information do I disseminate? How important is that information to my subordinates? Do I keep too much information to myself because disseminating it is time consuming or inconvenient? How can I get more information to others so they can make better decisions?

3. Do I tend to act before information is in? Or do I wait so long for all the information that opportunities pass me by?

4. What pace of change am I asking my organization to tolerate? Is this change balanced so that our operations are neither excessively static nor overly disrupted? Have we sufficiently analyzed the impact of this change on the future of our organization?

5. Am I sufficiently well-informed to pass judgment on subordinates' proposals? Can I leave final authorization for more of the proposals with subordinates? Do we have problems of coordination because subordinates already make too many decisions independently?

6. What is my vision for this organization? Are these plans primarily in my own mind in loose form? Should I make them explicit to guide the decisions of others better? Or do I need flexibility to change them at will?

7. How do my subordinates react to my managerial style? Am I sufficiently sensitive to the powerful influence of my actions? Do I fully understand their reactions to my actions? Do I find an appropriate balance between encouragement and pressure? Do I stifle their initiative?

8. What kind of external relationships do I maintain, and how? Do I spend too much of my time maintaining them? Are there certain people whom I should get to know better?

9. Is there any system to my time scheduling, or am I just reacting to the pressures of the moment? Do I find the appropriate mix of activities or concentrate on one particular function or problem just because I find it interesting? Am I more efficient with particular kinds of work, at special times of the day or week? Does my schedule reflect this? Can someone else schedule my time (besides my secretary)?

10. Do I overwork? What effect does my work load have on my efficiency? Should I force myself to take breaks or to reduce the pace of my activity?

11. Am I too superficial in what I do? Can I really shift moods as quickly and frequently as my work requires? Should I decrease the amount of fragmentation and interruption in my work?

12. Do I spend too much time on current, tangible activities? Am I a slave to the action and excitement of my work, so that I am no longer able to concentrate on issues? Do key problems receive the attention they deserve? Should I spend more time reading and probing deeply into certain issues? Could I be more reflective? Should I be?

13. Do I use the different media appropriately? Do I know how to make the most of written communication? Do I rely excessively on face-to-face communication, thereby putting all but a few of my subordinates at an informational disadvantage? Do I schedule enough of my meetings on a regular basis? Do I spend enough time observing activities firsthand, or am I detached from the heart of my organization's activities?

14. How do I blend my personal rights and duties? Do my obligations consume all my time? How can I free myself from obligations to ensure that I am taking this organization where I want it to go? How can I turn my obligations to my advantage?

never work the tangible bits and pieces of information into a comprehensive picture of their world.

To create this comprehensive picture, managers can supplement their own models with those of specialists. Economists describe the functioning of markets, operations researchers simulate financial flow processes, and behavioral scientists explain the needs and goals of people. The best of these models can be searched out and learned.

In dealing with complex issues, the senior manager has much to gain from a close relationship with the organization's own management scientists. They have something important that the manager lacks—time to probe complex issues. An effective working relationship hinges on the resolution of what a colleague and I have called "the planning dilemma."[16] Managers have the information and the authority; analysts have the time and the technology. A successful working relationship between the two will be effected when the manager learns to share information and the analyst learns to adapt to the manager's needs. For the analyst, adaptation means worrying less about the elegance of the method and more about its speed and flexibility.

Analysts can help the top manager schedule time, feed in analytical information, monitor projects, develop models to aid in making choices, design contingency plans for disturbances that can be anticipated, and conduct "quick and dirty" analyses for those that cannot. But there can be no cooperation if the analysts are out of the mainstream of the manager's information flow.

You can't teach swimming or management in a lecture hall.

The manager is challenged to gain control of his or her own time by turning obligations into advantages and by turning those things he or she wishes to do into obligations. The chief executives of my study initiated only 32% of their own contacts (and another 5% by mutual agreement). And yet to a considerable extent they seemed to control their time. There were two key factors that enabled them to do so.

First, managers have to spend so much time discharging obligations that if they were to view them as just that, they would leave no mark on the organization. Unsuccessful managers blame failure on the obligations. Effective managers turn obligations to advantages. A speech is a chance to lobby for a cause; a meeting is a chance to reorganize a weak department; a visit to an important customer is a chance to extract trade information.

Second, the manager frees some time to do the things that he or she—perhaps no one else—thinks important by turning them into obligations. Free time is made, not found. Hoping to leave some time open for contemplation or general planning is tantamount to hoping that the pressures of the job will go away. Managers who want to innovate initiate projects and obligate others to report back to them. Managers who need certain environmental information establish channels that will automatically keep them informed. Managers who have to tour facilities commit themselves publicly.

The Educator's Job

Finally, a word about the training of managers. Our management schools have done an admirable job of training the organization's specialists—management scientists, marketing researchers, accountants, and organizational development specialists. But for the most part, they have not trained managers.[17]

Management schools will begin the serious training of managers when skill training takes a serious place next to cognitive learning. Cognitive learning is detached and informational, like reading a book or listening to a lecture. No doubt much important cognitive material must be assimilated by the manager-to-be. But cognitive learning no more makes a manager than it does a swimmer. The latter will drown the first time she jumps into the water if her coach never takes her out of the lecture hall, gets her wet, and gives her feedback on her performance.

In other words, we are taught a skill through practice plus feedback, whether in a real or a simulated situation. Our management schools need to identify the skills managers use, select students who show potential in these skills, put the students into situations where these skills can be practiced and developed, and then give them systematic feedback on their performance.

My description of managerial work suggests a number of important managerial skills—developing peer relationships, carrying out negotiations, motivating subordinates, resolving conflicts, establishing information networks and subsequently disseminating information, making decisions in conditions of extreme ambiguity, and allocating resources. Above all, the manager needs to be introspective in order to continue to learn on the job.

No job is more vital to our society than that of the manager. The manager determines whether our social institutions will serve us well or whether they will squander our talents and resources. It is time to strip away the folklore about managerial work and study it realistically so that we can begin the difficult task of making significant improvements in its performance.

References

1. All the data from my study can be found in Henry Mintzberg, *The Nature of Managerial Work* (New York: Harper & Row, 1973).

2. Robert H. Guest, "Of Time and the Foreman," *Personnel*, May 1956, p. 478.

3. Rosemary Stewart, *Managers and Their Jobs* (London: Macmillan, 1967); see also Sune Carlson, *Executive Behaviour* (Stockholm: Strombergs, 1951).

4. Francis J. Aguilar, *Scanning the Business Environment* (New York: Macmillan, 1967), p. 102.

5. Unpublished study by Irving Choran, reported in Mintzberg, *The Nature of Managerial Work*.

6. Robert T. Davis, *Performance and Development of Field Sales Managers* (Boston: Division of Research, Harvard Business School, 1957); George H. Copeman, *The Role of the Managing Director* (London: Business Publications, 1963).

7. Stewart, *Managers and Their Jobs*; Tom Burns, "The Directions of Activity and Communication in a Departmental Executive Group," *Human Relations* 7, no. 1 (1954): 73.

8. H. Edward Wrapp, "Good Managers Don't Make Policy Decisions," HBR September-October 1967, p. 91. Wrapp refers to this as spotting opportunities and relationships in the stream of operating problems and decisions; in his article, Wrapp raises a number of excellent points related to this analysis.

9. Richard E. Neustadt, *Presidential Power* (New York: John Wiley, 1960), pp. 153-154; italics added.

10. For a more thorough, though rather different, discussion of this issue, see Kenneth R. Andrews, "Toward Professionalism in Business Management," HBR March-April 1969, p. 49.

11. C. Jackson Grayson, Jr., in "Management Science and Business Practice," HBR July-August 1973, p. 41, explains in similar terms why, as chairman of the Price Commission, he did not use those very techniques that he himself promoted in his earlier career as a management scientist.

12. George C. Homans, *The Human Group* (New York: Harcourt, Brace & World, 1950), based on the study by William F. Whyte entitled *Street Corner Society*, rev. ed. (Chicago: University of Chicago Press, 1955).

13. Neustadt, *Presidential Power*, p. 157.

14. Leonard R. Sayles, *Managerial Behavior* (New York: McGraw-Hill, 1964), p. 162.

15. See Richard C. Hodgson, Daniel J. Levinson, and Abraham Zaleznik, *The Executive Role Constellation* (Boston: Division of Research, Harvard Business School, 1965), for a discussion of the sharing of roles.

16. James S. Hekimian and Henry Mintzberg, "The Planning Dilemma," *The Management Review*, May 1968, p. 4.

17. See J. Sterling Livingston, "Myth of the Well-Educated Manager," HBR January-February 1971, p. 79.

MANAGEMENT'S NEW GURUS

BUSINESS IS HUNGRY FOR FRESH APPROACHES TO THE GLOBAL MARKETPLACE

A 1990s management quiz:

(1) Do you work in a "learning organization"?

(2) Is the boss talking about "business process reengineering"?

(3) Is your company's "organizational architecture" sound?

(4) Are you a "time-based competitor"?

(5) Is your company leveraging its "core competencies"?

Say what? If you aren't familiar with these buzzwords and the management gurus who coined them, you can hardly consider yourself today's thoroughly modern manager. Worse, you and your company may fail to gain competitive advantage from the thriving marketplace of business ideas.

Sure, you've read bits and pieces of Peter F. Drucker's 25 books, and you've digested the best of W. Edwards Deming's ideas about quality. But Drucker is now 82, Deming 91. Tom Peters, perhaps the most-quoted guru of the day, remains durable (page 21). But he has delivered much the same be-true-to-your-customer message for years. Yet the corporate landscape is shifting fast: Competition is increasingly global, technology is developing quickly, and the work force is changing profoundly. **NEW LINGO.** These pressures are leaving managers hungrier than ever for fresh approaches. U. S. companies spent $13.9 billion on outside advice last year—up from $7 billion only five years ago. American readers shelled out more than $500 million last year on business books, the traditional calling card for any Drucker wannabe. That appetite for ideas is why a whole new generation of management gurus, mostly in their forties, is

jockeying to take the place of the grand old men of American business thought.

These champions of change are creating a new business language, along with new ideas designed to help companies manage better. While most of these pundits are corporate outsiders—academics, consultants, and speechgivers—many already boast power and influence in boardrooms and on factory floors around the world. Among their client companies, there's a growing sense that the key resource of business isn't capital, personnel,

MICHAEL HAMMER

A former MIT computer science professor, he has become a missionary for massive organizational change. Hammer, 44, uses the term 'reengineering' to advocate the radical redesign of work. He urges companies to organize around process—say, the filling of a customer order—instead of by functional departments, such as finance and marketing. Has worked with Aetna Life & Casualty, Hallmark Cards, and Texas Instruments

or plant, but knowledge and information. "Ideas are key," says Robert W. Galvin, who as chairman of Motorola Inc. brought that company to the forefront of the quality movement. "We listen. We read. Management thinkers are very influential. They are the developers and promulgators of key ideas."

Of course, many new management ideas are yesterday's theories warmed over and disguised under a sauce of new buzzwords. Others are mere fads, feel-good illusions peddled by false prophets who convince managers that their solutions make large-scale change easy. "The gurus are selling hope, confidence, the future, and happiness, and all these guys are great sellers," cautions Michael A. Stephen, president of Aetna Life & Casualty Co.'s international operations. "But change is a painful process, and there's no gain without pain. I have the battle scars to prove it."

If much of what the gurus offer in their endless rounds of seminar-giving, speechifying, and scribbling is dross, there's real gold out there, too. A few of these new oracles of modern management are having a profound impact on some of the nation's biggest companies. For example, Eastman Kodak Co. and American Express Co. have heeded the preaching of Michael Hammer, who coined the term "reengineering" to describe the fundamental rethinking and radical redesign of a business system: Both of these companies have appointed senior officers for reengineering.

ESOTERICA. It's the same story at Xerox Corp. Chairman Paul A. Allaire is no pushover for fashionable B-school nostrums: Much current management literature is, he says, "pure rubbish." But not so the work of David Nadler, president of Delta Consulting Group and the hidden figure behind Xerox' major reorganization this year. An academic turned consultant, the 43-year-old Nadler is the current guru of organizational architecture, a

GEORGE STALK JR.

A vice-president of Boston Consulting, he popularized the idea that companies can use speed for a competitive edge. Coined the term 'time-based competition'—which he uses to explain why companies need to heed 'cycle times' in every process. Consults with GE, IBM, Square D, and Wausau Paper

term he uses to describe a new form of corporate structure that evolves around "autonomous work teams" in "high-performance work systems."

The lingo may be esoteric, but Allaire views Nadler's ideas as a means to provoke new thinking inside the company. "If you've been in a company long enough, you're part of the culture yourself, and it's hard to step back and listen to new ideas," Allaire says. "He can help facilitate the process and can provide perspective."

The new gurus aren't rewriting Drucker, the most enduring management thinker of our time. More often than not, they're updating him by adding new ideas and tools to what Drucker has called "the practice of management." Besides Nadler and Hammer, the hottest and most influential new gurus include Peter M. Senge, a soft-spoken researcher at Massachusetts Institute of Technology, who focuses on how managers and corporations learn; C. K. Prahalad, a University of Michigan professor who is shaking up strategic planning; Edward E. Lawler III, a California academic who's expanding the frontiers of employee empowerment; and George Stalk Jr., a consultant who is the chief proponent of time-based competition.

The new gurus aren't all proselytizing from the same text, but they do have several tenets in common. For starters, theirs is generally a sterner religion than the happy-talk evangelism of *The One-Minute Manager*, that one-minute best-seller of the 1980s. Nearly all these preachers shun incremental change. They urge managers to think in radical terms, dramatically overhauling entire operations at a stroke.

WIDE NET. They also tend to agree that smaller is usually better. Most believe that management should organize itself on the basis of process, such as fulfilling an order, instead of functions, such as marketing or manufacturing. That takes an organization's focus off its own internal structure and puts it on meeting customers' needs, where it belongs. They generally agree that time can be squeezed out of every job; that self-managed teams throw more challenge and meaning into employment; and that companies sorely need to create networks of relationships with customers, suppliers, and competitors to gain greater competitive advantage.

Many of these thinkers also cast unusually wide conceptual nets, basing their ideas on theories and experiences borrowed from the nonbusiness world. Nadler, for example, takes much of his inspiration from the history and philosophy of architecture, which he uses as a metaphor to guide managers through change. Charles Handy, a popular British thinker, draws lessons from John Keats and George Bernard Shaw. In challenging managers to act more boldly, for instance, Handy notes that Shaw once observed that all progress depends on the unreasonable man.

The 44-year-old Hammer used his experience as a former computer-science professor to formulate his notion of reengineering. Hammer has crisscrossed the U.S. in the past year, giving more than 100 sermons on his precepts, which he unabashedly thinks of as commandments in a new management theology. "It's a theology because it requires a belief that there is a different way to do things," he says. "It requires faith."

Similarly, MIT's Senge uses psychology and education theory as metaphor in his concept of the "learning organization." He tells thousands of managers at

DAVID NADLER

Adviser to top management at AT&T, Corning, and Xerox, Nadler founded New York-based Delta Consulting. He focuses on 'organizational architecture,' a term he uses to describe a new form of organization that evolves around 'autonomous work teams' in 'high-performance work systems'

TENETS OF THE NEW GURUS

THE LEARNING ORGANIZATION
A conceptual framework for the organization of the future, it's the notion that learning is central to success. Management needs to see the big picture, to escape linear thinking, and to understand subtle interrelationships

REENGINEERING
The term for a fundamental rethinking and radical redesign of a business system. Urges an overhaul of job designs, organizational structures, and management systems. Work should be organized around outcomes, not tasks or functions

CORE COMPETENCIES
The idea is for companies to identify and organize around what they do best. Corporate strategy should be based not on products or markets, but on competencies that give a company access to several markets and are difficult for competitors to imitate

ORGANIZATIONAL ARCHITECTURE
A metaphor that forces managers to think more broadly about organization in terms of how work, people, and formal and informal structures fit together. Leads to autonomous work teams and strategic alliances

TIME-BASED COMPETITION
The belief that time is the equivalent of money, productivity, quality, and innovation. Proponents argue that time, like costs, is manageable and a source of competitive advantage throughout every process in the organization

DATA: BW

ILLUSTRATION BY RAY VELLA/BW

the likes of Ford Motor, Federal Express, and Procter & Gamble that corporations, like people, vary in their ability to assess and learn from their experiences. "Learning disabilities hurt organizations and industries badly," says Senge, who offers up his own tenets for how executives and their companies can learn better.

STEPPING BACK. At their most provocative, some of the new gurus are turning conventional wisdom on its head. Only a few years ago, managers were sold the logic that strong leadership and enduring corporate cultures were good things. But several management thinkers now believe all the focus on leadership was wrong because it undermined the concept of empowerment. Today's best managers, the theory goes, must step back to allow their workers to assume alternating roles as leaders in teams.

The romantic view of the strong, omniscient leader is largely a myth, maintains Robert Kelley, a consultant and business professor. He estimates that leaders on average contribute no more than 20% to the success of an organization, while so-called followers are responsible for the remaining 80%. Yet all the thinking, study, and literature focus exclusively on how to produce leaders, he says, often to the detriment of others who assume more passive roles. Similarly, some gurus now say strong corporate cultures, with their ingrained traditions, prevent companies from changing rapidly in response to the times.

Even corporate strategy—once hatched by vast departments of corporate planners at headquarters and later moved down in the organization to line managers—has undergone a complete metamorphosis in recent years. Prahalad, a 51-year-old guru of global strategy, says executives too frequently think of strategy as "fit" instead of "stretch." Companies plot strategy on the basis of their ability to match their existing resources with their ambitions. "If they fit, however, there's no opportunity for creativity and innovation because you're scaling down your ambitions to fit your

resources," says Prahalad, who advises AT&T, Kodak, and Philips. "Only when your aspirations and desires lie outside your resources does creativity occur, because you have to invent new ways of competing and change the rules of the game."

To foster that sort of thinking, the professor urges companies to focus on their "core competencies"—what they do best and what differentiates them from the competition. Then, he says, companies should search for ways to expand beyond their existing resources through licensing arrangements, strategic alliances, and supplier relationships. A case in point: Apple Computer Inc.'s alliance with Sony Corp. to manufacture Apple's highly successful Powerbook line of computers, which linked Apple's knack for designing easy-to-use products with Sony's miniaturization and the manufacturing knowhow necessary to make compact products.

Thanks to the freshness of his ideas, Indian-born Prahalad is regarded as the most influential thinker on strategy since Harvard business school's Michael E. Porter—no slouch as a guru himself. Prahalad, along with a London Business School colleague, now boasts his own video series and expects to publish his ideas in book form within the year.

RECYCLED? Yet much current management thinking sounds suspiciously recycled and repackaged. "High involvement," for example, is only the latest iteration of "empowerment," which in turn was just another name for an older notion. "The idea has been renamed more times than Elizabeth Taylor," laughs Lawler, one of the foremost thinkers in the arena of employee participation. "It all goes to the same issue: How do you move power, knowledge, information, and rewards downward in an organization?"

If the basic belief of empowerment isn't new, Lawler has advanced the ball with an appreciation for how profoundly a company must change to make empowerment work. It is extremely difficult, he says, for managers to give up

authority and for employees to translate that surrender of power by higher-ups into lasting increases in productivity.

"You've got to change the whole system," says Lawler, director of the University of Southern California's Center for Effective Organizations, which works with TRW, Hewlett-Packard, and Digital Equipment. "You create small business units, you flatten the organization, you change the work systems and the design, and you change the role of the manager." Lawler has advised General Mills Inc. on how to set up self-managed teams to run several plants. At some beverage plants, for example, four shifts of 20-person teams are informed of marketing plans and production costs. "They have at their fingertips all the data that would normally be held by management," says Daryl D. David, a human resources director. The self-managed teams do everything from scheduling production to rejecting products not up to quality standards, and they receive bonuses based on plant performance. Some 60% of General Mills' plants have been converted to such "high-performance work systems." The approach has produced significant gains in productivity, and the company is now moving to spread it to all operations.

While many of the new gurus are advocates of radical restructuring, that doesn't mean they applaud the downsizing so many corporations went through in the past few years. In the view of many, those maneuverings may have lowered overhead costs but did not necessarily make businesses more productive or responsive to the market. "If all you try to do is flatten your existing organization," says Hammer, "you'll kill it. The fat is not waiting around on top to be cut. It's marbled in, and the only way you get it out is by grinding it out and frying it out." Translation: Companies need to redesign totally—or reengineer—how the work gets done.

Hammer, a former IBM software engineer who taught computer science at MIT, began formulating his idea of rethinking work in the mid-1970s, when he was consulting with Citibank and Xerox

PETER SENGE

The soft-spoken Senge has captured the imaginations of many with his notion of 'the learning organization'—a phrase that has become a conceptual catchall of the new business organization. Senge, 44, encourages learning through exercises and games that force people to think differently about business problems. Director of MIT's Systems Thinking & Organizational Learning Program, he has consulted with Ford, Federal Express, and Herman Miller

EVER IN SEARCH OF A NEW TAKE ON EXCELLENCE

It was a more or less typical day for Tom Peters. He got out of bed at 3:15 a.m. for a predawn run through the rich countryside surrounding his Vermont farm. Later, swerving to avoid a porcupine that scampered across the dirt road, he drove his car into a ditch. After a neighbor pulled him out, he made it to the airport for a 5:30 a.m. private flight to New York, where he was to deliver yet another chest-thumping exhortation to a group of managers.

Peters, the former McKinsey & Co. consultant and co-author of the best-selling management book of all time, *In Search of Excellence,* has done thousands of speeches and seminars. But this one, on a summer morning before some 50 human resources officers, was different. It was his first chance to present material from his new book to be published this fall, *Liberation Management: Necessary Disorganization*

$25,000 a pop. Now he makes some 30 public appearances annually, at about $60,000 each. He also writes a weekly syndicated column, runs an executive-training company on the side, and appears in several PBS specials a year.

Admirers speak with near-adulation of the evangelical fervor Peters brings to the competitiveness debate. Critics say his often flippant comments are little more than sound bites. More important, however, he has undergone his own transformation from a cheerleader of what's right with the best of Big Business—a basic theme of *In Search*—to a champion of small to midsize companies and an outspoken critic of the status quo. The change largely results from his belief that smaller operations are easier to manage and that they tend to be more responsive to customers.

'**BONKERS.**' For three straight hours, Peters is out to show he's as relevant and provocative as ever. Pacing the floor, rocking

than laid off while doing something boring."
■ "The average decentralized corporation is not decentralized. It's a sham, a sick joke."

When Peters, 49, talks of companies that do it right, nearly all his examples are either small unknowns or professional service firms such as Arthur Andersen, Chiat/Day/Mojo, and his old employer McKinsey. One reason: Peters believes that the best models for the organization of the future are advertising agencies or consultancies. In such firms, most work is performed by cross-functional project teams that use their collective intellect to satisfy visible customers. People take initiative, start projects, seek customers, and build their own networks of contacts to accomplish goals.

Such companies "trade in pure knowledge," Peters says. "Functional departments are virtually nonexistent, and all the work is organized around loosely linked teams of people." The changing nature of the economy, from a world in which resources were key to one in which knowledge and information are crucial, is the driving force behind this change. To survive, managers have to act more like consultants, creating projects and challenging norms.

The audience, from such companies as American Express and Olin, listens to him, then politely asks a few questions and disbands. Later, back on his 1,300-acre Vermont farm with its llamas and sheep, he hears that many in the audience thought his presentation wasn't relevant to them.

Peters can't hide his disappointment. "I'd like them to get the message," he

> **TOM PETERS** The author of *In Search of Excellence* now makes about 30 public appearances a year—most of them chest-thumping exhortations to groups of managers—at $60,000 a pop

for the Nanosecond Nineties. Even Peters seemed jittery.

HIGH HOOPLA. Since the publication of *In Search* a decade ago, and of two best-selling sequels, the iconoclastic Peters has become the most quoted observer of American business. In a world of advice-giving fads and frills, where so many fade out quickly, Peters has shown remarkable durability. So has his Tokyo-based, former McKinsey colleague Kenichi Ohmae, 49, whose ruminations on global business have forced executives to think more clearly in terms of an international marketplace. The Japanese-born thinker was among the first to argue for partnerships among U.S., European, and Asian companies. Ohmae has proved the most prolific of the McKinsey-rooted thinkers, writing 38 books in 20 years. He received 930 requests for speeches last year. Peters' original partner, Robert H. Waterman Jr., has chosen to keep a lower profile, preferring to remain an active consultant.

At the height of the *Excellence* hoopla, in the early to mid-1980s, Peters was giving 150 to 200 speeches a year—at

back and forth, he expounds on everything from the need for "minimalist headquarters" to "deintegration," or the falling apart of companies that try to do everything themselves. He speaks of "buckyborgs," his term for clusters of 50- to 60-person business units, and of "brainware," the need to compete on the basis of intelligence instead of hardware. And he hasn't lost his knack for the audacious comment:

> **KENICHI OHMAE** The McKinsey veteran has written 38 books in the past 20 years and received 930 requests for speeches last year

■ "If the marketplace has gone bonkers, you better have a bonkers organization. Straitlaced folks are not going to make it in a world that's not straitlaced."
■ "Middle managers are cooked geese. Raise hell and at least go down in flames. You're better off getting fired for doing something interesting rather

says. "I'm frustrated because we're dealing with intractable business problems, and it's the frustration of being a reasonably well-known explainer who's not doing anything when it comes to explaining." Ah, but who ever said the life of a guru was going to be easy?

By John A. Byrne in New York

21

on the use of information systems. "Most organizations were using computers to automate antiquated paper practices," he says. "They were merely paving cowpaths." Believing that companies should use technology to rethink the way they did business, not simply to automate current practice, he quit his MIT job in 1982 to launch his own Cambridge (Mass.) consulting firm. But it wasn't until 1987 that he thought of the term "reengineering" to describe how companies must radically redesign work.

FIEFDOMS. After he published an article on the subject two years ago in *Harvard Business Review*, Hammer found himself and his ideas hot property. More than 1,500 managers and executives have since rushed to attend his three-day seminars. He has signed a contract with HarperCollins Publishers Inc., which expects to publish his book on reengineering early next year.

Behind the hoopla is an intriguing idea: that companies should be organized around process instead of function. "Something as simple as filling an order might go through a dozen different functions in some companies," Hammer says. "Each has its own fiefdom with its own concerns and objectives." Such function-based organization introduces errors, adds costs, and causes delays.

Hammer's reengineering approach offers ways to streamline—an alluring notion to cost-conscious managers. ITT Sheraton Corp., with 450 hotels around the world, is in the midst of reengineering its operations. Executive Vice-President John W. Herold Jr. was impressed by Hammer's spiel a few years ago. Herold invited him to headquarters to talk with senior management, then dispatched 22 of his top operating executives to Hammer's three-day seminars.

The upshot: "We threw away the book and invented a new hotel," says Herold. The typical 300-room Sheraton Hotel had required up to 40 managers and 200 employees. By eliminating narrowly defined jobs and rethinking antiquated procedures, ITT found it could run a reengineered version of 250 suites with only 14 managers and 140 employees—with higher customer satisfaction. "We redesigned the processes of the company and eliminated everything we didn't need to do," says Herold. "Most of the managers were filling out reports for bosses."

TIME PRESSURE. Hammer's ideas overlap somewhat with another hot movement in management thinking: the push for time-based competition. The chief proponent of the idea, George Stalk, and his partners at Boston Consulting Group Inc. had been startled in the late 1970s by how much faster several Japanese companies got products to market than

did their U.S. competitors. In one consulting study after another, Stalk heard clients talk about the speed of development. "What made it connect was that everyone knew time was important to business, but no one knew how to manage time," he says.

By 1985, he had thought up the term "time-based competition" to describe the focus of his consulting efforts. In the late 1980s, Stalk was regularly mapping, measuring, and monitoring a given process—whether it was the development of a product or the fulfillment of an order—to form the basis of a time-based competition practice of some 12 consultants within BCG. Today, more than 100 consultants at BCG alone largely work with major corporate clients to implement the idea, at fees of about $250 an hour. And Stalk's catchy phrase has spawned a litter of similar terms to describe the same thing, from "cycle-time reduction" to "time-compression management."

Whatever the phrases, they are all familiar to Nadler, who has captured a strong corporate following for his advice on organizational design. The former Columbia University business school professor established New York's Delta

Consulting in 1981 as an alternative to such strategy-based shops as McKinsey & Co., Bain & Co., and Stalk's BCG. His idea: to bring together the strategic issues with the behavioral dynamics of organizations.

The philosophical framework for his firm is what he dubs the "congruence model of effectiveness." It's how the four key elements of an organization—work, people, the formal structure of a company, and the informal structure and process—fit together. Sound a bit dense? Says Nadler: "It's a language system, a way to take something complex and overwhelming and make it easy for managers to understand."

That system is used to study an existing company and to then design the "organizational architecture" of a new one. Allaire of Xerox, for example, is said to walk around the company with a sketch of the congruence model in one of his notebooks. Xerox used Nadler's methodology to guide it through its latest reorganization, which breaks the company into smaller, more autonomous, and theoretically more responsive units.

The internal group of Xerox managers who developed the new architecture of the company called itself the "future-

---

MORE GURUS AND THEIR TENETS

CHARLES HANDY Half philosopher, half futurist, this clever British thinker maintains that "discontinuous change" requires dramatically new approaches to work and organization. A lecturer at the London Business School, Handy, 60, is the author of *The Age of Unreason,* a handbook loaded with new, catchy phrases to help managers cope with change.

JOHN KOTTER The Harvard Business School's guru on leadership, he believes that most U.S. companies are over-managed and underled. Kotter, 45, says that organizations need to combine strong leadership—defined as the ability to cope with a changing environment—with strong management, or the ability to cope with complexity.

EDWARD E. LAWLER III He dislikes the term "empowerment," but this guru at the University of Southern California is one of the foremost thinkers in what is now called "high-performance involvement." Lawler, 54, advises companies to break themselves down into small units, give employees exceptional say in what they do, and reward them for taking responsibility.

C. K. PRAHALAD A brilliant teacher at the University of Michigan, Prahalad may well be the most influential thinker on corporate strategy today. With Gary Hamill, a colleague at the London Business School, Prahalad, 51, urges firms to focus their strategies around "core competencies"—what they do best—and to leverage those and future competencies.

GERALD ROSS Co-founder of a Greenwich (Conn.) consulting firm called Change Lab International, Ross is a change-management expert who has worked with such companies as Aetna Life & Casualty and Bristol-Myers Squibb. Ross, 48, maintains that the "new molecular organization will be built around markets, not products or functions."

SHOSHANNA ZUBOFF Author of *In the Age of the Smart Machine,* this thoughtful Harvard business school professor speaks of the need not to "automate" but to "informate"—to use smart machines in interaction with smart people. Zuboff, 40, is currently studying "model companies" that employ technology to change the nature of work.

tecture" team. Over the 15 months of the project, Nadler worked closely with the team. One result: A new, three-level organization chart shows Xerox' corporate staff at the bottom, supporting the business teams and districts at the top. More important, profit-and-loss responsibility, once focused in the chief executive's suite, has moved down to 20 business-team general managers. Units and teams now have complete beginning-to-end responsibility for a Xerox product.

PLAYING GAMES. No matter how dazzling the insight or brilliant the theory, however, it will be of little use if an organization and its people can't learn from it. That's where the idea of the "learning organization," popularized by Senge, comes in. One way to improve learning, he says, is to create opportunities for managers to practice in a risk-free environment, not unlike a rehearsal for an actor or an exhibition game for a ball player. "People who have studied how human beings learn come again and again to the world of play or what we call a practice field," says Senge. "By moving managers between a performance field and a practice field, you can improve the learning process."

To do that, Senge brings senior executives and front-line managers together to play simulation games that allow them to gain better insights into how each of their decisions affects the others. His approach is being used by managers at numerous companies, from Ford to Federal Express. And he has many enthusiastic supporters in the business community. As chief executive of Hanover Insurance Co., William J. O'Brien used Senge as a consultant for eight years to teach his management team such techniques. "I'm not saying it gives absolute answers, but it gives the human mind a more informed way to look at business," says O'Brien.

For every Senge or Nadler who has already won the ears of the corporate elite, there are dozens of other aspirants who hope someday to become the next Drucker or Deming. Some of them and their ideas will go the way of the hula-hoop. But others are likely to have a lasting impact on the practice of management and the shape of U.S. corporations. Whether or not you agree with them, that fact alone makes the current crop of pundits worth listening to.

By John A. Byrne in New York

How to Spot
Unsuccessful Executives

They treat subordinates unfairly, don't listen, discuss problems endlessly without acting, fail to grasp the big picture, and mismanage time.

Woodruff Imberman

Dr. Imberman is president, Imberman and DeForest, Inc., a Chicago, Ill., management consultants firm.

EVERY BOOKSTORE is full of volumes describing what makes an effective executive. Daily newspapers carry syndicated columns written by gurus who depict the methods and behavior of successful CEOs. Major magazines such as *Fortune* and *Time* regularly publish feature articles on various "shining lights" in the business world.

Few publications, however, care to depict the behavior of *unsuccessful* executives, which usually manifests itself in disregarding subordinates, inability to listen, failing to see the big picture, and talking rather than doing.

Disregarding subordinates. The unsuccessful manager almost always is conscious of the need to pander to superiors. While he rushes to meet their whims, just as often he disregards the need to be considerate of subordinates. He orders things to be done, rather than motivating anyone to do them. ("Increase productivity! Improve quality!

Get the lead out! Group machines into cells for synchronous production! Don't give me excuses! Do it!")

When such executives *do* deal with subordinates, their attitude tends to be full of artificial cordialities. The sole purpose is to manipulate. When they say "no," they usually give no reason. They engender no loyalty among their staff. They really do not believe their success is related to that of subordinates.

The ABC Apparel Manufacturing Co. had 1,200 workers in several plants. A project leader with some status in the parent company was promoted to plant manager in an outlying factory where girls' dresses and casual wear were produced for Wal-Mart, KMart, Ames, etc. Upon assuming his new job, he decided to impress by concentrating on cutting costs that affected the price of producing garments.

Previously, overtime was voluntary. Since there was nothing in the union contract on the subject, the new plant manager unilaterally posted a notice that employees must work overtime when ordered by management, and proceeded to enforce the

rule. Most plant employees were women with family obligations. Soon, four were disciplined for refusing overtime. Grievances were filed. In the meantime, productivity in the plant declined. This led to a query from headquarters.

The "call out" problem was handled similarly. A maintenance employee called to work outside his regular scheduled hours was paid a minimum of four hours regular pay or one-and-one-half times his regular rate for time worked, whichever was greater. When the emergency job was completed, the employee went home to rest for his regular shift. Sometimes, he worked only one hour, but received four hours pay.

The new plant manager unilaterally changed the rule without discussing the matter with maintenance employees or the union. Under the new rule, whenever a worker was called out for an emergency job, he would be assigned to a second and perhaps a third task in order to fill out the four hours. The union objected, but the manager felt that, if the company was paying for four hours work, it certainly should receive four hours work.

The plant began to have difficulty in calling out emergency workers. Wives would tell the plant representative when he phoned that their husbands were not at home. An emergency job left undone because of employee resentment resulted in a one-day shutdown of a department.

Finally, a two-week strike broke out at contract time. Money was said to be the major issue, but newspaper stories in the community—the reporters interviewed a number of strikers and their spouses—indicated that the trouble was due almost entirely to the manager's unilateral arbitrary actions. Behind that, of course, lay the manager's disdain for subordinates' opinions, which undermined the company effort to achieve workforce cooperation on cost containment.

Inability to listen. In considering policies, the successful executive listens for the intangibles as well as tangibles. What is the staff's feeling about the new computerized machining equipment? Is the bar code printer too slow? What are we getting out of the employee suggestion boxes? Are the department heads unfair or tyrannical? Can we shorten the time it takes to develop designs? Why the current increase in employee absenteeism? The unsuccessful executive rarely bothers listening for such intangibles.

Employee attitude surveys which may engender uncomplimentary views about management are pooh-poohed. Interviews, focus groups, and employee audits that tap worker opinions sometimes may produce adverse sentiments concerning equipment, materials, lighting, heating, bathroom cleanliness, arbitrary supervisory practices, or management policies. The unsuccessful manager discounts such observations as mere "employee gripes," unworthy of serious attention. Yet, from long business consulting experience, I can attest that many of such comments, while intangible, basically are constructive and point to opportunities for improvements in productivity, quality, and cost savings.

One manager of a plant producing engine components for the automotive market, after losing a National Labor Relations Board election to a friendly independent (company) union, negotiated a two-year "sweetheart" contract with the victorious group of well-disposed southern employees. In his first contract year, the executive had no patience to listen to worker complaints, so grievances mounted. The plant manager forced arbitration six times over petty grievances, winning five. In his second year, he had six arbitration cases over similar minor issues and won them all. He overlooked the point that the arbitration process will produce decisions, but will not resolve intangible human problems.

In the third year, the docile company union revolted and affiliated with the United Auto Workers Union, which demanded new terms that the plant manager declared unacceptable. A three-week strike ensued. Thereafter, productivity went way down, and the shipping schedules showed a similar decline.

Unsuccessful executives take pride in being realistic. They often mean that they concentrate only on the tangible facts. They regard intangibles as ephemeral, wishy-washy, hot air. For example, such executives will maintain loudly that a labor contract is nothing more than an agreement to purchase labor service at such-and-such a price, and that it is no different from a contract to buy vacuum fluorescent displays, a label printer / applicator, or a carload of steel. Such executives will be unable to sense that this failure to grasp the intangible difference will earn the company endless ill-will.

In certain situations—particularly *financial* positions—an executive's ability to concentrate only on the tangibles may be valuable. Where people and motivation are involved, however, trouble ensues when intangible feelings and attitudes are disregarded.

Intelligence is not enough

Failing to see the big picture. There is no evidence that one has to be very bright or have excessive book learning to be a good manufacturing executive. An MBA education doesn't guarantee success in any industry. As J. Sterling Livingston pointed out in the *Harvard Business Review,* "A great many executives who mistakenly believe that grades are a valid measure of leadership potential have expressed concern over the fact that fewer and fewer of those 'top third' graduates . . . are embarking on careers in business. What those executives do not recognize, however, is that academic ability does not assure that an individual will be able to learn what he needs to know to build a career in fields that involve such broad matters as leading, changing, developing, or working with people."

Livingston was not talking about the grasp of technical marketing or financial details drilled into MBAs. He was alluding to general functions all manufacturing executives must be able to execute—planning, directing, controlling, evaluating, etc. In that connection, unsuccessful executives very often do not see the bigger picture, getting lost in the details instead.

Many executives have been promoted because of their attention to detail. Consider a quality inspector in a company producing pressure gauges and flowmeters. He needs to know if the incoming material is consistent, machine settings are proper, and operator practices are up to standard, as well as actual vs. expected variations at each processing stage. He has to worry about quality documentation, maintaining a formal gauge calibration system to ensure that there are no excessive weight disparities and seeing that there are no significant deviations, either in size average or within machine variation.

He does a good job and is promoted to quality manager, reporting to the manufacturing vice president. As a *manager,* the ability to assign tasks to subordinates (without looking over their shoulders) and devote time and thought to broader issues may not come easy to a "detail man." For some people, this graduation never takes place because they can not help involving themselves in the details. Conceptualization—the bigger picture—does not interest them.

While many people talk about the "Peter Principle" (individuals rise to the level of their incompetence), few understand what accounts for the phenomenon of promoting a man beyond his abilities. Incapacity to accept broader and broader horizons—in short, the inability to see the larger scene—is what accounts for it. Some individuals never let go of the details because they are most comfortable in that area. They usually are unsuccessful as major executives precisely for that reason.

Talking rather than doing. Of all the hallmarks of unsuccessful executives, the tendency to discuss issues endlessly instead of acting is the universal characteristic. Executives are faced daily with decisions. While many are minor, major ones do have to be made, often in concert with other executives. Do we need a jumbo die jig to handle larger rolls? Should we think about having our punch press operations done outside instead of in-house? Should we consider a branch plant in Puerto Rico? Should we hire that consultant to help manage the transition to a profit-sharing program? We need new forklift trucks; should we switch brands?

Invariably, the unsuccessful executive will be reluctant to reach a firm decision, even if all possible facts are laid out. He always wants to keep discussing the proposition, to talk some more, rather than do anything. Talk often is regarded by some executives as a form of action, and continuing to discuss the decision is regarded as doing something constructive. To continue talking requires no change in behavior, adjustment of routine, upheaval of standard procedure, or risk to anyone's status. That always suits the unsuccessful executive, since change is perilous and may lead to unforeseen consequences.

This tendency to talk instead of acting, if it encourages other executives to follow along, may lead to slow death of the company. Study the Fortune 500 of 20 years ago and compare them with today's leaders. Only a handful of corporations are on both lists. Many of the others slowly withered, in good part because talk was accepted in place of action.

While no one unsuccessful executive exhibits *all* the undesirable traits to the degree described above, the tendency to talk instead of acting is characteristic of *every* unsuccessful manager. Dealing with such executives is a very frustrating experience.

To avoid these pitfalls, junior and senior executives should be required to take in-house courses to promote management development. To be effective, such programs must be realistic and custom-tailored (not out of books) for each company. Executives with these types of shortcomings can be identified by their reactions and comments to realistic case studies. As a result, they can be guided into the proper executive slot to suit their talents and avoid being promoted into positions in which they can not function in the best interests of the company. Most firms have room for all sorts of executives, but square pegs will not function well in round holes.

MANAGING IN THE MIDST OF CHAOS

It's not just you and your company. The entire corporate world seems to be going crazy as companies cut costs but demand more. Here's how you can weather the storm.

John Huey

CALL IT whatever you like—reengineering, restructuring, transformation, flattening, downsizing, rightsizing, a quest for global competitiveness—it's real, it's radical, and it's arriving every day at a company near you. Some companies opt for dramatic change as a preemptive strategy, others because they've run out of alternatives. Either way, when it hits, it hurts. For managers chosen to lead the charge against the reigning corporate culture, urgency becomes the watchword, while fear and uncertainty take over in the ranks. To the survivors, the revolution feels something like this: scary, guilty, painful, liberating, disorienting, exhilarating, empowering, frustrating, fulfilling, confusing, challenging. In other words, it feels very much like chaos. Because even when it is orchestrated from above by a sure hand connected to a clear eye, the result is *still* chaos.

In this climate the hot new skill for leaders has become the ability to manage chaos—culturally, structurally, emotionally—while participating in the radical transformation of the way your company does business. With CEOs focused on strategy and middle-management ranks decimated, the skill is most critical at the level of the senior manager, two or three layers below the top. These are the folks where the rubber meets the road, those who must embrace the revolution and then actually make it happen—now.

Meet four such executive revolutionaries.

REPORTER ASSOCIATE *Andrew Erdman*

All share—and proselytize—the management philosophies and techniques of the moment: a belief in worker teams, customer focus, employee empowerment. Follow them around for a day. Listen to what they say and how they say it. See how they deal with people, how they feel about their jobs, how they worry. In the process you should gain new insights into—and useful survival lessons from—American corporations in the midst of managing through the turmoil.

■ Duane Hartley, 49, is general manager of Hewlett-Packard's microwave instruments division. The upheaval in the computer business hit H-P hard, but the company confronted its problems much earlier than IBM or Digital Equipment, its larger East Coast rivals. Despite painful downsizing that affected 6,800 of its workers over the past seven years, H-P has preserved much of its culture of divisional autonomy while continuing to focus on change. Says Hartley: "We really got caught up in the success of the defense industry. And as somebody once put it, 'When you're successful, you forget quickly and learn slowly.' I think that happens everywhere. Organizations get successful, then they lose their sense of urgency and end up having to go through some kind of transition to get it back."

■ Jim Eibel, 56, is vice president of sales and service at Ameritech's largest subsidiary, Illinois Bell. Since the breakup of AT&T in 1984, Ameritech has been one of the top-performing Baby Bells, but the company feels it must destroy the old Bell system culture in order to survive the dramatic transformation taking place in telecommunications. Says Eibel: "Today 20% of our revenues come from competitive operations. In five years 95% will be competitive—with cable TV operators, long-distance carriers, and other Baby Bells vying for the same businesses. If we wait to change our culture until we've got a fully competitive marketplace, we'll be IBM or GM."

■ Willow Shire, 44, is corporate vice president at Digital Equipment Corp., responsible for selling computer systems to the hospital, pharmaceutical, Social Security, and government health industries. Unlike the situation at Ameritech, Digital's revolution was launched as a matter of survival. Changing market forces have so severely battered the world's No. 3 computer maker that its once revered corporate culture has become an obsolete burden. Concedes Shire: "Morale is very low. When I first came here 16 years ago, I was surrounded by intelligent, bright, aggressive, vibrant people who were excited about what they were doing. Now people are tired, frustrated, and frightened. We need to regain some of that old value."

■ Rebecca McDonald, 40, is president of Tenneco's natural gas marketing subsidiary. When CEO Michael Walsh arrived at Tenneco 18 months ago, the diversified company was hemorrhaging with unexpected losses, and the natural gas business was already moving from a regulated to a market-driven industry. Says McDonald: "Corporate arrogance was our culture. We said: 'Here are the services we think our customers need,' but we never asked them. The hierarchy suppressed new ideas and made us very risk averse." Today, she says, "it's a blank page, a chance to do everything over. How can that not be exciting?" As for managing the ensuing chaos, "It's my specialty. I don't mind a muddle at all."

These are all veteran managers who have embraced change, and who—though stressed by the challenges they face—seem energized by the process. Not everyone is so adaptable. Change is most difficult for lower-level executives accustomed to getting orders from above, and compliance from below, says William Bridges, a consultant to many corporations on the subject of transition: "Fifteen percent of the people out there don't need anything to get them ready. They're just waiting to be turned loose. Another 15% will never learn the new skills no matter what." Today's managers have to concentrate on the remaining 70%: Win them over or winnow them out.

Part of the problem lies in the chaotic nature of the mission, which has two paradoxical thrusts: (A) keep everything running and increasing in profitability, while at the same time . . . (B) change everything.

Says Noel Tichy, a University of Michigan management professor and author, who is exporting to other companies what he learned as a consultant for General Electric CEO Jack Welch—the icon of the corporate management revolution: "The toughest part is designing a new organization while you operate the old one. You can't slamdunk the new way. You have to run the two systems in parallel."

In Santa Rosa, California, Duane Hartley's Hewlett-Packard unit has been in revolution for a while now. As a general manager at H-P since 1985, Hartley—who joined a company assembly line just out of high school 31 years ago—has been in the thick of the change, and he is still devoting much of his time to matters of corporate culture. Today his schedule is filled with "coffee talks," informal chats between senior management (who want to keep everyone up to date on corporate goals and the progress toward them) and employees (who want to voice their gripes and fears). At the first of six such sessions in various plants covering different shifts, Hartley begins by sharing the results of a recent downsizing that reduced by 300 his regional operation of 3,300 employees.

"I believe our structure is now correct to compete anywhere in the world," Hartley tells the coffee sippers. But the first question concerns a rumor that one plant is going to merge with another, and that layoffs

will continue. Without overcommitting himself, Hartley tries to calm fears. Finally he says, "Okay, do I sound enough like Bill Clinton for you?"

Hartley comes from the taproot of H-P, the test and measurement side of the business, which since its founding just before World War II has earned its money as a supplier of expensive, high-performance, engineer-operated instruments to the defense industry. By the mid-Eighties, though, orders for such equipment had begun to dry up, while inflation continued to drive costs higher. And by the late Eighties, the computer side of H-P was experiencing similar problems. So John Young, CEO at the time, issued a new statement of purpose for all of Hewlett-Packard: to evolve from a company driven by hardware into one focused on customer solutions.

"I know that once we've positioned ourselves as a competitive company, my job won't exist anymore."

Sure, you've heard that before. And at Hartley's coffee talks, you hear it again and again. The reason is that in H-P's case the first result out of the box was a stunning success: the highly profitable LaserJet printer line, which was developed by a maverick group in Boise, Idaho, that broke practically every H-P rule in the book. Engineering-proud H-P actually built the product partly under license from other companies, including Canon, and made it compatible with other personal computers, not just its own. H-P customers can now get the print quality of machines that once cost $100,000 for less than $2,000.

"That became our paradigm for the rest of the company," says Hartley. Put another way, the LaserJet model changed H-P's corporate culture. Hartley keeps his workers focused on the importance of developing similar products, ones with low costs and wide markets. So instead of depending on dwindling sales of its high-performance measurement instruments, the unit sells tens of millions of dollars in customer-friendly testing devices for such service workers as cable TV installers, cellular radio operators, even candymakers trying to determine how much moisture is in a gumball.

H-P never really larded on the administrative layers and imperial trappings for which IBM is so famous. Duane Hartley maintains offices in two plants, both of them partitioned cubbyholes erected in the middle of

the room, posted with signs that say things like "Leadership is an activity, not a position." When workers encounter the big boss in the hall, they invariably smile and blurt out a "Hi, Duane." He likes it that way. "Approachability is a big deal," he says.

At the sessions, he shares all kinds of information: the profitability of the division and its contribution to overall profitability for H-P, market share, candid results of the employee satisfaction survey. He reports on current corporate strategy. And then he announces the date of the first division beer bust. The beer, he says, should get there "just in time."

The questions from the troops demonstrate a high degree of sophistication. Afterward several employees always remain behind to talk to Hartley about their problems—although one wants to talk with him just about his hot-rod collection. Another stops by to say: "Thanks for your leadership, Duane. It makes a difference."

Over a quick lunch in one of his plant cafeterias, Hartley reflects on what he's trying to do: "Right now I'm probably spending 75% of my energy on matters that could be called corporate culture. I don't think people really enjoy change, but if they can participate in it and understand it, it can become a positive for them."

Is all of this stressful for Hartley? "I don't worry about losing my job. What I lose sleep over is making the right decisions to keep all my people on the payroll. I don't want to disappoint them." Hartley cautions managers in similar positions about focusing too much on themselves. "Like any other crisis you go through, self-doubt can set in," he says. "I think lots of managers take it too personally and start thinking of themselves like football fans think of quarterbacks—they give themselves too much credit and take too much blame—instead of thinking about how strong the team is and how much of a difference a strong company can make."

The revolution has claimed the careers of some of Hartley's colleagues, but he expresses little guilt—no serious bouts with "survivor syndrome." Of those who don't make the cut, says Hartley, "they don't listen. They don't listen to the customers, the market, the field, their own employees. They just flat get out of touch."

COMMUNICATION, appropriately, is the big job for Ameritech's Jim Eibel, a 31-year veteran of the former Bell system responsible for some 18,000 employees. He devotes most of his time these days to moving his workers away from what was once the company's most treasured asset: the Bell culture. "In our old monopoly environment, we believed the company was entitled to customers and to profit, and every one of us was entitled to employment," he says. "Today I know that once we've positioned ourselves as a competitive company, this job—my job—won't exist any more. I just hope my name will still be on a box somewhere in the organization chart."

With Ameritech in the midst of a complete reorganization, many employees share Eibel's personal goal. Over the past year and a half, Illinois Bell alone has eliminated about 25% of its 5,000 managers. For employees of the paternalistic old Bell system—some of whom boast up to 40 years' service—wholesale layoffs are a serious shock.

Says Eibel: "The craft [union] people say, 'You owe it to us to tell us what's going to happen.' But all we can honestly say is, 'Hey, if you can tell us how many customers we'll manage to attract—and keep—we can give you an answer.'" With regulatory authorities opening up the telecommunications business to competition almost daily—Congress's granting cable TV the right to provide phone service, for exam-

ple—Eibel works at getting everyone in the company to comprehend just how much the world is changing. "If you just look around and see what's going on out there, you can get awfully motivated."

Like every other company in revolution, Ameritech is reinventing itself—culturally and structurally—to focus on the needs of its customers. "Before," says Eibel, "big customers would ask for things—say, First Chicago requesting a revised volume-discount structure—and it would take us two or three years to respond."

Now Ameritech can get to work on it right away because it is organized into teams focused on each large customer. "Basically, before, we told everybody what to do, and if they had any questions, they called the boss," says Eibel. "Now everyone in the team has some say in designing the process, and everyone is accountable for results. Eventually we want everyone to have some money at risk in the outcome as well, through bonuses or other compensation tied to unit productivity."

RESISTANCE to the new way of doing things is palpable at today's Vision and Values session, a touchy-feely seminar aimed at achieving what the consultants call buy-in from some 40 workers seated in groups of five around tables equipped with paper easels. Though Eibel is in charge of these workshops and often runs them, he is just an observer at this meeting.

"Hey, we know you're cutting down on your work force," says one clearly agitated employee, "but don't you realize you're screwing the customer when you do it?"

"We agree with you," says seminar leader Mike Tatom, Eibel's general manager of customer service in the Chicago area. "We know we can't just keep cutting expenses. We know we have to grow revenues. But to do that we need to make sure we're getting the best use out of our resources."

Everyone is asked to use the easels to write out his or her personal commitment to the new Team Ameritech. A hint of the

CORPORATE CULTURE SHOCK: AN IBM–APPLE COMPUTER JOINT VENTURE

So here's Joe Guglielmi, a 30-year veteran IBM executive, sitting—tieless—in his spartan office beside Route 280 in Cupertino, California. The support staff consists of Jo Ann Vander Vennet, his administrative assistant. And the computer on the desk is a Macintosh. Whoa, Joe! Is this the twilight zone, or what?

Well, almost. It's Taligent, the software joint venture between IBM and Apple, of which Guglielmi, 51, is the chief executive. The technological challenge—to develop an object-oriented operating system to compete with Microsoft and Next—is tough. The social engineering challenge—to create a new corporate culture out of the collision of two diametrically opposed operating philosophies—may be even tougher. Call it Big Blue comes to Steve's garage.

Does this sound like corporate culture shock? "Yes, there's a dramatic difference," admits Guglielmi. "IBM is a very hierarchical company. Plans go up, are consolidated, and come back down as one worldwide strategy. Apple is a group of empowered individuals doing great things with great technology. Decisions are made at very low levels all the time." But while the Apple way lends itself to much greater speed—a necessity in high-tech industry—both systems have their downsides, Guglielmi says. Everyone knows hierarchy

slows things down, but you should recognize too that "empowerment without process leads to anarchy."

Because most of Taligent's 260 or so employees come from either Apple or some other loose Silicon Valley culture, Guglielmi's first big hurdle was a dress code. "They asked about it right away. I told them I wouldn't comment on the way they dressed if they wouldn't comment on the way I dressed." (He's prone to slick sports parkas and aviator shades—just the right look for his sporty Jaguar.)

Guglielmi admits to missing the support structure that was such a part of his former culture: "When I was running the applications software business for IBM, I had a senior secretary, an assistant, and an office worker to handle the mail. When I traveled, it was usually with one or two other people minimum. Today it's me and Jo Ann. I travel alone, which took some retraining. And I do my own mail."

Comfortable as all that support was, he says, he sees now that it has a distinct negative side: insulation. "An executive at IBM really has to work hard to stay in touch with what's going on. If you never experience the problem—but only read about it—you're so detached it's hard to imagine coming up with the solution."

What he misses least about IBM is the

hierarchical decision-making process. Still, Guglielmi—an ardent IBM loyalist—does try to impose some of what he feels are the best aspects of IBM culture on to the new company, and not surprisingly, he meets resistance from the former Apple folks.

"I like to measure performance," he says, "and that requires some discipline. I ask questions like 'What's your process for doing this?' or 'How do you know you can repeat it?' 'I'm tired of folklore,' I tell them. 'I want some data.'" At first, says Guglielmi, the natural instinct of the Apple folks is to resist, to say, "'You can't do this, you can't keep track of this or that process.' But then they try it, and if it works, they love it. If it doesn't, we try something else."

So forbidding is the IBM culture these days, says Paul Carroll, a journalist who is completing a book about IBM's troubles, that it has become a negative icon to those who would succeed. According to Carroll, when a group of IBM executives led a spinoff of some IBM operations and created their own company, called Lexmark International, one of their first acts was to install Big Blue's bulky procedures manual in the middle of the plant floor—encased in Lucite. They wanted everyone to remember it as historically significant. They didn't want anyone using it.

revival meeting, or of a new age self-help cult, is in the air. "Who's ready to take the challenge?" asks Tatom. "What can you do individually to help serve our customers better?" In response each employee stands and reads his or her commitment to the group. "My personal commitment is to become a team player and be more receptive to change," says Stan Mathies, an older worker who then can't help muttering: "I still got a problem with that."

For all the emphasis on empowerment at Ameritech, there is also fear—at least some of it is purposefully induced. Ameritech's CEO, William Weiss, has let it be known around the company that he is a great admirer of GE's Welch and has even hired some of GE's consultants to spur along Ameritech's transformation. At GE, where he eliminated 170,000 jobs, Welch earned the reputation as one of America's toughest bosses and acquired a variety of unflattering nicknames—"Neutron Jack" stuck—for his summary firings. Ameritech is building its own reputation within the former Bell system. In at least one case, a senior official of long standing was escorted to the door and told that his office effects would be forwarded to his home. Ameritech says it gave terminated employees the choice to pack up their own things or to have them sent home.

Aside from its questionable ethics, this conduct produces paranoia, says one former high-ranking Ameritech officer who left voluntarily. "Some managers are saying that paternalism has made American business soft and less competitive. But in the old days we could recruit good people to the Bell system and keep them for less money than the competition because we could tell them they would be taken care of for life. That culture had some value. Yet it's all being tossed aside as worthless, mostly in the name of stripping out costs. I'm not sure the net gain from productivity is really going to be there in the long run."

Jim Eibel is clearly uncomfortable with some parts of the process. "I've had some sleepless nights," he says. "You have some tough things to do, and it's not easy. I am very close friends with two of the people who left, and I had a lot of personal concern for them and what happened after." How to cope with it? "When you go through one of these things," he says, "it's important that you really do believe in it, that you're fully committed to the necessity for change."

IS THE ROUGH STUFF really required? Tenneco CEO Michael Walsh, who has eliminated thousands of jobs himself, doesn't think so. "This Nazi approach is just so unnecessary," he says. "It's stupid and unproductive and inhumane. Just because an individual doesn't fit into a certain employment situation doesn't mean he or

she isn't a good person. Besides, the biggest leadership challenge is to help good people change, not to get rid of them."

Tenneco's Rebecca McDonald says that since Walsh arrived, "there's a lot more opportunity here for everybody—except people who can't be flexible, people who have no tolerance for ambiguity." Walsh, she says, was and is very clear, and very consistent, about his expectations. "He put it out there and said, 'This is what I believe in: things like quality, creativity, cost control. No surprises. No excuses.' And he has always been open to criticism."

To communicate what the new boss wants, McDonald says, consistency is critical: "You walk the walk as well as talk the talk. You structure the environment to foster the changes." But, she admits, not everyone sees the logic. "You hear a lot of rationalization: 'This is just the flavor of the month, so I don't have to do it. This was good enough before. Maybe the problem isn't me; maybe it's with all of you.' When that happens, we say: 'You may be right. Some other organizations out there aren't embracing this. Maybe you'd be happier with them.' It used to be you fired people because they'd messed up a deal or lost some money. Now they have to go if quality isn't the most important thing to them."

Her experience belies the "old dog, new tricks" cliché. "It's not at all a question of age," she says. "We see a lot of kids just out of college with preconceptions of what business is going to be like, and they just can't adjust. But many of our older people are terribly relieved by all this. Maybe they've been doing the right things all along—taking care of the customers—in spite of the system, and they've been frustrated. All of a sudden they feel appreciated, almost discovered."

What's more, McDonald, who had been the youngest vice president ever at another company in the good-old-boy-dominated gas industry, Panhandle Eastern, has some provocative thoughts on the role women play in the new chaotic environment. "You hear a lot of talk about changing the way we teach little girls because they're taught to listen and accommodate, while little boys are taught to win at all costs. I wonder if, really, we shouldn't rethink the way we're teaching boys. The rigidity that comes from expecting to win at all costs doesn't necessarily play to the new skill sets for corporate America."

Those management skills include dealing with needs, issues, and market forces that are not often clearly defined. "Women have a higher tolerance for ambiguity because we've always been responsible for tending to the emotional needs of others—which are very fluid. We learn to read between the lines and come up with creative solutions for accommodating people," says McDonald.

"What I'm suggesting isn't touchy-feely at all. Results, results, results are still the bottom line. I'm just saying that women are especially suited to today's demands: listening, communicating, getting to the root of the problem. It's what we're trained for."

In Massachusetts, at Digital Equipment, Willow Shire agrees: "Women are used to juggling four or five things all the time. Most of us have never had the luxury of focusing on one thing at a time." A history of disenfranchisement helps too. "We were never invested in the old boy club," she says. "So when it's time to tear down the old system, we have nothing to lose."

That time came to Digital last fall when the struggling computer maker ousted its CEO and founder, Ken Olsen. His replacement, Bob Palmer, quickly began restructuring the company around nine new business units, including Shire's. Like Jim Eibel, Shire devotes much of her time to purging the old corporate folkways from her organization. "We are in the process of a cultural revolution," she says. "First, we have to get rid of that old engineering idea: 'Build a good box, and they will come.' And we have to focus on accountability. In the past, if you were terribly charming and quite influential, you could pretend that you were successful. But we didn't focus on the customer, and we paid no attention to the underlying profitability of what we were doing."

Two examples of what she means:

Recently she learned that one of her salesmen had never called on the head of a large Veterans Administration hospital to which he had been selling disk drives for three years. She forced him to take her on a sales call and learned that the hospital director had invested in an array of sophisticated computer projects—all Hewlett-Packard equipment. Says Shire, with disgust: "Yet here we are patting ourselves on the back because we've got a multimillion-dollar contract to sell disk drives."

And: Another salesman flew the management staff of a hospital client from Alabama to Massachusetts to tour Digital's Alpha AXP chip manufacturing plant. Examining the client's history, Shire determined that Digital was actually losing money on its business. "I asked the salesman, 'Where is your profitability on this trip?' But I could tell he simply had no idea why the plant tour was a bad move."

How will she get the reform she wants? By choosing the right people for the job—and letting the rest go. "There's a lot of nervousness around here," she says. "And there should be." One item on her agenda today captures the mood: a meeting with 20 or so managers assigned to task forces charged with helping to define the new division. It soon becomes apparent that the folks in the room—mostly men—have no idea whether jobs will be waiting for them once the division structure is in place. Only two participants, both women, who are in effect Shire's COO and CFO, are confident they have positions. Everyone else is auditioning for jobs, which Shire tells the group "will be posted."

AMID ALL THIS reorganization, Shire still has to focus on the customer, which is why today she is also meeting with representatives of Australia's national health care system. After some technical chitchat about systems for transmitting medical images to physicians in the outback, the Australians want to talk about things like "partnering" and "commitment."

"Look," Shire tells the Australians, "selling equipment is boring to me. Shipping boxes isn't exciting to me. Coming up with solutions to save lives and improve the quality of health care *is* exciting." Fine, but the

> ## "There's a lot of nervousness around here," says DEC's Willow Shire. "And there should be."

Australians want to know who would be their personal hand-holder should their business go to Digital. Shire turns to her sales representative, whom she has corrected several times during the presentation, and says a bit ominously, "You're the contact until you're not."

In everything she does—running through the halls between meetings, for example—Shire exudes urgency. As she says over and over to her employees: "We are out of time. There is no more time." She means this both

in the larger sense—"We must return to profitability before too many quarters pass"—and in the immediate sense; anyone late to one of her meetings is fined $1, the proceeds of which are donated to St. Jude Children's Research Hospital in Memphis. Since she has only until July 1 to get her new unit staffed and moving, Shire worries that waging the revolution so quickly might break things unnecessarily. "I don't want to lay off revenue-producing people just for the sake of laying off. And I don't want orders sitting in a drawer somewhere waiting to be filled. It's all very exciting. Am I scared? I'm scared to death."

Jim Eibel, Rebecca McDonald, Willow Shire, Duane Hartley. All are senior managers who worked their way through the old corporate hierarchies. Now, for the success of their companies and their own careers, they must lead the way through today's chaos to create new ways of doing business, new ways of thinking, new ways of managing people—whole new corporate cultures.

Can You Manage
in the
New Economy?

*There may be a formula, but it's not nice and neat. And, not so incidentally,
the experts differ on the details of the "new" economy.*

John S. McClenahen

• Looking Beyond U.S. Borders. • Relating to the Needs
of Customers and Employees. • Redefining Processes. •
Engendering Trust. • Encouraging Teamwork.

*American industry must do all these things if it is to
succeed in global markets during the rest of the 1990s and
on into the 21st century. You've read and heard about
these practices for a decade—at least since Chairman &
CEO John F. Welch Jr. set a revolution in motion at
General Electric Co. in the early 1980s. You've also been
told that American companies need to be both more disciplined and more flexible. And you have probably been
advised that managers need to be entrepreneurs and agents
of change. You're about to encounter these ideas again in
the following five thoughtful perspectives on managing in
a new economy. But among the positions put forth by
management consultants and educators you'll find some
differences—in reasoning and emphasis, in suggested
courses of action, and in the perceived nature of the
economy.*

P. RANGANATH NAYAK

"The impression one gets is that there is a tremendous recession
underway. There isn't," claims P. Ranganath Nayak, a senior
vice president at Arthur D. Little Inc. (ADL), Cambridge,
Mass. "In fact, the economy of the United States has been
growing at pretty much historic rates for some time now." Some
segments of U.S. industry are hurting—a result of overinvesting
in capacity and other past management misjudgments, he allows. Autos, for example.

But Dr. Nayak points to the nation's "troubled" computer
industry and cites Hewlett-Packard Co., Microsoft Corp., Sun
Microsystems Inc., Intel Corp., and Dell Computer Corp. as
companies that "are going gangbusters." Part of the mistaken
impression that the country is in for a prolonged period of slow
growth and low business profits derives from corporate downsizing, including the massive layoffs such companies as General
Motors, IBM, and Sears have announced during the last several
months, believes Dr. Nayak. Confronted by billions of dollars in
losses, these companies are seeking the keys to turnarounds.

"IT'S DIFFICULT FOR A COMPANY THAT IS PROSPEROUS ALSO TO REMAIN AUSTERE, BUT THAT IS THE REAL CHALLENGE OF MANAGEMENT."

Sensitive to the human costs and social toll of the resulting
unemployment, Dr. Nayak is nevertheless encouraged that large
U.S. companies have begun to thin their ranks. "Companies are
finally beginning to prepare for the future." Indeed, if Dr.
Nayak had his way, the firms would be on perpetual diets. He's
convinced that big, bulky companies become inbred, overconfi-
dent, and insulated from competitive pressures. Their managers
become self-centered and begin to believe the purpose of the
business is to serve their ends. Notably, they do not detect the
warning signs of trouble.

"Warnings are there long, long before a crisis actually
begins," Dr. Nayak contends. GM wasn't listening 20 years ago
when the marketplace was telling it to make high-quality,
reasonably priced small cars, he states. Also back in the 1970s,
Detroit's automakers used to take *Consumer Reports* magazine

to task for criticizing their cars when they should have regarded the magazine as a voice of their customers, he says. And, more recently, "Ross Perot sounded an alarm at General Motors, and he got thrown out—or bought out," he recalls. "That is [the kind of thing] that eventually kills companies." Yet the ADL consultant is not ready to sign death certificates for GM, IBM, and several other large U.S. firms now struggling to get their acts in order. He believes they can again be very profitable and command leadership positions in their industries.

But they must be vigilant. They must be disciplined. They must keep close to their customers and carefully eye their competition. And they must resist bulking up.

"It's difficult for a company that is prosperous also to remain austere, but that is the real challenge of management," says Dr. Nayak.

Clearly, Dr. Nayak likes what he has seen at Microsoft Corp., the $3 billion, highly successful Redmond, Wash.-based software producer. There are tight controls on hiring, no first-class travel for anyone (not even Chairman William H. Gates III) no limousines, no perks, Dr. Nayak reports.

He contrasts Microsoft's austerity with the out-of-control hiring and spending that he says characterize "a lot" of big companies when good times get rolling. Wrongly assuming that the company's continued growth will be constrained by its current complement of workers and facilities, management adds to the payroll and to capacity. And once that has happened, "all it takes is one year of slow growth and the company is in trouble," says Dr. Nayak. Terrific profits can turn into serious losses, and the company is back into the "horrible cycle of firing thousands of people and demotivating those who are left. And you can't satisfy your customers with demotivated employees."

"We are developing a mental model which says a new kind of capitalism is [emerging] and that there are three kinds of capital that most managers need to worry about," Dr. Nayak relates. "One is finance, which is the traditional thing we have thought about. One is the attitude of your customers toward you and their satisfaction with what you do. And the third is the dedication of your employees. You need to husband and conserve and build all three kinds of capital simultaneously."

Put another way, Dr. Nayak is saying the job of a company is to create value for all its stakeholders—shareholders, customers, and employees—and all at the same time. "If that idea gets truly imbedded in managers' minds, then it becomes difficult to go astray," he contends.

As a kind of reality check, Dr. Nayak suggests managers should periodically ask themselves seven questions:

- Why am I in business?
- Who are my stakeholders?
- Do I know what they want and how satisfied they are?
- If I know what they want, why am I not giving them what they want?
- What am I going to do about it?
- Can I do more than my stakeholders expect?
- Can I increase value delivered to stakeholders faster than my competitors?

WILLIAM BEST

William Best, A. T. Kearney Inc.'s Hong Kong-based vice president for Asia, differs with Dr. Nayak on the U.S. economic outlook. "The U.S. is in persistent slow growth," he insists. "Despite recent Clinton promises, with the budget and trade deficits where they are for the foreseeable future it's going to be a long time before the U.S. climbs out of its economic misery." Consequently, "one of the things management has to do is to focus on international markets that are going to be the engine of growth in the future." The major opportunities are not on the eastern side of the Atlantic Ocean where Europeans, saddled with high unemployment and Eastern European integration, are constructing a protectionist moat that makes it easier to compete within the European Community than from outside, claims Mr. Best. But great growth markets do exist in Southeast Asia and China, he states. For example, in China's Guandong province, just to the north of Hong Kong, inflation-adjusted economic growth is 20% to 30% a year, more than six times the rate INDUSTRY-WEEK projects for the U.S. in 1993. However, to succeed in Asia, U.S. and other Western companies must stop viewing the region only as the home of low-cost labor, says Mr. Best. With the exception of firms such as Coca-Cola Co. and

---

"COMPANIES THAT OVERLOOK THE ASIAN OPPORTUNITY ARE COMMITTING WHAT IS TANTAMOUNT TO COMPETITIVE SUICIDE."

Du Pont Co., companies "have overlooked [Asia] as a place to sell consumer and industrial goods," the Kearney consultant says. Major opportunities exist in China for U.S. chemical companies, for example, and there's active interest in pharmaceuticals. Chinese "hospitals are changing the way they administer drugs, and there are some regulatory changes going on that are going to make that market grow faster than normal," he says. "Companies that overlook the Asian opportunity are committing what is tantamount to competitive suicide." To succeed, U.S. firms also need a physical presence in Asia; they can't sit back in Milwaukee or Moline or Toledo or Tampa, says Mr. Best. "They have to study the opportunities themselves. They've got to become insiders in the marketplace. This is why Motorola is investing about $120 million in Tianjin in China. [Motorola] is going to become an insider; it is going to have first-to-market advantages that other companies are just not going to have." Motorola says its facility, announced last June, will contain assembly and test operations for discrete semiconductors and integrated circuits, pagers, cellular radiotelephones, automobile electronic ignitions and regulators, and two-way radios.

Mr. Best counsels U.S. companies to look first to one project in one country—and not initially try to do something in 13 or 14 countries simultaneously. Kearney studies show that Western companies that make it in Asia "tend to really focus their efforts on a few countries where they can achieve critical mass in a reasonable period of time and then, after success has been secured, move on to the other opportunities in Asia." Significantly, he says, for most Western companies human resources constitute the biggest constraint on success. "They just don't have the managers on staff who can come to Asia and be successful in Asia," he states. "Essentially what it comes down to is getting an Asian manager to a point where you trust him to manage your investment in a manner consistent with corporate expectations."

But "there is only a handful of companies that have reached that point," Mr. Best says. "Unfortunately, you can't just go to your competitor and pull out a great manager—as you can in the U.S." Take China, he suggests. The country lacks "management that can operate along Western norms. You can always get a manager out of one of the Chinese factories, but he will continue to manage the old way. He won't manage the way your company would manage. It'll take 10 years before you can develop a senior manager who understands your corporate culture and understands the Western system well enough to take it over."

WILLIAM F. GLAVIN

The intensity of global competition in the "new" economy will make it impossible for any area of the world to have a lock on any industry, any product, or any service, asserts William F. Glavin, president of Babson College, Wellesley, Mass., and a former vice chairman of Xerox Corp. "We are going to have multiple countries competing in the same businesses. Fulfilling customer requirements with lower cost will be the driving factor in successes. And the people who spend their time looking at how to do things differently, more cost-effectively, and right the first time are the ones most likely to succeed.

Slow growth? That's something Mr. Glavin is not sure about. However, "I think we will not have the kinds of profit margins that we have had before. But there's still money to be made. There still will be returns on equity and investments that are adequate—and better than what you could do by putting your money in the stock market or buying bonds."

Get out of businesses that clearly aren't going to make it, he counsels. But be very wary of the current back-to-the-core movement, he also cautions. Mr. Glavin reasons there is nothing inherently wrong with the out-of-the-mainstream businesses many firms got into over the years. Indeed, those businesses can be viable and profitable—with proper management, he contends. But what back-to-the-core "says to me is that the management of a particular company can't manage some of those other businesses," states Mr. Glavin.

"Well, maybe you can't manage diverse businesses. But somebody else can. So why don't you hire people who could do that for you and let them run it on their own?" he asks, rhetorically.

Example: General Motors! "Although I think GM's management has been one of the total disasters in my lifetime in industry, there's one thing that GM did that really is pleasantly surprising to me. It set up EDS [Electronic Data Systems Corp.]

and Hughes [GM Hughes Electronics Corp.] with their own stock. Those companies are run as if they were not owned by General Motors. And they're able to make good business decisions and have good management. EDS recently came out with record earnings! And the rest of General Motors is in trouble."

"YOU HAVE TO START WITH THE CONFIDENCE TO TAKE RISKS AND THEN BE WILLING TO TAKE RISKS IN ENVIRONMENTS THAT ARE NOT WITHIN YOUR OWN UNDERSTANDING."

The problem, reiterates Mr. Glavin, is not diverse businesses collected under a corporate umbrella. Indeed, "what makes us think that the managers who are selling off non-core businesses can manage the core businesses?" he wonders. "Why couldn't they have managed those other businesses?" Mr. Glavin's telling reply is that the managers were inflexible, tried to control everything from corporate headquarters, and didn't have the entrepreneur's willingness to take risks. *They* were the problem.

Significantly, taking risks—while recognizing the limits of one's own experiences and doing something about them—will be critical to global business successes, believes Mr. Glavin. "You have to start with the confidence to take risks and then be willing to take risks in environments that are not within your own understanding," he states. And "you have to hire competent people who know the areas you are weak in," he stresses.

Among the most successful entrepreneurs who are Babson College graduates there is a common characteristic: the willingness to hire people "who are smarter than they are in those areas in which they recognize they don't have talent," says the college's president. "Most people think entrepreneurs have such huge egos that they won't hire anybody because they believe they know all the answers. But the great successful entrepreneurs have hired others with needed specific expertise."

LOUIS E. LATAIF

The management of U.S. industry will face three special challenges during the decade ahead, believes Louis E. Lataif, dean of Boston University's School of Management, a former president of Ford of Europe, and former Ford Motor Co. vice president for worldwide quality and marketing.

- Competition will no longer be limited to North America—for U.S. companies of *any* size.
- Social changes, including the two-career family, are likely to make people less mobile and cause companies to be more flexible in their human-resources policies.
- Companies "necessarily" will be less hierarchical, and that will require new management skills.

"Many companies, I think, are going to do work cooperatively with competitors and other companies on specific projects—what some people call the 'virtual' corporation," says Dean Lataif. "I am not of the school that says that is what *all* corporations will be like. But I do sense that there will many more cooperative ventures undertaken among normally noncooperating entities." A current example: Ford and Nissan linked in the production of a minivan that's sold through Lincoln-Mercury dealerships—with a separate version sold through Nissan dealers.

"Most compelling from my standpoint is the idea that we will be managing process . . . rather than function, which is the way we have all been taught to manage," Dean Lataif states. The emphasis, he indicates, will be on integrating the *interdependent* functions involved in producing or adding value to goods and services for customers, and not on simply optimizing design, manufacturing, marketing, and each of the other functional elements.

Dean Lataif believes bigness is not the major problem confronting large American companies. "Size alone is not a deterrent to success," he states. Procter & Gamble Co., a $29.4 billion firm, regularly seems to reinvent and rejuvenate itself, he notes.

Rather, because companies, like people, have life cycles, "part of what we have to learn is how to keep a big organization freshened with . . . youthful vigor—irrespective of its chronological age," he says. "Bob Galvin [chairman of the executive committee at Motorola] articulates the philosophy of 'Ready, Fire, Aim.' " Instead of analyzing innovation to death, "he tries to create an atmosphere where people will invent, try something on a scale that doesn't bet the whole store, and undertake the analysis while experimenting," says an approving Dean Lataif.

Another way to help keep companies competitive, he says, is to anticipate product maturity and innovate on the upside of the demand curve. In other words, don't wait for the peak. Example: Japanese "re-invention" of video cassettes. Even as global demand grows for the original, relatively large cartridge, several Japanese firms are developing new sizes and shapes and are not waiting for customers to beg for them, he states. "You hear that expressed now in some TQM [total quality management] circles as: 'Fix it when it isn't broken.' "

How does Dean Lataif size up the "new" economy? Essentially as history repeating itself. "I don't have any reason to believe that the normal ebb and flow of the economic cycle is likely to be any different in the years ahead than it has been in the past." For example, the notion that profits are now going to be irrevocably compressed "is not something that I can logically buy into." Yes, as a result of greater competition, some mature, commodity-type industries may have a more difficult time making profits, he allows. "But even in the automobile business, where they've been through a very bad patch the last few years, I have every confidence that in the next several years the U.S. auto companies are going to realize some superb profit years."

NOEL TICHY

A University of Michigan School of Business professor, Noel M. Tichy's perspective on managing in the new economy could fill a book. In fact, it does: *Control Your Destiny or Someone Else Will: How Jack Welch Is Making General Electric the World's Most Competitive Company,* co-authored with Stratford Sherman (Currency Doubleday, 1993).

The essence of his message: To survive in a highly competitive global environment, U.S. industry must restructure, refocus, and then keep the revolution alive.

Restructuring means cutting out overcapacity and getting rid of bloated bureaucracies. "It is to take the unnecessary, non-value-added customer work out and to get back to the essentials," states Dr. Tichy. "You actually want to recreate a 'Mom and Pop' shop, where everybody wakes up every day worried about everything from receivables to value added to the customer." Restructuring involves "flattening" the organization—dramatically reducing the number of layers from the bottom to the top of a business. It means wider spans of control for a new complement of fewer management positions. It means fewer reports and meetings. It means more risk-taking and, hopefully, greater speed.

For middle managers, it means that everything they once learned about goal setting, work planning, and doing appraisals no longer works, says Dr. Tichy. With as many as 20 to 30 people now reporting to a single person, "you have to form teams, [and] you have to develop new ways of goal setting, individual work planning, and coordinating," he states.

Refocusing is "how do we make a buck in the global marketplace?—all the good strategic-positioning stuff," quips Dr. Tichy. It is, he says, repeatedly and objectively asking management guru Peter Drucker's question: "If we weren't in this business today, would we start it today?" At GE, it was Mr. Welch stating that if a business were not No. 1 or No. 2 in its field, it was to be fixed, closed, or sold, relates the University of Michigan professor.

Keeping the revolution going may be the toughest task of all because it says that a state of change is to be the normal state, and that runs counter to human nature, says Dr. Tichy. To overcome the natural inertia, it takes dissatisfaction with the status quo, a vision of the future, *and* a first step toward change—whether the issue is improving individual physical fitness or overhauling a big corporation, he states. "The leader ends up having to manipulate all three of those: to create dissatisfaction where there isn't enough; to give the focus, the vision; and then to be very practical and pragmatic on first steps. Otherwise you're dealing with an abstraction."

At GE, the vehicle for sustaining Jack Welch's revolution is an off-site, "town-hall," continuous-improvement process dubbed Work-Out. As Dr. Tichy explains it, people at all levels come together to revisit the business' vision. They look for ways to eliminate reports, approvals, measurements, meetings, and policies that don't add customer value. And they use process mapping to try to get better quality and greater speed out of everything they are doing.

"The point of Work-Out is to give people better jobs," says Mr. Welch in Dr. Tichy's book. "When people see that their ideas count, their dignity is raised. Instead of feeling numb, like robots, they feel important. They *are* important."

Business in the 21st Century

Businesses must master the "forgetting curve" to cope with new challenges such as environmentalism and an emerging "cyberpunk" society.

Edith Weiner

Edith Weiner is president of Weiner, Edrich, Brown, Inc., 200 East 33rd Street, New York, New York 10016. This article is based on her presentation at "Business & The Future: Planning to Survive and Progress through the '90s and into the 21st Century," a World Future Society conference held on September 11–13, 1991, in New York City.

Some years ago, I saw a marvelous cartoon depicting an alien spaceship that had been observing life on Earth. The alien scouts reported the following conclusions: Earth is inhabited by metallic creatures called cars, and each car owns at least one two-legged slave who cares for it. Each morning, the slave goes outside its home and wakes up the car. The car is taken for its nourishment to what is called a gas station, and then it goes to its social club to be with other cars. The club is called a parking lot. Meanwhile, the slave goes to work to earn money to take care of the car. At the end of the slave's work day, the car bids farewell to its friends at the parking lot and the slave takes it back to its home. On days when the slave is not making money for the car, it washes the car, or takes it for a drive and shows it a lot of different places.

This cartoon cleverly points out

that, viewed by new eyes, alien eyes, the world can be interpreted in very different ways. Businesses that hope to thrive in the next decade and beyond must seek out new perspectives. Too many enterprises are currently based on outdated interpretations of the world, its inhabitants, its social structures, and the ways that markets behave.

Pretend for a moment that we are aliens—that we are not loaded down with the baggage of memory, of experience, of preconceived ideas about what is and what should be.

Suppose we were to invent the financial-services sector today, from scratch. This sector includes life insurance, disability insurance, pensions, and savings and investment vehicles. What do we see with our new eyes? We observe the huge numbers of working women, and particularly single or divorced working mothers, and we see the enormous numbers of women who outlive men in their very old years. We also see many more women taking care of disabled men than men taking care of disabled women. Thus, we conclude that the primary market for all forms of financial services should be women, and we start from there. The reality is, however, that the modern financial-services business grew up over the course of 200 years and evolved with

a male-oriented market; only in the past 20 years has it *begun* to recognize women as a serious market.

Mastering the Forgetting Curve

Let's look at retailing. This is one of many business sectors affected by "disintermediation," the bypassing of traditional channels for the delivery of goods and services in the marketplace. For example, people no longer go only to general practitioners or hospitals for health care. There are specialists, homeopaths, outpatient clinics, do-it-yourself tests and remedies, health clubs and spas, nutrition centers and stores, health maintenance organizations, preferred provider organizations, diet books, exercise videos, and on and on.

As for retailing, suppose we own a clothing store that sells things like slacks and blouses and skirts. But today, these same items are sold through catalogs, on television, on sidewalks, through purchase clubs, etc. Why would anyone want to travel to our store and buy the clothing in person? Why should they take the time?

Maybe it's because they like to try on clothing before buying it. If so, why are our fitting rooms tiny stalls in the back of the store, with limited numbers of garments allowed to be tried on at one time? Why don't they occupy 30% of the floor space, each

From *The Futurist*, March/April 1992, pp. 13-17. *The Futurist*, published by the World Future Society, 7910 Woodmont Ave., Suite 450, Bethesda, MD 20814.

room large, with different lighting and seating options so customers could see how the clothes really look on them?

In a changing business environment, clothing retailers' memory and experience prevent them from recognizing fitting rooms as the major attraction of a store. A major challenge to businesses that wish to survive and thrive in the next decade is to stop worrying only about the learning curve. Any bright individual or management team can quickly rise on the learning curve. Executives must come to value and master the forgetting curve. Forgetting is much more difficult than learning. But it holds the key to tomorrow, whereas many business people expend much of their energy and resources merely peering through the keyhole.

The image of the keyhole conjures up another kind of alien world: Alice in Wonderland, with Alice peering through a keyhole to see the elusive white rabbit vanish. She is far too big to pass through the door, but she is given two options—or tools, if you will—to potentially achieve her goal. One is a solid that says "eat me" and winds up making her too big. Another is a liquid that says "drink me" and leaves her too tiny to reach the key. Eventually, Alice figures out that if she eats some and drinks some and eats some and drinks some, she'll be just the right size.

Businesses seem to be doing exactly that as they experiment with management styles and concepts of success. First, Japan emulates the United States, then the United States emulates Japan, then both emulate each other in fits and starts. In the next decade, businesses will be picking and choosing those things about each other that seem to spell success and trying to shed those that portend failure.

For the past several decades, one management guru after another has come along and provided a theory or formula that spread through business circles, became adopted as a panacea at great cost, creating internal turmoil, only to be uprooted a few years later by the new wave of management theory. This activity will only get stronger in the 1990s. Eat some, drink some, eat some, drink some . . . eventually, a number

of businesses will find their own right combination to fit through Alice's door. But getting through will not necessarily mean being successful. Keeping the white rabbit in sight doesn't mean catching it.

The Cyberpunk Scenario

What's on the other side of the door? What does the future hold for business? To answer that, we have to begin with a scenario of what the future holds in general.

For some years now, Anthony Burgess's science-fiction novel *A Clockwork Orange* has appeared to be unfolding in reality. Society is becoming increasingly polarized: Those with wealth and access to all manner of advanced technology are juxtaposed against a growing alienated, illiterate, sociopathological underclass. This phenomenon is occurring all over the world, and not just in urban areas. Growing gang membership, abandoned and orphaned children, drug running and AIDS babies, malnutrition, the spread of guns and violence, deteriorating economic prospects—all of these factors weigh heavily on much of the world's young, giving rise to the main social characteristics of what is called the cyberpunk future.

Cyberpunk is a term that combines cybernetics—or the human–machine interface—with punk, that nihilistic, defeatist, and street-culture-oriented view of life and the future. In a cyberpunk society, the haves will increasingly seek to remove and protect their persons and property from the have-nots. Thus, security—in all its manifestations—is likely to be one of the fastest-growing and largest businesses of the twenty-first century.

The cyberpunk vision of the future also foresees the rise of all-powerful global corporations, superseding the relevance of nation-states. This, too, is not an unreasonable assumption to make as we head into the twenty-first century. The recent geopolitical boundaries that we have called nation-states have been undergoing serious attacks. Again, let us become aliens and observe the earth as if for the first time. What do we see?

We see economic activity going on 24 hours a day, seven days a week, around the globe via satellite and

computer technologies that know no national boundaries. We see interdependent markets and economies tied into each other, with powerful and growing feedback loops, such that no area of the world has sure control over its own domestic finances, industries, and economic policy. We see ecological issues that respect no lines drawn on maps. The magnitude of and solutions to most environmental problems are beyond any one nation's control.

We see massive movements of human beings around the globe, such that waves of people from the Southern Hemisphere are migrating north, creating whole new cultures and geographical affiliations. We see information, whether via television or fax machines, making a mockery of cultural and national isolationism and exposing everyone, everywhere, to what many never had access to before. And we see peoples reuniting and breaking apart based on heritage and common belief systems as opposed to geopolitics and governments.

If we see these aspects of our changing world through our new, unbiased alien eyes, we know that they portend great changes ahead for business in the twenty-first century. As global corporations begin to inherit the charges once given to the nation-states, including those of instigating wars and petitioning for peace, we will hear more talk of such things as corporate culture, corporate flags, corporate security forces, corporate democracy, corporate credos, corporate social responsibility, and the global work force.

And, paradoxically, as sociopolitical agendas and infrastructure needs desperately call for more and more taxation of business, business will be courted everywhere around the world based on tax relief and favorable regulatory conditions.

The Stewardship Ethic

Environmentalism experienced a major shift in the late 1970s, and that shift will continue to shake the foundations of business well into the twenty-first century.

A decade ago, in even the most conservative churches of the industrialized nations, something groundbreaking was occurring: The Book of Genesis was being reinterpreted.

Where once it had been translated as saying that man has *dominion over* the earth and all its resources, it was now being taught that humankind has *stewardship for* the earth and its resources.

Dominion is an industrial model which implies that mankind is at the top of a hierarchy and entitled to exploit all of nature and even other humans for its own ends. Stewardship, however, says that there is no hierarchy, that humanity is given the task of caring for and preserving the earth and all its resources, to return them in as good or better shape to each succeeding generation. These two interpretations of Genesis are as different as night and day. The stewardship model has begun to take hold around the globe, and it has come to affect all manner of commerce and enterprise.

Animal testing, for example, has become as contested an issue as it is because many in mainstream society have concluded not that it's not *nice* to hurt animals, but that it's not our *right* to hurt animals. They believe that animals and humans have equal footing in the natural scheme of things, and we're supposed to care for rather than exploit them.

It is stewardship, rather than Marxism or socialism or communism, that will provide the future counterpoint to capitalism. In the years ahead, stewardship will underpin the great bulk of policy in the United States and worldwide, whether in politics (as in the Green parties sprouting up across the globe), in business practices (as in the clarion call to focus on management ethics and stakeholder rights), or in social-priority shifts (as in the concern for family, community, church, and education as the cornerstones of the next generation's success). It is critical for any large business that wants to succeed into the twenty-first century to fully understand this tidal wave of change sweeping over humanity.

Integrity Pays Off

In line with the stewardship ethic, a subtle shift will take place over the next five years in the discussion about, and focus on, quality. Quality was the buzzword of the late 1980s, as management circles focused on a new economic quantifier in a competitive environment—the amount of perfection or flawlessness in its goods that a company could deliver to the consumer. This was seen as Japan's edge, which the United States once had and then gave away. Sloppy work habits, careless attention to detail, and mismatches between customer wants and product performance were all studied under microscopes and attacked with injections of quality circles, suggestion boxes, whistle-blowing policies, computerization, market research, executive speeches, and profit-sharing plans. These measures will all continue in the 1990s, as quality becomes a cornerstone of doing business, a commodity without which a business may not survive.

But quality will begin to be superseded by another factor, something more basic than quality and from which quality automatically flows. And that is integrity.

Integrity is not an economic or quantitative measure of performance, but an attitudinal and value-based method of doing business. While I wish I could say that only businesses which operate with the highest degree of integrity will succeed, that will not be the case. In a cutthroat market environment, many companies will abandon ethics for quick profits. If we want to know which current companies will survive and thrive over the next 10 years, we cannot base the answer on integrity. But if we want to know which companies will survive the next 25 years, then we look to companies that consider the needs of their employees, their customers, and society at large, companies that embody concern and affection, service and caring, honor and fairness. Integrity may cost dearly in the short run, but it pays off well and long into the future.

Speaking about a cutthroat market environment, there is one handicap that U.S. companies will continue to encounter as they expand around the world: a lack of familiar distribution infrastructures. The United States is the strongest retail environment in the world. But in most other countries, personal sales, family business, and community-based commerce are strong, if not domi-nant. In the United States, only the life insurance business and a few companies, like Avon and Amway, have longtime experience in this new distribution environment.

Other Challenges to Business

There are dozens and dozens more challenges that businesses face as they square off with the future. A few of these include:

1. The mapping of the human genome, which will result in the cracking of the human genetic code. This will not only revolutionize health insurance and social inter-action (prospective couples will wish to know each other's genetic infor-mation), but also affect the bases of capital accumulation in countries around the world: their pension and life insurance businesses.

2. The changing nature of house-holds. The idea of a "typical" family or household makeup is becoming more and more obsolete. Of special note in the 1990s will be the rising numbers of men living alone and of seniors in shared arrangements with nonrelated individuals.

3. The burgeoning health insur-ance crisis. This will lead to "health wars" in which activists for one dis-ease (such as breast cancer) will chal-lenge the emphasis placed on an-other (such as AIDS), or in which constituents for one group (such as those pressing for neonatal care for the young) will attack the priorities of other groups (such as those asking for Alzheimer's funding for the old). Scarce funding and escalating costs will not only force some forms of ra-tioning, but will also take signifi-cantly more dollars directly out of consumers' pockets, potentially dampening what might otherwise have been a major boost in the sav-ings rates of nations with a maturing population.

4. The growth and proliferation of underground and gray economies around the world, casting much eco-nomic data in doubt and siphoning off profits from legitimate busi-nesses. The underground economy in the United States is estimated to be anywhere from 15% to 30% of the size of the gross national product. That would place it in the same range as the size of the aboveground GNP of Canada.

5. The increasing countertrade within and between all countries, including but not limited to barter arrangements. Tax and accounting systems will be greatly challenged by this method of business, which in the early 1990s already accounts for more than 20% of world commercial activity.

6. Desktop publishing, which will challenge not only existing media but all forms of communication. With a few thousand dollars' investment in computers and printers, anyone can become a purveyor of slick, professional-quality messages to more and more limited and targeted audiences.

A publication called *Factsheet Five* reviews the thousands of "zines" (small-circulation magazines) now being published. Some have subscription lists as small as a few dozen. Zines service every manner of interest, profession, belief system, or need.

7. The melding of rural, suburban, and urban populations and environments into what, for want of a better term, might be called rurbania. While so many center cities are closed down and abandoned after 6 p.m., farflung rural malls are open seven days a week until 10 p.m. The countryside is now dotted with satellite dishes, on lawns and in barnyards. Traditional notions of what differentiates downtown from outskirts from boondocks are all breaking down as businesses push outward, urban refugees seek space and safety, rural populations flock to suburbs for jobs, and values and expectations migrate as well.

8. Virtual reality. Sophisticated computer technology now allows individuals to interact with other people or many environments in a simulated but highly realistic fashion. Already, biophysicists can "walk" into molecules and explore them from many angles, and architects can "enter" buildings drawn but not yet built, to see and test their construction ideas. In Japan, consumers in a furniture showroom are able to experience themselves inside their own kitchens, creating alternative arrangements of cabinets until they strike upon the setup they wish to buy.

9. The challenge of intellectual property. Ownership of ideas, processes, and customer information becomes harder to determine in an economy that's more and more dependent upon intelligence—whether embedded in the human mind or in computer software. As employees switch companies and technology migrates across national boundaries, issues of licensing, trademark, and copyright will provide one more feeding frenzy for the world's overpopulation of lawyers. Already, a potentially important advance in energy—superconducting—is involved in multiparty patent contests that may take a decade to resolve.

10. The aging of industrial societies as a counterpoint to the youth of the Third World. Aging will alter lifestyles, the nature and makeup of work forces, the goods and services wanted and needed, and the public-policy choices made on a wide variety of issues, from lifelong education to health care.

One could add a number of other issues: the rising cost of college education, leading to a mismatch between true talent and paper credentials and to the possible return of apprenticeships; the economic importance of Latin America as a future area for serious attention and development; the buying of politicians through campaign funds that have turned many Western governments, and most notably that of the United States, into checkbook democracies, where only the rich and connected may play and where special interests dominate; the demographic pressures that are creating havoc in Japan; the rise of fundamentalist Protestantism, fueling capitalism in countries where Catholicism and socialism once flourished.

To cope with and profit from these developments, businesses must view them from new perspectives. Only by seeing through alien eyes can businesses picture the real future rather than the extrapolated one.

HOW WE WILL WORK IN THE YEAR 2000

The world of business is changing fundamentally. Cynics will deride the result as a freelance economy, but others will discover in it a new freedom.

Walter Kiechel III

THE YEAR 2000 will dawn on a Saturday, perfect for nursing recollections of the Nineties and soberly contemplating the era ahead. Ruminative types among the approximately 133 million people then in the work force will look back on a decade of change all the more head-spinning for its seemingly chaotic, devolutionary quality.

The average size of a U.S. company, measured by the number of individuals it employs, will have decreased. More people will have set up in business for themselves. Many of the industrial colossi, long the pillars of our economy, will have broken up or hollowed out. Taking the place of the hierarchically layered giants will be not just one type of organization but a variety of them, with names such as spider's web.

What Americans do on the job will have changed too, so much so as to cry out for a new definition of work. The old blue-collar elite will have ceded pride of place to an ascendant class, technical workers, who program computers or conduct laboratory tests or fix copiers. Almost everyone, up through the highest ranks of professionals, will feel increased pressure to specialize, or at least to package himself or herself as a marketable portfolio of skills. Executives and what used to be called managers will have undergone probably the most radical rethinking of their role.

And more and more of the population will be caught up in the defining activity of the age: scrambling. Scrambling for footing on a shifting corporate landscape—cynics will call it a freelance economy—where market forces have supplanted older, more comfortable employment arrangements. Scrambling to upgrade their software, their learning, their financial reserves. Scram-

REPORTER ASSOCIATE *Ani Hadjian*

bling even to carve out moments of tranquillity under a banner blazoned FIGHT STRESS, a banner flapping like a Tibetan prayer flag in the gales of change.

Stephen R. Barley, a professor at Cornell's School of Industrial and Labor Relations, builds on the work of others to argue that until recently, "the economies of the advanced industrial nations revolved around electrical power, the electric motor, the internal combustion engine, and the telephone." The development of these "infrastructural technologies" made possible the shift from an agricultural to a manufacturing economy, in the process precipitating "urbanization, the growth of corporations, the rise of professional management, the demise of religion, and the disintegration of the extended family."

Now, Barley writes, the evidence suggests that another shift is taking place, with implications likely to be just as seismic: "Our growing knowledge of how to convert electronic and mechanical impulses into digitally encoded information (and vice versa) and how to transmit such information across vast distances is gradually enabling industry to replace its electromechanical infrastructure with a computational infrastructure."

You already know part of the punch line from this not unfamiliar tale: The computational infrastructure, computers at its heart, takes over progressively more of the work that can be routinized—and ever more can, with the new technology—from guiding machines that make things to transmitting information within the organization or across its boundaries. Bingo, you've got flexible manufacturing, program trading, and point-of-purchase terminals wired into the supplier's factory.

Experts on such transformation, people like futurist Tom Mandel at SRI International in Menlo Park, California, correct

our impression that new technology drives changes in how we work; rather, it enables them. Posit increased competition through the Eighties, the maturity of existing infrastructural technologies, even a falling rate of profit overall for the postwar U.S. economy. The result of such pressures, argues Mandel, is that "people in business are rethinking, reinventing, reengineering, whatever you want to call it, the structure of work. When they sit down to ask, 'Can we do this a better way?' technology helps provide the answer."

FOR MANY companies evolving their way toward 2000, a big part of the answer is to get smaller, or to stay small from the outset. Look at the numbers: IBM now employs 302,000 people, down from 406,000 in 1985; Digital Equipment, 98,000, down from 126,000 in 1989. But then these two old-line computer companies compete against the likes of Apple, with 15,100 employees, Microsoft, with 13,800, and Novell, with 3,500, each of whose market capitalization—the total value of its outstanding stock—exceeds Digital's. AT&T, down to 312,000 people, recently saw the future and sought a piece of it, in the form of a one-third interest in McCaw Cellular, which employs 5,000.

Note that all these companies, the relatively small and the getting-smaller, are in industries central to the new computational infrastructure—what can only be seen as growth industries. If you want to gaze at employment prospects further out on the technology horizon, consider Genentech, the largest biotechnology company. It employs 2,100.

Unfair, the argument might come back: In comparing IBM with an Apple or a Microsoft you're comparing companies at very different stages of corporate development.

The younger outfits, as they mature, will surely add lots more employees.

If they do, they will be bucking the trend. Research by professors Erik Brynjolfsson and Thomas W. Malone of MIT's Sloan School indicates that while the average number of employees per company increased until the 1970s, it has been decreasing since then, particularly in manufacturing.

Why should more economic activity be devolving upon smaller companies? The work done at MIT points again to technology's enabling effects. Brynjolfsson found that even as the typical company in his study eliminated 20% of its employees over ten years, it tripled its investment in information technology. The investment generally preceded the downsizing, but the dynamic was considerably more subtle than a straightforward substitution of computational power for bodies. "Because computers tend to replace more routine workers while augmenting knowledge workers, they change the relative advantages and disadvantages of different types of organization," he explains. "Routine work is organized well in large hierarchical companies. Innovation and knowledge-work type activities"—presumably something like higher-order thinking and analysis—"thrive best under the incentives of small firms." Just ask any of the legion of millionaires at Microsoft.

Malone suggests that the true potential of computers and computer networks, and their effect on organizations, may lie less in their computational power and more in their capacity to take over "coordination activities"—from processing orders to keeping track of inventory to posting accounts. Computerized coordination can be substituted for human effort: Empty out those back offices full of clerks or those plusher spaces inhabited by managers passing information up and down the chain of command. Companies can do more coordination: *Voilà*, elaborate airline reservation systems with fares being constantly adjusted and, because for the first time the airlines can keep track of who goes where, frequent-flier programs.

The biggest effect may be a relatively unexpected one. Malone finds it somewhat surprising, but by now pretty clear, "that the increasing use of information technology appears likely to increase the importance of market mechanisms as a way of coordinating economic activity"—market mechanisms as opposed to a company's internal control systems and procedures. To oversimplify cartoonishly, the benefits of vertical integration melt away. The company discovers that compared with making a product or doing a service in-house, it's cheaper to outsource from one of the many outfits scrambling for the business over the computational infrastructure.

SO WE ALL end up working in so-called network organizations, right, hooked in with customers and suppliers via technology and the company itself perhaps structured as a network to mirror its various outside interfaces, pardon the expression? If you've been keeping up on your reading, you will think of the modular or virtual corporation—should the trendies ever agree on a definition for the latter—an outfit pared down to its core competencies and sending out for everything else.

Ah, but it isn't that simple. "There's been a lot of attention, even press attention, to the network organization," sniffs professor James Brian Quinn from Dartmouth's Tuck School of Business. "But when we looked into the way organizations were really developing, the network was only one of about five different new forms. Each of the others was not strictly a network," but each has a distinctive logic behind it.

Quinn's new treatise, *Intelligent Enterprise* (Free Press), the closest approximation we have to a textbook on the emerging economy, describes, for example, the "radically flat organization." Hundreds of separate sites—stores, offices—transmit information to a single headquarters where it's digested, decisions are made, and directions in turn sent back to the sites, which don't need to be in touch with one another. Anyone recognize Wal-Mart here, or Merrill Lynch, with its 12,700 far-flung account executives?

For the Tuck professor, networks are central only to what he calls spider's web organizations, so named for "the lightness yet completeness of their interconnection." Here the examples to bear in mind are an Arthur Andersen Consulting or a McKinsey & Co., an investment banking house or a law firm. The accumulated knowledge in such an organization resides mostly in the heads of its people or in case teams—in network talk, both are at the "nodes"—who don't require, much less want, guidance from a hierarchical superior. What the nodes do require is lots of communication with one another to keep themselves abreast of what each has learned from the latest assignment.

Grant that no single organizational form will take the place of the old multilayer ziggurat as the new corporate model. Still, if you could pick only one to study for its lessons on how work will be structured and employees accommodated in the year 2000, put your chips on the network, Quinn's spider's web.

This not because more companies will come to resemble consulting firms—though more will—but because the vertical division of labor, based on ranks in a hierarchy, is giving way to a horizontal division, based on individuals' specialties. In the fu-

ture, the key question for most people will be not "Where do you stand on the corporate ladder?"—sounds of its demolition already ring through the land—but "What do you know how to do?" Pay will be tied less to a person's position or tenure and more to the changing market value of his skills.

CORNELL'S BARLEY, who has probably done the most to identify this trend, came at it from study of a remarkably overlooked echelon of the American labor force—technical workers. These folks don't jibe with our traditional stereotypes of white collar and blue, which may be why we haven't accorded them sufficient notice or respect. As described by Barley, they "often wear white collars, carry briefcases, conduct relatively sophisticated scientific and mathematical analysis, and speak with an educated flair." But many also "use tools and instruments, work with their hands, make objects, repair equipment, and perhaps most important, get dirty." They range from medical technologists to paralegals, from so-called test-and-pay technicians—really—to the person who hooked up the personal computer in your office.

Their ranks are growing. Indeed, if you wonder where the good jobs are going to be in the Nineties, look here. Together with professionals—accountants, scientists, engineers, and the like—whom they increasingly resemble and with whom the Census Bureau lumps them, they already represent about 16% of the work force. If the projections hold, some experts think that by 2000 they could be the biggest segment at 20%, or over 23 million people, substantially exceeding the number of manufacturing operatives and laborers. To the extent that any segment in the employment statistics approximates that much and loosely used term "knowledge workers," these people, along with their professional brethren, are it.

Barley attributes the rise of technical workers to a number of forces. Scientific knowledge has been growing exponentially, by some estimates doubling every six to ten years since the 1960s. Concomitantly, professionals scrambling to keep up with the latest learning have become increasingly specialized, in the process "hiving off" their more routine duties—taking X-rays, for example—to individuals less highly trained. Large professional service organizations—big hospitals, large consultancies, and law firms—can afford to support such increasingly narrow specialization.

But the biggest force behind the ascendance of technicians has been that ol' devil, or angel, technology. Over the past four decades, Barley notes, emerging technologies have created entirely new types of job: air traffic controller, nuclear technician, broadcast engineer, materials scientist. And then, of course, there's the computational infrastructure. Ask Barley what generalizations he can make about technical workers and he shoots back, "The only occupation that we studied where computers aren't integral to the task being done was emergency medical technician."

What technical workers also have in common, and why they're out front in shifting the division of labor, is that they don't fit well within hierarchical organizations. If you don't believe this, just imagine how effective you would be acting the straw boss to the person who arrives to fix your copying machine.

In Barley's theorization, and more than slightly academic language, "vertical divisions of labor encode expertise in rules, procedures, and positions," meaning that the organization itself is the primary vessel for accumulated learning. A horizontal division, by comparison, "rests on the assumption that knowledge and skills are domain-specific"—reflecting a specialty—"and too complex to be nested" within a hierarchy. Like traditional professionals working within an organization, the technical worker ends up with dual loyalties: some to his employer, but usually more to his specialty.

Which helps explain the attitude of such workers toward their nominal superiors. "When technical people talk about managers they don't discount them," says Barley. "What they do is to impute substantive expertise to managers, saying, 'Well, they know how to make policy' or 'They know about marketing.' So on those issues, they will defer to the managers' wisdom. What they don't defer to is a general, overarching authority based on the hierarchical structure."

Barley's concept of a horizontal division of labor clearly has import beyond technical workers. It fits perfectly with the growing importance of smaller, focused organizations. Whom would you expect to find in such outfits if not specialists, those human repositories of core competency? The concept also explains why companies increasingly turn to multifunctional teams to tackle the new.

It sheds light, too, on the growing unwillingness of many in supervisory positions—and just about all baby-boomers—to describe themselves as managers. Ask a woman with 100 people accountable to her what she does for a living, and she will probably say something like, "Oh, I'm in finance." This isn't just boomer egalitarianism. It reflects an intuition that Barley's technical workers are right: If a manager doesn't have substantive expertise—a specialty, if you will—he had better acquire it soon, for by the year 2000 that's what he will be paid for.

Much that nowadays passes for managerial skill probably won't fill the bill then. As Barley points out, a lot of what one learns going up the ranks in a big hierarchical company is "contextual"—the rules and procedures we use here at General Motors, or the Equitable. How useful is such knowledge at another company, especially a smaller one? How much will have been rendered obsolete by computer coordination, anyway?

Not all coordination will be computerized, however, indicating one competence critical to the men and women who will take the place of today's managers. The problem, or opportunity, according to James Brian Quinn: "As more people get more skilled, they also tend to be somewhat more focused, and may not see the whole problem. Getting a team of specialists to come to an answer is a nontrivial event," requiring abilities akin to a diplomat's.

Indeed, in an economy where market forces increasingly dominate coordination, tomorrow's manager-replacements will have to excel at striking all kinds of deals. (Which may help explain why courses in negotiation have become so popular in recent years.) Deals to put together the best possible team. Deals for partnerships with other companies to jointly develop new products. Deals to obtain resources for less, whether from inside the company or out. Deals to eke out at least a modest profit when more and more product markets act like commodity businesses, what with all that information on features, quality, and price whizzing around the computational infrastructure.

PERHAPS paradoxically, a heart, or the ability to feign possession of one, may also be a requisite. Consultant Gifford Pinchot, co-author of the soon-to-be-published *End of Bureaucracy and Rise of the Intelligent Organization*, asserts that for all their Darwinian sharpness, the new masters of coordination will be paid as much "for their ability to make others feel that they care." How do you motivate employees whose specialized skills and ability to operate on their own make them virtually the equivalent of independent contractors? "You make them feel that they're considered meaningful," says Pinchot.

A touch warm-fuzzy-New-Age for your taste? It may seem less so in another context: Pinchot argues that the principle—making others feel you care as a core skill—will apply just as much to salespeople dealing with customers. Then recall the single key piece of learning from the past 20 years on how to manage customer service: An employee treats customers exactly the same way his manager treats him.

If all this—what technical workers do, what organizations and manager-replacements and salespeople will do—begins to sound like an endless daisy chain with one person or organization providing service to another, then you are starting to grasp the future. It's already a truism that America is becoming, or has become, a service economy. Truly understanding this, though, goes beyond knowing the statistics—that service businesses account for three-quarters of U.S. GDP, for example, and a still larger share of employment. Beyond realizing that further decline in manufacturing jobs is inevitable. Beyond figuring out that it's stupid to deride service jobs as mere burger flipping. Who gets paid more, after all, the executives of an average manufacturing company or the partners—service workers all—in an average investment banking house?

TRULY UNDERSTANDING the emerging economy takes a change of mind-set or, inevitably, of paradigm: from thinking of business as making things, or churning out product, to realizing that it consists instead of furnishing services, even within what has traditionally been thought of as manufacturing. Much of the quality movement can be understood as building more service into a product. When an Allied-Signal or Eastman Kodak breaks down its operations into the steps by which it adds value, maybe as part of "reengineering its core processes," what is the company doing but identifying a sequence of services performed along the way that eventually leads to the customer?

"Products are a happy way of capturing services," explains Quinn, illustrating the coming view. "A car embodies convenient transportation service and it will until we can either physically move you in some other manner or give you the same experience through, say, electronics. Virtual reality could do the latter." Begin thinking like this and you can fully appreciate the prediction of Lord William Rees-Mogg, former editor of the *Times* of London: "In the future, more business will be based on intangibles than on tangibles."

You can also speculate with greater intelligence on the growth industries of tomorrow. In a sense, 140 years ago Henry David Thoreau posed the fundamental issue for the computational infrastructure, in the process suggesting why, finally, it's so unsatisfying to talk of "the information age" or knowledge workers. Thoreau wrote: "We are in great haste to construct a magnetic telegraph from Maine to Texas; but Maine and Texas, it may be, have nothing important to communicate." Information for what purpose? Knowledge to serve what human aim or itch? Where's the juice?

Many of the best businesses of the year 2000 will deliver not just services, but experiences. According to this line of thought, the flagship companies of corporate America in the 21st century will be not Intel or Microsoft—providers of rolling stock and switches to the computational infrastructure—But Walt Disney Co. or, blush to say, Time Warner, parent of FORTUNE's publisher. Half the U.S. population east of the Mississippi has visited Disney World in Orlando, Florida, at least once. Today entertainment represents the second-biggest U.S. export, after aerospace. Employment in travel services has been growing 4% a year on average over the past decade.

Other new enterprises will rise up around small ways of making our lives easier that we don't even realize we need now. Just as we didn't understand that we needed to conduct so much business face to face around the globe until jet travel made this possible. Just as teleconferencing may be starting to convince us that electronic face to face is almost as effective, often cheaper, and easier on aging boomer bodies.

Opportunities will abound, too, in services that can't be subsumed by the computational infrastructure because they require a human touch. These aren't merely the janitorial and maid jobs that the Bureau of Labor Statistics projects as among the fastest-growing types of work in the Nineties, measured in the sheer number of positions added. (The total is expected to rise by over 500,000 from the current three million.)

Expect to see a substantial increase in the ranks of what might be termed nurturant service workers. Example: home health care providers, people who tend the sick or recuperating in the patient's home, where convalescents can be treated for much less than in hospitals. How big could the category of nurturant service workers become? Jim Davidson, co-author with Rees-Mogg of a slightly grim predictive work entitled *The Great Reckoning*, notes that about a tenth of the labor force at the start of the 20th century was in domestic service—household help.

Americans won't take that kind of job, the Zoë Bairds of this world might argue. No, probably not if it entailed viewing themselves as servants. "But if they saw themselves as independent professionals," counters Pinchot, "providing their services for a fee." Services like those of a licensed massage therapist, whose numbers have increased fourfold since 1987, or counseling psychologist, or exercise physiologist, the muscular type who oversees your exertions at the fitness center or serves as a high-end personal trainer. These are not just caring professions; they are, even better for their prospects, anti-stress professions.

It will take a major change in our collective social ethic to convince many Americans, particularly men over 40 who worked in giant companies, that jobs like these carry with them anything like the dignity of big-shouldered manufacturing. (But then, how dignified was it really to labor on an assem-

bly line, or to boss those who did?) The proof will come in the answers to three huge questions at the heart of the historic change now under way.

Can technology help make service jobs as productive as manufacturing jobs have been, in ways that are high-paying to the worker and generally enriching to the society? Recent evidence suggests it can (FORTUNE, May 3). How many Americans have the basic education and the flexibility to become technical workers or new-style service workers? Finally, how many of us are ready for the changes in the very nature of work that the emerging economy will bring with it?

The basic imperative of the computational infrastructure is to push toward the day when, for humans, there is no more business as usual. The decisions kicked to workers by machines will require literacy, numeracy, a capacity for critical thinking and for innovation. Paul Saffo of the Institute for the Future explains what this means, particularly for manufacturing jobs: "Work will become intervention, humans intervening in processes set in motion by us but maintained by our new tools." In his air-conditioned cubicle, the sole remaining human on the factory floor monitors dials and gauges; when they show something awry, his response must be immediate but not automatic, his instincts informed by his intelligence. Scramble.

WORK will be learning, too. Ho-hum, another truism—the need for lifelong learning. But attend to Stephen Barley again, this time on how technical workers acquire their skills: "Most of these people will tell you that if they got anything at all out of their formal education it was only a disciplined way of thinking. It's quite possible that practitioners, when it comes to their own technology, know more than what they could get out of a formal course. Take microcomputer support specialists, the people who maintain microcomputers and local area networks. They read trade magazines, they go to trade shows, they collect information produced by vendors, they piece together bits and pieces from the forefront of technology and then try to integrate it with the needs of their organization. What you see them doing is scrambling to stay on top of change." Specialists of all stripes will face this same challenge.

Many of the walls we have traditionally built around work, in part to contain it, will tumble. The computational infrastructure will benefit us by allowing more people to live and work where they want to, probably far from cities, hooked up electronically to their market, their database, or the rest of

the organization. The trend will be spearheaded by independent professionals, technicians, and small organizations, particularly those willing to work on a project basis—what used to be called piecework. nicians, and small organizations, particularly those willing to work on a project basis—what used to be called piecework.

Nick Davis, the man on the cover, moved to Bozeman, Montana, two years ago mostly because it seemed like a great place to raise his children. He found, though, that "electronics are so user-friendly these days" and the data available over various networks so complete that his three-person money management firm, Montana Investment Advisors, can analyze more companies than he could as a Paine Webber broker in New York City and then Denver. Davis devotes the hour a day he used to spend commuting in Colorado to serious study of the piano. Then there's the nearby skiing, of course, and fly-fishing.

But for those who work where they live, it won't all be cozily tapping at the keyboard by the fireplace with the dog curled at their feet. There will be the next project to hustle up, the computer message or fax or phone to be answered forthwith—that's what service is about—the next client visit to drag off to, perhaps somewhat more difficult to launch from Coeur D'Alene, Idaho, than from Los Angeles or Chicago.

"The notion of a workday as we have known it is one of the first casualties of all this," argues Saffo, and not just for the new cottage workers. "Nine-to-five is an artifact of Taylorist thinking," when labor could be measured in the factory or office, and left there when evening came. Harder to leave behind the problem of getting those three specialists to agree when you have no formal authority over them. Or the beeper that signals a glitch in machines back at the plant. Or those sales figures you might go over just one more time on your home PC.

The danger is that we'll be so busy scrambling, so market-driven, that we miss the bigger opportunity presented us by the future—namely, a new freedom. Says MIT's Tom Malone: "Information technology reduces the constraints on information flow and coordination that have limited what we could do in the past. In that sense, we're becoming richer," just as education or wealth give one more options. "To me that raises the importance of what it is we want to do in the first place."

Will we be prepared, for example, to push back from the computer terminal to spend more time with people we love, even if it means missing the next deal and the money to buy the latest gadget? Or willing to walk out into the air and think on what there is to value about ourselves beyond our work?

Good questions for a Saturday.

Case I: *Robin Hood*

Robin Hood awoke just as the sun was creeping over the crest of the hill in the very middle of Sherwood Forest. He was not the least rested, for he had not slept well that night. He could not get to sleep because of all the problems he was going to have to face today.

Certainly his campaign against the sheriff was going well, perhaps too well. It had all started out as a personal quarrel between the two of them, but now it was much more than just that. There was a price on his head of 1000 pounds, and there was no doubt that he was causing the sheriff a great deal of trouble, as taxes went uncollected or undelivered to the Crown, and rich men could not sleep soundly at night anywhere near Sherwood.

Things had changed since the early days, however. In those days it was just a small band of men, united in their cause against the sheriff, and for that matter, against Prince John, for the sheriff was simply doing John's bidding. But that was no longer the case. The fame of the Merry Men had grown and with it their numbers. He used to know each man as both a friend and companion, but now he didn't even know all of their names. Little John continued to keep discipline among the men as well as maintaining their skills with the bow, while Will Scarlet kept an eye on the sheriff, as well as any rich prospect who was foolish enough to travel Sherwood. Scarlock took care of the loot as he always had, and Much the Miller's Son continued to keep the men fed.

All this success was leading to problems. Game was, frankly, getting scarce as the number of men in the band increased, and the corresponding demand for food grew. Likely targets for the Merry Men were getting hard to find as more and more wealthy travelers were giving Sherwood a wide berth, as they were reluctant to part with their gold. Finally, the Sheriff and his men were getting better. Robin had always had the advantage of knowing Sherwood better than any man alive, but now there were at least several men who knew it almost as well as he, and some of them wore the colors of Prince John.

All this was leading Robin to reconsider his old ways. Perhaps a simple transit tax through Sherwood might be a part of the answer. But that might destroy his support among the people of the forest, and it had been rejected by the Merry Men, who were proud of their motto "Rob from the rich and give to the poor!" Besides, he needed the support of the poor, as they were his main source of information on the movements of the sheriff.

Killing the sheriff was not the answer. He would just be replaced, and, aside from quenching Robin's personal thirst for revenge, the new sheriff might be even more treacherous. Robin hated his enemy, but he had the advantage of knowing the sheriff's strengths and weaknesses. He would not know a new man's talents.

Prince John, on the other hand, was a vicious tyrant, a good part of which stemmed from his very weakness. The Barons were growing more restless every day, and the people simply hated him. They wanted King Richard back from his jail in Austria. Robin had been discreetly approached by several nobles loyal to Richard to join in the effort to free the King with the promise of a full pardon for him and all his men should they succeed. But Robin knew that if they failed, John would burn Sherwood and the rest of England to the ground to reap his vengeance. Theft and unrest in the provinces were one thing, intrigue at court was another.

Robin knew the days of the Merry Men were numbered. Even as they grew stronger, they grew weaker. Time was on the side of the sheriff, who could draw on all the power of the Crown if he had to, and, if Robin became too much of a threat, would surely do so.

Just then the horn blew for the traditional English breakfast of bread and ale. Robin would have breakfast with the Merry Men and then confer with Will Scarlet, Little John, and Scarlock.

Using the Case of *Robin Hood*

Robin Hood is a perfect example of a manager facing the problems of success. Robin's very success has created his problems.

Questions for Discussion

1. What are some of the problems facing Robin and the Merry Men?
2. What are some of the situations in the environment that will have an impact on whatever Robin decides to do?
3. What are some of the alternatives that Robin is considering for dealing with his problems? Can you identify some additional alternatives?
4. What do you think the reaction of Merry Men will be? The sheriff? The people?
5. What do you think Robin should do?

Exercise I: Managerial Development

1. Identify the best manager with whom you personally have interacted within the last seven years:
2. Why did you select that person? I selected him/her because:
   A. s/he:
   B. s/he:
   C. s/he:
3. Of the attributes you listed above, which is the most important for you? A, B, or C?
4. Why do you feel that is the most important attribute of a manager?
5. Identify the best employee with whom you personally have interacted within the past seven years.
6. Why did you select that person? I selected him/her because:
   A. s/he:
   B. s/he:
   C. s/he:
7. Of the attributes you listed above, which is the most important? A, B, or C?
8. Why do you feel that is the most important attribute of an employee?

Using the Exercise for *Managerial Development*

This exercise has been developed to give you the opportunity to establish a role model for managerial and employee behavior. It provides a useful tool for determining your attitude toward what makes a good manager and a good employee.

It might be particularly useful to do the exercise during the first few days of class, discuss it, and then, at the end of the term, redo the exercise to determine if there has been any changes in your perception of the best manager and employee and what they did.

It is recommended that you keep the papers so that they can be used for reference during a class discussion of managerial and employee behavior. The names of the individuals are not important. The ideas, perceptions, and attitudes of those people are what count.

Planning

Managers must plan. Planning must be accomplished before action takes place. The question is, how should managers plan and decide on a course of action?

There are various styles, methods, and techniques a manager can use in planning and decision making. As Victor Vroom demonstrates in his classic article "A New Look at Managerial Decision Making," the way the decision is made will be a key factor in the implementation of the plan. People who feel they have some participation in making important decisions that will affect them are far more likely to support the plan enthusiastically than are people who feel the decision is a fiat from the upper reaches of the organizational chart. Of course, some decisions a manager can make alone, or in consultation with a few people. The important point is to select the appropriate planning/decision-making style so that the action will have the greatest chance for success. The way to accomplish this is to involve the people who will be most directly concerned with the implementation of that decision.

It is basic to the function of a manager that he or she must make decisions. It is not possible for the policy manual to cover every situation that can arise. Managers must be able to interpret the goals and objectives of the plans they have devised and make decisions for the good of the organization—not an easy task. Since there is always a degree of uncertainty in an important decision, the organization is also obligated to provide the manager with support and resources so that the decisions will succeed. These include not only a recognition and knowledge of the firm and its plans, but an understanding of the organization's internal and external environment.

Planning must consider the internal strengths and weaknesses of the organization, including finance, human resources, manufacturing, distribution, and marketing. Capitalizing on strengths while minimizing the impact of weaknesses is vital to successful planning. Strategic decision making also involves an assessment of the environment, as well as an understanding of the corporate culture, as seen in "How Corporate Culture Drives Strategy." Organizations must interact with their surroundings. Those who manage and plan for organizations must recognize that the only constant is change. Everything is fluid: people, places, and things, and "managing the strategic agenda" will be a key to success.

Finally, there are many ways to plan and make strategy. The effectiveness of the plans depends on the nature and needs of the business, the styles of the people, and the goals and plans of the firm. The four basic questions in strategic planning are: (1) Where have we been? (2) Where are we now? (3) Where do we want to go? (4) How do we want to get there? These questions must be answered by each firm's management as he or she plans for the organization in a changing and uncertain world.

Looking Ahead: Challenge Questions

Decision making can vary in approach and style. What styles would you use in certain situations?

The job of the manager is to make decisions. What can organizations do to assist managers in decision making?

Strategic analysis is a very big part of the planning process. What are some factors managers must consider when planning for the firm?

Unit 2

A NEW LOOK AT MANAGERIAL DECISION MAKING

Victor H. Vroom

Victor H. Vroom, Professor, Yale University

All managers are decision makers. Furthermore, their effectiveness as managers is largely reflected in their track record in making the right decisions. These right decisions in turn largely depend on whether or not the manager has utilized the right person or persons in the right ways in helping him solve the problem.

Our concern in this article is with decision making as a social process. We view the manager's task as determining how the problem is to be solved, not the solution to be adopted. Within that overall framework, we have attempted to answer two broad sets of questions: What decision-making processes should managers use to deal effectively with the problems they encounter in their jobs? What decision-making processes do they use in dealing with these problems and what considerations affect their decisions about how much to share their decision-making power with subordinates?

The reader will recognize the former as a normative or prescriptive question. A rational and analytic answer to it would constitute a normative model of decision making as a social process. The second question is descriptive, since it concerns how managers do, rather than should, behave.

Towards a Normal Model

About four years ago, Philip Yetton, then a graduate student at Carnegie-Mellon University, and I began a major research program in an attempt to answer these normative and descriptive questions.

We began with the normative question: What would be a rational way of deciding on the form and amount of participation in decision making that should be used in different situations? We were tired of debates over the relative merits of Theory X and Theory Y and of the truism that leadership depends upon the situation. We felt that it was time for the behavioral sciences to move beyond such generalities and to attempt to come to grips with the complexities of the phenomena with which they intended to deal.

Our aim was ambitious—to develop a set of ground rules for matching a manager's leadership behavior to the demands of the situation. It was critical that these ground rules be consistent with research evidence concerning the consequences of participation and that the model based on the rules be operational, so that any manager could see it to determine how he should act in any decision-making situation.

Table 1 shows a set of alternative decision processes that we have employed in our research. Each process is represented by a symbol (e.g., AI, CI, GII) that will be used as a convenient method of referring to each process. The first letter in this symbol signifies the basic properties of the process (A stands for autocratic; C for consultative; and G for group). The Roman numerals that follow the first letter constitute variants on that process. Thus, AI represents the first variant on an autocratic process, and AII the second variant.

Conceptual and Empirical Basis of the Model

A model designed to regulate, in some rational way, choices among the decisions processes shown in Table 1 should be based on sound empirical evidence concerning the likely consequences of the styles. The more complete the empirical base of knowledge, the greater the certainty with which we can develop the model and the greater will be its usefulness. To aid in understanding the conceptual basis of the model, it is important to distinguish among three classes of outcomes that bear on the ultimate effectiveness of decisions. These are:

1. The quality or rationality of the decision.
2. The acceptance or commitment on the part of subordinates to execute the decision effectively.
3. The amount of time required to make the decision.

The effects of participation on each of these outcomes or consequences were summed up by the author in *The Handbook of Social Psychology* as follows:

The results suggest that allocating problem solving and decision-making tasks to entire groups requires a greater

From *Readings in Management*, 1986, pp. 132-148. Originally from *Organizational Dynamics*, Vol. 1, No. 4, Spring 1972, pp. 66-80. © 1972 by American Management Association, Inc., New York. All rights reserved. Reprinted by permission of the publisher.

TABLE 1

TYPES OF MANAGEMENT DECISION STYLES

AI   You solve the problem or make the decision yourself, using information available to you at that time.

AII   You obtain the necessary information from your subordinate(s), then decide on the solution to the problem yourself. You may or may not tell your subordinates what the problem is in getting the information from them. The role played by your subordinates in making the decision is clearly one of providing the necessary information to you, rather than generating or evaluating alternative solutions.

CI   You share the problem with relevant subordinates individually, getting their ideas and suggestions without bringing them together as a group. Then *you* make the decision that may or may not reflect your subordinates' influence.

CII   You share the problem with your subordinates as a group, collectively obtaining their ideas and suggestions. Then *you* make the decision that may or may not reflect your subordinates' influence.

GII   You share a problem with your subordinates as a group. Together you generate and evaluate alternatives and attempt to reach agreement (consensus) on a solution. Your role is much like that of chairman. You do not try to influence the group to adopt *your* solution and you are willing to accept and implement any solution that has the support of the entire group.

(GI is omitted because it applies only to more comprehensive models outside the scope of this article.)

investment of man hours but produces higher acceptance of decisions and a higher probability that the decision will be executed efficiently. Differences between these two methods in quality of decisions and in elapsed time are inconclusive and probably highly variable. . . . It would be naive to think that group decision making is always more "effective" than autocratic decision making, or vice versa; the relative effectiveness of these two extreme methods depends both on the weights attached to quality, acceptance and time variables and on differences in amounts of these outcomes resulting from these methods, neither of which is invariant from one situation to another. The critics and proponents of participative management would do well to direct their efforts toward identifying the properties of situations in which different decision-making approaches are effective rather than wholesale condemnation or deification of one approach.

We have gone on from there to identify the properties of the situation or problem that will be the basic elements in the model. These problem attributes are of two types: 1) Those that specify the importance for a particular problem of quality and acceptance, and 2) those that, on the basis of available evidence, have a high probability of moderating the effects of participation on each of these outcomes. Table 2 shows the problem attributes used in the present form of the model. For each attribute a question is provided that might be used by a leader in diagnosing a particular problem prior to choosing his leadership style.

In phrasing the questions, we have held technical language to a minimum. Furthermore, we have phrased the questions in Yes-No form, translating the continuous variables defined above into dichotomous variables. For example, instead of attempting to determine how important the decision quality is to the effectiveness of the decision (attribute A), the leader is asked in the first question to judge whether there is any quality component to the problem. Similarly, the difficult task of specifying exactly how much information the leader possesses that is relevant to the decision (attribute B) is reduced to a simple judgment by the leader concerning whether or not he has sufficient information to make a high quality decision.

We have found that managers can diagnose a situation quickly and accurately by answering this set of seven questions concerning it. But how can such responses generate a prescription concerning the most effective leadership style or decision process? What kind of normative model of participation in decision making can be built from this set of problem attributes?

Figure 1 shows one such model expressed in the form of a decision tree. It is the seventh version of such a model that

TABLE 2

PROBLEM ATTRIBUTES USED IN THE MODEL

Problem Attributes	Diagnostic Questions
A. The importance of the quality of the decision.	Is there a quality requirement such that one solution is likely to be more rational than another?
B. The extent to which the leader possesses sufficient information/expertise to make a high-quality decision by himself.	Do I have sufficient information to make a high-quality decision?
C. The extent to which the problem is structured.	Is the problem structured?
D. The extent to which acceptance or commitment on the part of subordinates is critical to the effective implementation of the decision.	Is acceptance of decision by subordinates critical to effective implementation?
E. The prior probability that the leader's autocratic decision will receive acceptance by subordinates.	If you were to make the decision by yourself, is it reasonably certain that it would be accepted by your subordinates?
F. The extent to which subordinates are motivated to attain the organizational goals as represented in the objectives explicit in the statement of the problem.	Do subordinates share the organizational goals to be obtained in solving this problem?
G. The extent to which subordinates are likely to be in conflict over preferred solutions.	Is conflict among subordinates likely in preferred solutions?

we have developed over the last three years. The problem attributes, expressed in question form, are arranged along the top of the figure. To use the model for a particular decision-making situation, one starts at the left-hand side and works toward the right asking oneself the question immediately above any box that is encountered. When a terminal node is reached, a number will be found designating the problem type and one of the decision-making processes appearing in Table 1. AI is prescribed for four problem types (1, 2, 4, and 5); AII is prescribed for two problem types (9 and 10); CI is prescribed for only one problem type (8); CII is prescribed for four problems types (7, 11, 13, and 14); and GII is prescribed for three problem types (3, 6, and 12). The relative frequency with which each of the five decision processes would be prescribed for any manager would, of course, depend on the distribution of problem types encountered in his decision making.

Rationale Underlying the Model. The decision processes specified for each problem type are not arbitrary. The model's behavior is governed by a set of principles intended to be consistent with existing evidence concerning the consequences of participation in decision making on organizational effectiveness.

There are two mechanisms underlying the behavior of the model. The first is a set of seven rules that serve to protect the quality and the acceptance of the decision by eliminating alternatives that risk one or the other of these decision outcomes. Once the rules have been applied, a feasible set of decision processes is generated. The second mechanism is a principle for choosing among alternatives in the feasible set where more than one exists.

Let us examine the rules first, because they do much of the work of the model. As previously indicated, the rules are intended to protect both the quality and acceptance of the decision. In the form of the model shown, there are three

rules that protect decision quality and four that protect acceptance.

1. *The Information Rule.* If the quality of the decision is important and if the leader does not possess enough information or expertise to solve the problem by himself, AI is eliminated from the feasible set. (Its use risks a low-quality decision.)

2. *The Goal Congruence Rule.* If the quality of the decision is important and if the subordinates do not share the organizational goals to be obtained in solving the problem, GII is eliminated from the feasible set. (Alternatives that eliminate the leader's final control over the decision reached may jeopardize the quality of the decision.)

3. *The Unstructured Problem Rule.* In decisions in which the quality of the decision is important, if the leader lacks the necessary information or expertise to solve the problem by himself, and if the problem is unstructured, i.e., he does not know exactly what information is needed and where it is located, the method used must provide not only for him to collect the information but to do so in an efficient and effective manner. Methods that involve interaction among all subordinates with full knowledge of the problem are likely to be both more efficient and more likely to generate a high-quality solution to the problem. Under these conditions, AI, AII, and CI are eliminated from the feasible set. (AI does not provide for him to collect the necessary information, and AII and CI represent more cumbersome, less effective, and less efficient means of bringing the necessary information to bear on the solution of the problem than methods that do permit those with the necessary information to interact.)

4. *The Acceptance Rule.* If the acceptance of the decision by subordinates is critical to effective implementation, and if it is not certain that an autocratic decision made by the leader would receive that acceptance, AI and AII are eliminated from the feasible set. (Neither provides an opportunity for

FIGURE 1
Decision Model

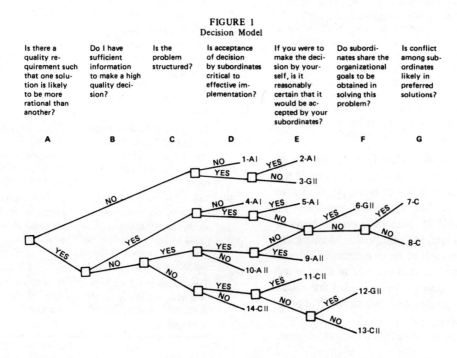

subordinates to participate in the decision and both risk the necessary acceptance.)

5. *The Conflict Rule.* If the acceptance of the decision is critical, and an autocratic decision is not certain to be accepted, and subordinates are likely to be in conflict or disagreement over the appropriate solution, AI, AII, and CI are eliminated from the feasible set. (The method used in solving the problem should enable those in disagreement to resolve their differences with full knowledge of the problem. Accordingly, under these conditions, AI, AII, and CI, which involve no interaction or only "one-on-one" relationships and therefore provide no opportunity for those in conflict to resolve their differences, are eliminated from the feasible set. Their use runs the risk of leaving some of the subordinates with less than the necessary commitment to the final decision.)

6. *The Fairness Rule.* If the quality of decision is unimportant and if acceptance is critical and not certain to result from an autocratic decision, AI, AII, CI, and CII are eliminated from the feasible set. (The method used should maximize the probability of acceptance as this is the only relevant consideration in determining the effectiveness of the decision. Under these circumstances, AI, AII, CI, and CII, which create less acceptance or commitment than GII, are eliminated from the feasible set. To use them is to run the risk of getting less than the needed acceptance of the decision.)

7. *The Acceptance Priority Rule.* If acceptance is critical, not assured by an autocratic decision, and if subordinates can be trusted, AI, AII, CI, and CII are eliminated from the feasible set. (Methods that provide equal partnership in the decision-making process can provide greater acceptance without risking decision quality. Use of any method other than GII results in an unnecessary risk that the decision will not be fully accepted or receive the necessary commitment on the part of subordinates.)

Once all seven rules have been applied to a given problem, we emerge with a feasible set of decision processes. The feasible set for each of the fourteen problem types is shown in Table 3. It can be seen that there are some problem types for which only one method remains in the feasible set, others for which two methods remain feasible, and still others for which five methods remain feasible.

When more than one method remains in the feasible set, there are a number of ways in which one might choose among them. The mechanism we have selected the principle underlying the choices of the model in Figure 1 utilizes the number of man-hours used in solving the problem as the basis for choice. Given a set of methods with equal likelihood of meeting both quality and acceptance requirements for the decision, it chooses that method that requires the least investment in man-hours. On the basis of the empirical evidence summarized earlier, this is deemed to be the method furthest to the left within the feasible set. For example, since AI, AII, CI, CII, and GII are all feasible as in Problem Types 1 and 2, AI would be the method chosen.

To illustrate application of the model in actual administra-

TABLE 3

PROBLEM TYPES AND THE FEASIBLE SET OF DECISION PROCESSES

Problem Type	Acceptable Methods
1.	AI, AII, CI, CII, GII
2.	AI, AII, CI, CII, GII
3.	GII
4.	AI, AII, CI, CII, GII*
5.	AI, AII, CI, CII, GII*
6.	GII
7.	CII
8.	CI, CII
9.	AII, CI, CII, GII*
10.	AII, CI, CII, GII*
11.	CII, GII*
12.	GII
13.	CII
14.	CII, GII*

*Within the feasible set only when the answer to question F is Yes.

tive situations, we will analyze four cases with the help of the model. While we attempt to describe these cases as completely as is necessary to permit the reader to make the judgments required by the model, there may remain some room for subjectivity. The reader may wish after reading the case to analyze it himself using the model and then to compare his analysis with that of the author.

CASE I. You are a manufacturing manager in a large electronics plant. The company's management has recently installed new machines and put in a new simplified work system, but to the surprise of everyone, yourself included, the expected increase in productivity was not realized. In fact, production has begun to drop, quality has fallen off, and the number of employee separations has risen.

You do not believe that there is anything wrong with the machines. You have had reports from other companies that are using them and they confirm this opinion. You have also had representatives from the firm that built the machines go over them and they report that they are operating at peak efficiency.

You suspect that some parts of the new work system may be responsible for the change, but this view is not widely shared among your immediate subordinates who are four first-line supervisors, each in charge of a section, and your supply manager. The drop in production has been variously attributed to poor training of the operators, lack of an adequate system of financial incentives, and poor morale. Clearly, this is an issue about which there is considerable depth of feeling within individuals and potential disagreement among your subordinates.

This morning you received a phone call from your division manager. He had just received your production figures for the last six months and was calling to express his concern. He indicated that the problem was yours to solve in any way that you think best, but that he would like to know within a week what steps you plan to take.

2. PLANNING: Management Classic

You share your division manager's concern with the falling productivity and know that your men are also concerned. The problem is to decide what steps to take to rectify the situation.

Analysis
Questions—
  A (Quality?) = Yes
  B (Managers Information?) = No
  C (Structured?) = No
  D (Acceptance?) =Yes
  E (Prior Probability of Acceptance?) = No
  F (Goal Congruence?) = Yes
  G (Conflict) = Yes
Problem Type—12
Feasible Set—GII
Minimum Man-Hours Solution (from Figure 1)—GII
Rule Violations—
  AI violates rules 1, 3, 4, 5, 7
  AII violates rules 3, 4, 5, 7
  CI violates rules 3, 5, 7
  CII violates rule 7

CASE II. You are general foreman in charge of a large gang laying an oil pipeline and have to estimate your expected rate of progress in order to schedule material deliveries to the next field site.

You know the nature of the terrain you will be traveling and have the historical data needed to compute the mean and variance in the rate of speed over that type of terrain. Given these two variables, it is a simple matter to calculate the earliest and latest times at which materials and support facilities will be needed at the next site. It is important that your estimate be reasonably accurate. Underestimates result in idle foremen and workers, and an overestimate results in tying up materials for a period of time before they are to be used.

Progress has been good and your five foremen and other members of the gang stand to receive substantial bonuses if the project is completed ahead of schedule.

Analysis
Questions—
  A (Quality?) = Yes
  B (Manager's Information?) = Yes
  D (Acceptance?) = No
Problem Type—4
Feasible Set—AI, AII, CI, CII, GII
Minimum Man-Hours Solution (from Figure 1)—AI
Rule Violations—None

CASE III. You are supervising the work of 12 engineers. Their formal training and work experience are very similar, permitting you to use them interchangeably on projects. Yesterday, your manager informed you that a request had been received from an overseas affiliate for four engineers to go abroad on extended loan for a period of six to eight months. For a number of reasons, he argued and you agreed that this request should be met from your group.

All your engineers are capable of handling this assignment and, from the standpoint of present and future projects, there is no particular reason why anyone should be retained over any other. The problem is somewhat complicated by the fact that the overseas assignment is in what is generally regarded as an undesirable location.

Analysis
Questions—
  A (Quality?) = No
  D (Acceptance?) = Yes
  E (Prior Probability of Acceptance?) = No
  G (Conflict?) = Yes
Problem Type—3
Feasible Set—GII
Minimum Man-Hours Solution (from Figure 1)—GII
Rule Violations—
  AI and AII violate rules 4, 5, and 6
  CI violates rules 5 and 6
  CII violates rule 6

CASE IV. You are on the division manager's staff and work on a wide variety of problems of both an administrative and technical nature. You have been given the assignment of developing a standard method to be used in each of the five plants in the division for manually reading equipment registers, recording the readings, and transmitting the scorings to a centralized information system.

Until now there has been a high error rate in the reading and/or transmittal of the data. Some locations have considerably higher error rates than others, and the methods used to record and transmit the data vary among plants. It is probable, therefore, that part of the error variance is a function of specific local conditions rather than anything else, and this will complicate the establishment of any system common to all plants. You have the information on error rates but no information on the local practices that generate these errors or on the local conditions that necessitate the different practices.

Everyone would benefit from an improvement in the quality of the data; it is used in a number of important decisions. Your contacts with the plants are through the quality-control supervisors who are responsible for collecting the data. They are a conscientious group committed to doing their jobs well, but are highly sensitive to interference on the part of higher management in their own operations. Any solution that does not receive the active support of the various plant supervisors is unlikely to reduce the error rate significantly.

Analysis
Questions—
  A (Quality?) = Yes
  B (Manager's Information?) = No
  C (Structured?) = No
  D (Acceptance?) = Yes
  E (Prior Probability of Acceptance?) = No
  F (Goal Congruence?) = Yes
Problem Type—12
Feasible Set—GII
Minimum Man-Hours Solution (from Figure 1)—GII
Rule Violations—
  AI violates rules 1, 3, 4, and 7
  AII violates rules 3, 4, and 7
  CI violates rules 3 and 7
  CII violates rule 7

Short Versus Long-Term Models

The model described above seeks to protect the quality of the decision and to expend the least number of man-hours in the process. Because it focuses on conditions surrounding the making and implementation of a particular decision rather than any long-term considerations, we can term it a short-term model.

It seems likely, however, that the leadership methods that may be optimal for short-term results may be different from those that would be optimal over a longer period of time. Consider a leader, for example, who has been uniformly pursuing an autocratic style (AI or AII) and, perhaps as a consequence, has subordinates who might be termed "yes men" (attribute E) but who also cannot be trusted to pursue organizational goals (attribute F), largely because the leader has never bothered to explain them.

It appears likely, however, that the manager who used more participative methods would, in time, change the status of these problem attributes so as to develop ultimately a more effective problem-solving system. A promising approach to the development of a long-term model is one that places less weight on man-hours as the basis for choice of method within the feasible set. Given a long-term orientation, one would be interested in the possibility of a trade-off between man-hours in problem solving and team development, both of which increase with participation. Viewed in these terms, the time-minimizing model places maximum relative weight on man-hours and no weight on development, and hence chooses the style farthest to the left within the feasible set. A model that places less weight on manhours and more weight on development would, if these assumptions are correct, choose a style further to the right within the feasible set.

We recognize, of course, that the minimum man-hours solution suggested by the model is not always the best solution to every problem. A manager faced, for example, with the problem of handling any one of the four cases previously examined might well choose more time-consuming alternatives on the grounds that the greater time invested would be justified in developing his subordinates. Similar considerations exist in other decision-making situations. For this reason we have come to emphasize the feasible set of decision methods in our work with managers. Faced with considerations not included in the model, the manager should consider any alternative within the feasible set, and not opt automatically for the minimum man-hours solution.

As I am writing this, I have in front of me a "black box" that constitutes an electronic version of the normative model discussed on the preceding pages. (The author is indebted to Peter Fuss of Bell Telephone Laboratories for his interest in the model and his skill in developing the "black box.") The box, which is small enough to fit into the palm of one hand, has a set of seven switches, each appropriately labeled with the questions (A through G) used in Figure 1. A manager faced with a concrete problem or decision can "diagnose" that problem by setting each switch in either its "yes" or "no" position. Once the problem has been described, the manager depresses a button that illuminates at least one or as many as five lights, each of which denotes one of the decision processes (AI, AII, etc.). The lights that are illuminated constitute the feasible set of decision processes for the problem as shown in Table III. The lights not illuminated correspond to alternatives that violate one or more of the seven rules previously stated.

In this prototype version of the box, the lights are illuminated in decreasing order of brightness from left to right within the feasible set. The brightest light corresponds to the alternative shown in Figure 1. Thus, if both CII and GII were feasible alternatives, CII would be brighter than GII, since it requires fewer man-hours. However, a manager who was not under any undue time pressure and who wished to invest time in the development of his subordinates might select an alternative corresponding to one of the dimmer lights.

Toward a Descriptive Model of Leader Behavior

So far we have been concerned with the normative questions defined at the outset. But how do managers really behave? What considerations affect their decisions about how much to share their decision-making power with their subordinates? In what respects is their behavior different from or similar to that of the model? These questions are but a few of those that we attempted to answer in a large-scale research program aimed at gaining a greater understanding of the factors that influence managers in their choice of decision processes to fit the demands of the situation. This research program was financially supported by the McKinsey Foundation, General Electric Foundation, Smith Richardson Foundation, and the Office of Naval Research.

Two different research methods have been utilized in studying these factors. The first investigation utilized a method that we have come to term "recalled problems." Over 500 managers from 11 different countries representing a variety of firms were asked to provide a written description of a problem that they had recently had to solve. These varied in length from one paragraph to several pages and covered virtually every facet of managerial decision making. For each case, the manager was asked to indicate which of the decision processes shown in Table I they used to solve the problem. Finally, each manager was asked to answer the questions shown in Table II corresponding to the problem attributes used in the normative model.

The wealth of data, both qualitative and quantitative, served two purposes. Since each manager had diagnosed a situation that he had encountered in terms that are used in the normative model and had indicated the methods that he had used in dealing with it, it is possible to determine what differences, if any, there were between the model's behavior and his own behavior. Second, the written cases provided the basis for the construction of a standard set of cases used in later research to determine the factors that influence managers to share or retain their decision-making power. Each case depicted a manager faced with a problem to solve or decision to make. The cases spanned a wide range of managerial problems including production scheduling, quality control, portfolio management, personnel allocation, and research and development. In each case, a person could readily assume the role of the manager described and could indicate which of the decision processes he would use if he actually were faced with that situation.

In most of our research, a set of thirty cases has been used and the subjects have been several thousand managers who were participants in management development programs in the United States and abroad. Cases were selected systematically. We desired cases that could not only be coded unambiguously in the terms used in the normative model but that would also permit the assessment of the effects of each of the problem attributes used in the model on the person's behavior. The solution was to select cases in accordance with an experimental design so that they varied in terms of the seven attributes used in the model and variation in each attribute was independent of each other attribute. Several such standardized sets of cases have been developed, and over a thousand managers have now been studied using this approach.

To summarize everything we learned in the course of this research is well beyond the scope of this paper, but it is possible to discuss some of the highlights. Since the results obtained from the two research methods—recalled and standardized problems—are consistent, we can present the major results independent of the method used.

Perhaps the most striking finding is the weakening of the widespread view that participativeness is a general trait that individual managers exhibit in different amounts. To be sure, there were differences *among* managers in their general tendencies to utilize participative methods as opposed to autocratic ones. On the standardized problems, these differences accounted for about 10 percent of the total variance in the decision processes observed. These differences in behavior between managers, however, were small in comparison with differences *within* managers. On the standardized problems, no manager indicated that he would use the same decision process on all problems or decisions, and most used all five methods under some circumstances.

Some of this variance in behavior within managers can be attributed to widely shared tendencies to respond to some situations by sharing power and others by retaining it. It makes more sense to talk about participative and autocratic situations than it does to talk about participative and autocratic managers. In fact, on the standardized problems, the variance in behavior across problems or cases is about three times as large as the variance across managers!

What are the characteristics of an autocratic as opposed to a participative situation? An answer to this question would constitute a partial descriptive model of this aspect of the decision-making process and has been our goal in much of the research that we have conducted. From our observations of behavior on both recalled problems and on standardized problems, it is clear that the decision-making process and has been our goal in much of the research that we have conducted. From our observations of behavior on both recalled

problems and on standardized problems, it is clear that the decision-making process employed by a typical manager is influenced by a large number of factors, many of which also show up in the normative model. Following are several conclusions substantiated by the results on both recalled and standardized problems: Managers use decision processes providing less opportunity for participation (1) when the possess all the necessary information than when they lack some of the needed information, (2) when the problem that they face is well-structured rather than unstructured, (3) when their subordinates' acceptance of the decision is not critical for the effective implementation of the decision or when the prior probability of acceptance of an autocratic decision is high, and (4) when the personal goals of their subordinates are *not* congruent with the goals of the organization as manifested in the problem.

So far we have been talking about relatively common or widely shared ways of dealing with organizational problems. Our results strongly suggest that there are ways of "tailoring" one's approach to the situation that distinguish managers from one another. Theoretically, these can be thought of as differences among managers in decision rules that they employ about when to encourage participation. Statistically, they are represented as interactions between situational variables and personal characteristics.

Consider, for example, two managers who have identical distributions of the use of the five decision processes shown in Table I on a set of thirty cases. In a sense, they are equally participative (or autocratic). However, the situations in which they permit or encourage participation in decision making on the part of their subordinates may be very different. One may restrict the participation of his subordinates to decisions without a quality requirement, whereas the other may restrict their participation to problems with a quality requirement. The former would be more inclined to use participative decision processes (like GII) on such decisions as what color the walls should be painted or when the company picnic should be held. The latter would be more likely to encourage participation in decision making on decisions that have a clear and demonstrable impact on the organization's success in achieving its external goals.

Use of the standardized problem set permits the assessment of such differences in decision rules that govern choices among decision-making processes. Since the cases are selected in accordance with an experimental design, they can indicate differences in the behavior of managers attributable not only to the existence of a quality requirement in the problem but also in the effects of acceptance requirements, conflict, information requirements, and the like.

The research using both recalled and standardized problems has also enabled us to examine similarities and differences between the behavior of the normative model and the behavior of a typical manager. Such an analysis reveals, at the very least, what behavioral changes could be expected if managers began using the normative model as the basis for choosing their decision-making processes.

A typical manager says he would (or did) use exactly the

same decision process as that shown in Figure 1 in 40 percent of the situations. In two thirds of the situations, his behavior is consistent with the feasible set of methods proposed in the model. In other words, in about one third of the situations his behavior violates at least one of the seven rules underlying the model.

The four rules designed to protect the acceptance or commitment of the decision have substantially higher probabilities of being violated than do the three rules designed to protect the quality or rationality of the decision. One of the acceptance rules, the Fairness Rule (Rule 6) is violated about three quarters of the time that it could have been violated. On the other hand, one of the quality rules, the Information Rule (Rule 1), is violated in only about 3 percent of occasions in which it is applicable. If we assume for the moment that these two sets of rules have equal validity, these findings strongly suggest that the decisions made by typical managers are more likely to prove ineffective due to deficiencies of acceptance by subordinates than due to deficiencies in decision quality.

Another striking difference between the behavior of the model and of the typical manager lies in the fact that the former shows far greater variance with the situation. If a typical manager voluntarily used the model as the basis for choosing his methods of making decisions, he would become both more autocratic and more participative. He would employ autocratic methods more frequently in situations in which his subordinates were unaffected by the decision and participative methods more frequently when his subordinates' cooperation and support were critical and/or their information and expertise were required.

It should be noted that the typical manager to whom we have been referring is merely a statistical average of the several thousand who have been studied over the last three or four years. There is a great deal of variance around that average. As evidenced by their behavior on standardized problems, some managers are already behaving in a way that is highly consistent with the model, while others' behavior is clearly at variance with it.

A New Technology for Leadership Development

The investigations that have been summarized here were conducted for research purposes to shed some light on the causes and consequences of participation in decision making. In the course of the research, we came to realize, partly because of the value attached to it by the managers themselves, that the data collection procedures, with appropriate additions and modifications, might also serve as a valuable guide to leadership development. From this realization evolved an important by-product of the research activities—a new approach to leadership development based on the concepts in the normative model and the empirical methods of the descriptive research.

This approach is based on the assumption stated previously that one of the critical skills required of all leaders is the ability to adapt their behavior to the demands of the situation and that one component of this skill involves the ability to select the appropriate decision-making process for each problem or decision he confronts.

Managers can derive value from the model by comparing their past or intended behavior in concrete decisions with that prescribed by the model and by seeing what rules, if any, they violate. Used in this way, the model can provide a mechanism for a manager to analyze both the circumstances that he faces and what decisions are feasible under these circumstances.

While use of the model without training is possible, we believe that the manager can derive the maximum value from a systematic examination of his leadership style, and its similarities to and dissimilarities from the model, as part of a formal leadership development program.

During the past two years we have developed such a program. It is not intended to "train" participants in the use of the model, but rather to encourage them to examine their own leadership style and to ask themselves whether the methods they are using are most effective for their own organization. A critical part of the program involves the use of a set of standardized cases, each depicting a leader faced with an administrative problem to solve. Each participant then specifies the decision-making process that he would use if faced with each situation. His responses are processed by computer, which generates a highly detailed analysis of his leadership style. The responses for all participants in the course are typically processed simultaneously, permitting the economical representation of differences between the person and other participants in the same program.

In its present form, a single computer printout for a person consists of three $15'' \times 11''$ pages, each filled with graphs and tables highlighting different features of his behavior. Understanding the results requires a detailed knowledge of the concepts underlying the model, something already developed in one of the previous phases of the training program. The printout is accompanied by a manual that aids in explaining results and provides suggested steps to be followed in extracting full meaning from the printout.

Following are a few of the questions that the printout answers:

1. How autocratic or participative am I in my dealings with subordinates in comparison with other participants in the program?
2. What decision processes do I use more or less frequently than the average?
3. How close does my behavior come to that of the model? How frequently does my behavior agree with the feasible set? What evidence is there that my leadership style reflects the pressure of time as opposed to a concern with the development of my subordinates? How do I compare in these respects with other participants in the class?
4. What rules do I violate most frequently and least frequently? How does this compare with other participants? On what cases did I violate these rules? Does my

leadership style reflect more concern with getting decisions that are high in quality or with getting decisions that are accepted?

5. What circumstances cause me to behave in an autocratic fashion; what circumstances cause me to behave participatively? In what respects is the way in which I attempt to vary my behavior with the demands of the situation similar to that of the model?

When a typical manager receives his printout, he immediately goes to work trying to understand what it tells him about himself. After most of the major results have been understood, he goes back to the set of cases to reread those on which he has violated rules. Typically, managers show an interest in discussing and comparing their results with others in the program. Gatherings of four to six people comparing their results and their interpretation of them, often for several hours at a stretch, were such a common feature that they have recently been institutionalized as part of the procedure.

We should emphasize that the method of providing feedback to managers on their leadership style is just one part of the total training experience, but it is an important part. The program is sufficiently new so that, to date, no long-term evaluative studies have been undertaken. The short-term results, however, appear quite promising.

Conclusion

The efforts reported in this article rest on the conviction that social scientists can be of greater value in solving problems of organizational behavior if their prescriptive statements deal with the complexities involved in the phenomena with which they study. The normative model described in this paper is one step in that direction. Some might argue that it is premature for social scientists to be prescriptive. Our knowledge is too limited and the issues too complex to warrant prescriptions for action, even those that are based on a diagnosis of situational demands. However, organizational problems persist, and managers cannot wait for the behavioral sciences to perfect their disciplines before attempting to cope with them. Is it likely that models that encourage them to deal analytically with the forces impinging upon them would produce less rational choices than those that they now make? We think the reverse is more probable—reflecting on the models will result in decisions that are more rational and more effective. The criterion for social utility is not perfection but improvement over present practice.

Implement Entrepreneurial Thinking in Established Organizations

Donald F. Kuratko, *Department of Management, Ball State University*
Jeffrey S. Hornsby, *Department of Management, Ball State University*
Douglas W. Naffziger, *Department of Management, Ball State University*
Ray V. Montagno, *Department of Management, Ball State University*

Dr. Hornsby, Associate Professor and Coordinator of the Human Resource Management Department at Ball State, is particularly interested in compensation, honesty testing, small business personnel, and intrapreneurship; Dr. Kuratko, author of several books including Management *and* Entrepreneurship: A Contemporary Approach, *is the Stoops Distinguished Professor of Business and director of Ball State's Entrepre-*

neurship Program; Dr. Naffziger, an Assistant Professor of Entrepreneurship and director of the Small Business Institute at Ball State, concentrates his research on planning, start-ups, and other aspects of entrepreneurship; and Dr. Montagno, Professor of Management, has published numerous articles in his fields of interest—organizational behavior, human resource management, and international management.

Introduction

"Corporate Culture has more to do with the mind than with the organizational chart."

Thomas J. Peters

The current decade has witnessed a growth in corporate strategies focused heavily on creating a competitive advantage through entrepreneurship. This emphasis on entrepreneurial thinking developed during the "entrepreneurial economy" of the 1980s. Peter Drucker, the renowned management expert attributed the emergence of this economy to four major developments. First, the rapid evolution of knowledge and technology promoted high-tech entrepreneurial start-ups. Second, trends such as two wage-earner families, continuing education of adults, and the aging population, added fuel to the proliferation of newly developing ventures. Third, the venture capital market became an effective funding mechanism for entrepreneurial ventures. Fourth, and most important, American industry began to learn how *to manage entrepreneurship*.[1]

The thrust in entrepreneurship as a major force in American business has led to a desire by corporate managers to replicate this type of activity *inside* enterprises. While some researchers conclude that entrepreneurship and bureaucracies are mutually exclusive, others have reported numerous successful entrepreneurial ventures within the established corporate framework.[2] These ventures have been undertaken in companies such as 3-M, IBM, Hewlett-Packard, General Electric, and Polaroid. Today, there is a wealth of popular business literature on the new corporate revolution, reflecting the infusion of entrepreneurial thinking into larger bureaucratic structures. This infusion is called "corporate entrepreneurship" or "intrapreneurship."[3]

Steven Brandt described management's role in taking on the new challenges confronting corporations:

The challenge is relatively straightforward. The United States must upgrade its innovative prowess. To do so, U.S. companies must tap into the creative power of their members. Ideas come from people. Innovation is a capability of the many. That capability is utilized when people give commitment to the mission and life of the enterprise and have the power to do something with their capabilities.[4]

This new challenge must permeate enterprises seeking to achieve success in the 1990s and beyond. In order to implement entrepreneurial thinking, today's managers need to recognize newly developing strategies, assess the corporation's climate for readiness, and reinforce behavior with effective rewards. Thus, many of the traditional functions of management are present, but in newer, more innovative ways.

One current example of this movement is IBM. The dramatic changes that are occurring to create a "new IBM" are a direct result of the decentralizing of authority and decision making. These changes have turned some parts of this corporate entity into almost freestanding, independent companies.[5]

Strategies for Creating Corporate Entrepreneuring

There are a number of approaches an organization can take in creating corporate entrepreneurship. It is important to understand that when an entrepreneurial environment is created, the ethos of the original enterprise often changes dramatically. Traditions will be set aside in favor of new processes and procedures. Some people, uncomfortable with operating in this environment, will leave; others will thrive in a system that encourages creativity, ingenuity, risk taking, teamwork, and informal networking, all designed to increase productivity and make the organization more viable.

The key to creating an entrepreneurial environment is to develop and articulate a specific strategy for encouraging innovative activity. The following discussion outlines the steps that managers need to follow to establish an entrepreneurial strategy.

Assessment of Current Strategies for Entrepreneurial Activity

This process has four major components. The first involves an assessment of the current organizational situation. Several questions can help management in this task, and by applying the answers, managers may be able to assess the organization's environment and readiness for change.

- Has the company developed effective ways to access the resources needed to try new ideas? (Intrapreneurs need discretionary re-

sources to explore and develop new ideas.)
- Are the managers prepared to allow experimentation with new products or services?
- Does the organization encourage risk taking and tolerate mistakes?
- Are the employees more concerned with new ideas or with defending their turf?
- Is it easy to form autonomous project teams within the corporate environment?[6]

A second component of the assessment process is to determine whether there is an understanding of the innovation that management wishes to achieve. Since corporate entrepreneuring unleashes the creative talents of people in the organization, employees need to understand this vision from the perspective of top management.

The third component is to identify specific objectives for corporate entrepreneuring strategies and the programs needed to achieve them. Rosebeth Moss Kanter, a noted researcher on innovation, has described three steps toward innovation:[7] making sure that current system, structures, and practices do not present insurmountable roadblocks to the flexibility and fast action needed for innovation; providing the incentives and tools for entrepreneurial projects; and seeking synergies across business areas, so that new opportunities are discovered in new combinations at the same time that business units retain operating autonomy.

The fourth component requires managers to understand entrepreneurial thinking by employees. Initially, a "corporate entrepreneur" is one who develops a business idea that does not yet exist. In the beginning, the individual may be specialized in one area such as engineering, marketing, or research and development, but once the individual starts an "intraprise", he or she quickly begins to learn all facets of the project. The corporate entrepreneur soon becomes a generalist with multi-skills.

Corporate entrepreneurs tend to be action-oriented and goal-oriented, willing to do whatever it takes to achieve their objectives. They combine thinking and doing, planning and working, vision and action. Dedication to the new idea is paramount. As a result, corporate entrepreneurs often expect the impossible from themselves and consider no setback so great that it threatens the success of their venture. They are self-determined goal setters who go beyond the call of duty in achieving their goals.

When faced with failure or setback, corporate entrepreneurs remain optimistic. They do not admit that they are beaten. They view failure as a temporary setback to be learned from and dealt with, not as a reason to quit. In addition, they

TABLE I

CRITICAL ELEMENTS IN INTRAPRENEURIAL ENVIRONMENTS

The presence of explicit goals: These goals need to be mutually agreed upon by worker and management so specific steps are achieved.

A system of feedback and positive reinforcement: This feedback is necessary in order for potential inventors, creators, or intrapreneurs to realize there is acceptance and reward.

An emphasis on individual responsibility: Confidence, trust, and accountability are key features to the success of any innovative program.

Rewards based upon results: A reward system that enhances and encourages others to risk and to achieve must be established.

view themselves as responsible for their own destiny. They do not blame their failure on others, but rather focus on learning how they might have done better. By objectively dealing with their own mistakes and failures, they learn to avoid making the same mistake again, and this, in turn, is part of what helps make them successful.

Managers must be prepared to handle a corporate entrepreneur differently than a traditional manager. Understanding the critical differences in action, status, decisions, and problem solving will help the manager develop procedures and policies that motivate rather than inhibit the entrepreneur; corporate entrepreneurs *can* be developed.

Specific strategies for effectively managing entrepreneurial thinking and behavior will vary from firm to firm. Nevertheless, most are based on a common set of assumptions, that is, a proactive change of the status quo must occur and a new, flexible approach to the management of operations must be installed.

Implementing An Entrepreneurial Climate

Most managers agree that the term intrapreneur refers to entrepreneurial activities that receive organizational sanction and resource commitments for the purpose of innovative results.[8] In establishing the drive to innovate inside today's corporations, one approach is to concentrate on

developing a climate conducive to corporate entrepreneurs. When coupled with other specific strategies for innovation and research, these efforts can enhance the potential for inventors and venture developers. One researcher, after profiling inventors as a potential employee source for corporations, found that companies need to provide more nurturing and information sharing in order to attract these individuals.[9]

Several elements are critical in establishing the necessary climate. These include: the presence of explicit goals; a system of feedback and positive reinforcement; an emphasis on individual responsibility; and rewards based upon results.[10] Table I provides an explanation of these key elements.

To establish corporate entrepreneuring, companies need to provide the freedom and encouragement that intrapreneurs require to develop their ideas. This can be a problem, because top managers may not believe that entrepreneurial ideas can be developed in their environment. They also find it hard to implement policies that encourage freedom and unstructured activitity.

What can a corporate manager do to foster the intrapreneurial process? First, the manager needs to examine and perhaps revise his or her philosophy of management. Many enterprises have obsolete ideas about cooperative cultures, management techniques, and the values of managers and em-

TABLE II

SOURCES OF AND SOLUTIONS TO OBSTACLES IN CORPORATE VENTURING

Traditional Management Practices	*Adverse Effects*	*Recommended Actions*
Enforce standard procedures to avoid mistakes	Innovative Solution blocked, funds misspent	Make ground rules specific to each situation
Manage resources for efficiency and ROI	Competitive lead lost, low market penetration	Focus effort on critical issues, e.g., market share
Control against plan	Facts ignored that should replace assumptions	Change plan to reflect new learning
Plan long term	Non-viable goals locked in, high failure costs	Envision a goal, then set interim milestones, reassess after each
Manage functionally	Entrepreneur failure and/or venture failure	Support entrepreneur with managerial and multidiscipline skills
Avoid moves that risk the base business	Missed opportunities	Take small steps, build out from strengths
Protect the base business at all costs	Venturing dumped when base business threatened	Make venturing mainstream, take affordable risks
Judge new steps from prior experience	Wrong decisions about competition and markets	Use learning strategies, test assumptions
Compensate uniformly	Low motivation and inefficient operations	Balance risk and reward, employ special compensation
Promote compatible individuals	Loss of innovators	Accommodate "boat rockers" and "doers"

Source: Hollister B. Sykes and Zenas Block, "Corporate Venturing Obstacles: Sources and Solutions" *Journal of Business Venturing*, Winter 1989, p. 161.

ployees. "You see what you are programmed to see, and you restrict your seeing to the signals that favor your expertise."[11] The obstacles to corporate entrepreneuring usually reflect the unanticipated effects of traditional management techniques on new venture development. Although unintentional, the adverse impact of a particular traditional management technique can be so destructive that the individuals within an enterprise will tend to avoid corporate entrepreneurial behavior. Table II provides a list of traditional management techniques, their adverse effects (when the technique is rigidly enforced), and the recommended actions to change or adjust the practice.

Understanding these obstacles is critical in fostering corporate entrepreneuring. To gain support and foster excitement for new venture development, managers must remove the perceived obstacles and seek alternative management actions.[12]

Unfortunately, doing old tasks more efficiently is not the answer to new challenges. A new culture with new values must be developed. There are significant differences between new venture units and historical operating units in corporations. It is important for managers to recognize the differences if corporate entrepreneuring is to flourish. Bureaucrats and controllers must learn to coexist with, or give way to, the designer and entrepreneur. This is easier said than done. However, there are some steps that organizations can take to help restructure corporate thinking. These include: an early identification of potential intrapreneurs; top management sponsorship of intrapreneurial projects; the creation of both diversity and order in strategic activities; promotion of intrapreneurship through experimentation; and development of collaboration between entrepreneurial participants and the organization at large.[13]

Peter F. Drucker[14] noted that entrepreneurship operates through the tool of innovation. It is a discipline that can be learned and developed. Based on this premise, Donald F. Kuratko and Ray V. Montagno have developed a training program for corporate managers to develop entrepreneurial skills.[15] Their research has led to the identification of specific factors that help individuals within an organization develop more entrepreneurial behavior.[16] These factors — top management support, time, resources, and rewards — are within the domain of managers and, thus, become the primary tools to be used to develop entrepreneurial thinking. In addition, James Brian Quinn, an expert in the field of innovation, noted that the following characteristics are present in large corporations that are successful innovators:

Atmosphere and vision: innovative companies have a clear cut vision of an innovative company and the support necessary to sustain it.

Orientation to the market: innovative companies tie their visions to the realities of the marketplace.

Small flat organizations: most innovative companies keep the total organization flat and project teams small.

Multiple approaches: innovative managers encourage the parallel development of several projects.

Interactive learning: within an innovative environment, learning and investigation of idea cuts across traditional functional lines in the organization.

Skunkworks: every highly innovative enterprise uses groups that function outside traditional lines of authority. This eliminates bureaucracy, permits rapid turnaround, and instills a high level of group identity and loyalty.

Controlling and Evaluating Corporate Entrepreneurship

The final task for managers is the control and evaluation of corporate entreprenurship activities. As with traditional management functions, the evaluation process will be a key to the effective implementation of corporate entrepreneurship.

Vijay Sathe has suggested a number of areas that management must focus to control entrepreneurial behavior successfully. The first is to encourage, not mandate, entrepreneurial activity. Managers should use financial rewards and strong company recognition rather than rules or strict procedures. This is actually a stronger internal control and direction method than traditional parameters.

Another area is the proper control of human resource policies. Managers need to remain in positions long enough to learn an industry and a particular division. Rather than move managers around as is the case in many companies, Sathe suggests "selected rotation," where managers are exposed to different but related territories. This helps managers gain sufficient knowledge for new venture development.

A third factor is for management to sustain its commitment to entrepreneurial projects long enough for momentum to occur. There will be inevitable failures, but they must be regarded as learning experiences.

A final element mentioned by Sathe is to bet on people *not* on analysis. While analysis is always important for judging the progression of projects, it should be supportive rather than imposed. The supportive challenge can help the entrepreneur realize errors, test their convictions, and accomplish a self-analysis.[18]

Overall, the concept of relying on people is a major managerial requirement if corporate entrepreneurship is to prosper. Therefore, it is important to reward employees effectively for their risk-taking on these projects. In one study of typical employees[19] the following factors (and the percentage of people responding to them) were cited as leading to improved performance:

Job enables them to develop abilities 61%
Pay tied to performance 59%
Recognition for good work 58%
Job requires creativity 55%
Job allows them to think for themselves 54%
Interesting work 54%
Challenging job 53%
A great deal of responsibility 50%

While these factors are not exclusive to corporate entrepreneurs, they do reinforce the belief that employees are willing to work on new projects and challenging teams if the rewards are apparent. It should be mentioned that the exact rewards for corporate entrepreneuring are not yet agreed upon by most researchers.[20] Some managers believe that allowing the innovator to be in charge of the new venture is the best reward. Others would say that allowing the corporate entrepreneur more discretionary time to work on future projects should be the reward. Still others insist that special capital, called intracapital, should be set aside for the corporate entrepreneur to use whenever investment money is needed for further research ideas.

Summary and Conclusion

The major thrust behind corporate entrepreneurship is a revitalization of innovation, creativity, and managerial development in our corporation. The strategies and insights presented in this paper serve as a foundation for understanding how to manage entrepreneurial interests inside corporations.

However it is imperative that corporations establish specific goals for corporate entrepreneurship. Today's strategies for innovation will only be recognized as effective if there are concrete performance goals to measure progress against. For some organizations it may be the resurgence of creative ideas from employees while other companies may seek a more sophisticated goal of new product lines or new corporate divisions. The final measurement is important as a reinforcement of the process. In other words, organizations need to experience some concrete results from an innovative process that differs from the traditional short-term results focus. However, it is clear that corporate entrepreneurship is a complete redevelopment of our traditional corporate strategies and thinking. Thus, newer and more innovative methods of measurement will also accompany this transition in strategies.

Overall it appears that corporate entrepreneurship may possess the critical components needed for the future productivity of our organizations. If so, then recognizing how to assess the current environment for innovative activity, implementing an entrepreneurial climate, and controling corporate entrepreneurial activities can be a manager's key for developing entrepreneurial thinking in today's organizations.

END NOTES

1. Peter F. Drucker, "Our Entrepreneurial Economy" *Harvard Business Review*, January – February 1984, pp. 59–64.
2. W. Jack Duncan, Peter M. Ginter, Andrew C. Rucks, and T. Douglas Jacobs "Intrapreneurship and The Reinvention of The Corporation" *Business Horizons*, May – June 1988, pp. 16–21; Also see: C. Wesley Morse, "The Delusion of Intrapreneurship" *Long Range Planning*, Vol. 19, 1986, pp. 92–95.
3. Gifford Pinchott, III *Intrapreneuring*, (New York, Harper & Row, 1985).
4. Steven C. Brandt, *Entrepreneuring in Established Companies*, (Homewood, IL, Dow Jones/Irwin Co., 1986).
5. "The New IBM" *Business Week*, December, 16, 1991, p. 113.
6. Adapted from: Gifford Pinchott, *Intrapreneuring*, (New York: Harper & Row, 1985), pp. 198–199.
7. Rosebeth Moss Kanter, "Supporting Innovation and Venture Development in Established Companies," *Journal of Business Venturing*, Winter 1985, pp. 56–59.
8. See: Robert A. Burgelman, "Designs for Corporate Entrepreneurship," *California Management Review*, 1984, pp. 154-166; and also, Rosebeth M. Kanter, "Supporting Innovation and Venture Development in Established Companies," *Journal of Business Venturing*, Winter 1985, pp. 47–60.
9. Robert D. Hisrich, "The Inventor: A Potential Source for New Products," *Mid-Atlantic Journal of Business*, Winter 1985–86, pp. 67–79.
10. Burt K. Scanlan, "Creating a Climate for Achievement," *Business Horizons*, March-April 1981, pp. 5–9.
11. Gustaf Delin, "Rewiring Corporate Thinking," *Public Relations Journal*, August 1983, p. 12.
12. See: Hollister B. Sykes and Zenas Block, "Corporate Venturing Obstacles: Sources and Solutions" *Journal of Business Venturing*, Winter 1989, pp. 159–167; and also Ian C. McMillan, Zenas Block, and P. M. Subba Narasimha, "Corporate Venturing: Alternatives, Obstacles Encountered, and Experience Effects" *Journal of Business Venturing*, Spring 1986, pp. 17–191.
13. Robert A. Burgelman, "Corporate Entrepreneurship and

Strategic Management: Insight From a Process Study," *Management Science,* December 1983, pp. 1349–1363; and William E. Souder, "Encouraging Entrepreneurship in The Large Corporation." *Research Management,* May 1981, pp. 18–22.

14. Peter F. Drucker, *Innovation and Entrepreneurship,* (New York: Harper & Row, 1985).

15. Donald F. Kuratko and Ray V. Montagno. "The Intrapreneurial Spirit" *Training and Development Journal*, October 1989, pp. 83–87.

16. Donald F. Kuratko, Ray V. Montagno, and Jeff A. Hornsby (1990). Developing an Intrapreneurial Assessment Instrument for an Effective Corporate Entrepreneurial Environment. *Strategic Management Journal,* 11, 49–58.

17. James Brian Quinn, "Managing Innovation: Controlled Chaos" *Harvard Business Review,* May-June 1985, pp. 73–84.

18. Vijay Sathe, "From Surface to Deep Corporate Entreneurship" *Human Resource Management,* Winter 1988, pp. 389–411.

19. Robert W. Goddard, "How to Reward the 80s Employee" *Personnel Management,* April 1989, pp. 7–10.

20. See: Zenas Block and O. Ornati, "Compensating Corporate Venture Managers" *Journal of Business Venturing,* Spring 1987, pp. 41–51.

A BIBLE FOR BENCHMARKING, BY XEROX

To benchmark effectively, a company needs solid support from the top, but the concept also must be an integral part of the organization, cascading down to every employee.

ROBERT C. CAMP

Mr. Camp is manager of benchmarking competency quality and customer satisfaction at Xerox Corp. in Rochester, N.Y.

For Xerox, benchmarking sprang from a competitive crisis. One Sunday morning in the late 1970s, our vice president of manufacturing and engineering read in the paper that a U.S. dealer, supported by its overseas manufacturer, was selling a xerographic device equivalent to a Xerox device at a price equal to our manufacturing cost. To analyze the huge gap between the competitor's market price and our manufacturing cost, we first went the traditional route with a product tear-down/reverse engineering and a visit to our foreign affiliate, Fuji Xerox, which gave us a window into the competition. But the visit merely confirmed that we were 50 percent off the mark. So we decided to try benchmarking, and we haven't looked back. In fact,

after our first big successes, senior management required all organizations within Xerox to pursue benchmarking. After 12 years, we are, if anything, intensifying our benchmarking activities.

A Chinese proverb says, "If we don't change our direction, we might end up where we're headed." Benchmarking is a direction-setting exercise, and it is nothing more than a quality tool, just one of many ways to improve and become more productive. However, it has been extremely important for us, so you may want to know why and how it fits in with an overall quality agenda.

Our quality program is called "leadership through quality," and it encompasses three processes: quality, problem-solving and benchmarking. We have trained more than 100,000 employees in the quality process, which shows them our output, as well as who the customers are and what they want. The problem-solving pro-

cess is a simplified version of the quality process for employees on the line and in the field. It enables them to quickly and simply analyze their own jobs, leverage the personal talents best-suited to their work and improve their performances.

After instituting the first two processes, we realized that they didn't help employees understand where we wanted them to concentrate their improvement activities. That's where benchmarking comes in. It's the process of finding better practices, bringing them back and handing them off, first to quality teams and then to employee involvement teams to see how they can use the first two facets of the quality program to implement those practices.

A TOUGH YARDSTICK

The formal definition of benchmarking is the continuous process of measuring our products, services and practices against those of our toughest competitors or companies renowned as leaders. We have never changed this definition, because it embodies some very tough lessons we learned while introducing benchmarking.

The first lesson concerns the competition. Although you must focus strongly on the competition, if that's the sole objective, playing catch-up is the best you can do. Watching the competition doesn't tell you how to outdistance them. The mix of our benchmarking activities has changed 180 degrees. In the early days, we spent 80 percent of our benchmarking time looking at the competition. Today, we spend 80 percent of that time outside our industry, because we have found innovative ideas from business in other industries.

Other companies have done the same. For example, Remington Arms, a division of the Du Pont Co., makes shotguns, rifles and ammunition. Its customers asked for smoother, shinier ammunition shells. The Du Pont team members wanted to achieve that goal with competitive benchmarking in their own industry, but Du Pont engineers targeted instead the cosmetics industry, which makes smooth and shiny lipstick containers. So Du Pont did some benchmarking with Maybelline and incorporated some practices into its manufacturing process to accommodate customers' request. Anecdotes like that demonstrate why we look beyond our industry for ideas.

In the beginning, we associated benchmarking with numerical measurements. We still do, because we must be concerned about financial ratios like selling, general and administrative expenses as a percent of revenue. But that information doesn't say anything about the changes necessary to improve performance. Most businesses have learned to look for indicators of how competitors are doing things differently. But you can't stop there; you must understand what the practices are to incorporate and measure their effects.

The formal definition is pretty cumbersome, but the operational definition of benchmarking is "finding and implementing the best business practices." It doesn't have to be any more complicated than that.

Taken one step further, the operational definition includes customer satisfaction. This is Xerox's priority, and one way to please customers is showing them how easy it is to do business with us. The primary conduit for that objective is the company-client contact point, which includes taking and filling orders, repairing devices, creating invoices and collecting payments. Those processes must incorporate the best practices to ensure customer satisfaction. With that objective, employees can pursue benchmarking in a straightforward fashion, because they know what they are being asked to do.

The four major types of benchmarking are internal, functional, generic and competitive. Internal benchmarking holds that large organizations have multiples of the same unit set up to do the same thing, such as similar marketing offices, districts, multiple distribution centers and order-taking points. The company can compare practices among internal areas and determine which one is the benchmark, bringing the others up to the same performance level.

Xerox was not always good at that. We associated benchmarking with trips to other companies, something known in benchmarking circles as industrial tourism or "feel good" trips. We did not conduct these trips with the discipline necessary to uncover and thoroughly understand the best practices, but more important, we lacked the necessary perspective on our internal operations to make the trips valuable as external comparisons.

Functional benchmarking is the story of L.L. Bean. In the early 1980s, when most managers were transfixed with competitive benchmarking, the Xerox review team members asked, "Who's the benchmark?" They expected to hear names like Kodak, IBM, Cannon or Minolta. We said no: The benchmark is L.L. Bean. Now, imagine the surprised faces in that audience, because this was the first time we advocated looking out-side the industry. The audience said, "Wait a minute – we're a copying company. How could we possibly compare ourselves to this little outdoor specialty company up in Freeport, Maine?"

SURPRISING SIMILARITIES

But all companies take their customers' orders and, provided we maintain some common characteristics, we can compare ourselves to companies in other industries. L.L. Bean's products, like ours, don't come in nice little standard packages, as you might guess about a company that sells ax handles, red flannel shirts, boots and canoes. And the company picked its orders manually, as we did, but the similarities stopped there: L.L. Bean picked its orders three times faster.

How did we know L.L. Bean was three times faster? We researched several companies as potential bench-

---

NAVIGATING THE PROCESS

Ask five companies and you'll probably get five different benchmarking methods, but just for starters, here's the process Xerox uses:

PLANNING
1. Identify what is to be benchmarked.
2. Identify comparative companies.
3. Determine data collection method and collect data.

ANALYSIS
4. Determine current performance levels.
5. Project future performance levels.
6. Communicate benchmark findings and gain acceptance.

INTEGRATION
7. Establish functional goals.
8. Develop action plans.

ACTION
9. Implement specific actions and monitor progress.
10. Recalibrate benchmarks.

marking candidates, scanning topical publications on material handling and engineering and attending a conference at which some Bean executives spoke. A magazine article gave us enough information to estimate the company's productivity rate. Eventually, we called them and simply asked, and after confirming their rate, we decided to compare processes.

Today, generic benchmarking is one of our most important focal points. We have been trying to determine if we can dedicate precious resources to continuous improvement and in which areas. After benchmarking with several other prominent firms and conducting some studies, we recognized that we would get the greatest return by improving basic business processes. We identified 67 processes for one unit and assembled a plan to revamp all of those steps.

Let's take an example of each of

> **In the early days, we spent 80 percent of our benchmarking time looking at the competition. Today, we spend 80 percent of that time outside our industry.**

the four types, beginning with internal benchmarking. Quickly answering customer inquiries and complaints makes customers happy, so we set up a customer problem resolution process as the benchmark, derived from our sister affili-

ate, Xerox Canada. We did not have to leave the Xerox family to find benchmarks in this case.

Competitive benchmarking for us meant streamlining without compromising service. Before benchmarking, Xerox had four layers – four places where we stored and handled material, and we were 30 percent off the mark. Our competitor had two layers, at manufacturing and the service person. The cost and asset levels affecting the profits and losses or the balance sheet were almost directly proportionate to the number of layers. Since then, we have changed our structure to look more like our competitor's, without any loss of service quality.

L.L. Bean is a good example of functional benchmarking. The first rule of running an efficient warehouse is ensuring that the fast-moving merchandise is closest to the main aisle, a principle called velocity

FINANCE GETS ON THE BENCHMARKING EXPRESS

Benchmarking is a two-way street to John Newcomer, manager of finance business planning at Xerox's U.S. customer operations division. "There's always something to learn, even if you think you're at the top of the class," he says. The finance department evidently agrees with him, because it's benchmarking at a steady pace. In 1992, it conducted 22 studies at 24 companies, not counting informal benchmarking activities, Newcomer reports.

Although the finance group benchmarks with a variety of companies, including Kodak, AT&T, IBM, Abbott Laboratories, and Hewlett Packard, it favors those of roughly similar size and complexity. The company also participates in competitive studies, in which a company surveys other companies on a particular process or activity,

analyzes the data it receives and shares the results with the respondents, he says.

Benchmarking efforts have focused on taxes, financing businesses, financial accounting and, more recently, financial systems. These are all process-oriented areas to which benchmarking is easier to apply than in other areas of finance, such as traditional financial planning and investment areas, Newcomer points out.

Internal benchmarking is a key information conduit. Because of the overall benchmarking drive, "There is an ongoing transference of ideas between divisions in Xerox," although the divisions do not formally disseminate information, he notes. In keeping with that tradition, the customer operations division recently benchmarked Xerox of Canada to investigate the mechanics behind its quick monthly close.

The answer lay partly in the Canadian affiliate's early cutoff date for journal and data entries. To explore other methods of reducing cycle time for the monthly close, finance also will benchmark three external companies, according to Newcomer.

Benchmarking with Digital Equipment Corp. helped the finance department address a different question: How much of its financial resources were necessary to drive the business? By gauging its practices against Digital's, finance could more clearly see opportunities to reallocate resources. Also, the company was interested in Digital's financial architecture, especially the financial systems developed during the last 10 years. Through its discussions with Digital, Xerox learned to recognize possible pitfalls and the need for "realistic time frame and resource commitment expectations" in developing a superior financial management system, Newcomer says.

sequencing. The employee can push a cart with customer order boxes and pick the necessary items. In fact, L.L. Bean uses the number of feet that a picker travels daily as a productivity indicator.

But L.L. Bean did something else. The company recognized that orders came in randomly and were unlikely to coincide with the locations of the items, so it changed the order fulfillment system. Within a set time period, employees sorted the orders and put like items together, enabling the picker to make one trip and pick all the red flannel shirts necessary for that batch of orders. Xerox did not have a comparable system, which accounted for the productivity differences. For functional benchmarking, the practices are the most important consideration.

Generic process benchmarking for us is the scheme under which we roll up the 67 processes. In developing

In general, finance benchmarking "is a process that goes up and down the whole organization," he explains. The CFO of the U.S. customer operations division is very involved in the process, he reports, and a typical benchmarking team also includes senior analysts, first-line and sometimes second-line managers. The usual number of people on a team ranges from three to eight people.

What's next on the finance agenda? Newcomer says his department "will continue looking hard at cycle times for our various processes and the associated concept of more productivity." If finance can reduce its cycle times, the department eventually will be able to spend less time on creating information and more on analyzing it. And, since benchmarking is a nonstop activity at Xerox, "we will continue to examine ourselves and to emphasize the overall quality initiative that began 10 years ago." ✧ —*RLF*

this plan, we found that we needed some accountability. One individual is responsible for each major area, so process owners are designated for 10 areas and 67 processes. These individuals document their processes and ensure that they are benchmarked.

Process owners have another responsibility, because many processes are cross-functional. For instance, an order-taking process creates an invoice, so decisions must be made about resource levels. The designated individuals are responsible for making trade-offs in the company's best interest. Our scheme gives us accountability and management.

For Xerox, benchmarking is a 10-step process, as shown in the [box "Navigating the Process,"] but the first three steps are the most important: indentifying what to benchmark, who to benchmark and where to get the data and information. In the early days, we did not mandate which companies to benchmark; we simply told our people to do it. The result was problem-based benchmarking, which we still use. However, this is not necessarily the most goal-oriented approach, so we refocused our methodology on process-based benchmarking, which will be the foundation for most of our continuous improvement efforts during the next five to eight years.

A PLAN OF ATTACK

With 67 business processes, we needed a plan of attack. Since customer satisfaction is number one, we began by targeting the processes that affected customers most. That brought us to customer engagement, the second category. The other nine areas did not want to spend years waiting their turn, so we began a demonstration project for them.

Whom to benchmark is the second step. To develop a candidate list, we might begin by looking at a list of companies cited for excellence in their business practices — the type of ranking that various trade and business journals might compile. We would then conduct secondary research to pinpoint three to six com-

> **Ask your software provider which customers use its software packages well, because these companies may be the ones to benchmark. Other options include original research, focus groups, commissioned studies and site visits to companies.**

panies for a specific benchmarking activity, which allows us to be certain that we have found the benchmark.

To obtain benchmarking information, you can tap more than 5,000 electronic data bases. Pay attention to conferences, professional associations and anything published on the subject, including software. Ask your software provider which customers use its software packages well, because these companies may be the ones to benchmark. Other options include original research, focus groups, commissioned studies and site visits to companies.

Step 10, recalibrating, is also important. Typically, we recalibrate once annually on the manufacturing side. On the business or marketing side, recalibrating every three years is adequate. In both cases, recalibrating is necessary because the benchmark, like an Olympic record, will change.

The best way to accomplish positive change is to believe in a need for improvement, determine what to improve and give people a vision of the goal. Benchmarking achieves all those objectives by bridging the gap between internal and external practices. However, it is not an isolated quick fix, but a continuous practice that must harmonize with other company initiatives.

To make benchmarking an integral part of your organization, emphasize it in your business and operating plans and in operations reviews. (See the sidebar on page 64 for an account of finance benchmarking at Xerox.) If you don't ask for it, people won't do it. Employees must be aware of the concept and their roles and responsibilities in conducting benchmarking. On-demand training for teams is also important.

A FEW ENDNOTES

A competency center, of which I'm the head, is crucial. I do not benchmark, but I help the teams and sustain the benchmarking concept. If the organization must make an important decision, I remind the appropriate individuals to make certain we have benchmarked the activity or process.

When we are planning to benchmark, we commission a team. Also, we follow a process, and so should you, whether it's our 10-step process or another company's model. Documenting the process is another must.

With the help of benchmarking, we have cut unit manufacturing costs in half since the early 1980s, and parts acceptance is nearly 100 percent. In-process inventory has been reduced by two-thirds. Service labor costs have dropped, and in the distribution organization; where I spent 15 years of my career, we upped the productivity rate substantially.

The most recent development in benchmarking circles is the International Benchmarking Clearinghouse. As an adjunct of the American Productivity and Quality Center, Xerox has helped set up a single organization in the United States as a central repository for benchmarking products and services. We use it to help qualify and teach people before they benchmark with us.

We want effective benchmarking to become prevalent in the organization and for employees to recognize its importance. Our current chairman, Paul Allaire, says the primary objective of benchmarking is understanding exemplary business practices. Four things count in benchmarking: the process on which you focus, the organizations you visit, the best practices you find and the changes you institute. Target-setting is secondary.

Planning Deming Management for Service Organizations

Thomas F. Rienzo

Thomas F. Rienzo is a research engineer with Hercules Incorporated, Kalamazoo, Michigan.

The word "quality" carries an almost spiritual character in globally focused, highly competitive businesses. Articles extolling the virtues and techniques of quality are *de rigueur* in current American business periodicals. Quality is a universally acknowledged factor in successful businesses. Allen F. Jacobsen, chairman of the board and chief executive officer of 3M Company, says, "I'm convinced that the winners of the '90s will be companies that make quality and customer service an obsession in every single market [in which] they operate."

Corporate America has begun an ambitious effort to improve the quality of goods and services offered by American companies. These efforts, sustained by fierce global competition, will continue. The United States Commerce Department reported a trade deficit of $4.02 billion in June 1991 with an accumulated midyear 1991 merchandise trade deficit of $30.27 billion. That is an improvement over the $48.28 billion deficit measured through the first half of 1990. Currently, negative trade balances with Japan alone exceed $3 billion per month.

Because of this, many firms in the United States are attempting to emulate successful Japanese business performances. Japan's economic success is rooted in quality; Japanese quality is rooted in W. Edwards Deming.

DEMING: A BIOGRAPHICAL SKETCH

W Edwards Deming received his formal academic training in mathematics and physics, earning a Ph.D. from Yale in 1927. After completing his degree, he found employment in the U.S. Department of Agriculture applying statistical techniques to the effects of nitrogen on farm crops. While working there, Deming met Walter Shewhart, a statistician with Bell Telephone Laboratories. Shewhart had created methods of statistically measuring varia-

tion in industrial processes, called control charts, that permitted workers to distinguish between random variation and special causes affecting changes in manufacturing processes. Deming was impressed. He traveled regularly to New York to study with Shewhart, whose statistical philosophy and techniques form the heart of Deming's quality seminars today.

> *Management according to Deming demands a change in philosophy as well as in process.*

During World War II, Deming taught numerous courses in statistical quality control, using Shewhart control charts, to improve the quality of American war production. Though successful during those years, statistical techniques faded in the United States after the war ended. American companies, which operated in a seller's market with virtually no competition, considered Deming's methods of statistical process control time-consuming and unnecessary. By 1949 they were no longer part of corporate America. Deming himself lamented that "there was nothing—not even smoke" (Walton 1986).

Deming first brought his statistical quality control techniques and management philosophy to Japan in 1947. He found the Japanese eager students. By 1951, the Deming Prize, which recognized superlative achievement in quality, was established in Japan. In 1960, Deming became the first American to receive Japan's Second Order of the Sacred Treasure award because of his great impact upon Japanese industry.

Although he was an industrial superstar in Japan, Deming was not well known in the United States. He made a comfortable living as a statistical consultant, but most American business managers were not aware of his management meth-

From *Business Horizons*, Vol. 36, No. 3, May/June 1993, pp. 19-29. © 1993 by The Foundation for the School of Business at Indiana University. Reprinted by permission.

Figure 1
Production Viewed as a System

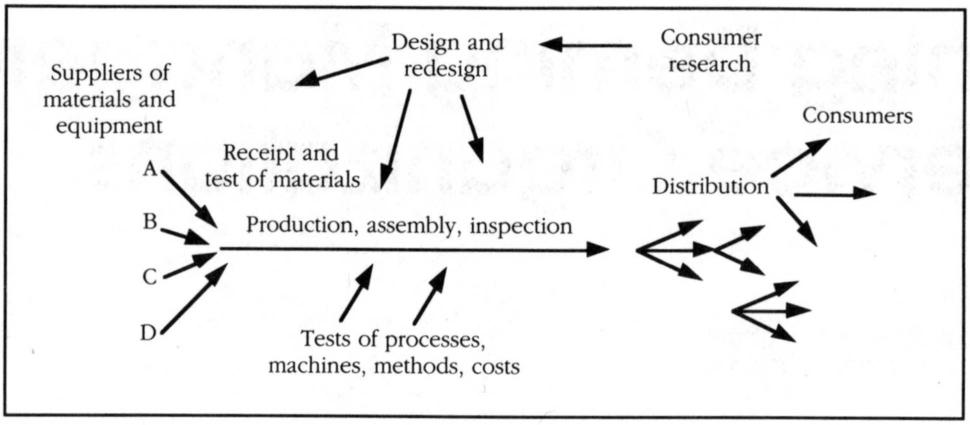

Source: Deming (1986)

ods, which formed the foundations of Japanese manufacturing excellence. American managers *were* aware, however, of stiff Japanese competition beginning in the 1970s. They realized that Japan was setting world quality standards for many manufactured goods.

One television show changed Deming's status in the United States. On June 24, 1980, NBC broadcast "If Japan Can . . . Why Can't We?" The final quarter hour of the show focused on Deming's contributions to Japan as well as on business improvements documented at Nashua Corporation, a U.S. company following the Deming quality philosophy. About four months before his 80th birthday, W. Edwards Deming became famous in America. Since that time his services and seminars have been in great demand throughout the world.

SYSTEM OF PROFOUND KNOWLEDGE

Deming claims that many firms cannot perform well from a long-term perspective because their managers do not know what to do. He is fond of repeating "There is no substitute for knowledge!" vigorously and frequently during his seminars.

American managers cannot provide answers to their problems because they do not know what questions to ask. William Scherkenbach (1990) claims the whole of Deming's management philosophy is directed toward asking the right questions. In Deming's view, insightful management hinges on the application of an awareness process he has labeled "profound knowl-

edge," which consists of four components:
1. Appreciation for a system
2. Theory of variation
3. Theory of knowledge
4. Psychology

These components are interdependent and interactive. Deming created his Fourteen Points for Management to provide a method of developing and implementing profound knowledge in the workplace.

Appreciation for a System

Deming defines a system as a series of functions or activities within an organization that work together for the aim of the organization. A system cannot function effectively without a clear aim, communicated to everyone capable of measurably affecting system operation. Complex systems, like businesses, must have full cooperation among components to accomplish their aims.

Managers are charged with the responsibility of optimizing systems; flow diagrams can help them understand what they are attempting to optimize. **Figure 1** shows Deming's perspective of production viewed as a system. Deming first used this chart in 1950 while explaining his quality management theories to Japanese business leaders. Flow diagrams help clarify relationships between system components, help define connections between processes, and provide insight into interactions. A systems approach to business activities also reveals that all processes have suppliers providing inputs and customers utilizing outputs. Most companies have a large number of processes whose suppliers and customers are internal to the corporation.

Theory of Variation

Systems are most efficiently optimized by concentrating on activities as far upstream as possible. Some understanding of variation is required to accomplish optimization. Variation always exists in any process, whether it involves equipment or people. Deming insists that managers have some means of distinguishing between changes in a process occurring at random, compared with changes resulting from some special cause affecting the process.

Statistical methods can help provide that distinction. Deming says, "Management is prediction!"[1] A process in statistical control is stable; as such, it furnishes a rational basis for prediction. Methods used to assess variation in systems are described in literature involving statistical process control.

Theory of Knowledge

Deming is convinced that hard work and best efforts are necessary though not sufficient conditions for achieving quality or satisfying a market. His Second Theorem declares, "We are ruined by best efforts misdirected."

Many shortcomings of American business do not result from a lack of effort, but from a lack of knowledgeable theory concerning subject matter that businesses attempt to manage. Deming believes that theory is essential: "Theory leads to questions. Without questions, experience and examples teach nothing. Without questions, one can only have an example. To copy an example of success, without understanding it with the aid of theory, may lead to disaster." He also claims, "There are no shortcuts to mastery of subject matter; there is no substitute for knowledge."

Deming expects managers to realize that they must concern themselves with issues that cannot be objectively measured. He frequently quotes Lloyd S. Nelson: "The most important figures for management are unknown and unknowable" (Deming 1986). The multiplying effect on sales attributable to happy customers, losses from annual ratings, or losses from inhibitors to pride of workmanship defies objective measurements.

Psychology

Psychology provides insight into human relationships and the ways in which people respond to circumstances in their lives. Deming is concerned about a knowledge of psychology in management because he sees current norms squeezing out workers' self-esteem and self-respect. He recommends eliminating a number of common management techniques that he believes are destructive, and offers suggestions for improve-

Figure 2
Faulty Management Practices and Suggestions for Improvement

FAULTY PRACTICE *Skills only required*	*BETTER PRACTICE* *Theory of Management Required*
Management of outcome with immediate action when figures deviate from expectations or standards.	Work on the system to reduce failure at the source. Avoid tampering. Instead, distinguish by appropriate techniques between special causes and common causes.
The so-called merit system—actually a destroyer of people.	Institute leadership. Reward cooperation.
Incentive pay for individuals—pay based on performance. The incentive is numbers, not quality.	Put all people on regular systems of pay. Provide leadership.
Problem report and resolution. This technique often results in tampering, making things worse.	Study the system. Learn methods to minimize net economic loss.
Work standards (quota and time standards) rob people of pride of workmanship and shut off any possibility of obtaining valid data to improve process.	Provide leadership. Everyone is entitled to pride of workmanship.
MBO—Management by Numbers ("Do it. I don't care how, just do it.")	Improve the system to get better results in the future.

Source: Deming notes from "Transformation for Management of Quality and Productivity," Seminar, February 19, 1991.

ment (see **Figure 2**). Deming believes that managers place too much emphasis on extrinsic motivation, thereby missing opportunities to help people achieve real satisfaction in their work lives.

THE VALUE OF PROFOUND KNOWLEDGE

Profound knowledge is crucial to the long-term operation of business because each component brings essential insight into optimization of the organization as a holistic entity, and success in business is measured by performance of the entire company. Appreciation for a system minimizes the damaging effects of suboptimization, in which one part of a company performs well at the expense of the business system. Theory of variation provides for recognizing a stable system in statistical control. Management is prediction, and rational prediction is possible *only* with processes in statistical control. Deming flatly rejects the contention that major

> "Profound knowledge can be applied in any area of human endeavor in which people attempt to achieve a goal through a system."

threats in business result from lack of effort: they result instead from not knowing what to do. Theory of knowledge tells us what to do. Psychology helps get everyone in the organization involved in its improvement.

Profound knowledge is itself a system. Components are interdependent and interactive. The aim of profound knowledge is optimum performance. Although Deming's management methods are presented in a business environment, profound knowledge can be applied in any area of human endeavor in which people attempt to achieve a goal through a system.

THE FOURTEEN POINTS FOR MANAGEMENT

Deming's Fourteen Points provide a method to develop and implement profound knowledge in business and guide long-term business plans and goals.

Point 1: Create constancy of purpose for improvement of product and service. Continuation of a business requires a core set of values and a purpose that do not change with time. Constancy of purpose means accepting obligations that include innovation, research, education, and continuous improvement of product and service design.

Point 2: Adopt the new philosophy. The new philosophy seeks to optimize holistic systems rather than suboptimize components. It eschews management practices that rob people of their pride of workmanship, and seeks profound knowledge as the basis for plans and decisions.

Point 3: Cease dependence on mass inspection. Inspection to improve quality is too late, ineffective, and costly. Quality does not come from inspection, but rather from improvements in the process. No amount of inspection affects process quality.

Point 4: End the practice of awarding business on the basis of price tag alone. Price has no meaning without a measure of the quality being purchased. Reliance on price must be replaced by evaluations of the effects of purchased goods and services on the operation of all processes involved in their use. Purchasers and suppliers should move from adversarial positions to cooperative ones.

Point 5: Improve constantly and forever the system of production and service. Quality should be built in at the design stage, and systems should be redesigned continually for improved quality. Variation should be minimized as

systems draw nearer and nearer toward operating at optimum points. Statistical tools and operational definitions (definitions determined by use in practice) can be extremely useful in implementing this point. They can provide the means with which to measure improvement.

Point 6: Institute training. Training should be based on system optimization and customer satisfaction. It should be a springboard from which workers can develop pride of workmanship. Training should provide managers and workers with the tools they will need to evaluate processes and improve systems. Deming recommends at least some training in statistical thinking so workers can appreciate variation.

Point 7: Adopt and institute leadership. Real leadership requires profound knowledge. Deming states that leaders must know the work they supervise. They must be empowered and directed to inform higher-level management about conditions that need correction. Higher-level management must act on that information. Leadership is the engine that drives systems toward optimization.

Point 8: Drive out fear. Deming (1986) claims that "no one can put in his best performance unless he feels secure." Fear begets misinformation, hidden agendas, and padded numbers. It may induce workers to satisfy a rule or a quota at the expense of the best interests of the company. All these consequences make system optimization very difficult.

Point 9: Break down barriers between staff areas. This point is a direct result of an integrated, systemic view of business processes. Optimization of systems is impossible unless all components recognize their systemic function and have some feedback concerning the way their activities are affecting system performance. Interstaff teams provide the best means to break down barriers between staff areas and enhance communication.

Point 10: Eliminate slogans, exhortations, and targets for the work force. Deming claims that posters and exhortations are directed at the wrong people. Posters represent the hope that workers could, by some additional effort, accomplish the goals set by management. Managers must learn that the responsibility for improving the business system is theirs, not the workers'. If posters and exhortations ask people to do what the system will not allow them to do, the only result will be disillusionment and frustration.

Point 11a: Eliminate numerical quotas for the work force. Deming views a quota as "a fortress against improvement of quality and productivity." He continues, "I have yet to see a quota that includes any trace of a system by which to help anyone do a better job" (1986). Quotas do not consider quality. They cannot provide data valuable in improving the system; they destroy pride in workmanship.

Point 11b: Eliminate numerical goals for people in management. Numerical goals are set when managers do not know the capabilities of the systems they are managing. They are generally set in ignorance or, at best, on the basis of what seems reasonable by experience. Stable systems do not need numerical goals. Output will be determined by system capability. Unstable systems have no capability. There can be no basis for setting a numerical goal in an unpredictable system.

Point 12: Remove barriers that rob people of pride of workmanship. This point recommends that all workers be given the tools and training they need to do a job in which they can take pride. It requires managers to listen to workers and act upon their suggestions and requests. Listening and follow-up action, which are hard work, need to be reinforced by high-level management. Some organizations seem more interested in bureaucratic procedures than their own employees.

Point 13: Encourage education and self-improvement for everyone. Systems will improve as a result of applied knowledge, which is linked to education. Deming writes, "In respect to self-improvement, it is wise for anyone to bear in mind that there is no shortage of good people. Shortage exists at the high levels of knowledge; this is true in every field." Deming recommends life-long learning, whether in formal or informal settings. Committed, knowledgeable people have the best chance of optimizing systems in which they work.

Point 14: Take action to accomplish the transformation. If business systems are to be optimized, everyone must be involved. The leadership for this involvement rests clearly with management. Managers must show the work force that they are serious about adopting a systems view of their business. They must demonstrate their concern for worker interests, provide adequate training to measure system performance, and measure attempts to improve it.

DEMING'S FOURTEEN POINTS AS MORAL PRINCIPLES

The Fourteen Points are not a list of action items. They are more similar to a code of conduct or a value system that provides a frame of reference with which to view the world. They are similar to the Ten Commandments—statements of principles that are considerably easier to list than to implement. Implementation requires judgment and guidance. Deming preaches a philosophy of life that is very similar to that of major religions: continuous, lifelong improvement from conversion to new core beliefs. The Deming philosophy really does require a transformation in thinking. Deming is guiding firms on a pilgrimage that takes time and perse-

verance, and he freely admits that there is no quick fix, no instant pudding. There will be struggle and some degree of pain, but the potential rewards are tremendous.

The journey Deming proposes demands faith. He comments on innovation as an obligation of his first point (Deming 1986): "One requirement for innovation is faith that there will be a future." When he writes, "He that would run his company on visible figures alone will in time have neither company nor figures," and tells us that the most important figures for management are unknown and unknowable, he is advocating acting by faith. How else can anyone deal with what is not visible, or what is unknowable, except by faith?

> "Deming is guiding firms on a pilgrimage that takes time and perseverance, and he freely admits that there is no quick fix, no instant pudding."

APPLICATION OF THE FOURTEEN POINTS IN SERVICE INDUSTRIES

Although quality as preached by Deming and others has been seen as principally applying to the manufacturing sector, there is no question that service businesses also can benefit from adopting Deming's philosophy in their firms. Below are some examples of successful implementations of this philosophy.

Windsor Export Supply

Windsor Export Supply is a division of Ford Motor Company. Its 250 employees take orders for parts from Ford's foreign manufacturing plants, most of which are located in South America. It also fills orders for Ford parts from customers outside the Ford organization.

Once an order is placed with Windsor, it purchases parts from Ford's North American plants, arranges shipment, and collects payment. In the early 1980s, orders began diminishing for the division in the face of stiff Japanese competition. Ford's manufacturing capacity had also grown overseas, and demand was declining for North American parts. Although Windsor was still profitable, Ford executives sought advice from Deming on improving the performance of the Windsor organization.

Windsor was the first service group at Ford to receive training in the Deming management philosophy. Ford's initial efforts with Deming focused on the factory floor. There were many barriers to pride of workmanship at Windsor. Managers were surprised to learn that white-collar service employees felt the same kind of frustrations in their jobs as blue-collar factory workers. Harry Artinian of the Ford statistical methods office noted, "If you took the white shirts and ties off those people and put them in overalls, you'd hear the same words" (Walton 1986).

Deciding what parts of the Windsor process to measure and optimize was a complicated procedure. In manufacturing, the accounting system highlights scrap, rework, and excess inventory. Those kinds of figures do not exist for service functions. The process of targeting significant inhibitors to performance at Windsor depended upon the knowledge and experience of the company's managers. The management team responsible for instituting Deming methods began with training and flow diagrams, hoping to get one good project as a consequence. Worker response was encouraging, and six projects were initiated.

One successful project involved freight auditing. Windsor would receive invoices from freight carriers through a contracted auditor, who completed the company paperwork and issued instructions for payment to the Ford accounts payable office in Oakville, Ontario. The contracted auditor was chosen to take advantage of "state-of-the-art" methods. But late payments and missing information were routine occurrences. Past due bills mounted, occasionally for months. Almost everyone involved in the system was frustrated.

The freight auditing optimization team measured elapsed time between the date Windsor received an invoice and the date Oakville issued a check. Using control charts, the team found that the system was stable with an average response time of 14 days, but as many as 35 days might pass between invoice receipt and issuance of a check. The team used cause-and-effect diagrams to identify reasons for delay. They found keypunch errors, misfiling, missing codes, and misplaced bills. Attempts to resolve those problems with the contracted auditor proved unsuccessful, so Windsor took over the auditing function, making a number of changes to correct problem areas. The final result of these efforts was a drop in average response time to six days and a reduction in the proportion of rejected bills at Oakville from 34 percent to less than 1 percent.

Parkview Episcopal Medical Center

Parkview Episcopal Medical Center is one of two hospitals serving Pueblo, Colorado. Hospital Corporation of America, which manages the facility, designated it as a "role model" hospital for quality improvement. Strict limitations in revenue prompted Parkview to undertake the cultural changes associated with Deming management. Ninety-five percent of its patient base is made up of Medicare and Medicaid beneficiaries, HMO

members, and the medically indigent. "With that amount of fixed payment," CEO Michael Pugh says, "it's clear that we have to do something different to survive" (Koska 1990).

Pugh was introduced to the Deming quality management philosophy for the first time in the spring of 1988. By autumn, many Parkview senior managers had received quality training. Pugh established a Quality Improvement Council of senior managers to help guide the implementation of Deming's "new philosophy." The hospital jumped on Deming Point 6, "Institute Training," with a vengeance. Quality improvement teams were formed to address hospital problems under the direction of a group of managers trained specifically to lead them. Almost all department managers attended a week-long course on statistics taught by a consultant. All hospital employees were scheduled to attend a quality awareness course.

Pugh estimates that it takes two to three years to integrate Deming quality methods into organizational culture. He advises managers to expect a steep employee learning curve. As Parkview moves further into its new philosophy, Pugh notes definite improvements in employee morale. The hospital turnover rate was less than 12 percent in 1990, compared with rates of 15 to 18 percent in previous years. Cost savings are more difficult to quantify, but quality improvement teams in operating room (OR) scheduling and food service delivery provided the hospital with more than $10,000 in annual savings in each department during 1990.

Parkview's approach to surgery scheduling provides an example of its utilization of the Deming approach to quality. The hospital had a history of not meeting early morning surgery schedules; 48 percent of morning surgical procedures began late, affecting operating times for the remainder of the day. Therefore, an OR quality improvement team was formed that included nurses, technicians, and physicians. The group tracked actual causes for delays, finding two common system causes: either the surgeon was late, or the OR was not ready. The team tried to encourage surgeons to arrive on time by 1) reminding physicians that they were expected to be on time for surgeries; 2) not permitting any surgeon who was late to surgery two times in one month to schedule the first case of the day; and 3) posting the names of late doctors in the physicians' lounge.

When the team examined instances when the OR was not ready to begin surgery at the scheduled 7:30 a.m. starting time, it discovered that extensive surgeries, such as total knee or hip replacements, were most likely to start late. The OR staff, coming in at 7:00 a.m., was unable to prepare instrumentation for extensive operations in 30 minutes. The team suggested moving starting times for major surgeries to 8:00 a.m. Leann Leuer, R.N., director of surgical services, commented, "By changing the rules a little bit we still start on time. Morale has improved because staff has more time to set up, and the surgeons aren't angry because they don't have to stand around waiting." As a result of the team's efforts, the number of late surgeries dropped from 48 to 8 percent.

GENERIC APPLICATION OF THE DEMING MANAGEMENT PHILOSOPHY

The Fourteen Points must be fully integrated into an entire business to realize the full benefits of Deming's management philosophy. However, Deming does not see this generally being done. He recognizes that statistical quality control has permeated unique processes on the shop floor, but he estimates that only about 3 percent of the benefits of his management transformation lie in this area. The big gains are in overall business strategy and company-wide systems.

Why have firms concentrated on unique shop floor processes and largely ignored company-wide systems, where Deming estimates that 97 percent of the benefits of the "new philosophy" wait to be tapped? Lack of effort is not a satisfactory explanation; in Deming's perspective, it rarely is. Many high-level American managers have not moved beyond unique shop-floor quality control because they have not accepted the Fourteen Points as desirable moral principles, or because they do not know how to bring the Deming philosophy into their company systems. Generic guidelines for implementing the philosophy throughout entire organizations would be helpful for managers who accept Deming's teach-

ing but do not know how to get beyond statistical quality control at the shop floor.

Guidelines for Implementing Deming Management

The Deming quality philosophy requires adopting a corporate culture based on his Fourteen Points for management. Because high-level managers are responsible for corporate culture, they must be the first converts to the new philosophy to provide an environment in which Deming's ideas can have lasting effects. Conversion begins at the top and travels down through the organization. Following adoption of the new philosophy, high-level managers need training in statistical thinking and the Fourteen Points. They should also create flow diagrams for systems under their authority to help them understand what they are charged with optimizing. **Figure 3** presents a generic flow diagram. It is created by first considering the needs and desires of customers, then working back through business processes to suppliers. Declaration of systems aims follows with an attempt to implement the Fourteen Points in the organization. Once aims are declared, training of middle management can begin.

The Shewhart Cycle, also called the PDCA cycle, can be a helpful procedure in implementing the Fourteen Points. It is shown in **Figure 4**. In the cycle, changes or experiments are planned and carried out. The effects are studied to determine whether changes have improved the system or offer any insight into prediction. A number of cycle iterations may be necessary before satisfactory results are achieved.

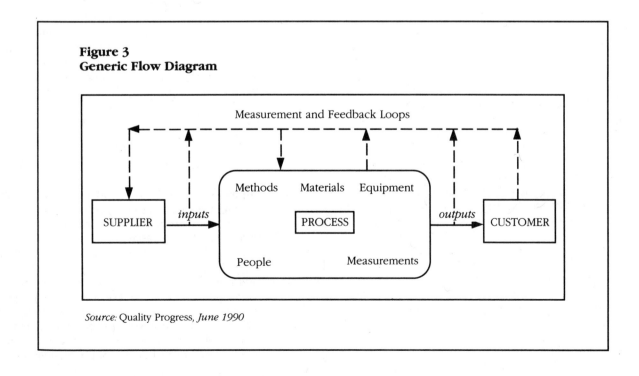

Figure 3
Generic Flow Diagram

Source: Quality Progress, *June 1990*

2. PLANNING: Decision Support Systems

Responsibilities of Management

The Deming philosophy must first transform upper management. Training, system diagrams, and the PDCA cycle are critical in implementing the Fourteen Points. Wherever possible, upper management should take action to improve the business system.

Once systems aims are declared, middle managers can begin learning the new philosophy. They must also be trained in statistical methods and the Fourteen Points. To better understand the systems for which they are responsible, middle managers should create flow diagrams, recognizing the aims that their systems are supposed to serve. Middle managers are close enough to the front lines of their businesses that they can use their training to target the largest system inhibitors to performance facing their sections of the company.

A variety of process tools are available to aid middle managers in bringing attention to large performance inhibitors. Flow diagrams increase understanding of systems. Cause-and-effect diagrams help clarify relationships between business components. Pareto charts and histograms demonstrate frequency of occurrences. Run charts and scatter diagrams show trends in process performance. Control charts allow managers to distinguish between common process variation and special causes that need immediate attention. These tools are discussed in detail in many statistical quality control texts.

Although middle management generally identifies significant system inhibitors to performance, lower management and non-management employees are in the best position to generate recommendations for improvement and deal with special causes that are not part of the system. One highly effective way of approaching inhibitors to performance is through interdisciplinary teams that target specific problems or opportunities.

Training is essential for the teams to function effectively. All employees should be exposed to the Deming philosophy, be informed of system aims, and learn statistical methods of measuring process performance. The PDCA cycle and process tools previously discussed are crucial ingredients for process optimization. Lower-level managers and workers can deal immediately with unique special causes outside their statistically stable systems. After study, they can also recommend ways of improving systems to upper management.

Company-wide implementation of Deming concepts, at all levels, is shown in **Figure 5**:

• Upper management is responsible for creating a corporate culture consistent with Deming's philosophy, instituting the Fourteen Points, understanding business supersystems, and declaring system aims. Upper management also must act to improve corporate business systems,

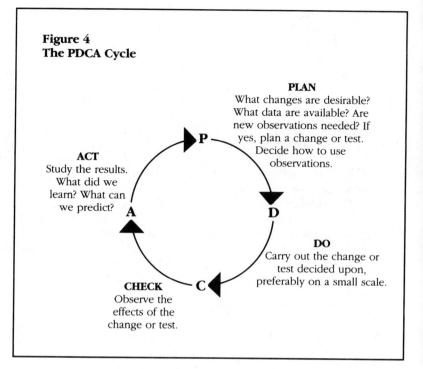

Figure 4
The PDCA Cycle

PLAN
What changes are desirable? What data are available? Are new observations needed? If yes, plan a change or test. Decide how to use observations.

ACT
Study the results. What did we learn? What can we predict?

DO
Carry out the change or test decided upon, preferably on a small scale.

CHECK
Observe the effects of the change or test.

often at the request of lower levels of management.

• Middle managers must adopt the new philosophy, understand systems for which they are responsible, implement the Fourteen Points, and target for attention significant inhibitors to performance. They too must take action to improve their business processes, frequently in response to recommendations from lower levels of management.

• Lower management and non-managerial workers must be instructed in the new philosophy and receive training to measure system performance and recognize special causes of variation. They must seek solutions to significant problems, often through interdisciplinary teams. Lower-level managers can take immediate action on special causes of process variation and recommend system changes to higher management. Deming concepts cannot be successfully applied without open communication among managerial levels.

Rules of Implementation

Figure 6 lists key activities involved in instituting Deming management methods on a company-wide basis, with general rules guiding their implementation. Systems are understood beginning with customer needs and desires, but optimized beginning with suppliers. Adoption of the new philosophy is accomplished top-down, as is the identification of significant inhibitors to performance. Solutions to overcoming those inhibitors, however, are developed bottom-up. Line workers and first-line management can act on special causes of variation, but management

Figure 5
Implementing Deming Concepts Company-wide

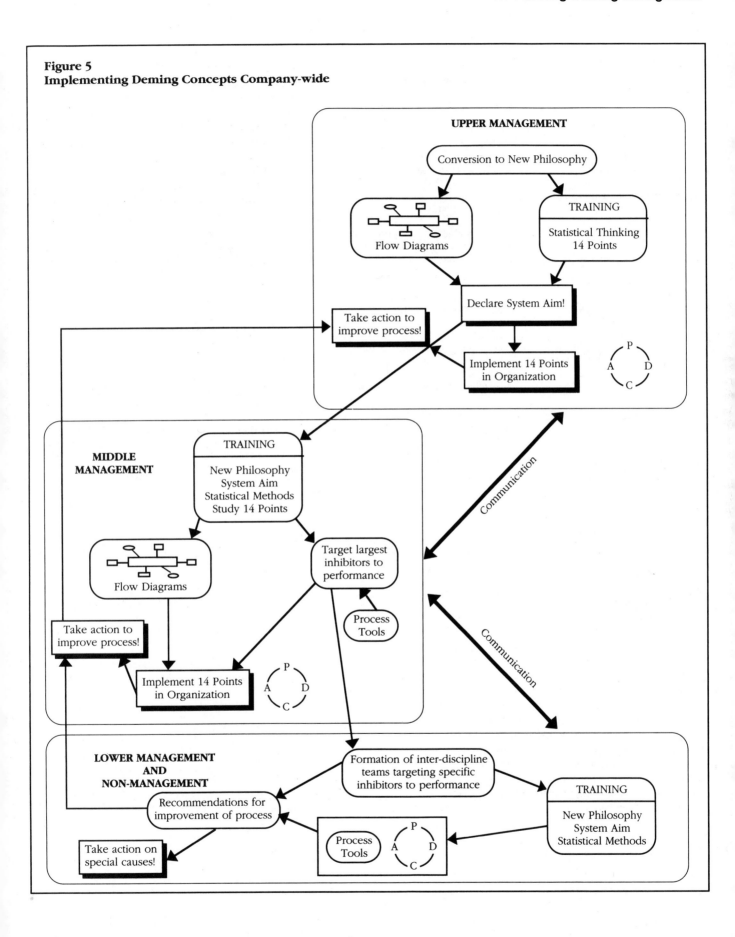

Figure 6
General Rules of Implementation

Activity	Rule of Implementation
Understanding systems through flow diagrams	Create flow diagram by beginning with customers and work back to suppliers
Optimizing systems with the aid of flow diagrams	Begin with suppliers and work forward to customers
Adopting the new philosophy	Adopt top-down, beginning with upper management
Identifying significant system problems and opportunities, and setting priorities in seeking solutions	Identify problems and opportunities top-down, frequently starting with middle management
Seeking solutions to problems involving common causes	Solutions emerge bottom-up from teams of workers and first-line supervision
Acting to correct special cause problems	Comes from workers and first-line supervision, unless higher-level management is needed to authorize substantial monetary expenditure
Acting to correct common cause problems	Comes from management at appropriate level, after receiving recommendations from problem-solving team

alone can make changes to improve common cause variations inherent in the system.

Cultural change is essential in any organization attempting to adopt Deming management because its major challenge comes not in planning, but in execution. Mary Walton (1990) explains the development of a Deming quality lifestyle as a sequence of five stages:

Stage 1: The Decision to Adopt. Management recognizes that historic ways of doing business no longer produce desired results.

Stage 2: Incubation. The quality message is transmitted throughout the organization, emphasizing that upper management is committed to change. Vision and mission statements are created.

Stage 3: Planning and Promotion. Company quality needs are determined and plans are developed to introduce the quality transformation throughout the company.

Stage 4: Education. Employees are trained in statistical thinking and given tools to evaluate and improve the systems in which they work.

Stage 5: Never-ending Improvement. Quality techniques become enmeshed in every operation of the organization. Quality becomes a part *of* business activities, not apart *from* business activities.

Continuous improvement is a never-ending journey that requires time, effort, and perseverance. Groups not truly converted to Deming's value system may well abandon the Fourteen Points when initial feelings of enthusiasm wane. The Deming philosophy is also paradoxical. Profound knowledge demands tremendous amounts of data and information, yet Deming insists that managers act on faith to manage what is invisible and unknowable.

W. Edwards Deming has preached his gospel of management transformation for more than 44 years. It is time for more American companies to listen to his message.

Notes

1. This and all other non-referenced Deming quotations are from his "Transformation Seminar" given at the Adam's Mark Hotel, Philadelphia, February 19-22, 1991.

References

W. Edwards Deming, *Out of the Crisis* (Cambridge, Mass.: MIT Center for Advanced Engineering Study, 1986).

Lucinda Harper, "Trade Deficit Shrank in June to $4.02 Billion," *Wall Street Journal*, August 19, 1991, p. A2.

A.F. Jacobsen, speech, quoted in *Business America*, March 25, 1991, p. 4.

Mary T. Koska, "Adopting Deming's Quality Improvement Ideas: A Case Study," *Hospitals,* July 5, 1990, pp. 58-64.

William W. Scherkenbach, *The Deming Route to Quality and Productivity: Road Maps and Roadblocks* (Rockville, Md.: Mercury Press, 1990).

Mary Walton, *Deming Management at Work* (New York: Putnam Publishing Group, 1990).

Mary Walton, *The Deming Management Method* (New York: Putnam Publishing Group, 1986).

How Corporate Culture Drives Strategy

Malcolm J. Morgan

Malcolm J. Morgan is Senior Lecturer in Accounting and Finance at the European School of Management, Oxford.
This article is a summary of a paper presented to the 'Seminaire Francophone d'Analyses Strategiques Europeenes' held at the European School of Management, boulevard Malesherbes, Paris on 27 May 1991.

The paper argues that corporate culture can be a practical management tool and should be incorporated into the organizational processes aimed at managing strategic change. Differing definitions of culture are examined and the conclusion is drawn that its best practical use is as a contingent variable within an open systems framework of strategic analysis. A contingency framework for the cultural analysis of organizations is then constructed in which key situational variables impacting upon the strategic process are identified. This model is then used to analyse the cultural problems facing Ford in its efforts to absorb Jaguar Cars into its organization. The process is further illustrated by reference to what is deemed to be a successful example of cultural analysis—the acquisition and integration of Zanussi by Electrolux.

The current heightened level of interest among the business community in the concept of corporate culture has a practical manifestation. In the main this interest can be attributed to the two major factors on most European businessmen's minds. The first is the increasing intensity of economic turbulence which leads to major organizational change and the second, the power of the Japanese economy which threatens every established Western business, however successful.

Business turbulence invariably leads firms anxious not only about their survival, but also concerned about achieving real growth, into mergers, acquisitions and diversification strategies in order that those objectives might be achieved. Invariably, such forays into what might be relatively unknown business territory are preceded by exhaustive financial, marketing and general management analysis.

Increasingly, however, the separate cultures of the different organizations are being considered as part of that analytical process. As one writer expressed it ' . . . although an organization's culture may be taken for granted when it is in harmony with a company's business, changes that don't take culture into account are fraught with peril' (Wilkins, 1983).

WHAT DO WE MEAN BY 'CULTURE'?

Perhaps because culture is such a common term, we believe we 'know' what it means without explanation, which is precisely why organization scholars need to be cautious in using it. For academics, culture provides a conceptual bridge between micro and macro levels of analysis, that is, a bridge between organizational behaviour at the operational level in the corporation and strategic management. For practitioners, it provides a more human way of understanding their organizational worlds, by more closely matching their daily experiences in the organization with the real and changing world of business.

How then can we weave together the separate threads of 'management' and 'culture'? These themes are distinct, but they are in fact quite compatible with one another. They are both consistent with what has been called the functionalist paradigm (Burrell and Morgan, 1979), the system structural view (Van De Ven and Astley, 1981), and the social practice paradigm (Ritzer, 1975). They are both derived from similar basic assumptions about the nature of the social world, of organizations, and of human nature.

Both assume that the 'social world' of the organization expresses itself in terms of general and contingent relationships among its more obvious and observable elements, referred to normally as 'variables' (Morgan

Reprinted with permission from *Long Range Planning*, Vol. 26, No. 2, April 1993, pp. 110-118. © 1993 by Pergamon Press, Ltd., Oxford, England.

and Smircich, 1980). Both approaches share the view of organizations as organisms, existing in an environment that presents imperatives for behaviour in the pursuit of survival and ultimate success. In an organizational sense these imperatives are the ability, indeed the necessity, of the organization to adapt to changes in its environment. In the first case, 'culture' is part of the environment and is seen as an identity enhancing force. In the second case, organizational culture is seen as a result of human enactment. In both approaches, organizations and cultures are to be known through the study of patterns of relationships both across and within boundaries. The desired outcomes of research into these patterns are statements of relationships that will have applicability to those trying to manage organizations. Underlining the interest in comparative management and corporate culture is the search for predictable means for organizational control and improved means for organization management. Because both of these research approaches have these basic purposes, the issue of causality is of critical and common importance.

In 1979, Pondy and Mitroff advocated that organization theory should move 'beyond open system models of organization' to a 'cultural model'—a model that would be concerned with the higher mental consciousness of human behaviour, such as language and the creation of meaning. They were suggesting that the culture metaphor replace the open systems metaphor as an analytical framework in organizational analysis. The growth of published research in this area stands as evidence that there is indeed a trend in this direction.

However, it is also apparent that the open systems analogy continues to be a dominant mode of thought in organizations. The suggested step that should now be taken is that of incorporating the idea of culture within that open systems framework, in other words explicitly identifying culture as a factor within the organizational framework.

The insights that might emerge from linking the two concepts of culture and organization are a function of the dynamic which exists between the basic concepts of culture and organization. This will be coloured by the perspective that the individual researcher brings to his or her enquiry. As a result the significance of culture for organization studies and analysis can only be considered against the broader context of basic assumptions and purposes related to the research model adopted. In other words, when we question whether or not a cultural model is a useful one, we need to ask more precisely, 'useful for whom, for what purpose and in what context?' By considering together all the research efforts stemming from the linking of culture and organization, the differences in interest and purposes pursued by organization scholars are emphasized and, as a result, the different intellectual strands more obviously stand out.

Some researchers give high priority to the principles of prediction, generalizability, universality, and the control of variables within the data set; where others are concerned by what appear to them to be more fundamental issues of meaning and the processes by which organizational life is made possible and therefore more acceptable to those living it. Some management scholars seek to chart patterns of beliefs and attitudes, as well as managerial practices across countries (Hofstede, 1981, 1986). Those who research dimensions of corporate culture seek to chart the ways these dimensions are inter-related and how they influence critical organizational processes and outcomes. Underlining both these areas of enquiry are the desires for a statement of relationships that will have applicability for those managing organizations. This is the critical area upon which this current piece of analysis is focused. Culture has long been recognized as a contingent variable in the process of strategy formulation (Ansoff, 1981). Alternative approaches to organizational analysis stemming from cognitive organizational theories have been identified.

HOW CAN WE USE 'CULTURE' CONSTRUCTIVELY?

We might bring together some of these ideas into an analytical model which links the culture-influencing factors within the company like structure, motivation and compensation systems, control systems and value systems with those in the environment within which the firm is operating. Included in this latter set of environmental culture-influencing variables would be technology, industry structure, competitive characteristics as well as economic, social and political institutions specifically relevant to the individual firm.

Such an analytical model is illustrated in a general form in Figure 1. It demonstrates the hypothesis developed in the paper so far, that no one optimum type of organizational culture exists or can be formulated. This contingency approach includes all situational factors, comprising the technical, political, social, financial and personnel environment within which the firm operates. It concerns itself with the interaction of environmental forces, technology, formal structures, behavioural forces and decision making processes. Thus management systems should be 'situationally specific'; different environments require different organizational relationships for optimum effectiveness. The challenge is to discover the appropriate factors for a given situation. In this paper we have argued that a recognition of the impact of corporate culture is an essential step in this analytical process. In this context it must be clearly understood that within this analytical framework these internal and external factors have only an indirect effect.

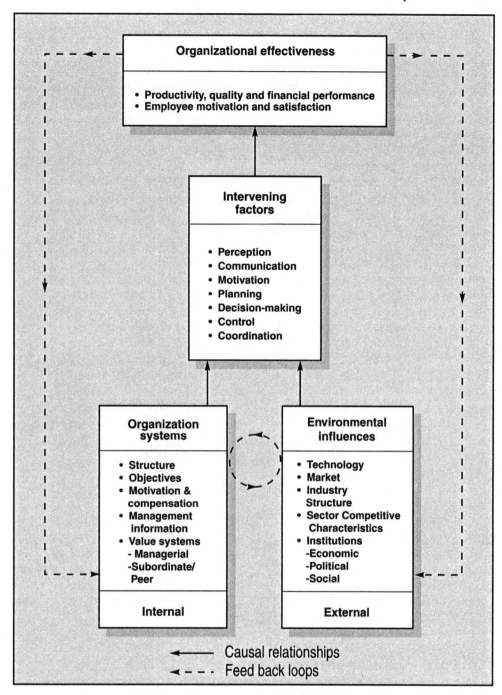

Figure 1. Analysing organizational culture

As with most factors within the business system it assumes even greater importance at certain critical points in the development of the organization. It may be stating the obvious, but firms need to pay culture particular attention when they confront the following types of conditions:

(1) Diversification opportunities
(2) Changes in competitive strategy
(3) Rapid growth
(4) Serious conflict between groups within the organization
(5) Retrenchment

What needs to be developed here is a structured view of what managers and scholars can do to understand, influence and even use culture to help solve organizational problems.

So far we have identified corporate culture as a contingent variable within each organization's managerial framework. In order to take our analysis a step forward we could usefully adopt a systems approach by stating that variables within the organization are only important insofar as they affect the achievement of its stated objectives one way or another.

2. PLANNING: Strategic Analysis

The achievement of those stated objectives will be affected by successful processes within the organization–operational, administrative and strategic. Such processes are in turn affected by the operation of, and changes to, key inputs to them from various parts of the organization. Critical amongst all these elements are those that are most vital to organizational performance. This is so because they are directly related to the ability and motivation of large groups of people to co-ordinate and direct their efforts productively.

In order to explore this further it makes sense to focus attention on those places in the organization or those periods in its history when cultural issues are closest to the surface. Most of those instances are covered by the five broad categories listed above. Specifically, we would identify three periods when organizational culture becomes more apparent and these are:

(1) When employees change roles

(2) When subcultures conflict

(3) When top management makes and implements critical decisions about company direction and style

For the purposes of illustration, let us concentrate our analysis on the last point above. The reasons for doing this are mainly that top management's behaviour reveals organizational culture more clearly because those at this level are the most visible members of the organization, and they are perceived as controlling such desired rewards as promotions, budget allocations, and work assignments.

Specifically, top management can assert assumptions or prerogatives in two ways:

(1) Through their personal behaviour, and

(2) Through the formal systems they create

They are thus in a unique position to reinforce existing culture or change it in response to important stimuli. We should nevertheless keep in mind that the shared and taken-for-granted assumptions which make up corporate culture are the result of complex social processes and are therefore not easily or quickly altered. Nevertheless we can identify employee role changes, subculture clashes and top management behaviour as particularly important inputs into our systems model where managers or others might try to nudge or redirect culture.

FORD AND JAGUAR

Figure 2 contains material from the *Financial Times*, 1 May 1991 and will be used to illustrate this analytical process.

It can be seen from this material that Ford has a major task on its hands bringing Jaguar into 'the modern world', particularly given the recession taking place in the world car industry since the takeover.

The case illustrates the fact that two firms operating in the same industrial sector, in the same markets and essentially using the same manufacturing technology can develop vastly different approaches to achieving organizational effectiveness. Ford's problems (and, by definition, those of Jaguar) are extremely complex despite the fact that both companies operate in the same socio-political environment, make the same products and share the same objectives.

Despite this, in analysing Jaguar's position after the takeover, Ford may have been forgiven for thinking that they had in fact moved into a quite different cultural environment than that which they were used to. When commenting on the state of Jaguar's factories Bill Hayden, previously vice-president of Ford's European manufacturing group said, '. . . I've been to car plants around the world. Apart from some Russian factories in Gorky, Jaguar's was the worst I had ever seen'. Add to this the production orientation of the

---

Figure 2. Jaguar to stay in the red with £70m loss

Jaguar, the U.K. luxury car maker and a subsidiary of Ford of the U.S., is expected to report later this month a pre-tax loss of around £70m for 1990, a further deterioration from a loss of £49.3m in 1989.

Mr Bill Hayden, Jaguar chairman, said financial pressures were forcing a delay of up to 12 months in development programmes of crucial new models for the second half of the decade.

Jaguar, taken over by Ford in late 1989 for £1.4bn, was hit hard last year by the recession in the U.K. luxury and executive car market and by the weakness of the U.S. dollar. The U.S. is its largest single market.

World sales fell 9.8 per cent last year to 42,754 with a 25.1 per cent U.K. fall. Production was cut by 13 per cent to 41,883.

The pressure on the luxury car market has intensified this year. In the first quarter, Jaguar's world sales plunged 45.4 per cent to only 6774 while output fell 57.8 per cent to 5339 from 12,652 a year ago.

In North America first-quarter sales were 2278, a 54.7 per cent drop from a year earlier. First quarter sales in the U.K. fell 43.2 per cent to 2104 and in the rest of Europe by 34.5 per cent to 1582. The only bright spot was Japan, where sales were unchanged at 590.

The company has taken drastic action to lower output and cut costs. It stopped production for 6 weeks in the first quarter in order to cut bloated stock levels.

Jaguar forecasts 1991 output of about 34,500 cars and sales of 36–37,000, the lowest levels since 1984 when it was privatized.

It is completing a programme to cut its workforce by around 1050 through early retirement and voluntary redundancies. Up to 500 more jobs could be cut by the end of the year.

Source: Reprinted with permission from *The Financial Times,* 1 May 1991.

company and its almost total disregard for the consumer and many comparisons can in fact be made with Communist controlled manufacturing entities.

This comparison becomes almost too stark when we note that it is not so long since Jaguar was rescued from collapse by Government intervention and was State controlled until as recently as 1984. Given these circumstances it could be argued that no real cultural change has taken place since the move into the private sector.

Figure 3. A slow road to the modern world

Ford's takeover of Jaguar, the U.K. luxury carmaker, appears—in the short term—to have been un unmitigated disaster. Losses are mounting, as sales and production plummet. Demand for luxury cars in Jaguar's two biggest markets, the U.K. and the U.S., seems to be in freefall. Worldwide sales in the first quarter have dropped by 45.4 per cent and production by 57.8 per cent.

Amid the gloom, however, Jaguar chairman Bill Hayden insists that there are glimmers of hope. Mr Hayden, previously vice-president of Ford of Europe's manufacturing group, came to Jaguar after the U.S. carmaker's takeover 16 months ago.

He says the first benefits of the company's landmark 1991–1992 labour agreement are beginning to show through in much higher productivity; and, he adds, Jaguar is set to reach quality levels with the launch today of a revamped XJS coupe and convertible range, which it had previously never dreamed of attaining.

The takeover was hardly cheap. Ford paid £1.38bn to gain its foothold in the world luxury car market. It is competing head on with the most prestigious German luxury car makers—Mercedes-Benz, BMA and Porsche—as well as with the upstart competition from Japan—Toyota's Lexus and Nissan's Infiniti ranges.

To make matters worse, Ford—which is the world's second largest car producer—made its play for Jaguar just before the bottom began to drop out of its own core North American automotive operations, and its profits began to plunge in Europe.

In the final quarter last year, the Ford group ran up a net loss of $519m (£307.1m), its first quarterly loss for 8 years. Yesterday it announced an $884m loss for the first quarter of 1991.

It was clear from the outset that the Jaguar name, rather than the physical assets, was the attraction. Of the £1.38bn purchase price, the net assets were valued at £249m, while the goodwill cost £1.133bn.

Ford never expected too much of the plants. Yet within months of arriving at Jaguar, Mr Hayden was declaring publicly that he was 'appalled'.

In one interview, he said: 'I've been to car plants around the world. Apart from some Russian factories in Gorky, Jaguar's factory was the worst I'd ever seen.'

Jaguar management admits that the first 16 months of Ford ownership has been traumatic. But the company insists that substantial progress is being made in modernizing its manufacturing and product development operations.

'Jaguar was quite an introverted company', says Mr Hayden, 'it muddled through but was not aware of competitive standards outside.'

Undoubtedly helped by the rapidly worsening economic environment, Jaguar has managed to revolutionize its labour practices. The 2-year agreement reached last November represents the biggest change in working practices in the company's history. It has finally eradicated shopfloor arrangements which had been defunct elsewhere in the U.K. motor industry for 10 to 15 years.

Mr Hayden says that direct labour productivity in the current year will be about 18 per cent higher than a year ago.

'We were not in a position to put industrial engineers on the shopfloor to time standard work and carry out process checks. Now we can and do.'

The notorious system of 'job and finish'—whereby there was tacit agreement that workers left the assembly line when a certain number of units had been produced, regardless of when the shift ended—has been stopped. There is now 'bell-to-bell working'.

Mr Hayden claims that the demarcation lines among the semi-skilled workers have been abolished. 'Before jobs were allocated by the unions. It was a metal finisher's job or a TGWU (Transport and General Workers Union) job. You could not allocate one to the other. Changing schedules or remaining the lines was impossible.'

Jaguar workers had also previously refused to take on tasks outside their narrowly-defined duties, such as detailing problems, assisting in statistical process control or carrying out quality calculations. 'All that has gone', says Mr Hayden.

At the same time, group leaders are being appointed from among the hourly workers to assist in tracking quality and production problems.

The unions previously decided the allocation of overtime. Management has now regained control, although it publishes its requirements to avoid suspicions that it is abusing its newly-won powers.

Ford's ownership of Jaguar has had an equally purgative affect on the company's engineering and product development functions. Long-held plans for a new sports car—the heir to Jaguar's legendary E-Type—were finally scrapped last year. The company realized it was unable to meet the cost, specification and performance criteria which it had established for the project.

At the same time, the management put in place by Ford has insisted on tough quality standards. The launch of the revamped XJS coupe and convertible range has been delayed for about 4 months until the required standards could be reached. Jaguar has spent about £50m on revising the range—priced from £33,400 to £50,600. The revisions amount to the most comprehensive changes made since the XJS was launched in 1975.

Mr Hayden has introduced Ford's uniform product assessment system for measuring quality. He insists that the new XJS will be introduced with the defects per vehicle cut to only one-third the level of a year ago.

In the long-term, Ford has heady ambitions for Jaguar. The company plans to more than treble output by the end of the decade to over 150,000 cars a year. It will do this by replacing its XJ6 luxury saloon range and also introducing a smaller, sportier Jaguar model to challenge the likes of the BMW 3 and 5 Series.

The ambitions will cost another £1bn, however, for development and capital investment costs, and Ford will need a steady nerve in its present troubled times.

Source: Reprinted with permission from *The Financial Times,* 1 May 1991.

2. PLANNING: Strategic Analysis

Several of the issues raised in the *Financial Times* article can be matched with elements in our analytical model in Figure 1 and these are shown in comparative terms in Figures 4 and 5. Figure 4 deals with internal variables and Figure 5 with external factors. Of course, such a superficial comparison should not allow us to escape from the extreme complexities of the problems facing Ford. They do however, allow us to understand the interaction of some of the key factors.

The changes that Ford have made, or which are impending, reflect that organization's priorities for Jaguar. In a very real sense therefore they are now being filtered through what Ford's approach to the intervening variables is. It is Ford's culture which now dominates and which influences perceptions of productivity, quality and financial performance as well as how they want to enhance employee motivation and satisfaction. Major changes need to be brought about in Jaguar's perception of the problems as well as the communication, motivation, planning, decision-making and control aspects of those problems.

Perhaps the essential point to make is that Ford appears to know what is wrong, has addressed the cultural issues and is working with a company that is part of the same national culture. And yet, as the figures in the case study show, there is no guarantee that they will be successful in turning the company around. Even if we recognize the influence of corporate cultures, and set about changing them there are no guarantees of success. It is as well to recognize this in relation to the efficacy of an open systems approach – just because you identify the key elements in a problem, it does not mean that you can solve it. Cultural analysis is not a panacea, but it represents an improved approach. Just how much better that approach is we will now examine.

CULTURAL ANALYSIS: A SUCCESSFUL EXAMPLE

Recent European management literature contains numerous examples of this process at work (Franck, 1990; Hyde *et al.*, 1991; and Ghoshal and Haspeslagh, 1990).

One of the most relevant cases to the process was examined by Ghoshal and Haspeslagh (1990). It is fitting that this case won the 1990 European Foundation for Management Development competition for the best Case Study submitted under a General European theme, as it deals with the acquisition and integration of Zanussi by Electrolux, the manufacturing giants of Southern and Northern Europe.

It was accepted from a business point of view that the acquisition was sound, that there were not many overlaps to their businesses and that Electrolux was strong where Zanussi was weak. Therefore, a critical element in the integration of the two organizations

Internal factors	Jaguar	Ford	Changes made or impending
Motivation and compensation	Piece work 'Job and finish' Lower earnings	Day work 'Bell to bell' Higher earnings	Renegotiated working practices agreement putting management back in control
Managerial value systems	Introverted 'Jaguar is best'	Open 'Market decides'	Comparative targets established for objective evaluation
Market orientation	Niche	Mass	Broaden product range to compete with BMW and Mercedes
Management information systems	Weak	Very strong	Introduction of new systems and personnel

Figure 4. A comparison of Jaguar and Ford: key factors influencing corporate culture

External factors	Jaguar	Ford	Changes made or impending
Manufacturing technology	Poor quality	State of the art	Huge capital investment programme (£1bn)
Market structure	Fragmented	Concentrated	Major review of distribution and dealer network
Competitive characteristics	Elitist Production-oriented	Pluralist Market-oriented	Bringing Jaguar into the modern world through the introduction of a wide range of up to date management techniques
	'Take it or leave it'	'Ford gives you more'	The introduction of a quality and marketing oriented culture giving the buyer value for money

Figure 5. A comparison of Jaguar and Ford: key factors influencing corporate culture

was the 'cultural fit' that needed to be established between them for the highest effectiveness of the organization to be achieved. This centred around not only the obvious differences between Nordic and Latin culture, but also the particular corporate culture of the two organizations. This process will be viewed from the perspective of our model in Figure 1.

It is refreshing to note that managers at Electrolux appeared to take the same open systems view that is represented in this model. They regarded each acquisition as unique and as having therefore to be dealt with differently. Such an attitude had been developed from the experience of more than 200 acquisitions in 40 countries over a period of 20 years. The two firms had a great deal in common in respect of the external variables affecting each of them, ignoring national cultural differences, and this was evident in the areas of: Technology, Market, Industry Structure, and Sector Competitive Characteristics.

But the cultures used by each organization to address and control these factors (crudely, 'the way we do things around here') were very different.

Some of the differences in corporate culture between Electrolux and Zanussi, as presented by Ghoshal and Haspeslagh (1990) are listed in Figure 6.

Essentially, Figure 6 examines only the External Cultural Factors that can be individually identified from Figure 1. This allows us to consider separately the internal factors specific to each firm which affected the cultural differences between them.

Ghoshal and Haspeslagh then go on to describe actions taken, in the main by Electrolux, to integrate these separate cultures into a whole. A number of

these incidents are telling and reflect an identification on the part of the managers involved of the key elements, outlined by Figure 1, in our analysis. A few examples will suffice.

Organization–from this viewpoint Zanussi had been dominated from its formation in 1916 by the Zanussi family. This domination was abruptly halted in the late 1960s when the head of the family died, with several other senior executives, in an air crash. This led to a period of stagnation in the company's fortunes which lasted until the approach by Electrolux.

However, their response to this managerial crisis was correctly identified by the senior Electrolux managers involved as a key element in the integration of the two companies. They began to *bridge the gap* between the family dominated approach to management evident in Zanussi and the professional manager tradition in Electrolux by appointing Italian managers from their SKF division as Chairman and Managing Director of the newly acquired company.

Strategy–traditionally, Zanussi's strategy had been to retain the top management in an acquired company but to replace the whole of the middle management cadre. This aspect of Zanussi's culture was obviously widely known to its middle managers, many of whom had benefited from it in the past. As a result, however they expected Electrolux to behave in the same way–a case of cultural expectation based on experience which had existed for several years.

A survey on the organizational climate in 1987 revealed that the top 60 Zanussi managers at that time showed strong support for the steps being taken toward integration. This sentiment was echoed by the

External factors	Zanussi	Electrolux
1. Organization:		
Traditional management	Family	Professional
Structure	Independent units	Integrated units
2. Strategy:		
Growth	Conglomerate	Focused
Investment emphasis	Peripheral	Core business
Post-acquisition focus	Middle management	Top management
3. Finance:		
Control orientation	Decentralized	Centralized
Importance	Low	High
Evaluation emphasis	Profits/costs	Return on investment
4. Human relations:		
Industrial relations	Union dominated	Democratic
Worker-management	Closed	Open
5. Operations:		
Capacity utilization	Low	High
Innovation	Absent	Priority
Quality	Poor	Total quality
6. External relations:		
Suppliers	High risk customer	'Blue chip'
Customers	Weak	Market oriented

Figure 6. Cultural differences between Zanussi and Electrolux

1000 or so front line managers in the organization. The problem, however, appeared to be in the management group between these two strata—the middle managers. Recognizing the basis of their fear, the senior management of the merged organization decided that they would *deal directly with front line managers* if their own subordinates showed signs of a lack of commitment to the agreed mission statement. This decision was made public and a clear sign was given to these senior managers that if they did not give this commitment, then their time with the company might be limited.

Finance—control had been weak within the Zanussi organization since the late 1960s whereas Electrolux prided itself on its clarity of objectives and supporting information systems. This area was one which was consistently addressed early in any acquisition strategy and the case of Zanussi was no exception. Cost and profit targets had been the prevailing technique at Zanussi and these were now *replaced by Return on Investment criteria* supported by relevant detailed information systems. The objective was to illustrate clearly the reasons why capital was being invested in particular areas within the organization. This was to ensure that a certain objectivity prevailed, and was seen to prevail. This approach was aimed at the 'them and us' argument and to demonstrate the integrated nature of the new organization, rather than the dominance of one company over the other. One of the benefits of this approach was a huge investment in the Porcia project, one of the biggest undertaken by Electrolux.

Human Resources—a key difference between the two companies was the closed, union-dominated environment of Zanussi vs the much more open, democratic culture that was evident in Electrolux. A number of key steps were taken by the acquiring company to break down these differences and to bring the separate companies closer together in cultural terms. The labour relations position at Zanussi at the time of acquisition was not acceptable to Electrolux and in a symbolic gesture, the only middle manager that was dismissed from the company post-acquisition was the Zanussi industrial relations manager.

In addition, in mid-1985 medium- and long-term plans for the organization were *discussed with union leaders* in some detail. Apparently, the meeting was characterized by an extremely open style on the part of the management which took the unions by surprise. After some serious negotiations the company's plans were accepted and an agreement was signed by all parties. This was not the end of labour relations difficulties, but the solution to subsequent problems was made easier by this visionary approach.

Operations—Zanussi's management in this area had resulted in low capacity utilization, the stagnation of innovation and the manufacture of poor quality products, all of which were anathema to Electrolux. In a culturally significant step to overcome at least one of these problems—low capacity utilization, *Electrolux guaranteed to source 700,000 units from Zanussi*. This decision was given wide publicity, both inside and outside the company, as evidence of the partnership forged between the two companies.

External Relations—the problem area which we have examined, and many others, had caused Zanussi to be regarded as a high risk customer and a poor quality supplier. Electrolux, using their leverage as a 'blue chip' company turned this to the advantage of the new organization. They forced suppliers into *immediate material price cuts of 2 per cent* in order to reflect the severe reduction in the level of risk when trading with the new company. Eventually, gains of 17 per cent would be achieved in this area.

We have tried to pick out in this analysis some of the qualitative steps taken by Electrolux managers to close the identified culture gap between the two companies. It is not successful management arising from increased production or better marketing, but these steps will create the common culture where such things can be achieved. It is the recognition of the *symbolic* aspects of business that comprise corporate culture.

CONCLUSIONS

This article has been written to clarify the differences between the ways the concepts of culture and organization have been linked. Also we have tried to explain how culture influences strategy formulation. There are important differences in the approaches outlined here. Whether you treat culture as a background factor, or as a way of conceptualizing an organization, the idea of culture focuses attention on the expressive, non-rational qualities of the experience of the organization.

The attraction of a cultural analysis is that it encourages us to question our assumptions, raising issues of context and meaning, and bringing to the surface the underlying values for which an organization and its members might stand—the key elements which make the difference between success and failure.

The rational model of organization analysis largely ignores these matters (Denhardt, 1981). Although many organizational scholars have conducted research on the values of individual managers, they have devoted much less energy to questioning the values embedded within companies and to examining the context in which 'corporate society' is meaningful. The cultural method of analysis encourages us to recognize that the practice of organizational enquiry and the practice of corporate management are the products of a social culture, with particular values. In our present day these values are efficiency, orderliness, and even organization itself. An important role for academics and managers is not to celebrate organization as a value but to question the ends it serves and the efficacy with which it achieves or fails to achieve those ends.

It is difficult for us, researchers and managers alike, to both live in our cultural context and to question it. It is also difficult to research organizational cultures and to examine and criticize one's own assumptions and values. But that is what a cultural framework for management and organizational research urges us to do. We must not shirk our responsibility.

BIBLIOGRAPHY

H. I. Ansoff, *Strategic Management,* Macmillan, London (1981).

G. Burrell and G. Morgan *Sociological Paradigms and Organisational Analysis,* Heinemann, London (1980).

R. B. Denhardt, *In the Shadow of Organization,* Regent's Press, Lawrence, KS (1981).

S. Ghoshal and P. Haspeslagh, The acquisition and integration of Zanussi by Electrolux: a case study, *European Management Journal,* **8,** (4), 414–433, December (1990).

Franck, Guillaume, Mergers and acquisitions: competitive advantage and cultural fit, *European Management Journal,* **8** (1), 40–43, March (1990).

G. Hofstede, *Culture's Consequences: International Differences in Work Related Values,* Sage, Beverley Hills, CA (1980).

G. Hofstede, The usefulness of the organizational culture concept, *Journal of Management Studies,* **23** (3), 253–257, May (1986).

D. Hyde, J. Ellert and J. P. Killing, The Nestlè takeover of Rowntree: a case study, *European Management Journal,* **9** (1), 1–17, March (1991).

G. Morgan and L. Smircich, The case for qualitative research, *Academy of Management Review,* **5,** 491–500 (1980).

L. R. Pondy and I. I. Mitroff, Beyond open system models of organization, in L. L. Cummings and B. M. Staw (Eds), *Research in Organizational Behaviour,* **1,** 3–39, JAI Press, Greenwich, Conn. (1979).

G. Ritzer, *Sociology: A Multiple Paradigm Science,* Allyn and Bacon, Boston (1975).

A. H. van de Ven, and W. G. Astley, Mapping the field to create a dynamic perspective on organization design and behaviour, in A. H. van de Ven and W. F. Joyce (Eds), *Perspectives on Organization Design and Behaviour,* pp. 427–468, Wiley, New York (1981).

A. L. Wilkins, The cultural audit: a tool for understanding organizations, *Organizational Dynamics,* pp. 24–38, Autumn (1983).

Case II: *The Fairfax County Social Welfare Agency*

The Fairfax County Social Welfare Agency was created in 1965 to administer services under six federally funded social service grants:

- The Senior Citizens' Developmental Grant (SCD).
- The Delinquent Juvenile Act Grant (DJA).
- The Abused Children's Support Grant (ACS).
- The Job Development and Vocational Training Grant (JDVT).
- The Food Stamp Program (Food).
- The Psychological Counseling and Family Therapy Fund (Counseling).

The agency's organizational structure evolved as new grants were received and as new programs were created. Staff members—generally the individuals who had written the original grants—were assigned to coordinate the activities required to implement the programs. All program directors reported to the agency's executive director, Wendy Eckstein, and had a strong commitment to the success and growth of their respective programs. The organizational structure was relatively simple, with a comprehensive administrative department handling client records, financial records, and personnel matters. (See below.)

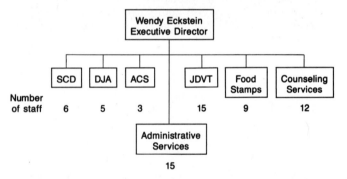

The sense of program "ownership" was intense. Program directors jealously guarded their resources and only reluctantly allowed their subordinates to assist on other projects. Consequently, there was a great deal of conflict among program directors and their subordinates.

The executive director of the agency was concerned about increasing client complaints regarding poor service and inattention. Investigating the matter, Eckstein discovered that:

1. Staff members tended to "protect" their clients and not refer them to other programs, even if another program could provide better services.
2. There was a total absence of integration and cooperation among program directors.
3. Programs exhibited a great deal of duplication and redundancy; program directors acquired administrative support for their individual programs.

Eckstein concluded that the present client or program-based structure no longer met the agency's needs. A major reorganization of this county social welfare agency is being considered.

Discussion Questions

1. What structural attributes of the agency could be causing the client complaints?
2. What actions could Eckstein take without actually changing the organization's structure?
3. Redesign the structure of the agency to improve cooperation and increase efficiency. How would you implement your newly designed structure?

Using the Case on *The Fairfax County Social Welfare Agency*

This case provides an outstanding opportunity to use Vroom's model of decision-making. Included with this discussion is some material developed by the Center for Creative Leadership, which takes Vroom's model and creates a schematic for decision purposes.

It is suggested that the instructor make a copy of the material for each of you or, perhaps, make an overhead for use in the classroom as you try to decide which decision-making approach would be best.

Questions for Discussion

1. How do you think Ms. Eckstein should proceed with making her decision?
2. What parts of the agency are going to be affected by the decision?
3. What are some of the likely outcomes from various decision-making approaches that Eckstein could use?

Exercise II: *NASA Exercise*

As you approach the moon for a rendezvous with the mother ship, the lateral dissimilar malfunctions, forcing your ship and crew to land some 17 craters, or 145 Earth miles, from the mother ship. The touchdown results in a great deal of damage to the ship but, luckily, none to the crew. Survival is dependent upon reaching the mother ship. The most critical items must be chosen for the trip.

Instructions: Below are the only 15 items left intact after the landing. Rank the items in order of importance they hold to you and your crew in reaching the rendezvous point. Place 1 by the most important item, 2 by the next most important, and so on, through all fifteen items. You should complete this section in 10 minutes.

Your Decision	Articles	Group Decisions
_____	Box of matches	_____
_____	Food concentrate	_____
_____	50 feet of nylon rope	_____
_____	Parachute silk	_____
_____	Portable heating unit	_____
_____	Two .45 caliber pistols	_____
_____	One case of dehydrated Pet milk	_____
_____	Two 100-pound tanks of oxygen	_____
_____	Stellar map of the moon's constellation	_____
_____	Self-inflating life raft	_____
_____	Magnetic compass	_____
_____	Five gallons of water	_____
_____	Signal flares	_____
_____	First-aid kit containing injection needles	_____
_____	Solar-powered FM receiver/transmitter	_____

Because you have survived as a group, the most appropriate decision-making method is group consensus. Each member of the group has to agree upon the rank order. Because the consequence of a wrong decision is so severe—death—you want to be as logical as you can and avoid arguments. In addition, you want to be sure to agree with that ranking that somewhat meets your solution. Be sure not to employ any voting, averaging, or trading techniques that might stifle and embitter one of your companions on this survival journal. (Answers may be found at the end of the Index.)

Scoring

1. Subtract the group score on each item from your individual score on each item. Write down the difference. For example, you put down an item as 3 on your list, and the group ended up ranking it 6. There is a net difference of 3.

2. Add all the net differences together to get your par score.

3. Collect all the scores in the group, add them, then divide by the number of people in the group.
   Your net difference-score _____
   Average Individual score _____

4. Now take the NASA-computed rankings and compare the group's ranking with it, computing the net difference between the group's ranking and the correct ranking.
   Net Difference Score—Group and Correct _____

What do these differences mean?

Organizing

- **Management Classic (Article 13)**
- **Elements of Organization (Article 14)**
- **Job Design (Articles 15 and 16)**
- **Designing and Changing the Organization (Article 17)**
- **Case III: Resistance to Change**
- **Exercise III: Organizing**

After the managers of an organization have planned a course of action, they must organize the firm to accomplish their goals. Many early writers in management were concerned with organization. Frederick W. Taylor was one of the first to apply scientific principles to organizing work. He was followed by Frank and Lillian Gilbreth, pioneers in the field of time and motion studies. Their work contributed to the development of the assembly line and other modern production techniques.

The question that constantly confronts managers today is how best to organize the firm, given the internal and external environments, how to approach the problem, not only from the company's perspective, but from the perspective of the economy as a whole. Are large organizations better than small ones? Each has advantages and disadvantages. Which is better able to compete in the global environment, against organizations from different countries with different expectations and rules? Add to this that society is evolving and new types of organizations will be needed in the future, as explained by Peter Drucker in "The Coming of the New Organization."

There are two ways a company can grow. One is to merge with and acquire other firms. The second is to expand the current businesses internally by building upon their already established business units. A recent trend in American industry has been to grow via the merger and acquisition route, but growing internally can often be more rewarding.

People are not machines; they are looking for fulfilling and enjoyable work. Managers must, therefore, design jobs to be interesting and rewarding. The days of assembly-line workers doing the same task over and over are numbered. Such positions are being replaced by jobs that vary in the types of tasks the worker performs each day. The content of jobs that have traditionally been low in requirements for mental ability and effort is also changing. Grease monkeys now need college degrees, as explained in "High Skills Under the Hood." Another change is that quality control is now each worker's responsibility. No longer can a worker pass the defects down the line for someone else to fix.

Today, firms must be designed to meet the increasingly competitive environment of a global economy. Organizations must learn to do more with fewer resources and fewer people; management overlap and deadwood can no longer be tolerated. Ford found this out, as explained in "A Decisive Response to Crisis Brought Ford Enhanced Productivity." Middle management is where the cuts have come and where they will continue to come. The future for middle managers will be increasingly competitive as businesses evolve with greater expectations, while the rewards for management in terms of pay and other incentives may decline. The opposite side of this coin is that the middle manager who is able to survive and prosper in this environment will be a better leader, having been tempered in a much hotter furnace than his or her predecessors.

To remain competitive in a rapidly changing environment, organizations must evolve to meet the rapidly developing global economy with which they will have to interact. These "new and improved" organizations will have the world as their market and as their competitor. They must be able to foresee changes in their environment and to react quickly to turn those changes to their advantage. Organizations will need strength and flexibility to meet these changes or they will suffer the fate of the dinosaur that failed to adapt to a new environment.

Looking Ahead: Challenge Questions

Organizations can grow either by acquisition or internally. Which way is best for the economy?

Job design is an evolving process that is leading to more interesting work. Can you think of any examples of jobs that would benefit from better and more complete job design?

Organizations are changing as they prepare to enter the future. What are some pressures that are causing this evolution? What are some of the results?

Unit 3

THE COMING OF THE NEW ORGANIZATION

Peter F. Drucker

Peter F. Drucker is Marie Rankin Clarke Professor of Social Sciences and Management at the Claremont Graduate School, which recently named its management center after him. Widely known for his work on management practice and thought, he is the author of numerous articles and books, the most recent of which is The Frontiers of Management *(E. P. Dutton/Truman Talley Books, 1986). This is Mr. Drucker's twenty-fourth contribution to HBR.*

The typical large business 20 years hence will have fewer than half the levels of management of its counterpart today, and no more than a third the managers. In its structure, and in its management problems and concerns, it will bear little resemblance to the typical manufacturing company, circa 1950, which our textbooks still consider the norm. Instead it is far more likely to resemble organizations that neither the practicing manager nor the management scholar pays much attention to today: the hospital, the university, the symphony orchestra. For like them, the typical business will be knowledge-based, an organization composed largely of specialists who direct and discipline their own performance through organized feedback from colleagues, customers, and headquarters. For this reason, it will be what I call an information-based organization.

Businesses, especially large ones, have little choice but to become information-based. Demographics, for one, demands the shift. The center of gravity in employment is moving fast from manual and clerical workers to knowledge workers who resist the command-and-control model that business took from the military 100 years ago. Economics also dictates change, especially the need for large businesses to innovate and to be entrepreneurs. But above all, information technology demands the shift.

Advanced data-processing technology isn't necessary to create an information-based organization, of course.

As we shall see, the British built just such an organization in India when "information technology" meant the quill pen, and barefoot runners were the "telecommunications" systems. But as advanced technology becomes more and more prevalent, we have to engage in analysis and diagnosis—that is, in "information"—even more intensively or risk being swamped by the data we generate.

The large business 20 years hence is more likely to resemble a hospital or a symphony than a typical manufacturing company.

So far most computer users still use the new technology only to do faster what they have always done before, crunch conventional numbers. But as soon as a company takes the first tentative steps from data to information, its decision processes, management structure, and even the way its work gets done begin to be transformed. In fact, this is already happening, quite fast, in a number of companies throughout the world.

We can readily see the first step in this transformation process when we consider the impact of computer technology on capital-investment decisions. We have known for a long time that there is no one right way to analyze a proposed capital investment. To understand it we need at least six analyses: the expected rate of return; the payout period and the investment's expected productive life; the discounted present value of all returns through the productive lifetime of the investment; the risk in not making the investment or deferring it; the cost and risk in case of failure; and finally, the opportunity cost. Every accounting student is taught these concepts. But before the advent of data-processing capacity, the actual analyses would have taken man-years of clerical toil to complete. Now anyone with a spreadsheet should be able to do them in a few hours.

The availability of this information transforms the capital-investment analysis from opinion into diagnosis, that is, into the rational weighing of alternative assumptions. Then the information transforms the capital-investment decision from an opportunistic, financial decision governed by the numbers into a business decision based on the probability of alternative strategic assumptions. So the decision both presupposes a business strategy and challenges that strategy and its assumptions. What was once a budget exercise becomes an analysis of policy.

Information transforms a budget exercise into an analysis of policy.

The second area that is affected when a company focuses its data-processing capacity on producing information is its organization structure. Almost immediately, it becomes clear that both the number of management levels and the number of managers can be sharply cut. The reason is straightforward: it turns out that whole layers of management neither make decisions nor lead. Instead, there main, if not their only, function is to serve as "relays"—human boosters for the faint, unfocused signals that pass for communication in the traditional pre-information organization.

One of America's largest defense contractors made this discovery when it asked what information its top corporate operating managers needed to do their jobs. Where did it come from? What form was it in? How did it flow? The search for answers soon revealed that whole layers of management—perhaps as many as 6 out of a total of 14—existed only because these questions had not been asked before. The company had had data galore. But it had always used its copious data for control rather than for information.

Information is data endowed with relevance and purpose. Converting data into information thus requires knowledge. And knowledge, by definition, is specialized. (In fact, truly knowledgeable people tend toward overspecialization, whatever their field, precisely because there is always so much more to know.)

The information-based organization requires far more specialists overall than the command-and-control companies we are accustomed to. Moreover, the specialists are found in operations, not at corporate headquarters. Indeed, the operating organization tends to become an organization of specialists of all kinds.

Information-based organizations need central operating work such as legal counsel, public relations, and labor relations as much as ever. But the need for service staff—that is, for people without operating responsibilities who only advise, counsel, or coordinate—shrinks drastically. In its *central* management, the information-based organization needs few, if any, specialists.

Traditional departments won't be where the work gets done.

Because of its flatter structure, the large, information-based organization will more closely resemble the businesses of a century ago than today's big companies. Back then, however, all the knowledge, such as it was, lay with the very top people. The rest were helpers or hands, who mostly did the same work and did as they were told. In the information-based organization, the knowledge will be primarily at the bottom, in the minds of the specialists who do different work and direct themselves. So today's typical organization in which knowledge tends to be concentrated in service staffs, perched rather insecurely between top management and the operating people, will likely be labeled a phase, an attempt to infuse knowledge from the top rather than obtain information from below.

Finally, a good deal of work will be done differently in the information-based organization. Traditional departments will serve as guardians of standards, as centers for training and the assignment of specialists; they won't be where the work gets done. That will happen largely in task-focused teams.

This change is already under way in what used to be the most clearly defined of all departments—research. In pharmaceuticals, in telecommunications, in papermaking, the traditional *sequence* of research, development, manufacturing, and marketing is being replaced by *synchrony:* specialists from all these functions work together as a team, from the inception of research to a product's establishment in the market.

How task forces will develop to tackle other business opportunities and problems remains to be seen. I suspect, however, that the need for a task force, its assignment, its composition, and its leadership will have to be decided on case by case. So the organization that will be developed will go beyond the matrix and may indeed be quite different from it. One thing is clear, though: it will require greater self-discipline and even greater emphasis on individual responsibility for relationships and for communications.

To say the information technology is transforming business enterprises is simple. What this transformation will require of companies and top managements is much harder to decipher. That is why I find it helpful to look for clues in other kinds of information-based organizations, such as the hospital, the symphony orchestra, and the British administration in India.

A fair-sized hospital of about 400 beds will have a staff of several hundred physicians and 1,200 to 1,500 paramedics divided among some 60 medical and paramedical specialties. Each specialty has its own knowledge, its own training, its own language. In each specialty, especially the paramedical ones like the clinical lab and physical therapy, there is a head person who is a working specialist rather than a full-time manager. The head of each specialty reports directly to the top, and there is little middle management. A good deal of the work is done in ad hoc teams as required by an individual patient's diagnosis and condition.

The best example of a large and successful information-based organization had no middle management at all.

A large symphony orchestra is even more instructive, since for some works there may be a few hundred musicians on stage playing together. According to organization theory then, there would be several group vice president conductors and perhaps a half-dozen division VP conductors. But that's not how it works. There is only the conductor-CEO—and every one of the musicians plays directly to that person without an intermediary. And each is a high-grade specialist, indeed an artist.

But the best example of a large and successful information-based organization, and one without any middle management at all, is the British civil administration in India.[1]

The British ran the Indian subcontinent for 200 years, from the middle of the eighteenth century through World War II, without making any fundamental changes in organization structure or administrative policy. The Indian civil service never had more than 1,000 members to administer the vast and densely populated subcontinent—a tiny fraction (at most 1%) of the legions of Confucian mandarins and palace eunuchs employed next door to administer a not-much-more populous China. Most of the Britishers were quite young; a 30-year-old was a survivor, especially in the early years. Most lived alone in isolated outposts with the nearest countryman a day or two to travel

away, and for the first hundred years there was no telegraph or railroad.

The organization structure was totally flat. Each district officer reported directly to the "Coo," the provincial political secretary. And since there were nine provinces, each political secretary has at least 100 people reporting directly to him, many times what the doctrine of the span of control would allow. Nevertheless, the system worked remarkably well, in large part because it was designed to ensure that each of its members had the information he needed to do his job.

Each month the district officer spent a whole day writing a full report to the political secretary in the provincial capital. He discussed each of his principal tasks—there were only four, each clearly delineated. He put down in detail what he had expected would happen with respect to each of them, what actually did happen, and why, if there was a discrepancy, the two differed. Then he wrote down what he expected would happen in the ensuing month with respect to each key task and what he was going to do about it, asked questions about policy, and commented on long-term opportunities, threats, and needs. In turn, the political secretary "minuted" every one of those reports—that is, he wrote back a full comment.

On the basis of these examples, what can we say about the requirements of the information-based organization? And what are its management problems likely to be? Let's look first at the requirements. Several hundred musicians and their CEO, the conductor, can play together because they all have the same score. It tells both flutist and timpanist what to play and when. And it tells the conductor what to expect from each and when. Similarly, all the specialists in the hospital share a common mission: the care and cure of the sick. The diagnosis is their "score"; it dictates specific action for the X-ray lab, the dietitian, the physical therapist, and the rest of the medical team.

Information-based organizations, in other words, require clear, simple, common objectives that translate into particular actions. At the same time, however, as these examples indicate, information-based organizations also need concentration on one objective or, at most, on a few.

Because the "players" in an information-based organization are specialists, they cannot be told how to do their work. There are probably few orchestra conductors who could coax even one note out of a French horn, let alone show the horn player how to do it. But the conductor can focus the horn player's skill and knowledge on the musicians' joint performance. And this focus is what the leaders of an information-based business must be able to achieve.

Yet a business has no "score" to play by except the score it writes as it plays. And whereas neither a first-

1. The standard account is Philip Woodruff, *The Men Who Ruled India,* especially the first volume, *The Founders of Modern India* (New York: St. Martin's, 1954). How the system worked day by day is charmingly told in *Sowing* (New York: Harcourt Brace Jovanovich, 1962), volume one of the autobiography of Leonard Woolf (Virginia Woolf's husband).

rate performance of a symphony nor a miserable one will change what the composer wrote, the performance of a business continually creates new and different scores against which its performance is assessed. So an information-based business must be structured around goals that clearly state management's performance expectations for the enterprise and for each part and specialist and around organized feedback that compares results with these performance expectations so that every member can exercise self-control.

Who depends on me for information? And on whom do I depend?

The other requirement of an information-based organization is that everyone take information responsibility. The bassoonist in the orchestra does so every time she plays a note. Doctors and paramedics work with an elaborate system of reports and an information center, the nurse's station on the patient's floor. The district officer in India acted on this responsibility every time he filed a report.

The key to such a system is that everyone asks: Who in this organization depends on me for what information? And on whom, in turn, do I depend? Each person's list will always include superiors and subordinates. But the most important names on it will be those of colleagues, people with whom one's primary relationship is coordination. The relationship of the internist, the surgeon, and the anesthesiologist is one example. But the relationship of a biochemist, a pharmacologist, the medical director in charge of clinical testing, and a marketing specialist in a pharmaceutical company is no different. It, too, requires each party to take the fullest information responsibility.

Information responsibility to others is increasingly understood, especially in middle-sized companies. But information responsibility to oneself is still largely neglected. That is, everyone in an organization should constantly be thinking through what information he or she needs to do the job and to make a contribution.

This may well be the most radical break with the way even the most highly computerized businesses are still being run today. There, people either assume the more data, the more information—which was a perfectly valid assumption yesterday when data were scarce, but leads to data overload and information blackout now that they are plentiful. Or they believe that information specialists know what data executives and professionals need in order to have information. But information specialists are tool makers. They can tell us what tool to use to hammer upholstery nails into a chair. We need to decide whether we should be upholstering a chair at all.

Executives and professional specialists need to think through what information is for them, what data they need: first, to know what they are doing; then, to be able to decide what they should be doing; and finally, to appraise how well they are doing. Until this happens MIS departments are likely to remain cost centers rather than become the result centers they could be.

Most large businesses have little in common with the examples we have been looking at. Yet to remain competitive—maybe even to survive—they will have to convert themselves into information-based organizations, and fairly quickly. They will have to change old habits and acquire new ones. And the more successful a company has been, the more difficult and painful this process is apt to be. It will threaten the jobs, status, and opportunities of a good many people in the organization, especially the long-serving, middle-aged people in middle management who tend to be the least mobile and to feel most secure in their work, their positions, their relationships, and their behavior.

To remain competitive—maybe even to survive—businesses will have to convert themselves into organizations of knowledgeable specialist.

The information-based organization will also pose its own special management problems. I see as particularly critical:

1. Developing rewards, recognition, and career opportunities for specialists.
2. Creating unified vision in an organization of specialists.
3. Devising the management structure for an organization of task forces.
4. Ensuring the supply, preparation, and testing of top management people.

Bassoonists presumably neither want nor expect to be anything but bassoonists. Their career opportunities consist of moving from second bassoon to first bassoon and perhaps of moving from a second-rank orchestra to a better, more prestigious one. Similarly, many medical technologists neither expect nor want to be anything but medical technologists. Their career opportunities consist of a fairly good chance of moving up to senior technician, and a very slim chance of becoming lab director. For those who make it to lab director, about 1 out of every 25 or 30 technicians, there is also the opportunity to move to a bigger, richer hospital. The district officer in India had practically no chance for professional growth except possibly to be relocated, after a three-year stint, to a bigger district.

Opportunities for specialists in an information-based business organization should be more plentiful than they are in an orchestra or hospital, let alone in the Indian civil service. But as in these organizations, they will primarily be opportunities for advancement within the specialty, and for limited advancement at that. Advancement into "management" will be the exception, for the simple reason that there will be far fewer middle-management positions to move into. This contrasts sharply with the traditional organization where, except in the research lab, the main line of advancement in rank is out of the specialty and into general management.

More than 30 years ago General Electric tackled this problem by creating "parallel opportunities" for "individual professional contributors." Many companies have followed this example. But professional specialists themselves have largely rejected it as a solution. To them—and to their management colleagues—the only meaningful opportunities are promotions into management. And the prevailing compensation structure in practically all businesses reinforces this attitude because it is heavily biased towards managerial positions and titles.

There are no easy answers to this problem. Some help may come from looking at large law and consulting firms, where even the most senior partners tend to be specialists, and associates who will not make partner are outplaced fairly early on. But whatever scheme is eventually developed will work only if the values and compensation structure of business are drastically changed.

The second challenge that management faces is giving its organization of specialists a common vision, a view of the whole.

Who will the business's managers be?

In the Indian civil service, the district officer was expected to see the "whole" of his district. But to enable him to concentrate on it the government services that arose one after the other in the nineteenth century (forestry, irrigation, the archaeological survey, public health and sanitation, roads) were organized outside the administrative structure, and had virtually no contact with the district officer. This meant that the district officer became increasingly isolated from the activities that often had the greatest impact on—and the greatest importance for—his district. In the end, only the provincial government or the central government in Delhi had a view of the "whole," and it was an increasingly abstract one at that.

A business simply cannot function this way. It needs a view of the whole and a focus on the whole to be shared among a great many of its professional special-

ists, certainly among the senior ones. And yet it will have to accept, indeed will have to foster, the pride and professionalism of its specialists—if only because, in the absence of opportunities to move into middle management, their motivation must come from that pride and professionalism.

One way to foster professionalism, of course, is through assignments to task forces. And the information-based business will use more and more smaller self-governing units, assigning them tasks tidy enough for "a good man to get his arms around," as the old phrase has it. But to what extent should information-based businesses rotate performing specialists out of their specialties and into new ones? And to what extent will top management have to accept as its top priority making and maintaining a common vision across professional specialties?

Heavy reliance on task-force teams assuages one problem. But it aggravates another: the management structure of the information-based organization. Who will the business's managers be? Will they be task-force leaders? Or will there be a two-headed monster—a specialist structure, comparable, perhaps, to the way attending physicians function in a hospital, and an administrative structure of task-force leaders?

The decisions we face on the role and function of the task-force leaders are risky and controversial. Is theirs a permanent assignment, analagous to the job of the supervisory nurse in the hospital? Or is it a function of the task that changes as the task does? Is it an assignment or a position? Does it carry any rank at all? And if it does, will the task-force leaders become in time what the product managers have been at Procter & Gamble: the basic units of management and the company's field officers? Might the task-force leaders eventually replace department heads and vice presidents?

Signs of every one of these developments exist, but there is neither a clear trend nor much understanding as to what each entails. Yet each would give rise to a different organizational structure from any we are familiar with.

With middle management sharply cut, where will the top executives come from?

Finally, the toughest problem will probably be to ensure the supply, preparation, and testing of top management people. This is, of course, an old and central dilemma as well as a major reason for the general acceptance of decentralization in large businesses in the last 40 years. But the existing business organization has a great many middle-management positions that are supposed to prepare and test a person. As a result, there are usually a good many people to choose from when filling a senior management slot. With the number of middle-management positions sharply cut, where will the information-based organization's top executives come from? What will be their preparation? How will they have been tested?

Decentralization into autonomous units will surely be even more critical than it is now. Perhaps we will even copy the German *Gruppe* in which the decentralized units are set up as separate companies with their own top managements. The Germans use this model precisely because of their tradition of promoting people in their specialties, especially in research and engineering; if they did not have available commands in near-independent subsidiaries to put people in, they would have little opportunity to train and test their most promising professionals. These subsidiaries are thus somewhat like the farm teams of a major-league baseball club.

We may also find that more and more top management jobs in big companies are filled by hiring people away from smaller companies. This is the way that major orchestras get their conductors—a young conductor earns his or her spurs in a small orchestra or opera house, only to be hired away by a larger one. And the heads of a good many large hospitals have had similar careers.

Can business follow the example of the orchestra and hospital where top management has become a separate career? Conductors and hospital administrators come out of courses in conducting or schools of hospital administration respectively. We see something of this sort in France, where large companies are often run by men who have spent their entire previous careers in government service. But in most countries this would be unacceptable to the organization (only France has the *mystique* of the *grandes 'ecoles)*. And even in France, businesses, especially large ones, are becoming too demanding to be run by people without firsthand experience and a proven success record.

Thus the entire top management process—preparation, testing, succession—will become even more problematic than it already is. There will be a growing need for experienced businesspeople to go back to school. And business schools will surely need to work out what successful professional specialists must know to prepare themselves for high-level positions as *business* executives and *business* leaders.

Since modern business enterprise first arose, after the Civil War in the United States and the Franco-Prussian War in Europe, there have been two major evolutions in the concept and structure of organizations. The first took place in the ten years between 1895 and 1905. It distinguished management

from ownership and established management as work and task in its own right. This happened first in Germany, when Georg Siemens, the founder and head of Germany's premier bank, *Deutsche Bank,* saved the electrical apparatus company his cousin Werner had founded after Werner's sons and heirs had mismanaged it into near collapse. By threatening to cut off the bank's loans, he forced his cousins to turn the company's management over to professionals. A little later, J. P. Morgan, Andrew Carnegie, and John D. Rockefeller, Sr. followed suit in their massive restructurings of U.S. railroads and industries.

We can identify requirements and point to problems; the job of building is still ahead.

The second evolutionary change took place 20 years later. The development of what we still see as the modern corporation began with Pierre S. du Pont's restructuring of his family company in the early twenties and continued with Alfred P. Sloan's redesign of General Motors a few years later. This introduced the command-and-control organization of today, with its emphasis on decentralization, central service staffs, personnel management, the whole apparatus of budgets and controls, and the important distinction between policy and operations. This stage culminated in the massive reorganization of General Electric in the early 1950s, an action that perfected the model most big businesses around the world (including Japanese organizations) still follow.[2]

Now we are entering a third period of change: the shift from the command-and-control organization, the organization of departments and divisions, to the information-based organization, the organization of knowledge specialists. We can perceive, though perhaps only dimly, what this organization will look like. We can identify some of its main characteristics and requirements. We can point to central problems of values, structure, and behavior. But the job of actually building the information-based organization is still ahead of us—it is the managerial challenge of the future.

---

2. Alfred D. Chandler, Jr. has masterfully chronicled the process in his two books *Strategy and Structure* (Cambridge: MIT Press, 1962) and *The Visible Hand* (Cambridge: Harvard University Press, 1977)—surely the best studies of the administrative history of any major institution. The process itself and its results were presented and analyzed in two of my books: *The Concept of the Corporation* (New York: John Day, 1946) and *The Practice of Management* (New York: Harper Brothers, 1954).

CAN GM REMODEL ITSELF?

The company can make great cars. But can it make money on them? As losses pile up and cash dwindles, CEO Stempel orders major cuts—but needs to do more.

Alex Taylor III

TO FULLY FATHOM the depth and pervasiveness of the ailments that forced General Motors to order the greatest upheaval in its modern history, consider the 1992 Cadillac Seville STS. GM is billing the redesigned $38,000 luxury sedan as its flagship, the embodiment of its engineering superiority, its answer to Mercedes and Lexus. The car is vastly superior to the model it replaces and has won several awards from enthusiast publications.

And yet its introduction was delayed for a year because of design problems. A new multivalve V-8 engine planned for the car won't be ready until 1993. Production ran behind schedule owing to difficulties with the paint system, among other things. The plant in Hamtramck, Michigan, where the Seville is built, has operated at little more than 50% of capacity since it opened in 1985, rendering it perpetually uneconomic.

Such are the wonders and the woes of the world's biggest manufacturing company. GM is capable of achievements bordering on brilliance. Today it builds the best cars and trucks in its history. In the 1992 model year it is introducing 16 new vehicles—the most ever. J.D. Power & Associates ranks Cadillac and Buick among the industry's ten top makes for customer satisfaction. GM is a world leader in several critical technologies, including antilock brakes and electric cars.

But the company is foundering. Even with the massive cutbacks announced by Chairman Robert Stempel in mid-December, it lags behind its major competitors in almost every measure of efficiency. By some key standards—how many worker-hours it takes to assemble a car, for instance—GM is an astounding 40% less productive than Ford. In 1991 GM lost, on average, $1,500 on every one of the more than 3.5 million cars and trucks it made in North America. It ended the year with barely more than 35% of a U.S. market that bought fewer than 13 million new cars and light trucks; in 1979 the market exceeded 14 million and GM commanded 46% of it. Efforts to reform the company have been crippled by a stubborn middle-management bureaucracy, as well as the take-no-prisoners attitude of the United Auto Workers. Union locals still strike at the drop of a wrench to protest work rule changes designed to improve efficiency.

Much is at stake, not only for GM but for the entire automotive industry and the U.S. economy. In North America, GM employs 429,000 hourly and salaried workers, enough to populate Fort Worth, the U.S.'s 30th-largest city. Some 21% are blacks and other minorities—the largest minority work force of any private employer. GM's 30,000 suppliers and 10,000 dealers provide jobs for another big city's worth of people. The company is America's largest consumer of steel, rubber, glass, plastic, and carpeting. Thirty-nine years ago GM's then-president, "Engine Charlie" Wilson, remarked that what was good for the country was good for General Motors, and vice versa. He was lambasted for saying so, but it is hard to envision a prosperous U.S. without a prosperous auto industry—and a prosperous GM.

GM's long decline has taken a toll among its more perceptive managers, who see a company that has succeeded at a critical task it set for itself—building better cars and trucks—but has yet to confront the enormous structural problems that afflict it. Says one: "There is a monumental challenge ahead of us. We can make great products. But can we do that and make money?" Spirits were buoyed somewhat by news of December's changes. Says another insider: "We did something we should have done in the mid-Eighties. I think Bob Stempel has taken charge, and what he is doing will create a lot of internal change."

Salvaging GM requires not reform but further upheaval. In addition to eliminating the jobs of thousands of white-collar workers and closing half a dozen more of its 33 assembly plants, it needs to restructure radically to get more efficient at everything it does. That will mean sacrificing some long-standing GM shibboleths, such as maintaining a separate marketing operation for each of its six car divisions—Chevrolet, Pontiac, Oldsmobile, Buick, Cadillac, and Saturn. Keeping the company going financially will not be easy: After spending an astounding $90 billion in the 1980s on new plants, equipment, and acquisitions, GM is nearly broke.

The company's future is in the hands of CEO Stempel, 58. After 33 years with GM, including five on the board of directors, Stempel, an engineer, knows cars—and GM—inside and out. But like everybody else there, he is the product of a highly centralized and insular culture that has always had huge resources and abundant time to bring to bear on any problem.

A onetime football player several inches over six feet tall, Stempel has made thousands of friends at GM during his 18-month tenure as CEO because of his loyalty, his skill at promoting teamwork, and his willingness to delegate. He has been known to return memos to subordinates with the handwritten message, "Why are you sending this to me? This is your decision."

REPORTER ASSOCIATES *Alicia Hills Moore and Wilton Woods*

FOR ALL HIS TALENTS, some critics say, he sometimes gets lost in details, deliberates overlong on problems, and prefers evolutionary, not revolutionary solutions. He has refused to consider changes in the cumbersome six-division marketing system and has promised never to reorganize the company. Stempel resolutely avoids public exposure when he can, leaving to deputies the operating levers that move the company. Says a Chicago management consultant who has often worked at GM: "I've heard guys in the organization ask, 'Where's Bob?' He has a lot going for him. But it isn't clear that he's using the chips he's got to make the organization move." Declaring they were too busy working out details of the cutbacks, Stempel and all six other members of GM's management committee declined to be interviewed by FORTUNE for this article. Understandably, few of the dozens of people inside or outside GM who commented for this story wanted to be quoted by name.

A series of horrific events in the fall of 1991 forced Stempel to move. One top GM official allowed that even the direst of pessimists could not have foreseen the company's predicament. Despite a sunburst of new models and heavy buyer incentives, GM was selling 600,000 fewer cars and trucks than in 1990; bread-and-butter Chevrolet alone accounts for two-thirds of the drop. After losing $2 billion in 1990, GM now faced a companywide deficit of nearly $3 billion for 1991. Seeing GM running short of cash, and with economic recovery nowhere in sight, Standard & Poor's announced in November that it was putting GM on a credit watch. For a company that once routinely luxuriated in triple-A ratings, the prospect of a downgrading was not only an embarrassment but a financial menace. Borrowing costs for GMAC, which is GM's finance arm, could increase by $200 million or more annually.

The company's deteriorating fiscal condition got the attention of GM's board of directors. At their regular December 9 meeting, in Washington, D.C., the directors pushed Stempel to move faster to cut costs by closing plants and getting rid of white-collar workers. Several days later, a sign of urgency and confusion in high places emerged: GM had to delay the closing of a $1 billion stock sale because it hadn't accounted for the multibillion-dollar cost of the write-offs required for the downsizing when it priced the stock.

THE CUTBACKS finally announced on December 18 will help get GM's payroll and production capacity more in line with its sales. By 1995, GM will close six assembly plants and 15 other factories, reducing its capacity by one-fifth so that it can operate profitably with a 35% market share. In the process, it will cut 74,000 blue- and white-collar jobs, trimming its work force to half the size it was in 1985. But while *productivity*—the number of cars produced per worker—will improve, *efficiency*—the number of worker-hours required per car—will not. Likewise, the cuts surely got the attention of managers in GM's famous "frozen middle" but did nothing to refocus their energies, restore potency to GM's waning brands, or unshackle a company tied down by a contract that forces GM to pay its blue-collar workers whether they are on the job or not.

GM has been closing plants for nearly a decade, but this could be the most expensive round ever. It now has to consider shuttering facilities that were either built or extensively modernized in the 1980s. Five of the plants that make midsize GM cars are scheduled for consolidation into four or fewer. Four of them were built new or completely renovated in the 1980s at a cost of $1 billion each.

With characteristic loyalty, Stempel has refused to replace his longtime sidekick and onetime rival, President Lloyd Reuss, 55. Reuss has suffered a number of career setbacks. He put middle-American Buick into a long skid by introducing European-style performance models for younger buyers and created an unwieldy, top-heavy bureaucracy at GM's small-car group, Chevrolet-Pontiac-Canada. Yet in 1990, Stempel insisted over board opposition that Reuss be named president. (The board withheld the title of chief operating officer.) Several sources report that when news of Reuss's appointment was broadcast throughout GM in 1990, a number of white-collar workers booed and jeered. Says Ronald Glantz, longtime auto analyst at Dean Witter in San Francisco: "If Lloyd Reuss were to quit tomorrow, it would add a couple of points to the stock."

The man being talked about as Reuss's successor is John F. "Jack" Smith Jr., 53, vice chairman and head of international operations. Smith, a son of Massachusetts who retains his Boston accent, won acclaim for helping turn around GM's European operations in the mid-1980s. He is known as a down-to-earth, results-oriented manager.

Surely not all of GM's problems are its alone. Ford and Chrysler have also suffered mightily in the recession, laying off tens of thousands of workers and scaling back their horizons. Their dwindling fortunes have devastated Detroit, the seventh-largest U.S. city. Auto parts suppliers all over the Midwest are failing, and unemployment in Michigan has flirted with double digits. But Ford and Chrysler have one advantage over GM: They have been through the wringer before, when both companies nearly went bankrupt in the early 1980s.

Although Detroit auto men are reluctant to criticize each other, a high executive at one of GM's competitors described its problems this way: "GM has been operating by the philosophy that, one, there is no problem that is so intractable that we cannot solve it by throwing money at it, and two, we've got all the money in the world, and if that isn't enough, we'll get some more.' It is not working, and the cash has been just hemorrhaging."

By the end of 1991's third quarter, in fact, GM was down to $3.5 billion in cash—half the amount it usually keeps on hand to meet payrolls and pay suppliers. Estimated fourth-quarter losses of $700 million even before the write-off, plus dividend payments of $285 million, meant that the company needed the $1 billion from the preferred stock offering just to stay even. Smaller Ford had $7.3 billion, and even Chrysler, often described as troubled, had $2.5 billion—much more in proportion to its revenues than GM. In mid-December, GM's stock fell to a four-year low of $26.875 per share. Long-term GM investors have taken a terrible beating. While the S&P 500 has more than quadrupled since 1965, GM common stock, adjusted for splits, is worth little more than half what it was then—even without adjusting for inflation.

GM has been paying out more than it takes in for nearly two years, so it desperately needs fresh capital to replenish its bank account. Altogether in 1991 it issued $2.4 billion in new common and preferred stock and took the unusual step of selling and leasing back some $650 million worth of assembly plant equipment. Since 1985, GM's long-term debt has more than doubled and now amounts to a steep 35% of equity. Because the auto business is nearly stagnant, that level of debt will put a drag on earnings and make it tough for GM to borrow more. The board cut the dividend from $3 to $1.60 a share in February and is likely to slash it further.

GM's cash squeeze is limiting its strategic choices and weakening its potential for future gains. It now plans to reduce capital spending by $1.1 billion, or 8%, in 1992 and 1993. While Stempel says the cuts won't mean eliminating major new cars or trucks, analysts say GM has delayed for a year or more a number of important programs, including reworking the high-profit Chevrolet S-10 pickup. The plant in Linden, New Jersey, that was being readied to produce the new truck will now stand idle until 1994.

Fixing GM will be a mammoth undertaking. Like a man out in the cold wearing a thick down parka, GM was protected by its bulk. Says the same high-placed Detroit competitor: "There is a sense of invulnerable permanence at GM. There is not a single guy there who's had to deal with a tough situation like this before." At the same time, says a New York City consultant who knows GM intimately, "Stempel and his managers are clearly in a situation where if they don't take action in a continuous way, they can get weaker and weaker every day." Sympathetic consultants and industry experts suggest some drastic remedies to improve its sub-par performance:

■ **Reorganize.** Unlike any other auto company in the world, at GM neither the chief of design nor the head of research reports to the automaking side of the business. Instead, both report to the head of R&D, who in turn reports to another executive who runs the aerospace and computer divisions. Besides being cumbersome, the arrangement penalizes GM in two ways. Designers don't work closely with vehicle engineers in creating a new car, so development takes longer and costs more. Scientists don't either, so GM is slow to apply new technologies even though it is quick to develop them.

Where Stempel *has* moved organizations around, GM hasn't yet gained efficiency because it hasn't eliminated redundant operations or people. Last fall he finished combining four separate divisions that cast engine blocks and assembled engines and transmissions; he melded them into a single behemoth Powertrain Division that employs 67,500 (only a little less than Chrysler's entire U.S. payroll). But few have lost their jobs so far, and GM is only now getting around to reducing the number of basic engines it makes from nine to five. The company produces three different four-cylinder engines and imports a fourth, even though all are comparable in size and output.

■ **Instill accountability.** According to a thoughtful 1988 analysis by one high-ranking officer circulated among the top-most executives, fewer than 100 salaried workers out of well over 100,000 were dismissed annually for poor performance between 1977 and 1983. Even bad mistakes are sometimes rewarded with promotion. (The most vivid example in recent years involved Saturn's head of manufacturing, who left the job shortly after production snarled during the launch—and was promoted to a vice president's post.) Says a business school professor and management consultant who has studied GM closely: "The challenge for Stempel is to look people in the eye who may be his friends and tell them it's time to go home."

■ **Promote solutions, not programs.** GM is a hothouse of creative problem-solving ideas, but little gets accomplished. Says an automotive industry consultant familiar with GM: "They have programs that are going to solve every problem, but they never get solved. At the end of the day, the biggest problem Stempel has is to get the organization to actually do something rather than put out page after page describing new programs."

■ **Encourage candor.** The 1988 memo observes: "Our culture discourages frank and open debate. The rank and file of GM personnel perceive that management does not

receive bad news well." Communications with suppliers and customers also suffer. After proclaiming a new "partnership" with outside parts makers in 1991, GM declared they should cut prices 7% over three years. "They don't walk their talk," the CEO of one big supplier complained.

■ **Rationalize the product line.** The divisional marketing system created 70 years by Alfred P. Sloan has long since outlived its usefulness. Three GM divisions—Pontiac, Oldsmobile, and Buick—market cars that are similar in size and function, even if they no longer look so much alike, and generally sell for $14,000 to $28,000 with popular options. Oldsmobile sales slumped from one million in 1983 to slightly more than 400,000 in 1991, and its car market share has dropped from 10.9% to 5.2%. Since Olds buyers are almost identical to Buick's in age and income, it would make sense to retain the Olds brand but combine its operations with, say, Cadillac. To ease the transition for dealers, GM might have to offer financial incentives and make the changeover gradually.

■ **Get tough with the union.** Stempel agreed to a three-year UAW contract in 1990 that obligates GM to pay its 304,000 U.S. blue-collar workers even when they're on layoff. During slow periods when many plants are closed, GM pays 80,000 workers at least 95% of their regular wages and benefits in effect to stay home and watch TV. The contract ought to be renegotiated immediately to give GM more flexibility. In the early 1980s the union agreed to reopen the contract, but Stempel says they haven't heeded his requests this time. Penalizing the union for GM's mistakes is unfair, but so is life. If the company keeps on shrinking, there will be fewer jobs for union workers.

■ **Improve efficiency.** According to an internal GM analysis, 20 of its car assembly plants require an average of 35.7 worker-hours per vehicle, vs. 21.6 hours for Ford. Worse, GM needs 32.2 hours to 36.3 hours to put together such midsize models as the Chevy Lumina and Pontiac Grand Prix, while Ford can turn out the similarly sized Taurus and Mercury Sable with under 17.2 hours. Figuring labor at $31.50 an hour for wages and fringes, overall Ford has a $441 cost advantage on the factory floor alone.

■ **Increase flexibility.** In Arlington, Texas, the hot-selling Buick Roadmaster is built on the same line as the less popular Chevrolet Caprice Classic. The plant is now listed for possible closing. When it shut down temporarily in 1991 to keep Caprice inventories in check, supplies of the Roadmaster dried up. GM has to learn how to build more models in each plant and adjust production among the models more deftly to better balance output with demand.

■ **Cut production engineering costs.** GM lags behind Ford in the design and engineering of the tools and stamping dies needed to make new models. One Michigan-based manufacturing consultant says GM spends 20% to 25% more than Ford to get a factory ready for production—a potential $100 million difference. GM, for instance, traditionally designs its dies to produce several times more volume than they actually do.

■ **Speed new model development.** Although GM is making progress at getting cars to market quicker, it remains slower than its major competitors. Harvard business school professor Kim Clark, who has studied product development worldwide, believes that it takes GM 42 to 48 months to complete a redesign. That is six to nine months better than in the mid-1980s, but still nine to 12 months slower than the Japanese. Says Clark: "The average Japanese firm has almost double the development productivity and can get to market a year faster than the average U.S. firm."

To see an example of a successful automotive turnaround, Stempel need look only as far as his own European operation. A big money loser as recently as 1986, it was revived after judicious investment in new factories and cars. GM's German and British makes, Opel and Vauxhall, sold 1.6 million cars in 1991, returned nearly $2 billion in profits, and challenged Volkswagen and Fiat for European sales leadership. Furman Selz analyst Maryann N. Keller says Opel's plant in Rüsselsheim may be the most productive on the Continent. Opel boss Louis Hughes, who took the trouble to learn to speak German on the job, has smoothed relations with Germany's contentious labor unions.

GM Europe is not a perfect paradigm, however. Being 4,000 miles from headquarters, it is relatively free from bureaucratic interference. It is only a third as large as North American operations, markets only two car brands, and lacks any feeling of invulnerability because it has already endured a life-threatening crisis. Perhaps most important, it competes in a market that traditionally yields higher profit margins and where Toyota, Nissan, and Honda have not been major forces until recently.

Besides helping itself, GM could also do with some wisdom from Washington to help redirect the regulatory and legislative crosswinds that buffet the industry. Automakers and consumers alike need relief from drastic fuel-economy and clean-air legislation that will drive up costs by several thousand dollars a vehicle while producing little for the environment. Tax collectors ought to ensure that foreign automakers operating in the U.S. aren't using accounting tricks to avoid paying their fair share by, say, inflating on their books the price of parts imported from Japan. Loopholes that allow four-door trucks like sport utility vehicles and minivans to be labeled as cars when they land in the U.S., thus avoiding a 25% tariff, should be closed. Laws regulating local content of Japanese cars built in the U.S. ought to be redrawn so that it is no longer possible, say, for a Toyota Camry engine assembled in Kentucky to count as 100% American even if three-quarters of the parts were imported from Japan (FORTUNE, June 17, [1991]).

While the recession exposed and aggravated GM's problems, it didn't cause them. Poor assembly quality in the early 1980s, combined with indifferent design and inadequate product differentiation, eroded the value of GM's brands. GM fares particularly poorly with customers under 45, who grew up when things were going badly for GM and bought Japanese cars instead. As buyers grow older, General Motors worries that they may decide to move up from Hondas and Toyotas into Acuras and Lexuses, bypassing the Buicks and Cadillacs their parents drove. In trend-setting California, GM is picking up some lost ground, but it still trails the imports badly. It gets only 24.6% of sales, to 42% for the Japanese.

No list of GM's self-inflicted wounds could overlook the series of misguided decisions, acquisitions, and investments the company made during the 1980s. Ford and Chrysler committed similar errors, but nobody spent as much as GM and got so little for it. For example, GM put $77 billion into new plants and equipment to reduce labor costs. Investing that much money sensibly is almost impossible, and GM paid more than it should and bought more than it needed. Some robots it acquired in the mid-1980s stand unused today. The highly automated equipment never delivered the promised savings because GM did not train workers properly to use it, and—unlike Honda, say—failed to design new models for easy robot assembly.

In a costly effort to diversify, GM spent $2.5 billion for Ross Perot's EDS and $5.2 billion for Hughes Aircraft. EDS is paying off as a stand-alone business, though it hasn't created the synergies predicted when it wired GM into a single computer system. Hughes hasn't produced the off-the-shelf high technology GM wanted for its cars. A complicated scheme to reimburse the Hughes Medical Institute for its stock will eventually boost the total acquisition cost by $2.6 billion.

The cupboard is now bare. GM will finally have to learn how to make do with less or try to raise new equity.

Another 1980s legacy: By combining North American car operations in two groups—Chevrolet-Pontiac-Canada and Buick-Oldsmobile-Cadillac—in 1984, GM added another level of management to an already unwieldy bureaucracy without producing new efficiencies. Staff functions such as marketing, engineering, and strategic planning are now performed at three different levels in the company: corporate, group, and individual car division. The reorganization stripped the car divisions of what remained of their autonomy, compounding brand-identity problems and customer confusion. It also created 18 months of chaos, delaying new-model programs and contributing to an incredible six-point loss of market share in a single year.

And there is Saturn. Convinced that it couldn't build a profitable small car within its existing structure, GM created a new division, gave it $3.5 billion, and told it to do something revolutionary. Saturn has tried some new wrinkles in manufacturing techniques and labor agreements, advertising and distribution. While the car has been received enthusiastically by some buyers, it is priced so low (base model sticker: $8,195) that other Detroit auto executives say GM will never recover its investment. Some 18 months after start-up, the plant in Spring Hill, Tennessee, is still debugging production. Saturn cost GM an estimated $800 million in 1991 and could run almost as deeply in the red in 1992.

So GM now finds itself in the position of former Washington Redskins football coach George Allen, who, given an unlimited budget, proceeded to spend it all. Hugely profitable international operations as well as solid computer, aerospace, and finance subsidiaries have not prevented GM from piling up the biggest loss in corporate history over the past two years. The cupboard is now bare. GM will finally have to learn how to make do with less or try to raise new equity from what must by now be thoroughly disillusioned investors.

Great men demand great times. Bob Stempel has an opportunity that was denied all of his predecessors: the crisis required to bring about revolutionary change. Stempel said in December that he is making fundamental alterations in the way GM does business. If he fails, it would be a tragedy for Detroit, for the Midwest, for the U.S. economy, and for a million or more GM workers and retirees—not to mention all those potential customers for high-quality, made-in-America automobiles. But if he and the rest of GM management are successful, even his competitors will have reason to cheer the renewed vitality of an American corporate institution.

HIGH SKILLS UNDER THE HOOD

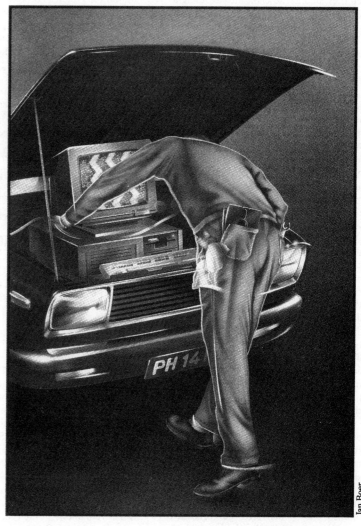

Jan Boer

BOB FILIPCZAK

Bob Filipczak *is staff editor of TRAINING Magazine.*

There's something under the hood of your new car that you should know about. It's a computer. And it doesn't contain a simple computer chip, like the kind you could pull out of a calculator. The computer in your 1993 car has enough power and smarts to act as your home computer, run your kids' Nintendo games, control the heating and humidity of every room in your house independently, run your sprinkler system so that it would react to changing soil moisture and manage your entire home security system. All at the same time.

Even if it were doing all that, this little box, about the size of a car stereo, would be using only about 40 percent of its memory and 60 percent of its communications capability. Instead of being an all-purpose housekeeper, however, it's running your car.

So when this technological marvel breaks down, to whom do you take it: Sam, the neighborhood grease monkey, or Ellie, the computer whiz next door? It's the perfect conundrum to illustrate the often-repeated maxim that we need to upgrade the skills of the work force because the abilities we'll need tomorrow will be markedly different from the ones needed today.

As an addendum to this line of reasoning, it is frequently said that our

Is anybody really serious about skilling up jobs? Carmakers are. Here's how Ford is teaching tomorrow's mechanics to be high-tech car doctors.

knowledge base is growing so rapidly that engineers graduating from college today will be "obsolete" in a few years if they don't continue to take courses and stay current with the literature. But technology expands the knowledge base in all sorts of ways and for all sorts of jobs—including the once-humble job of car mechanic.

Recognizing this, a number of companies have begun apprenticeship programs to try to build the workers of tomorrow from the ground up. Ford Motor Co., for instance, has devised a novel industry-education partnership in an attempt to produce car mechanics who will be a cross between Sam and Ellie. The program, called ASSET (Automotive Student Service Educational Training), involves community and vocational colleges, Ford dealerships, students, instructors and the Ford parent company.

ASSET's workings are relatively simple. A Ford dealership sponsors a student. When the student passes muster at one of the community colleges that houses an ASSET program, he starts a two-year journey that will give him two things when he completes the program: an associate degree and a job as a Ford technician. Instead of studying automotive technology in a generic course—where he would learn to fix anything from an Accord to a Zephyr—he learns how to handle only Ford and Lincoln-Mercury cars.

The practical design of this program is the kind of thing instructional designers have been advocating for decades: Give trainees lots of time to practice and make sure they have support on the job. In the ASSET program, students attend eight to 12 weeks of regular classroom training both for their associate degree and to learn the particulars of Ford automotive engineering.

Then the students go to their sponsoring dealership and practice what they've learned for another eight to 12 weeks. Then it's back to school to learn, followed by more back-and-forth, for the entire two years. With this design, students don't wait two years to see if what they were taught is applicable in the real world.

A smart way to do things? It certainly seems that way. And although Ford has set up an exemplary program, it's not the pioneer. General Motors started the first such program in 1979, which was called ASEP (Automotive Service Excellence Program). Chrysler, Toyota and Nissan have all followed suit with similar programs. Ford's effort, which started in 1985, now includes 59 programs around the country, with 1,300 current students and more than 1,700 graduates.

A great deal of time and thought went into ironing out the details of this cooperative effort. But Charlie Quinn, Ford's national ASSET director, downplays the complexity of the program and suggests that the only real necessity was to make sure everyone came to the table with something to offer and something to gain. That means educators, dealers, students and Ford itself all have something that the other groups need.

KEEPING CURRENT

ASSET was established to create highly skilled automotive technicians who could handle the increasingly complex nature of the cars Ford was producing. What are these so-called "high skills" the mechanics need? We already talked about the computer that controls a 1993 Ford, but there's more to it.

According to Ken Koeper, an ASSET instructor at Hennepin Technical College in Minneapolis, separate computer systems exist for anti-lock brakes, power steering, shocks, suspension, en-

> *The days of the grease monkey—the student who didn't do too well in school but was good with his hands—are vanishing.*

gine control, emissions and the keyless entry system on some of the fancier cars. The days of Sam the grease monkey—the student who didn't do well in school but was good with his hands—are vanishing. A student who wants a good job fixing cars today has to know his way around electronics, computer control systems, chemistry and physics in addition to all the automotive stuff that hasn't changed over the years.

What's more, future models promise to be even more demanding. Koeper says the changes that will be made in automotive technology in 1994 will outpace those made in the last 10 years combined. No wonder, then, that Ford decided it needed a new breed of car mechanic.

Koeper, who once was a technician for a Ford dealership, said he first glimpsed the yawning gap between what he knew and what he was supposed to know in the early 1980s, when computer systems were introduced into cars. Keeping current was a struggle for him and his coworkers. As an instructor, Koeper gets about six weeks of training every year from Ford to keep him up to date.

Technicians at dealerships often keep up by attending night classes at community colleges. It was clear to Ford, however, that the technicians of the future weren't going to be able to fix the cars of the future if they received only the generic education most community colleges offer. Thus began the ASSET program.

As a result of ASSET, Ford gets a work force of highly skilled technicians who can handle whatever the engineers decide to stick into the cars. What does the company offer in return? It recruits dealers for the program, provides money so the community colleges can recruit students, develops the entire curriculum, gives the school state-of-the-art testing equipment (always a boon to community and technical colleges) and maintains a fleet of cars for the students to work on. Add the six weeks of training every year for instructors and Ford's cost is about $2.5 million annually.

WHEELERS AND DEALERS

The payoff is clear for Ford and Lincoln-Mercury dealers as well. Having a ready pool of qualified technicians gives them one less thing to worry about as they try to run their businesses.

Each dealership that sponsors a student in the ASSET program is responsible for three things: to provide work uniforms during the two-year period, to hire the sponsored student after he completes the ASSET program and to pay the student for the work he does in the dealership during the work/study period. The wages, according to students, range from $5 to $6.50 an hour.

Some dealerships also offer their sponsored students financial support in the form of scholarships. These grants are used to pay some extra expenses the students might incur. As Quinn explains, some ASSET programs serve dealerships throughout a state or a group of states. Students who go to school in St. Louis, for instance, may be sponsored by a dealership 100 miles away. This poses a financial burden for the student who may need living quarters in two different places during the length of the program. Often, a dealer will pay some of these expenses.

For their part, students are expected to pay for their education and tools. Educational expenses include tuition for their general education courses, books (although Ford provides the books for automotive classes) and living expenses. The tools cost about $1,000, but Pat Garrity, ASSET program instructor at Cuyamaca

College in San Diego, doesn't make students buy all the tools at once. Students in his program can buy the tools as they need them, and Garrity has persuaded a manufacturer to sell the tools at a discount.

Overall costs for students who go through the ASSET program vary radically depending on geography. The tuition for a general education associate degree is the big variable; community colleges charge wildly different prices for their degrees. A California student, for example, can get through the two years for about $1,800; other programs can cost up to $20,000.

More than the money, however, is the commitment students must make to get through the ASSET program. As Garrity explains, these people are cramming the academic load of a two-year associate degree, a full year of work and a full year of automotive instruction into two years. That makes for an intense 24 months.

For some, like Gordon Wright, a 21-year-old student in Garrity's program, the academic track gets compressed to accommodate the ASSET schedule. Since the Cuyamaca program runs in nine-week cycles (nine weeks in class and nine weeks at the dealership) and the college runs its academic classes on 16-week cycles, Wright has to pack a 16-week course into nine. Garrity says it's not unusual for a student to put in 14-hour days at school just to keep up.

The return on investment for the students' time and money is a guarantee of a good job when it's all over. The starting salary for an automotive technician in a dealership usually runs between $25,000 and $35,000 a year. In addition to good compensation, the skills the ASSET student develops are recognized across the country by Ford and Lincoln-Mercury dealers, so the ASSET graduate has little trouble finding a job if she wants to move elsewhere. Quinn says that three years after graduation, about 60 percent of ASSET graduates are still working for the same dealership that sponsored them. More than 90 percent of ASSET graduates are still working for a Ford or Lincoln-Mercury dealer somewhere.

As the technology increases in complexity, graduates of this program have an advantage over technicians who have been in dealerships for 10 years or more. ASSET students have been baptized into the world of automotive technology with computer diagnostics and electronics instead of carburetors and camshafts. These students still will need continual updating to keep current, but they start their race against accelerating technology from a better vantage point than the beginning mechanic of 10 years ago.

KEEPING BUSY

The instructors for this program are a special breed of adult educators, with one foot in the academic world and one in the "real" world. The ideal candidate, according to Quinn, is someone with experience as a Ford dealership technician as well as some teaching experience.

Garrity, who didn't have all the credentials when he got the job, received 13 weeks of training to familiarize him with the technology and curriculum. Koeper became an instructor after working at a Ford dealership and teaching night classes in auto repair at the community college where he now works full time.

That last point is important. While Ford helps choose and train the instructors for the program, each teacher works at, and is paid by, the college that houses the ASSET program. That gives the college more control over what goes on, but it also means it has to pay an additional faculty member. For the school, the payoff is the prestige of a partnership with Ford and the ability to offer a program that guarantees a good job at the end. The school also gains access to the latest automotive technology, a persistent problem for many technical colleges.

The duties of ASSET instructors? They teach classes, obviously, and monitor the progress of the 12 to 24 students in each ASSET program. They also recruit and screen students, and oversee a career day during which dealers and potential students meet each other in a flurry of interviews. During the "work" part of the work/study program, Koeper says, the instructors do three on-site visits for every student to see how things are going at the dealerships. Six months after graduation, instructors conduct a follow-up visit.

Because of their close relationships with students over the two-year period, instructors can give guidance and personal attention to each individual. It's harder for students to fall through the cracks and easier for instructors to discover and correct minor problems before they become catastrophic.

For example, if a student is great in the classroom but can't actually do the work at the dealership, the instructor can uncover the problem during a site visit and try to resolve it after two quarters, not after two years. Quinn puts the attrition rate for ASSET students at about 25 percent, compared with about 60 percent for most community college programs.

JOHNNY CAN WORK WITH HIS HANDS

After students are screened for math and English skills and approved for admittance in the community or technical college, they can apply for the ASSET program. It usually has about three qualified applicants for every available slot, so there's no shortage of candidates. These hopefuls are then invited to a career day where Ford and Lincoln-Mercury dealers interview them for sponsorship in the ASSET program. Once they are sponsored, they're in.

Each dealer interviews a raft of candidates; in turn, most candidates interview with numerous dealers during the career day. Instructors will often suggest that students in a certain geographic area meet with nearby dealers. After all the interviews are done, dealers each choose their top three candidates and students do likewise. Then instructors match dealers with students.

Frank Rodgers, technical service manager for the ASSET program in Southboro, MA, recruits dealers into the program. The recruiting part of his job is easy, he says, because the program sells itself; dealers usually ask how they can get involved. Rodgers has seen career days that ended with perfect matches (meaning the dealer's first choice corresponded with the student's first choice) in 75 percent of the cases.

Wright has a less rosy view. When he participated in a career day in San Diego, he was disappointed to see how few dealers showed up. Since he wasn't chosen that day, he went out to find his own sponsor and succeeded.

Wright's classmate, Trish Pavin, bypassed the career day process and found her sponsor by rifling through the yellow pages. The service managers she talked with invited her to the dealerships to get a feel for the environment. Two dealers offered to sponsor her. The one she chose was more distant but more compatible.

Since Ford and the sponsoring dealerships are trying to build a new generation of automotive technicians, what exactly are they looking for? As Rodgers points out, the automotive industry used to be a dumping ground for high school students with subpar grades. The rationale was that "Johnny is good with his hands, so he can work on cars." Rodgers explains that "We don't want Johnny who's good with his hands. We want Johnny who's good with his mind, his hands, who can speak, read *and* comprehend." In other words, throw away your stereotype of the kind of individual you will encounter next time you drag your wounded car into a dealership.

Automotive technology has changed the face of dealerships

from a customer's point of view, says Rick Anthes, ASSET coordinator at St. Louis Community College in Missouri. In the past, if a mechanic was reading through a book while fixing your car, you would be worried that he didn't know what he was doing. Now, Anthes says, you should be worried if the mechanic is *not* consulting a manual when he's working on your car.

Clearly, both Ford and the dealerships want something more than just technical expertise from the ASSET graduates. In the interest of better customer service, dealers want graduates who can talk with customers intelligibly and explain technical concepts in layman's terms. In short, they want their mechanics to have something auto mechanics have never been known for in the past: people skills.

If Koeper finds a candidate he thinks could succeed but who needs remediation, he encourages the student to take some classes before the next career day. In many cases, students can increase their marketability in time to be admitted for the interviews with dealers. Garrity agrees that most of the students he sees need some remedial help but would still be good candidates for the program. He asserts, "I see some brilliant kids who can't pass the English competency test because they've only been speaking [English] for three years."

The technician who fixes your new Ford may not look very different today than he did 10 years ago. The average age for ASSET students is 24, and they are still dressed in blue uniforms with their names sewn on. But when an ASSET graduate bellies up to the opened hood and hooks a computer diagnostic workstation into your car's computer, you've got to know something has changed. Instead of looking at the engine and guessing what might be wrong, a mechanic may be reading a computer printout. Without question, this kind of technology demands a different kind of worker.

Ford and the other auto companies recognize this and have started building their work force for the future. According to Garrity, other industries are thinking about setting up similar systems; he cites a nursing program in California that sends student nurses through 20 hours of class instruction and 20 hours of work every week. But he maintains that Ford's handling of this industry-education partnership was exemplary. By coming in and involving all the interested parties and giving schools and instructors a lot of freedom within the curriculum, Ford laid the foundation for success.

Industry-education partnerships are certainly one possible answer when business leaders start asking, "Where are we going to get highly skilled workers for the future?" True, it takes money—a joint investment from business, industry, the educational community and even the workers themselves. That's the philosophy behind the heralded apprenticeship system in Germany, and one reason why the Germans aren't whining about the inadequacy of their work force. But there's no need to study Germany. "You don't have to look to Europe for the model. It's here already," Garrity says.

Fixing the new cars being developed isn't rocket science—yet. But automotive technology is a demanding field that requires expertise and flexibility. After being involved in ASSET, Rodgers is optimistic about the future. "It's just exciting," he says, "to see the individuals who are coming into the program, knowing they're going to be the ones taking care of us in the next century."

Golden Employees—In Their Golden Years

Small businesses are discovering that older workers are often "aged to perfection."

Sharon Nelton

The employees at Kuempel Chime Clock Works and Studio in Excelsior, Minn., are any business owner's dream. They get to work early. They're self-starters. They rarely get sick. They are meticulous about quality. They are honest. And they work hard.

The secret? They are older workers. Old, in fact. According to Bruce J. Hedblom, principal owner of the company, most of Kuempel's 20 employees are ages 62 to 84.

Throughout its 77-year history, says Hedblom, an owner since 1990, Kuempel has "targeted the older worker as the ideal employee." The company prepares kits for grandfather clocks and smaller clocks that customers assemble and finish themselves.

In an era when other companies are downsizing by pushing older employees out the door or luring them out with attractive retirement packages, Kuempel and a handful of other smaller companies are steadfast about maintaining a work force of seniors.

"Their work ethics are unbelievable. They're from the old school, the school of hard knocks. They're just great people," says Millie Newman, an owner of The Place, a discount clothing chain based in North Miami.

The Place has hired older workers since its founding 28 years ago because they can relate to the company's target customers, who are age 40 and over. Now the company has four stores in south Florida, and 63 of its 74 employees are 60 or over. Newman is 73.

"It is the policy of The Place to hire, not fire, the senior citizen," says Richard Walfish, Newman's son and partner.

Business owners like Hedblom, Newman, and Walfish emphasize that their employees disprove the myths about older workers. Such misperceptions arise on various subjects. Among them:

Absenteeism. "For the most part, our employees are in good health, and we certainly don't have any absentee problems that would be out of line with the normal population," says Hedblom.

The U.S. Department of Health and Human Services says older workers who stay in the labor force may represent a self-selected healthier group of older people.

"They take good care of themselves. We don't see many bleary eyes around here," laughs John H. Swon, one of Hedblom's partners.

Learning. Business owners and managers find seniors no more resistant to learning than younger workers. "They're scared of computer equipment," says April Tripp, a department manager at Enrich International, a multilevel marketing firm in Orem, Utah. "[But] that's very easily overcome with practice."

Kuempel's employees include a retired school principal, a former banker, and others who were hired with no experience in woodworking or clock repair. They've learned those skills on the job.

Benefits. While the costs of benefits such as health, disability, and life insurance often do increase with an employee's age, such benefits may not be a factor when an employee reaches 65. According to research conducted for the U.S.

Older Workers, Younger Bosses

To April Tripp, an older worker is anyone 40 or over. But then, she's only 25.

As a manager at Enrich International, a marketer of herbal and beauty products, in Orem, Utah, Tripp supervises 30 people; usually four or five are in the "older" category. "It can be a little difficult when I am the same age as [an employee's] youngest child," she says.

Any young supervisor could be mindful of these observations about older workers:

■ Don't be afraid to hire them. "As long as you treat them fairly with the other employees and don't show them any more or any less deference than you show anyone else, it can be a real productive experience," Tripp says.

■ Regard older workers as a valuable resource. They offer experience and special qualities, says Joan Kelly of the American Association of Retired Persons.

■ Don't be intimidated. Some older workers think their age qualifies them for higher pay, Tripp has found, but she's firm about not favoring any age group with higher pay.

■ Deal with resentment tactfully. Sometimes an older worker resents a younger boss. A tactic that has worked for Tripp is to put the employee in charge of a special project, which often makes the worker too busy to be resentful.

—*Sharon Nelton*

Small Business Administration, most older workers are retirees with health or pension plans.

Most of the workers at Kuempel and The Place are already on Medicare and Social Security. The Place provides no health insurance, while Kuempel provides health insurance for employees under 65 who work 30 or more hours a week. For employees over 65, Kuempel offers either a package to supplement Medicare or a stipulated amount of money per month to be applied to a Medicare supplement.

According to a joint survey by the American Association of Retired Persons (AARP) and the Society for Human Resource Management (SHRM), older workers are becoming a more important source of labor as the work force ages and as the shortage of skilled workers increases. However, the survey, which polled 5,000 SHRM members, indicates that older workers are "underutilized and undervalued."

One thing seniors bring to the workplace, says John Swon, is "a sense of calm. They don't get frantic very easily. They pace themselves to the point where they know just exactly what it takes to accomplish the task on the schedule that's been set. As a consequence of that, they don't make as many mistakes."

Recruiting and managing seniors may require some nontraditional approaches. Older people may already be convinced that employers don't want to hire them, says Joan Kelly, head of AARP's business partnerships program, so companies should recruit aggressively, emphasizing their need for experienced workers. She suggests recruiting through churches and senior-citizen clubs, holding a job fair for older workers, or offering "bounties" to employees who bring in prospective employees over a certain age.

Hedblom and Swon suggest that companies recruit older workers through senior newspapers, automobile-club publications, and nonprofit organizations that attract older volunteers.

Good management practices that succeed with other employees work with seniors, too. But older workers tend to require more flexibility on the part of their employers. For instance, they often prefer part-time work to keep their income below the level where they start losing Social Security benefits. (Workers under age 65 lose $1 for every $2 in earnings above $7,680; workers age 65 through 69 lose $1 in Social Security benefits for every $3 they earn above $10,560 annually. From age 70, a Social Security recipient can collect full benefits regardless of the amount of earned income.)

There's another factor: As Hedblom says, older workers are a "very active group." They want time for traveling and activities such as fishing, golf, and cards. Kuempel and The Place both offer part-time work and flexible schedules to accommodate their employees' desires.

Job sharing is another option, one that is offered at LinguiSystems, a publisher of special-education materials in East Moline, Ill., according to the company's manager of human resources, Kathy Herbst.

It's best not to overmanage older employees, suggests April Tripp. They need less "hand holding, watching, and guiding" than younger workers, she says. "They don't need to be told how to do [a task]. You just tell them what you need done and when you need it done, and they're off doing it."

Adequate training helps seniors overcome any fear of technology. The Place trains its employees in the use of its point-of-sale computers, and Richard Walfish says the seniors can operate them "just as well as anybody else, even better."

Business owners who develop an older work force can take advantage of the added marketing and public-relations value that such a work force offers. Kuempel has used photographs of its employees in catalogs to convey quality, craftsmanship, and stability.

The Place and its older workers gained coverage from *The Miami Herald* and a local television station earlier this year. The headline on the *Herald* story spotlighted the contribution that such workers can make to a firm's image. "At The Place," it said, "service is aged to perfection."

For More Information

A number of useful resources on older workers are available to employers. Write to Joan Kelly, Business Partnerships, American Association of Retired Persons, 601 E Street, N.W., Washington, D.C. 20049, regarding the following free publications and services. Publications are available in single copies only.

■ *How To Recruit Older Workers, How To Manage Older Workers,* and *How To Train Older Workers.* Include titles when ordering these 16-page booklets.

■ *Working Age,* a bimonthly newsletter on employment issues that affect middle-age and older people.

■ "The Older Workforce: Recruitment and Retention," a report on a survey conducted jointly by AARP and the Society for Human Resource Management.

■ The National Older Workers Information System (NOWIS), a database on company programs utilizing older workers. Topics include hiring, job redesign, benefits, and training.

Another useful publication, available from the Social Security Administration, is *How Work Affects Your Social Security Benefits.* Contact your local Social Security office or call 1-800-772-1213. Ask for SSA Publication No. 05-10069.

Team Spirit

A Decisive Response To Crisis Brought Ford Enhanced Productivity

Auto Maker Used Hard Times To Enlist Its Work Force In Battle for Lower Costs

New Attitude at Walton Hills

Neal Templin

Staff Reporter of THE WALL STREET JOURNAL

DEARBORN, Mich.—Ford Motor Co. sold nearly as many vehicles in 1988 as it did in 1978—using half as many production workers.

How did a company so big—with a union as powerful as the United Auto Workers—pull off such a feat?

Using a baseball analogy, Ford officials attribute it to singles and doubles, rather than any grand slam. They point to some basic, albeit painful, measures, such as massive layoffs. They also point to engineering advances enabling them to build cars with fewer parts; the bumper on the Taurus, for example, has only 10 parts, compared with more than 100 bumper parts on General Motors Corp.'s competing Pontiac Grand Prix.

But by far the most important and impressive factor in Ford's increased productivity involves increased cooperation by its work force. Over a period of years, Ford persuaded its employees, who historically had been suspicious of management, to work harder and smarter, and to help management find ways to cut costs.

The results can be seen at Ford's Walton Hills metal stamping plant outside Cleveland. Every year since 1985, workers there have helped reduce labor and overhead costs by an average of

3.2%. They've found other efficiencies as well; Bob Kubec, a metal-press operator at the plant, last year figured out a way to save four inches of sheet metal on every floor panel part he makes, an innovation that will save Ford $70,000 a year (and that won Mr. Kubec a $14,000 reward).

The Walton Hills plant isn't an anomaly. "At Ford plants, you see everyone walking somewhere with a purpose—doing something. At a GM plant, guys are just sitting on a bench watching the press line run, waiting for something to break," contends John McElroy, editor in chief of Automative Industries magazine.

The difference is quantifiable. Ford takes one-third fewer man-hours to build its cars than GM, giving Ford a cost advantage of $795 a vehicle, said a recent study by Harbour & Associates.

NO PAIN, NO GAIN

Industry observers say Ford's efficiency gains, which grew out of a financial crisis around 1980, illustrate how decisive action can sustain a big, old company in hard times and leave it strengthened for the future. That's a lesson bound to give hope to companies such as GM and International Business Machines Corp., which are burdened these days with weak sales and the need to reduce a bloated work force.

Indeed, GM just now is showing signs of following Ford's lead. Yesterday, UAW and GM officials unveiled an early-retirement plan that will allow the company to shed thousands of workers; GM has said it needs to slash 54,000 blue-collar jobs. In general, GM has made a push to improve its frayed relationship with the UAW in recent months.

"Jack Smith [GM's new president and chief executive officer] has talked openly about improving our relations with the UAW to meet the challenges we face," says Gerald A. Knechtel, GM's top labor negotiator. "Certainly, we feel we're making progress on that."

NET LOSSES

To be sure, Ford still has its problems. Ford posted a $158.9 million loss in the third quarter, largely because of heavy consumer discounts. Another loss is likely this quarter, but Ford is expected to be profitable for the full year. GM, by contrast, is expected to post a loss for the year of $1 billion or more.

And despite its productivity improvements, Ford still lags behind the top Japanese companies, notably Toyota Motor Corp. In assembly plants, Ford has nearly closed the gap, according to Jim Harbour of Harbour & Associates. But he says Ford still trails the Japanese in engine and stamping plants. Ford uses about 7 1/4 hours of labor to produce stampings for the average vehicle, down from 15 hours in 1980, Mr. Harbour estimates. The Japanese need only about 3 1/2 hours.

A SUDDEN DROP

From 1978 to 1982, Ford's annual vehicle sales dropped 47%, and it posted its first loss in 34 years. In the middle of that span, in early 1980, the company placed Harold A. Poling in charge of North American auto operations. He quickly ordered the closure of three assembly plants to save $1.5 billion a year and canceled a new V-8 engine program to save an added $500 million. Mr. Poling, now chairman, conceded at the time this was "very tough medicine."

Between 1978 and 1982, Ford also laid off half its work force. It turned increasingly to "outsourcing"—sending work that had always been done by its employees to outside contractors. By 1982, union officials were worried. "We were losing jobs rapidly, and we wanted to try and control it," says Donald Ephlin, then head of the UAW's Ford department.

The labor contract with Ford wasn't scheduled to expire until September of 1982, but in the early part of that year the UAW agreed to reopen it. Within weeks, the two sides forged a compromise that set the stage for Ford's comeback in the 1980s. The union agreed to moderate its wage increases over the next 2 1/2 years, while the company promised not to close any more plants in that period. Ford also agreed to notify the union before it farmed out any more work.

In the months that followed, the historically antagonistic relationship between employees and managers began to improve. Industry observers largely credit an employee involvement program that Ford officials introduced with much fanfare. Philip Caldwell, Ford's chairman in the early 1980s, made numerous visits to plants to solicit ideas from the rank and file. "It's stupid to deny yourself the intellectual capability and constructive attitude of tens of thousands of workers," says Mr. Caldwell, who's now retired.

SETTING AN EXAMPLE

Mr. Ephlin of the UAW says of Mr. Caldwell's plant visits: "It was very important not only for hourly workers but

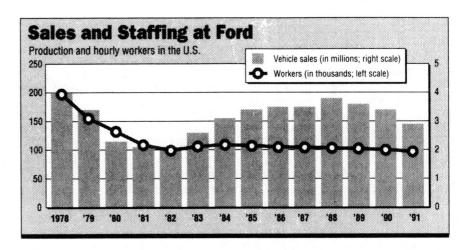

Sales and Staffing at Ford
Production and hourly workers in the U.S.

Vehicle sales (in millions; right scale)
Workers (in thousands; left scale)

for management to see him, so they understood this was policy from the top." Although GM implemented its own employee-involvement plan, Mr. Ephlin, who ran the UAW's GM department from 1983 to 1989, says Ford's received a lot more support from management.

In the mid-1980s, while GM spent $3 billion equipping its metal stamping plants with highly automated machinery designed to replace workers, Ford concentrated on increasing the productivity of its slimmed-down work force. "GM was determined to minimize the role of the hourly people," says Peter Pestillo, the Ford executive vice president who heads labor relations. "Our goal was to maximize the contribution of the hourly people." The outcome: GM's highly automated stamping plants now produce half as many stamped parts per worker as Ford's, partly because GM has done a poor job of operating its presses, experts say.

'WALKING MILLWRIGHT RULE'

The rewards of Ford's efforts to enhance productivity became apparent after sales started rising in 1983. Even as vehicle sales topped 3.8 billion in 1988—almost as many as in the pre-slump year of 1978—Ford managed to continue operating with half as large a work force as back then. As older workers retired, Ford hired back those who had been laid off, eventually offering jobs to virtually all its former workers who wanted them. Most returned with a new appreciation for the importance of profitability. Darrell Dalton, an assembly-line worker laid off at Walton Hills from 1979 to 1984, says, "Whatever it takes to keep this plant open, I'm willing to do."

The story of the Walton Hills plant parallels the recent history of Ford. Fifteen years ago, workers at the factory, known then as the Cleveland plant, prided themselves on a tough approach to management. "I believe we were the most militant local in the UAW," says Joseph D'Amico, longtime president of UAW local 420.

The local once went on strike—idling Ford nationwide—because there were no doors on the restrooms. And its labor contract contained some of the most expensive work rules in the Ford system. One, called the "walking millwright rule," required that millwrights accompany forklift drivers whenever machinery was being moved. The plant also had an antiquated quota system that allowed certain employees to knock off work in three or four hours after producing the quota of parts for their shift.

It was Ford's least productive stamping plant, and one day in 1980 Mr. Caldwell informed UAW officials of plans to shut it down. Overnight, union officials became obliging, asking for a chance to save the plant and then negotiating $15 million in projected annual savings by eliminating work rules. "I opened my eyes and saw what reality was," says Mr. D'Amico, the union leader. "If we didn't break down some barriers, we'd be history."

When workers gathered at a horse track near the plant to discuss the proposed concessions one Saturday, "there was a lot of booing and people shouting, 'Shut the plant down,'" recalls Mr. D'Amico. Some members set fire to their copies of the proposed agreement. But Mr. D'Amico told them to discuss it with their families and fellow workers, and four days later 88% voted to approve the accord.

But changing work rules was a lot simpler than changing attitudes. When Frank Calapa, who has earned seven awards for money-saving suggestions, cooperated with management in the early 1980s, it didn't sit well with fellow workers at the Cleveland plant. "They'd ask whose a— I was kissing," he says.

Likewise, low-level managers at the plant didn't exactly embrace the idea of employee involvement, often ignoring worker suggestions. "You'd go to a meeting and you'd come up with a suggestion and you'd never hear any more on it," recalls Ralph Mask, a 37-year veteran of the plant.

But Ford officials persisted in their efforts to end labor-management divisiveness. For instance, they sponsored joint trips to Japan for UAW officials and Ford executives to tour Japanese plants. After touring a Mazda Motor Corp. plant, the UAW's Mr. D'Amico recalls concluding that the Japanese didn't work harder; they simply did a better job of working together. "I learned the best way to accomplish anything is to talk," he says.

Ford also flew a group of workers to other company stamping plants, where they made an interesting discovery: Unlike the Cleveland plant, other plants repaired their own equipment following breakdowns, saving the time and cost of farming out the repairs. Mr. Mask was one of several workers who recommended making in-house repairs at the Cleveland plant. When management finally agreed, Mr. Mask says he became a believer in employee involvement.

A NEW-FOUND TRUST

Plant management also gave more autonomy to workers. For instance, Bob Kubec and his partner, Mark Asta, now run a transfer press—a highly technical press that stamps sheets of metal—with very little supervision.

Both men were involved in buying and setting up the press. Mr. Kubec made so many trips to Ford's Buffalo stamping plant to watch a similar press there that fellow workers in Cleveland dubbed him "Buffalo Bob." Meanwhile, Ford sent Mr. Asta to Japan, where the new press was being built, to suggest modifications before it was shipped.

Today, the Cleveland plant produces as much work with 2,000 employees as it did in the 1970s with more than 3,000. And it isn't called the Cleveland plant anymore; a few years ago, its name was changed to Walton Hills, the name of the community where it's located, to reflect the "burying of the old way of doing business," says Michael Murphy, a former top labor negotiator with Ford.

The plant still ranks "in the middle of the pack" among Ford stamping plants in productivity, says William R. Smith, the plant manager. And it is one of only two Ford stamping plants that haven't received the Q1 award, Ford's top internal quality award. But Mr. Smith believes it stands a good chance of winning soon.

AN EXCESS OF SUPPORT?

There are costs to the employee involvement program. At Walton Hills, seven UAW workers now perform such full-time duties as drug counseling and safety awareness. Ford's Mr. Pestillo believes the number of such jobs has gotten "a little out of control." But he says, "It's better to have a whole plant productive and to have four or five extra people" than to return to the old way of running things.

Unlike the old days, when Mr. D'Amico fought management at every turn, he sometimes joints it in urging changes these days. At a recent meeting, he told workers that the plant would be more competitive if it had only one classification for electricians, instead of separate classifications for maintenance and automation electricians. If workers agree to the change—as Mr. D'Amico believes will happen—he says the plant has a good chance of landing a new press that will bring in other jobs.

Mr. Smith, the manager, has changed, too. He says he used to break wristwatches while banging his fist during meetings with labor officials. He hasn't broken a watch in ages, he says.

On a recent afternoon, Mr. D'Amico and Mr. Smith sat comfortably around a table in Mr. Smith's office. "I don't see his job and my job as significantly different," says Mr. Smith. "I think we both take care of the plant and the people. We just come at it from different angles."

Case III: *Resistance to Change*

What This Incident Is About: Employees face the threat of the unknown when consultants arrive to study their performance. The incident involves the process of successful change: gaining acceptance, coordination, use of consultants, attitudes, and morale.

As office manager of the Duncan Paper Products Corporation, Robert Hale was responsible for the work of approximately 45 employees, of whom 26 were classified as either stenographers or file clerks. Acting under instructions from the company president, he agreed to allow a team of outside consultants to enter his realm of responsibility and make time and systems-analysis studies in an effort to improve the efficiency and output of his staff.

The consultants began by studying job descriptions, making observations, and recording each detail of the work of the stenographers and file clerks. After three days, they indicated to Hale and his employees that they were prepared to begin more detailed studies, observations, and interviews on the following day.

The next morning, five employees participating in the study were absent. On the following day, 10 employees were absent. Concerned, Hale investigated the cause of the absenteeism by telephoning several absentees. Each employee related approximately the same story. Each was nervous, tense, and tired after being viewed as a "guinea pig" for several days. One stenographer told Hale that her physician had advised her to ask for a leave of absence if working conditions were not improved.

Shortly after the telephone calls, the chief of the systems-analysis team explained to Hale that, if there were as many absences on the next day, his team would have to drop the study and proceed to another department. He said that a valid analysis would be impossible to conduct with 10 employees absent. Realizing that he would be held responsible for the failure of the systems analysis, Hale began to create and evaluate alternative actions that would provide the conditions necessary for the study. He was also concerned about implementing the procedural changes that he knew would be mandated after the study was completed. Hale was astute enough to realize that policies declared and orders issued are not always followed by instant compliance, even in the military, and that this wasn't a military situation.

Using the Case on *Resistance to Change*

This case is a classic example of how people will react to situations that are imposed upon them as opposed to situations in which they themselves have been active in producing. These employees are responding in this manner because they fear for their jobs and their well-being. They have no input into the decisions leading to the study, and they are refusing to cooperate with the company by simply not showing up for work. This passive/aggressive behavior is typical in this type of situation, although mass absenteeism is a very strong form of protest, just short of mass resignation.

Questions for Discussion

1. How do you think the company could have handled the situation so as to get greater cooperation?
2. What are some of the alternatives that Robert Hale could implement to get greater cooperation from the employees?
3. What do you think Robert Hale and the company should do?

Exercise III: *Organizing*

The purpose of this exercise is to increase your awareness of the importance of structure in organization. In addition, the exercise focuses on the importance of management in organizing a venture.

The Problem

Select one of the following situations to organize. Then read the background material before answering the questions.

- The registration process at your university or college
- A new hamburger fast-food franchise
- A Jet-ski rental in an ocean resort area

Do steps 1–7, below, as homework. In preparing your answers, use your own experience or think up logical answers to the questions.

Background

Organization is a way of gaining some power against an unreliable environment. The environment provides the organization with input, which includes raw materials, human resources, and financial resources. There is a service or product to produce that involves technology. The output is to be sold to a client, a group that must be nurtured. The complexities of the environment and the technology determine the complexity of the organization.

Planning Your Organization

1. In a few sentences, write the mission or purpose of your organization.
2. From the mission statement you should be able to write down specific things that must be done in order to accomplish the mission.
3. From the list of specifics that must be accomplished, an organizational chart can be devised. Each position on the chart will perform a specific task or is responsible for a specific outcome.
4. Add duties to each job position on your organizational chart. This will form a job description.
5. How would you ensure that the people you placed in these positions work together?
6. What degree of skill and abilities is required at each position and level in order to hire the right person for each position?
7. Make a list of the decisions that would have to be made while you planned and built the organization. Make a second list of those decisions you would have to make just after your organization began operating.

In Class

1. Form into groups of up to three members that organized the same project and share your answers to the questions.
2. Come to agreement on the way to organize, utilizing everyone's responses.
3. Present your group's approach to the class.

Directing

Managers spend most of their time directing the organization. They have learned, however, that just telling people what to do is not good enough. To achieve the maximum possible results, people must first clearly understand the firm's goals, and then management must find a way to motivate them. Abraham Maslow, while not the first to recognize the importance of motivation, did categorize and define a hierarchy of needs that individuals must fulfill. Maslow's hierarchy has become the basis of a vast array of research into motivation, and his article, "A Theory of Human Motivation," is included here. People who are motivated are far more likely to succeed than those who are not.

People enter business situations with a history of experiences, attitudes, and beliefs, and effectively communicating with them can be difficult. Open communication must be based upon trust. If there is fear or confusion as to where open communication leads, then communication will not be as effective as it could be. Managers must be able to communicate both in writing and orally. Effective communication involves the ability to design a letter, memo, or conversation so that both the sender and the receiver have a clear understanding of what was communicated and what is now expected of both parties. This frequently involves telling the receiver not only the message, but how the message was generated, because an employee's understanding of the reasons for an instruction can be the key to effective motivation.

Of all the various components of management, leadership is probably the most discussed, analyzed, and misunderstood. Indeed, some would argue that leadership and management are two separate and distinct activities. In "Developing Effective Leadership: An Interview with Henry Cisneros, Secretary, U.S. Department of Housing and Urban Development," Henry Cisneros, HUD secretary for the Clinton administration, discusses effective leadership development. Leadership may be over-discussed, but it is not well understood. Leaders come in all shapes and sizes. There have been good leaders and evil leaders; saints and brutes. They all shared certain characteristics. One is an idea that they are able to communicate to their followers and have them accept as their own. This results in motivation of the followers. The second characteristic is genuine caring, enthusiasm, and dedication to the dream and the people involved in striving for it.

A manager who is successful in communicating with, motivating, and leading people will experience enhanced performance and productivity. The Japanese have led other nations in this area with the application of many techniques, such as quality circles, However, not all forms of worker participation have resulted in enhanced productivity. American firms have also been applying new ideas in a variety of industries, including incentive plans, as outlined in "Incentive Plan Pushes Production."

In conclusion, effective managers are people who are able to successfully direct the organization. They know how to communicate, motivate, and lead, achieving enhanced productivity and performance that will accomplish the goals and mission of the organization in a fluid environment.

Looking Ahead: Challenge Questions

An effective manager must be able to communicate. How do you think managers could do so more effectively? Motivating people may be the single most difficult task for a manager. In what ways do you feel managers could better motivate their employees?

Leadership may be the least understood of all the functions a manager must perform. Who are some people who have best represented the qualities of leadership? What do they have in common?

Unit 4

A Theory of Human Motivation

Abraham H. Maslow

Abraham H. Maslow was born in 1908. He attended the University of Wisconsin, receiving a B.A. in 1930, an M.A. in 1931, and a Ph.D. in 1934. Maslow joined the faculty of Brandeis University in 1951, where he was professor and department chairman. While at Brandeis he completed his best known book, Motivation and Personality (1954) *in which he developed his famous hierarchy theory of needs. Maslow died on June 8, 1970.*

In a previous paper (13) various propositions were presented which would have to be included in any theory of human motivation that could lay claim to being definitive. These conclusions may be briefly summarized as follows:

1. The integrated wholeness of the organism must be one of the foundation stones of motivation theory.
2. The hunger drive (or any other physiological drive) was rejected as a centering point or model of a definitive theory of motivation. Any drive that is somatically based and localizable was shown to be atypical rather than typical in human motivation.
3. Such a theory should stress and center itself upon ultimate or basic goals rather than partial or superficial ones, upon ends rather than means to these ends. Such a stress would imply a more central place for unconscious than for conscious motivations.
4. There are usually available various cultural paths to the same goal. Therefore conscious, specific, local-cultural desires are not as fundamental in motivation theory as the more basic, unconscious goals.
5. Any motivated behavior, either preparatory or consummatory, must be understood to be a channel through which many basic needs may be simultaneously expressed or satisfied. Typically an act has *more* than one motivation.
6. Practically all organismic states are to be understood as motivated and as motivating.
7. Human needs arrange themselves in hierarchies of prepotency. That is to say, the appearance of one need usually rests on the prior satisfaction of another, more prepotent need. Man is a perpetually wanting animal. Also no need or drive can be treated as if it were isolated or discrete; every drive is related to the state of satisfaction or dissatisfaction of other drives.
8. *Lists* of drives will get us nowhere for various theoretical and practical reasons. Furthermore any classification of motivations must deal with the problem of levels of specificity or generalization of the motives to be classified.
9. Classifications of motivations must be based upon goals rather than upon instigating drives or motivated behavior.
10. Motivation theory should be human-centered rather than animal-centered.
11. The situation or the field in which the organism reacts must be taken into account but the field alone can rarely serve as an exclusive explanation for behavior. Furthermore the field itself must be interpreted in terms of the organism. Field theory cannot be a substitute for motivation theory.
12. Not only the integration of the organism must be taken into account, but also the possibility of isolated, specific, partial or segmental reactions.

It has since become necessary to add to these another affirmation.

13. Motivation theory is not synonymous with behavior theory. The motivations are only one class of determinants of behavior. While behavior is almost always motivated, it is also almost always biologically, culturally and situationally determined as well.

The present paper is an attempt to formulate a positive theory of motivation which will satisfy these theoretical demands and at the same time conform to the known facts, clinical and observational as well as experimental. It derives most directly, however, from clinical experience. This theory is, I think, in the functionalist tradition of James and Dewey, and is fused with the holism of Wertheimer (19), Goldstein (6), and Gestalt Psychology, and with the dynamicism of Freud (4) and Adler (1). This fusion or synthesis may arbitrarily be called a 'general-dynamic' theory.

It is far easier to perceive and to criticize the aspects in motivation theory than to remedy them. Mostly this is because of the very serious lack of sound data in this area. I conceive this lack of sound facts to be due primarily to the absence of a valid theory of motivation. The present theory then must be considered to be a suggested program or framework for future research and must stand or fall, not so much on facts available or evidence presented, as upon researches yet to be done, researches suggested perhaps by the questions raised in this paper.

THE BASIC NEEDS

The 'Physiological' Needs

The needs that are usually taken as the starting point for motivation theory are the so-called physiological drives. Two recent lines of research make it necessary to revise our customary notions about these needs, first, the development of the concept of homeostasis, and second, the finding that appetites (preferential choices among foods) are a fairly efficient indication of actual needs or lacks in the body.

Homeostasis refers to the body's automatic efforts to maintain a constant, normal state of the blood stream. Cannon (2) has described this process for (1) the water content of the blood, (2) salt content, (3) sugar content, (4) protein content, (5) fat content, (6) calcium content, (7) oxygen content, (8) constant hydrogen-ion level (acid-base balance) and (9) constant temperature of the blood. Obviously this list can be extended to include other minerals, the hormones, vitamins, etc.

Young in a recent article (21) has summarized the work on appetite in its relation to body needs. If the body lacks some chemical, the individual will tend to develop a specific appetite or partial hunger for that food element.

Thus it seems impossible as well as useless to make any list of fundamental physiological needs for they can come to almost any number one might wish, depending on the degree of specificity of description. We can not identify all physiological needs as homeostatic. That sexual desire, sleepiness, sheer activity and maternal behavior in animals, are homeostatic, has not yet been demonstrated. Furthermore, this list would not include the various sensory pleasures (tastes, smells, tickling, stroking) which are probably physiological and which may become the goals of motivated behavior.

In a previous paper (13) it has been pointed out that these physiological drives or needs are to be considered unusual rather than typical because they are isolable, and because they are localizable somatically. That is to say, they are relatively independent of each other, of other motivations and of the organism as a whole, and secondly, in many cases, it is possible to demonstrate a localized, underlying somatic base for the drive. This is true less generally than has been thought (exceptions are fatigue, sleepiness, maternal responses) but it is still true in the classic instances of hunger, sex, and thirst. It should be pointed out again that any of the physiological needs and the consummatory behavior involved with them serve as channels for all sorts of other needs as well. That is to say, the person who thinks he is hungry may actually be seeking more for comfort, or dependence, than for vitamins or proteins. Conversely, it is possible to satisfy the hunger need in part by other activities such as drinking water or smoking cigarettes.

In other words, relatively isolable as these physiological needs are, they are not completely so.

Undoubtedly these physiological needs are the most prepotent of all needs. What this means specifically is that in the human being who is missing everything in life in an extreme fashion, it is most likely that the major motivation would be the physiological needs rather than any others. A person who is lacking food, safety, love, and esteem would most probably hunger for food more strongly than for anything else.

If all the needs are unsatisfied, and the organism is then dominated by the physiological needs, all other needs may become simply nonexistent or be pushed into the background. It is then fair to characterize the whole organism by saying simply that it is hungry, for consciousness is almost completely preempted by hunger. All capacities are put into the service of hunger-satisfaction, and the organization of these capacities is almost entirely determined by the one purpose of satisfying hunger. The receptors and effectors, the intelligence, memory, habits, all may now be defined simply as hunger-gratifying tools. Capacities that are not useful for this purpose lie dormant, or are pushed into the background. The urge to write poetry, the desire to acquire an automobile, the interest in American history, the desire for a new pair of shoes are, in the extreme case, forgotten or become of secondary importance. For the man who is extremely and dangerously hungry, no other interests exist but food. He dreams food, he remembers food, he thinks about food, he emotes only about food, he perceives only food and he wants only food. The more subtle determinants that ordinarily fuse with the physiological drives in organizing even feeding, drinking or sexual behavior, may now be so completely overwhelmed as to allow us to speak at this time (but *only* at this time) of pure hunger drive and behavior, with the one unqualified aim of relief.

Another peculiar characteristic of the human organism when it is dominated by a certain need is that the whole philosophy of the future tends also to change. For our chronically and extremely hungry man, Utopia can be defined very simply as a place where there is plenty of food. He tends to think that if only he is guaranteed food for the rest of his life, he will be perfectly happy and will never want anything more. Life itself tends to be defined in terms of eating. Anything else will be defined as unimportant. Freedom, love, community feeling, respect, philosophy, may all be waved aside as fripperies which are useless since they fail to fill the stomach. Such a man may fairly be said to live by bread alone.

It cannot possibly be denied that such things are true but their *generality* can be denied. Emergency conditions are, almost by definition, rare in the normally functioning peaceful society. That is truism can be forgotten is due mainly to two reasons. First, rats have few motivations other than physiological ones, and since so much of the research upon motivation has been made with these animals, it is easy to carry the rat picture over to the human being. Secondly, it is too often not realized that culture itself is an adaptive tool, one of whose main functions is to make the physiological emergencies come less and less often. In most of the known societies, chronic extreme hunger of the emergency type is rare, rather than common. In any case, this is still true in the

United States. The average American citizen is experiencing appetite rather than hunger when he says "I am hungry." He is apt to experience sheer life-and-death hunger only by accident and then only a few times through his entire life.

Obviously a good way to obscure the 'higher' motivations, and to get a lopsided view of human capacities and human nature, is to make the organism extremely and chronically hungry or thirsty. Anyone who attempts to make an emergency picture into a typical one, and who will measure all of man's goals and desires by his behavior during extreme physiological deprivation is certainly being blind to many things. It is quite true that man lives by bread alone—when there is no bread. But what happens to man's desires when there *is* plenty of bread and when his belly is chronically filled?

At once other (and 'higher') needs emerge and these, rather than physiological hungers, dominate the organism. And when these in turn are satisfied, again new (and still 'higher') needs emerge and so on. This is what we mean by saying that the basic human needs are organized into a hierarchy of relative prepotency.

One main implication of this phrasing is that gratification becomes as important a concept as deprivation in motivation theory, for it releases the organism from the domination of a relatively more physiological need, permitting thereby the emergence of other more social goals. The physiological needs, along with their partial goals, when chronically gratified cease to exist as active determinants or organizers of behavior. They now exist only in a potential fashion in the sense that they may emerge again to dominate the organism if they are thwarted. But a want that is satisfied is no longer a want. The organism is dominated and its behavior organized only by unsatisfied needs. If hunger is satisfied, it becomes unimportant in the current dynamics of the individual.

This statement is somewhat qualified by a hypothesis to be discussed more fully later, namely that it is precisely those individuals in whom a certain need has always been satisfied who are best equipped to tolerate deprivation of that need in the future, and that furthermore, those who have been deprived in the past will react differently to current satisfactions than the one who has never been deprived.

The Safety Needs

If the physiological needs are relatively well gratified, there then emerges a new set of needs, which we may categorize roughly as the safety needs. All that has been said of the physiological needs is equally true, although in lesser degree, of these desires. The organism may equally well be wholly dominated by them. They may serve as the almost exclusive organizers of behavior, recruiting all the capacities of the organism in their service, and we may then fairly describe the whole organism as a safety-seeking mechanism. Again we may say of the receptors, the effectors, of the intellect and the other capacities that they are primarily safety-seeking tools. Again, as in the hungry man, we find that the dominating goal is a strong determinant not only of his current world outlook and philosophy but also of his philosophy of the future. Practically everything looks less important than safety (even sometimes the physi-

ological needs which, being satisfied, are now underestimated). A man, in this state, if it is extreme enough and chronic enough, may be characterized as living almost for safety alone.

Although in this paper we are interested primarily in the needs of the adult, we can approach an understanding of his safety needs perhaps more efficiently by observation of infants and children, in whom these needs are much more simple and obvious. One reason for the clearer appearance of the threat or danger reaction in infants is that they do not inhibit this reaction at all, whereas adults in our society have been taught to inhibit it at all costs. Thus even when adults do feel their safety to be threatened we may not be able to see this on the surface. Infants will react in a total fashion and as if they were endangered, if they are disturbed or dropped suddenly, startled by loud noises, flashing light, or other unusual sensory stimulation, by rough handling, by general loss of support in the mother's arms, or by inadequate support.[1]

In infants we can also see a much more direct reaction to bodily illnesses of various kinds. Sometimes these illnesses seem to be immediately and per se threatening and seem to make the child feel unsafe. For instance, vomiting, colic or other sharp pains seem to make the child look at the whole world in a different way. At such a moment of pain, it may be postulated that, for the child, the appearance of the whole world suddenly changes from sunniness to darkness, so to speak, and becomes a place in which anything at all might happen, in which previously stable things have suddenly become unstable. Thus a child who because of some bad food is taken ill may, for a day or two, develop fear, nightmares, and a need for protection and reassurance never seen in him before his illness.

Another indication of the child's need for safety is his preference for some kind of undisrupted routine or rhythm. He seems to want a predictable, orderly world. For instance, injustice, unfairness, or inconsistency in the parents seems to make a child feel anxious and unsafe. This attitude may be not so much because of the injustice per se or any particular pains involved, but rather because this treatment threatens to make the world look unreliable, or unsafe, or unpredictable. Young children seem to thrive better under a system which has at least a skeletal outline of rigidity, in which there is a schedule of a kind, some sort of routine, something that can be counted upon, not only for the present but also far into the future. Perhaps one could express this more accurately by saying that the child needs an organized world rather than an unorganized or unstructured one.

The central role of the parents and the normal family setup are indisputable. Quarreling, physical assault, separation, divorce or death within the family may be particularly terrifying. Also parental outbursts of rage or threats of punishment directed to the child, calling him names, speaking to him harshly, shaking him, handling him roughly, or actual physical punishment sometimes elicit such total panic and terror in the child that we must assume more is involved than the physical pain alone. While it is true that in some children this terror may represent also a fear of loss of parental love, it can also occur in completely rejected children, who seem to cling to the hating parents more for sheer safety and protection than because of hope of love.

Confronting the average child with new, unfamiliar, strange, unmanageable stimuli or situations will too frequently elicit the danger or terror reaction, as for example, getting lost or even being separated from the parents for a short time, being confronted with new faces, new situations or new tasks, the sight of strange, unfamiliar or uncontrollable objects, illness or death. Particularly at such times, the child's frantic clinging to his parents is eloquent testimony to their role as protectors (quite apart from their roles as food-givers and love-givers).

From these and similar observations, we may generalize and say that the average child in our society generally prefers a safe, orderly, predictable, organized world, which he can count on, and in which unexpected, unmanageable or other dangerous things do not happen, and in which, in any case, he has all-powerful parents who protect and shield him from harm.

That these reactions may so easily be observed in children is in a way a proof of the fact that children in our society feel too unsafe (or, in a word, are badly brought up). Children who are reared in an unthreatening, loving family do *not* ordinarily react as we have described above (17). In such children the danger reactions are apt to come mostly to objects or situations that adults too would consider dangerous.[2]

The healthy, normal, fortunate adult in our culture is largely satisfied in his safety needs. The peaceful, smoothly running 'good' society ordinarily makes its members feel safe enough from wild animals, extremes of temperature, criminals, assault and murder, tyranny, etc. Therefore, in a very real sense, he no longer has any safety needs as active motivators. Just as a sated man no longer feels hungry, a safe man no longer feels endangered. If we wish to see these needs directly and clearly we must turn to neurotic or near-neurotic individuals, and to the economic and social underdogs. In between these extremes, we can perceive the expressions of safety needs only in such phenomena as, for instance, the common preference for a job with tenure and protection, the desire for a savings account, and for insurance of various kinds (medical, dental, unemployment, disability, old age).

Other broader aspects of the attempt to seek safety and stability in the world are seen in the very common preference for familiar rather than unfamiliar things, or for the known rather than the unknown. The tendency to have some religion or world-philosophy that organizes the universe and the men in it into some sort of satisfactorily coherent, meaningful whole is also in part motivated by safety-seeking. Here too we may list science and philosophy in general as partially motivated by the safety needs (we shall see later that there are also other motivations to scientific, philosophical or religious endeavor).

Otherwise the need for safety is seen as an active and dominant mobilizer of the organism's resources only in emergencies, e.g., war, disease, natural catastrophes, crime waves, societal disorganization, neurosis, brain injury, chronically bad situation.

Some neurotic adults in our society are, in many ways, like the unsafe child in their desire for safety, although in the former it takes on a somewhat special appearance. Their reaction is often to unknown, psycho-logical dangers in a world that is perceived to be hostile, overwhelming and threatening. Such a person behaves as if a great catastrophe were almost always impending, i.e., he is usually responding as if to an emergency. His safety needs often find specific expression in a search for a protector, or a stronger person on whom he may depend, or perhaps, a Fuehrer.

The neurotic individual may be described in a slightly different way with some usefulness as a grownup person who retains his childish attitudes toward the world. That is to say, a neurotic adult may be said to behave 'as if' he were actually afraid of a spanking, or of his mother's disapproval, or of being abandoned by his parents, or having his food taken away from him. It is as if his childish attitudes of fear and threat reaction to a dangerous world had gone underground, and untouched by the growing up and learning processes, were now ready to be called out by any stimulus that would make a child feel endangered and threatened.[3]

The neurosis in which the search for safety takes its clearest form is in the compulsive-obsessive neurosis. Compulsive-obsessives try frantically to order and stabilize the world so that no unmanageable, unexpected or unfamiliar dangers will ever appear (14). They hedge themselves about with all sorts of ceremonials, rules and formulas so that every possible contingency may be provided for and so that no new contingencies may appear. They are much like the brain injured cases, described by Goldstein (6), who manage to maintain their equilibrium by avoiding everything unfamiliar and strange and by ordering their restricted world in such a neat, disciplined, orderly fashion that everything in the world can be counted upon. They try to arrange the world so that anything unexpected (dangers) cannot possibly occur. If, through no fault of their own, something unexpected does occur, they go into a panic reaction as if this unexpected occurrence constituted a grave danger. What we can see only as a none too strong preference in the healthy person, e.g., preference for the familiar, becomes a life-and-death necessity in abnormal cases.

The Love Needs

If both the physiological and the safety needs are fairly well gratified, then there will emerge the love and affection and belongingness needs, and the whole cycle already described will repeat itself with this new center. Now the person will feel keenly, as never before, the absence of friends, or a sweetheart, or a wife, or children. He will hunger for affectionate relations with people in general, namely, for a place in his group, and he will strive with great intensity to achieve this goal. He will want to attain such a place more than anything else in the world and may even forget that once, when he was hungry, he sneered at love.

In our society the thwarting of these needs is the most commonly found core in cases of maladjustment and more severe psychopathology. Love and affection, as well as their possible expression in sexuality, are generally looked upon with ambivalence and are customarily hedged about with many restrictions and inhibitions. Practically all theorists of psychopathology have stressed thwarting of the love needs as basic in the picture of maladjustment. Many clinical studies have therefore been made of this need and we know more about it perhaps than any of the other needs except the physiological ones (14).

One thing that must be stressed at this point is that love is not synonymous with sex. Sex may be studied as a purely physiological need. Ordinarily sexual behavior is multidetermined, that is to say, determined not only by sexual but also by other needs, chief among which are the love and affection needs. Also not to be overlooked is the fact that the love needs involve both giving *and* receiving love.[4]

The Esteem Needs

All people in our society (with a few pathological exceptions) have a need or desire for a stable, firmly based, (usually) high evaluation of themselves, for self-respect, or self-esteem, and for the esteem of others. By firmly based self-esteem, we mean that which is soundly based upon real capacity, achievement and respect from others. These needs may be classified into two subsidiary sets. These are, first, the desire for strength, for achievement, for adequacy, for confidence in the face of the world, and for independence and freedom.[5] Secondly, we have what we may call the desire for reputation or prestige (defining it as respect or esteem from other people), recognition, attention, importance or appreciation.[6] These needs have been relatively stressed by Alfred Adler and his followers, and have been relatively neglected by Freud and the psychoanalysts. More and more today however there is appearing widespread appreciation of their central importance.

Satisfaction of the self-esteem need leads to feelings of self-confidence, worth, strength, capability and adequacy of being useful and necessary in the world. But thwarting of these needs produces feelings of inferiority, of weakness and of helplessness. These feelings in turn give rise to either basic discouragement or else compensatory or neurotic trends. An appreciation of the necessity of basic self-confidence and an understanding of how helpless people are without it, can be easily gained from a study of severe traumatic neurosis (8).[7]

The Need for Self-Actualization

Even if all these needs are satisfied, we may still often (if not always) expect that a new discontent and restlessness will soon develop, unless the individual is doing what he is fitted for. A musician must make music, an artist must paint, a poet must write, if he is to be ultimately happy. What a man *can* be, he *must* be. This need we may call self-actualization.

This term, first coined by Kurt Goldstein, is being used in this paper in a much more specific and limited fashion. It refers to the desire for self-fulfillment, namely, to the tendency for him to become actualized in what he is potentially. This tendency might be phrased as the desire to become more and more what one is, to become everything that one is capable of becoming.

The specific form that these needs will take will of course vary greatly from person to person. In one individual it may take the form of the desire to be an ideal mother, in another it may be expressed athletically, and in still another it may be expressed in painting pictures or in inventions. It is not necessarily a creative urge although in people who have any capacities for creation it will take this form.

The clear emergence of these needs rests upon prior satisfaction of the physiological, safety, love and esteem needs. We shall call people who are satisfied in these needs, basically satisfied people, and it is from these that we may expect the fullest (and healthiest) creativeness.[8] Since, in our society, basically satisfied people are the exception, we do not know much about self-actualization, either experimentally or clinically. It remains a challenging problem for research.

The Preconditions for the Basic Need Satisfactions

There are certain conditions which are immediate prerequisites for the basic need satisfactions. Danger to these is reacted to almost as if it were a direct danger to the basic needs themselves. Such conditions as freedom to speak, freedom to do what one wishes so long as no harm is done to others, freedom to express one's self, freedom to investigate and seek for information, freedom to defend one's self, justice, fairness, honesty, orderliness in the group are examples of such preconditions for basic need satisfactions. Thwarting in these freedoms will be reacted to with a threat or emergency response. These conditions are not ends in themselves but they are *almost* so since they are so closely related to the basic needs, which are apparently the only ends in themselves. These conditions are defended because without them the basic satisfactions are quite impossible, or at least, very severely endangered.

If we remember that the cognitive capacities (perceptual, intellectual, learning) are a set of adjustive tools, which have among other functions, that of satisfaction of our basic needs, then it is clear that any danger to them, any deprivation or blocking of their free use, must also be indirectly threatening to the basic needs themselves. Such a statement is a partial solution of the general problems of curiosity, the search for knowledge, truth and wisdom, and the ever-persistent urge to solve the cosmic mysteries.

We must therefore introduce another hypothesis and speak of degrees of closeness to the basic needs, for we have already pointed out that *any* conscious desires (partial goals) are more or less important as they are more or less close to the basic needs. The same statement may be made for various behavior acts. An act is psychologically important if it contributes directly to satisfaction of basic needs. The less directly it so contributes, or the weaker this contribution is, the less important this act must be conceived to be from the point of view of dynamic psychology. A similar statement may be made for the various defense or coping mechanisms. Some are very directly related to the protection or attainment of the basic needs, others are only weakly and distantly related. Indeed if we wished, we could speak of more basic and less basic defense mechanisms, and then affirm that danger to the more basic defenses is more threatening than danger to less basic defenses (always remembering that this is so only because of their relationship to the basic needs).

The Desires to Know and to Understand

So far, we have mentioned the cognitive needs only in

passing. Acquiring knowledge and systematizing the universe have been considered as, in part, techniques for the achievement of basic safety in the world, or, for the intelligent man, expressions of self-actualization. Also freedom of inquiry and expression have been discussed as preconditions of satisfactions of the basic needs. True though these formulations may be, they do not constitute definitive answers to the question as to the motivation role of curiosity, learning, philosophizing, experimenting, etc. They are, at best, no more than partial answers.

This question is especially difficult because we know so little about the facts. Curiosity, exploration, desire for the facts, desire to know may certainly be observed easily enough. The fact that they often are pursued even at great cost to the individual's safety is an earnest of the partial character of our previous discussion. In addition, the writer must admit that, though he has sufficient clinical evidence to postulate the desire to know as a very strong drive in intelligent people, no data are available for unintelligent people. It may then be largely a function of relatively high intelligence. Rather tentatively, then, and largely in the hope of stimulating discussion and research, we shall postulate a basic desire to know, to be aware of reality, to get the facts, to satisfy curiosity, or as Wertheimer phrases it, to see rather than to be blind.

This postulation, however, is not enough. Even after we know, we are impelled to know more and more minutely and microscopically on the one hand, and on the other, more and more extensively in the direction of a world philosophy, religion, etc. The facts that we acquire, if they are isolated or atomistic, inevitably get theorized about, and either analyzed or organized or both. This process has been phrased by some as the search for 'meaning.' We shall then postulate a desire to understand, to systematize, to organize, to analyze, to look for relations and meanings.

Once these desires are accepted for discussion, we see that they too form themselves into a small hierarchy in which the desire to know is prepotent over the desire to understand. All the characteristics of a hierarchy of prepotency that we have described above, seem to hold for this one as well.

We must guard ourselves against the too easy tendency to separate these desires from the basic needs we have discussed above, i.e., to make a sharp dichotomy between 'cognitive' and 'conative' needs. The desire to know and to understand are themselves conative, i.e., have a striving character, and are as much personality needs as the 'basic needs' we have already discussed (19).

FURTHER CHARACTERISTICS OF THE BASIC NEEDS

The Degree of Fixity of the Hierarchy of Basic Needs

We have spoke so far as if this hierarchy were a fixed order but actually it is not nearly as rigid as we may have implied. It is true that most of the people with whom we have worked have seemed to have these basic needs in about the order that has been indicated. However, there have been a number of exceptions.

(1) There are some people in whom, for instance, self-esteem seems to be more important than love. This most common reversal in the hierarchy is usually due to the development of the notion that the person who is most likely to be loved is a strong or powerful person, one who inspires respect or fear, and who is self-confident or aggressive. Therefore such people who lack love and seek it, may try hard to put on a front of aggressive, confident behavior. But essentially they seek high self-esteem and its behavior expressions more as a means to an end than for its own sake; they seek self-assertion for the sake of love rather than for self-esteem itself.

(2) There are other, apparently innately creative people in whom the drive to creativeness seems to be more important than any other counterdeterminant. Their creativeness might appear not as self-actualization released by basic satisfaction, but in spite of lack of basic satisfaction.

(3) In certain people the level of aspiration may be permanently deadened or lowered. That is to say, the less prepotent goals may simply be lost, and may disappear forever, so that the person who has experienced life at a very low level, i.e., chronic unemployment, may continue to be satisfied for the rest of his life if only he can get enough food.

(4) The so-called psychopathic personality is another example of permanent loss of the love needs. These are people who, according to the best data available (9), have been starved for love in the earliest months of their lives and have simply lost forever the desire and the ability to give and to receive affection (as animals lose sucking or pecking reflexes that are not exercised soon enough after birth).

(5) Another cause of reversal of the hierarchy is that when a need has been satisfied for a long time, this need may be underevaluated. People who have never experienced chronic hunger are apt to underestimate its effects and to look upon food as a rather unimportant thing. If they are dominated by a higher need, this higher need will seem to be the most important of all. It then becomes possible, and indeed does actually happen, that they may, for the sake of this higher need, put themselves into the position of being deprived in a more basic need. We may expect that after a long-time deprivation of the more basic need there will be a tendency to reevaluate both needs so that the more prepotent need will actually become consciously prepotent for the individual who may have given it up very lightly. Thus, a man who has given up his job rather than lose his self-respect, and who then starves for six months or so, may be willing to take his job back even at the price of losing his self-respect.

(6) Another partial explanation of *apparent* reversals is seen in the fact that we have been talking about the hierarchy of prepotency in terms of consciously felt wants or desires rather than of behavior. Looking at behavior itself may give us the wrong impression. What we have claimed is that the person will *want* the more basic of two needs when deprived in both. There is no necessary implication here that he will act upon his desires. Let us say again that there are many determinants of behavior other than the needs and desires.

(7) Perhaps more important than all these exceptions are the ones that involve ideals, high social standards, high values and the like. With such values people be-

come martyrs; they will give up everything for the sake of a particular ideal, or value. These people may be understood, at least in part, by reference to one basic concept (or hypothesis) which may be called 'increased frustration-tolerance through early gratification.' People who have been satisfied in their basic needs throughout their lives, particularly in their earlier years, seem to develop exceptional power to withstand present or future thwarting of these needs simply because they have strong, healthy character structure as a result of basic satisfaction. They are the 'strong' people who can easily weather disagreement or opposition, who can swim against the stream of public opinion and who can stand up for the truth at great personal cost. It is just the ones who have loved and been well loved, and who have had many deep friendships, who can hold out against hatred, rejection or persecution.

I say all this in spite of the fact that there is a certain amount of sheer habituation which is also involved in any full discussion of frustration tolerance. For instance, it is likely that those persons who have been accustomed to relative starvation for a long time, are partially enabled thereby to withstand food deprivation. What sort of balance must be made between these two tendencies, of habituation on the one hand, and of past satisfaction breeding present frustration tolerance on the other hand, remains to be worked out by further research. Meanwhile we may assume that they are both operative, side by side, since they do not contradict each other. In this respect to this phenomenon of increased frustration tolerance, it seems probable that the most important gratifications come in the first two years of life. That is to say, people who have been made secure and strong in the earliest years, tend to remain secure and strong thereafter in the face of whatever threatens.

Degrees of Relative Satisfaction

So far, our theoretical discussion may have given the impression that these five sets of needs are somehow in a stepwise, all-or-none relationship to each other. We have spoken in such terms as the following: "If one need is satisfied, then another emerges." This statement might give the false impression that a need must be satisfied 100 percent before the next need emerges. In actual fact, most members of our society who are normal, are partially satisfied in all their basic needs and partially unsatisfied in all their basic needs at the same time. A more realistic description of the hierarchy would be in terms of decreasing percentages of satisfaction as we go up the hierarchy of prepotency. For instance, if I may assign arbitrary figures for the sake of illustration, it is as if the average citizen is satisfied perhaps 85 percent in his physiological needs, 70 percent in his safety needs, 50 percent in his love needs, 40 percent in his self-esteem needs, and 10 percent in his self-actualization needs.

As for the concept of emergence of a new need after satisfaction of the prepotent need, this emergence is not a sudden, saltatory phenomenon but rather a gradual emergence by slow degrees from nothingness. For instance, if prepotent need A is satisfied only 10 percent, then need B may not be visible at all. However, as this need A becomes satisfied 25 percent, need B may emerge 5 percent; as need A becomes satisfied 75 percent, need B may emerge 90 percent, and so on.

Unconscious Character of Needs

These needs are neither necessarily conscious nor unconscious. On the whole, however, in the average person, they are more often unconscious rather than conscious. It is not necessary at this point to overhaul the tremendous mass of evidence which indicates the crucial importance of unconscious motivation. It would by now be expected, on a priori grounds alone, that unconscious motivations would on the whole be rather more important than the conscious motivations. What we have called the basic needs are very often largely unconscious although they may, with suitable techniques, and with sophisticated people become conscious.

Cultural Specificity and Generality of Needs

This classification of basic needs makes some attempt to take account of the relative unity behind the superficial differences in specific desires from one culture to another. Certainly in any particular culture an individual's conscious motivational content will usually be extremely different from the conscious motivational content of an individual in another society. However, it is the common experience of anthropologists that people, even in different societies, are much more alike than we would think from our first contact with them, and that as we know them better we seem to find more and more of this commonness. We then recognize the most startling differences to be superficial rather than basic, e.g., differences in style of hairdress, clothes, tastes in food, etc. Our classification of basic needs is in part an attempt to account for this unity behind the apparent diversity from culture to culture. No claim is made that it is ultimate or universal for all cultures. The claim is made only that it is relatively *more* ultimate, more universal, more basic, than the superficial conscious desires from culture to culture, and makes a somewhat closer approach to common human characteristics. Basic needs are *more* common-human than superficial desires or behaviors.

Multiple Motivations of Behavior

These needs must be understood *not* to be *exclusive* or single determiners of certain kinds of behavior. An example may be found in any behavior that seems to be physiologically motivated, such as eating, or sexual play or the like. The clinical psychologists have long since found that any behavior may be a channel through which flow various determinants. Or to say it in another way, most behavior is multimotivated. Within the sphere of motivational determinants any behavior tends to be determined by several or *all* of the basic needs simultaneously rather than by only one of them. The latter would be more an exception than the former. Eating may be partially for the sake of filling the stomach, and partially for the sake of comfort and amelioration of other needs. One may make love not only for pure sexual release, but also to convince one's self of one's masculinity, or to make a conquest, to feel powerful, or to win more basic affection. As an illustration, I may point out that it would be possible (theoretically if not practically) to analyze a single act of an individual and see in it the expression of his physiological needs, his safety needs, his love needs, his esteem needs and self-actualization. This contrasts sharply with the more naive brand of trait psychology in which one trait or one motive accounts for a certain kind of act, i.e., an aggressive act is traced solely to a trait of aggressiveness.

Multiple Determinants of Behavior

Not all behavior is determined by the basic needs. We might even say that not all behavior is motivated. There are many determinants of behavior other than motives.[9] For instance, one other important class of determinants is the so-called field determinants. Theoretically, at least, behavior may be determined completely by the field, or even by specific isolated external stimuli, as in association of ideas, or certain conditioned reflexes. If in response to the stimulus word "table," I immediately perceive a memory image of a table, this response certainly has nothing to do with my basic needs.

Secondly, we may call attention again to the concept of 'degree of closeness to the basic needs' or 'degree of motivation.' Some behavior is highly motivated, other behavior is only weakly motivated. Some is not motivated at all (but all behavior is determined).

Another important point[10] is that there is a basic difference between expressive behavior and coping behavior (functional striving, purposive goal seeking). An expressive behavior does not try to do anything; it is simply a reflection of the personality. A stupid man behaves stupidly, not because he wants to, or tries to, or is motivated to, but simply because he *is* what he is. The same is true when I speak in a bass voice rather than tenor or soprano. The random movements of a healthy child, the smile on the face of a happy man even when he is alone, the springiness of the healthy man's walk, and the erectness of his carriage are other examples of expressive, nonfunctional behavior. Also the *style* in which a man carries out almost all his behavior, motivated as well as unmotivated, is often expressive.

We may then ask, is *all* behavior expressive or reflective of the character structure? The answer is no. Rote, habitual, automatized, or conventional behavior may or may not be expressive. The same is true for most 'stimulus-bound' behaviors.

It is finally necessary to stress that expressiveness of behavior, and goal-directedness of behavior are not mutually exclusive categories. Average behavior is usually both.

Goals as Centering Principle in Motivation Theory

It will be observed that the basic principle in our classification has been neither the instigation nor the motivated behavior but rather the functions, effects, purposes, or goals of the behavior. It has been proven sufficiently by various people that this is the most suitable point for centering in any motivation theory.[11]

Animal- and Human-Centering

This theory starts with the human being rather than any lower and presumably 'simpler' animal. Too many of the findings that have been made in animals have been proven to be true for animals but not for the human being. There is no reason whatsoever why we should start with animals in order to study human motivation. The logic or rather illogic behind this general fallacy of 'pseudosimplicity' has been exposed often enough by philosophers and logicians as well as by scientists in each of the various fields. It is no more necessary to study animals before one can study man than it is to study mathematics before one can study geology or psychology or biology.

We may also reject the old, naive behaviorism which assumed that it was somehow necessary, or at least more 'scientific' to judge human beings by animal standards. One consequence of this belief was that the whole notion of purpose and goal was excluded from motivational psychology simply because one could not ask a white rat about his purposes. Tolman (18) has long since proven in animal studies themselves that this exclusion was not necessary.

Motivation and the Theory of Psychopathogenesis

The conscious motivational content of everyday life has, according to the foregoing, been conceived to be relatively important or unimportant accordingly as it is more or less closely related to the basic goals. A desire for an ice cream cone might actually be an indirect expression of a desire for love. If it is, then this desire for the ice cream cone becomes extremely important motivation. If however the ice cream is simply something to cool the mouth with, or a casual appetitive reaction, then the desire is relatively unimportant. Everyday conscious desires are to be regarded as symptoms, as surface indicators of more basic needs. If we were to take these superficial desires at their face value we would find ourselves in a state of complete confusion which could never be resolved, since we would be dealing seriously with symptoms rather than with what lay behind the symptoms.

Thwarting of unimportant desires produces no psychopathological results; thwarting of a basically important need does produce such results. Any theory of psychopathogenesis must then be based on a sound theory of motivation. A conflict or a frustration is not necessarily pathogenic. It becomes so only when it threatens or thwarts the basic needs, or partial needs that are closely related to the basic needs (10).

The Role of Gratified Needs

It has been pointed out above several times that our needs usually emerge only when more prepotent needs have been gratified. Thus gratification has an important role in motivation theory. Apart from this, however, needs cease to play an active determining or organizing role as soon as they are gratified.

What this means is that, e.g., a basically satisfied person no longer has the needs for esteem, love, safety, etc. The only sense in which he might be said to have them is in the almost metaphysical sense that a sated man has hunger, or a filled bottle has emptiness. If we are interested in what *actually* motivates us, and not in what has, will, or might motivate us, then a satisfied need is not a motivator. It must be considered for all practical purposes simply not to exist, to have disappeared. This point should be emphasized because it has been either overlooked or contradicted in every theory of motivation I know.[12] The perfectly healthy, normal, fortunate man has no sex needs or hunger needs, or needs for safety, or for love, or for prestige, or self-esteem, except in stray moments of quickly passing threat. If we were to say otherwise, we should also have to aver that every man had all the pathological reflexes, e.g., Babinski, etc., because if his nervous system were damaged, these would appear.

It is such considerations as these that suggest the bold postulation that a man who is thwarted in any of his basic needs may fairly be envisaged simply as a sick man. This is a fair parallel to our designation as 'sick' of the man who lacks vitamins or minerals. Who is to say that a lack of love is less important than a lack of vitamins? Since we know the pathogenic effects of love starvation, who is to say that we are invoking value-questions in an unscientific or illegitimate way, any more than the physician does who diagnoses and treats pellagra or scurvy? If I were permitted this usage, I should then say simply that a healthy man is primarily motivated by his needs to develop and actualize his fullest potentialities and capacities. If a man has any other basic needs in any active, chronic sense, then he is simply an unhealthy man. He is as surely sick as if he had suddenly developed a strong salt hunger or calcium hunger.[13]

If this statement seems unusual or paradoxical the reader may be assured that this is only one among many such paradoxes that will appear as we revise our ways of looking at man's deeper motivations. When we ask what man wants of life, we deal with his very essence.

SUMMARY

1. There are at least five sets of goals, which we may call basic needs. These are briefly physiological, safety, love, esteem, and self-actualization. In addition, we are motivated by the desire to achieve or maintain the various conditions upon which these basic satisfactions rest and by certain more intellectual desires.

2. These basic goals are related to each other, being arranged in a hierarchy of prepotency. This means that the most prepotent goal will monopolize consciousness and will tend of itself to organize the recruitment of the various capacities of the organism. The less prepotent needs are minimized, even forgotten or denied. But when a need is fairly well satisfied, the next prepotent ("higher") need emerges, in turn to dominate the conscious life and to serve as the center of organization of behavior, since gratified needs are not active motivators.

Thus man is a perpetually wanting animal. Ordinarily the satisfaction of these wants is not altogether mutually exclusive, but only tends to be. The average member of our society is most often partially satisfied and partially unsatisfied in all of his wants. The hierarchy principle is usually empirically observed in terms of increasing percentages of nonsatisfaction as we go up the hierarchy. Reversals of the average order of the hierarchy are sometimes observed. Also it has been observed that an individual may permanently lose the higher wants in the hierarchy under special conditions. There are not only ordi-

narily multiple motivations for usual behavior, but in addition many determinants other than motives.

3. Any thwarting or possibility of thwarting of these basic human goals, or danger to the defenses which protect them, or to the conditions upon which they rest, is considered to be a psychological threat. With a few exceptions, all psychopathology may be partially traced to such threats. A basically thwarted man may actually be defined as a 'sick' man, if we wish.

4. It is such basic threats which bring about the general emergency reactions.

5. Certain other basic problems have not been dealt with because of limitations of space. Among these are (a) the problem of values in any definitive motivation theory, (b) the relation between appetites, desires, needs and what is 'good' for the organism, (c) the etiology of the basic needs and their possible derivation in early childhood, (d) redefinition of motivational concepts, i.e., drive, desire, wish, need, goal, (e) implication of our theory for hedonistic theory, (f) the nature of the uncompleted act, of success and failure, and of aspiration level, (g) the role of association, habit and conditioning, (h) relation to the theory of interpersonal relations, (i) implications for psychotherapy, (j) implication for theory of society, (k) the theory of selfishness, (l) the relation between needs and cultural patterns, (m) the relation between this theory and Allport's theory of functional autonomy. These as well as certain other less important questions must be considered as motivation theory attempts to become definitive.

Notes

1. As the child grows up, sheer knowledge and familiarity as well as better motor development make these "dangers" less and less dangerous and more and more manageable. Throughout life it may be said that one of the main conative functions of education is this neutralizing of apparent dangers through knowledge, e.g., I am not afraid of thunder because I know something about it.

2. A "test battery" for safety might be confronting the child with a small exploding firecracker, or with a bewhiskered face, having the mother leave the room, putting him upon a high ladder, a hypodermic injection, having a mouse crawl up to him, etc. Of course I cannot seriously recommend the deliberate use of such "tests" for they might very well harm the child being tested. But these and similar situations come up by the score in the child's ordinary day-to-day living and may be observed. There is no reason why these stimuli should not be used with, for example, young chimpanzees.

3. Not all neurotic individuals feel unsafe. Neurosis may have at its core a thwarting of the affection and esteem needs in a person who is generally safe.

4. For further details see (12) and (16, Ch. 5)

5. Whether or not this particular desire is universal we do not know. The crucial question, especially important today, is "Will men who are enslaved and dominated inevitably feel dissatisfied and rebellious?" We may assume on the basis of commonly known clinical data that a man who has known true freedom (not paid for by giving up safety and security but rather built on the basis of adequate safety and security) will not willingly or easily allow his freedom to be taken away from him. But we do not know that this is true for the person born into slavery. The events of the next decade should give us our answer. See discussion of this problem in (5).

6. Perhaps the desire for prestige and respect from others is subsidiary to the desire for self-esteem or confidence in oneself. Observation of children seems to indicate that this is so, but clinical data give no clear support for such a conclusion.

7. For more extensive discussion of normal self-esteem, as well as for reports of various researches, see (11).

8. Clearly creative behavior, like painting, is like any other behavior in having multiple determinants. It may be seen in "innately creative" people whether they are satisfied or not, happy or unhappy, hungry or sated. Also it is clear that creative activity may be compensatory, ameliorative or purely economic. It is my impression (as yet unconfirmed) that it is possible to distinguish the artistic and intellectual products of basically satisfied people from those of basically unsatisfied people by inspection alone. In any case, here too we must distinguish, in a dynamic fashion, the overt behavior itself from its various motivations or purposes.

9. I am aware that many psychologists and psychoanalysts use the term "motivated" and "determined" synonymously, e.g., Freud. But I consider this an obfuscating usage. Sharp distinctions are necessary for clarity of thought, and precision in experimentation.

10. Discussed fully in a subsequent publication.

11. The interested reader is referred to the very excellent discussion of this point in Murray's *Explorations in Personality* (15).

12. Note that acceptance of this theory necessitates basic revision of the Freudian theory.

13. If we were to use the word "sick" in this way, we should then also have to face squarely the relations of man to his society. One clear implication of our definition would be that (1) since a man is to be called sick who is basically thwarted, and (2) since such basic thwarting is made possible ultimately only by forces outside the individual, then (3) sickness in the individual must come ultimately from a sickness in the society. The "good" or healthy society would then be defined as one that permitted man's highest purposes to emerge by satisfying all his prepotent basic needs.

References

(1) A. Adler, *Social Interest* (London: Faber & Faber, 1938).
(2) W. B. Cannon, *Wisdom of the Body* (New York: Norton, 1932).
(3) A. Freud, *The Ego and the Mechanisms of Defense* (London: Hogarth, 1937).
(4) S. Freud, *New Introductory Lectures on Psychoanalysis* (New York: Norton, 1933).
(5) E. Fromm, *Escape from Freedom* (New York: Farrar and Rinehart, 1941).
(6) K. Goldstein, *The Organism* (New York: American Book Co., 1939).
(7) K. Horney, *The Neurotic Personality of Our Time* (New York: Norton, 1937).
(8) A. Kardiner, *The Traumatic Neuroses of War* (New York: Hoeber, 1941).
(9) D. M. Levy, "Primary Affect Hunger," *American Journal of Psychiatry*, 94 (1937), pp. 643-652.
(10) A. H. Maslow, "Conflict, Frustration, and the Theory of Threat," *Journal of Abnormal (Social) Psychology*, 38 (1943), pp. 81-86.
(11) A. H. Maslow, "Dominance, Personality and Social Behavior in Women," *Journal of Social Psychology*, 10 (1939), pp. 3-39.
(12) A. H. Maslow, "The Dynamics of Psychological Security-Insecurity," *Character and Personality*, 10 (1942), pp. 331-344.
(13) A. H. Maslow, "A Preface to Motivation Theory," *Psychosomatic Medicine*, 5 (1943), pp. 85-92.
(14) A. H. Maslow and B. Mittelmann, *Principles of Abnormal Psychology* (New York: Harper & Brothers, 1941).
(15) H. A. Murray et al., *Explorations in Personality* (New York: Oxford University Press, 1938).
(16) J. Plant, *Personality and the Cultural Pattern* (New York: Commonwealth Fund, 1937).
(17) M. Shirley, "Children's Adjustments to a Strange Situation," *Journal of Abnormal (Social) Psychology*, 37 (1942), pp. 201-217.
(18) E. C. Tolman, *Purposive Behavior in Animals and Men* (New York: Century, 1932).
(19) M. Wertheimer, Unpublished lectures at the New School for Social Research.
(20) P. T. Young, *Motivation of Behavior* (New York: John Wiley and Sons, 1936).
(21) P. T. Young, "The Experimental Analysis of Appetite," *Psychology Bulletin*, 38 (1941), pp. 129-164.

A 21ST CENTURY COMMUNICATION TOOL

Milan Moravec, Herman Gyr and Lisa Friedman

Milan Moravec is president of Moravec and Associates, a worldwide consulting, strategy and implementation firm based in Walnut Creek, Calif.

Herman Gyr and Lisa Friedman are principals of Co-Development Associates Inc., an organizational development firm based in Los Gatos and Palo Alto, Calif.

Upward feedback helps create an environment of shared leadership, in which managers listen to and act on employees' suggestions. It allows employees to assess their supervisors' management skills and provides a framework for talking about everyone's responsibility for pursuing the business vision. When employees give feedback to a manager and the manager acts on the information, the employees feel that they are, in a sense, authorizing the manager to act as their leader and to represent their interests. This is qualitatively different from complying with authority.

The idea is not for employees to vent their frustrations by criticizing their managers, but for the two to develop better ways of working and achieving together.

Still, it's critical for any organization contemplating an upward feedback system to make sure of two things:

● Those who participate must feel

By championing upward feedback, a growing number of companies including British Petroleum and AT&T, are challenging the traditional command-and-control and performance management systems.

minimum pain and optimum gain.

● New awareness must be translated into specific changes in behavior.

In the old approach to assessing attitudes toward management, employees filled out questionnaires that were then analyzed by outside consultants. The results were reported to the managers anonymously, and the managers were left to decide for themselves what, if any, action to take. Today's upward feedback systems are much more results-oriented and much more interactive, usually involving face-to-face sessions between employees and managers.

The prospect of being evaluated by their subordinates makes some managers decidedly uneasy. But in companies where everyone is aware of the need to improve communication and build trust, it is surprising how little resistance there is to upward feedback. One multinational organization, which was contemplating an upward feedback system as part of a "bureaucracy-busting" effort, surveyed managers and staff about the idea and received an enthusiastic response from both. They viewed upward feedback as a new opportunity for constructive communication and change.

Honesty without fear

How can the discomfort of this process be minimized without compromising candor? BP Exploration (BPX), a division of British Petroleum, created an approach that combines directness with consultant support.

At BPX, the upward feedback process begins with managers and supervisors distributing a questionnaire describing 23 management practices (for example, meeting frequently with employees to review their individual performance) to each of their direct reports, plus certain people in other departments with whom the manager interacts. These respondents rate the manager on each item.

When BPX initiated the system two years ago, the respondents submitted the questionnaires to a consultant who produced a confidential feedback report summarizing the responses. A trained upward feedback adviser returned the summary to the manager and the two discussed key findings. Now that everyone is more comfortable with the process and more skilled in using it, the subordinates anonymously enter the completed questionnaires onto an on-line computer system that collates, summarizes and sends a report directly to the manger via electronic mail.

The manager still has the option of discussing the feedback with a trained adviser, who can help identify areas that will be discussed at the next critical part of the process—a feedback meeting between the manager and his or her staff.

At this meeting, the manager and staff discuss areas of their relationship that, based on the survey results, need work. At this stage, it is important that participants be frank without putting each other on the spot. The manager might say, "Here's an area where my feedback indicates I need to improve. Whether you agree with this assessment or not, tell me what specifically I might be doing or not doing."

The manager can ask the feedback adviser to be present at the meeting to help keep it positive and objective. This person remains available to support both the manager and staff, but is not an ombudsman or mediator—only a facilitator whose focus is on producing tangible results for employees and management. Eventually, BPX expects that the facilitator

EXHIBIT 1
Ways To Deliver Upward Feedback

Delivery System	Advantages	Disadvantages
PC-driven	• Cost • Turnaround time • Flexibility	• Ability to aggregate data • Need for hardware • Control (may require special procedures)
Paper Surveys/ Automated Results	• Familiar approach • No need for PCs • Can easily aggregate data	• Cost • Turnaround time • Accuracy (keypunch errors) • Perceived confidentiality problems
Local Area Network Approach	• High-tech approach • Can aggregate data • Flexiblity • Allows for better control • Turnaround time	• Cost • Need for network • Possible loss of confidentiality from manager's standpoint
Voice Response (Telephone)	• High-tech approach • No learning curve • Can aggregate data • Turnaround time • Accessibility	• Cost • Survey size limitations • Inability to process open-ended questions

EXHIBIT 2
Are You Ready To Use Upward Feedback?

Not Ready	Ready
The work group has a new manager or has been working for a manager for less than three months.	The majority of group members have been working for the manager for the past three to six months.
The manager is not interested in change.	The work group will perceive a benefit from participating in the Leadership Assessment Program.
The manager is not interested in developing employees and will most likely not ask employees for help in shaping his or her developmental action plan.	The work group believes that the manager will use the feedback and make positive changes.
If the manager receives negative feedback, he or she may retaliate.	The manager's agenda is consistent with the upward assessment process.
The work group has several members on discipline.	The work group and manager will be together long enough to implement desired changes and action plans.
The work group's climate is unsure.	The work group's climate is stable.
The manager is due to leave the work group soon, or the work group's membership may change significantly in the near future.	Work group membership will not significantly change in the near future.

Source: Karen Stoneman, Edward Bancroft and Carole Halling

BPX gives managers a *Tactics Guide* to help them translate information into behavior.

will no longer be needed, and when the desired openness is achieved, anonymity will not be necessary either.

Through the process of mutual analysis and action planning, employees learn that they do make a difference, and that they share responsibility for the success of their work group. Managers learn to accept input from group members and to translate this input into personal development plans and departmental action. Managers as well as subordinates begin to ask: What do I need to do, and what do we as a team need to do, to move forward? All of them should realize that they are interdependent.

Benefits for managers

Should upward feedback systems be tied to managerial promotions and raises? This is a sensitive question, and one on which companies are divided. In many organizations, a manager's own manager is informed about feedback results, so it's difficult not to take them into consideration. Some companies make upward feedback a formal part of promotion and succession planning.

At BPX, managers are expected to develop an action plan stemming from the decisions they committed to at the feedback meetings. Managers then share the plan with their own supervisors, and it becomes part of

A Look at AT&T Call Servicing's Upward Feedback System

by Karen Stoneman, Edward Bancroft and Carole Halling

In the fall of 1991, AT&T Call Servicing—NeWest Region was in the process of completing its third round of quality skills training. Managers and operators throughout the region were then immersed in both the theory and the tools needed to make quality a reality in the operator offices.

The first step in this process was identifying what the organization expected of its managers in the area of quality. Although managers had participated in several quality seminars, the actions expected of managers were not found in any one place or program. The exercise of defining the questions for an assessment then took on added importance. Not only would the questionnaire serve as a tool for assessing present practices, it would also succinctly define the NeWest Region's quality expectations of its managers.

AT&T wanted a very short, well-defined set of practices. The process was begun by interviewing each senior manager. From these interviews a list of 13 behavior statements was developed. These behaviors were then reviewed by groups of middle managers, first-line supervisors and operators. Each group had valuable edits and items to add. The final list included 20 questions. It was presented to the senior team for comments and final changes. Once this was done, the region had an agreed upon set of Quality Leadership Actions on which to build an upward feedback assessment questionnaire.

This questionnaire is used by each senior manager with his or her direct reports for upward feedback. Administration and follow-up consultation are provided by internal consultants who are already assigned to these intact management teams. The process is now flowing to the next two levels of management. Managers are expected to thoroughly analyze their data, meet with their direct reports to discuss results, and develop an action plan based on the data.

The impact of the process has been immediate. Data reports became the basis for extensive team and individual development activity. Results are now being used as baseline measures for setting individual and team goals as the organization evolves into team-based management models. The instrument has already undergone a revision as the model for quality management evolves.

The next steps in the process include a PC-based version of the questionnaire. Managers will be able to collect responses to the short questionnaire on an ongoing basis to get needed feedback between formal administrations. Data will be tracked for trends. The trends will then drive training and organizational interventions.

the managers' performance management and personal development plan.

Integration of upward feedback into managerial development and evaluation helps ensure that managers act on the feedback. BPX makes it easier for managers by giving them a *Tactics Guide* to help them translate information into behavior.

Suppose, for example, a manager learns that she rates low on "meeting frequently with employees to review their performance." The manager might think, "I do performance reviews when they're required by company policy. What more is expected of me." The *Tactics Guide* spells out the behaviors: "Discuss performance frequently, formally and informally. Do not avoid talking to employees about performance problems. Prepare thoroughly for performance discussions." For each of these suggestions, the guide includes a page of "What To Do" and "How To Do It."

Best scenarios
Upward feedback systems work best when

● The corporate culture perceives learning and changing as key competencies for business success.

● Employees feel free to speak up, without fear of reprisal, about better ways of doing things.

● Managers view open communication—upward, downward and lateral—as essential in creating a flexible organization that senses and responds quickly.

● Managers use what they learn to establish strategy and make changes relevant to their personal success and the success of their department.

● Managers discuss the changes regularly with their employees so employees can see their input has made a difference, thus maintaining program credibility.

● Upward feedback is part of the total change architecture. It is coordinated with other programs such as self-managed work teams and total quality programs.

● Feedback ratings and meetings take place at least once a year, as well as a couple of months after a reorganization or after a new leader comes on board—before opinions and behaviors are set in concrete.

If it is conducted with sensitivity and a focus on results, upward feedback can be a driving force in the bureaucracy breakdown.

Evaluation surveys of upward feedback participants—managers and employees—in various organizations have elicited comments such as these:

"It's an opportunity for me to be heard."

"We feel able to give feedback at other times now."

"We had a chance to clarify perceptions and plan next steps."

"It's not as threatening as I thought it would be."

"It reminds me of what it takes to be a good manager."

HR professionals like upward feedback because once it's introduced, it becomes part of the normal communication process, rather than regarded as "another HR program."

AT&T Call Servicing
Sample Upward Feedback Instrument

To what extent does the manager...	Almost Always	Often	Sometimes	Seldom	Almost Never	Do Not Know
Planning						
1. Develop plans that accurately anticipate future needs.	6	5	4	3	2	1
2. Communicate a consistent and clear direction for the team.	6	5	4	3	2	1
3. Take actions that place the team above the individual.	6	5	4	3	2	1
Communication						
4. Communicate business issues in an understandable way.	6	5	4	3	2	1
5. Tell the truth about business issues and their effect on the team.	6	5	4	3	2	1
6. Help you and others understand your importance to overall business success.	6	5	4	3	2	1
Problem Solving						
7. Involve you and others when making decisions.	6	5	4	3	2	1
8. Address business problems in new and creative ways.	6	5	4	3	2	1
9. Use facts and measures as the basis for solving problems.	6	5	4	3	2	1
10. Identify problems completely before moving to solutions.	6	5	4	3	2	1

Source: Karen Stoneman, Edward Bancroft and Carole Halling.

AT&T and exhibit information provided by the following authors:

Karen Stoneman is a performance management consultant at The Wyatt Company's Chicago office.

Edward Bancroft is the director of performance management in the same office.

Carole Halling is a process effectiveness manager at AT&T Call Servicing Chicago.

Developing effective leadership: an interview with Henry Cisneros, Secretary, U.S. Department of Housing and Urban Development

Janice R. Joplin

About the Author

Janice R. Joplin is a doctoral candidate at the University of Texas at Arlington. She has a B.S. in management from the University of Maryland and Masters in management from Incarnate Word College. She has worked for the Department of Defense and served as a consultant to not-for-profit social service agencies and small businesses in the U.S., Italy, and Great Britain. Her dissertation topic is on leader development processes.

Executive Overview

More than ever, effective change is being called for from our nation's leaders. The changing of the guard to the boomer generation has caused a lot of speculation as to whether or not these new leaders have the right stuff. In this interview, conducted prior to his confirmation, Henry Cisneros, President Clinton's selection for Secretary of Housing and Urban Development, provides a rare glimpse of his role models and explains how formal training as well as historical figures have shaped and enhanced his leadership development.

Henry Cisneros, age forty-five, is regarded as an effective leader on many diverse fronts. President Clinton has selected him to serve as Secretary of Housing and Urban Development, a choice based in part on Cisneros' performance as a four-term mayor of San Antonio in the 1980s. As mayor, he exercised a developmental strategy that led the city to unprecedented levels of economic and cultural growth. From 1989, until being confirmed as Secretary of Housing and Urban Development in January 1993, he has been chairman and CEO of the investment firm Cisneros Asset Management, and continued to actively serve as a leader in many forums. Among his commitments, he served as one of five members of President Clinton's Transition Planning Foundation Board, and in 1991 he was appointed vice chairman of the board of the Dallas Federal Reserve Bank. His recent civic commitments included serving as a member of the board of the Rockefeller Foundation; as a trustee of the American Assembly; chairman of the National Civic League; as co-chairman of the National Hispanic Leadership Agenda; and as chairman of the committee building the domed stadium in San Antonio. He has been a leader in the Mexican American Legal Defense and Educational Fund's move to reallocate educational funding to economically and educationally deprived border areas of South Texas and he was called on by Los Angeles Mayor Tom Bradley to help the Hispanic community in the aftermath of the riots. He is a frequent speaker for events ranging from academic gatherings to opening a Boy's Club in a small Texas town, and is a writer on urban development.

From *Academy of Management Executive*, Vol. 7, No. 2, May 1993, pp. 84-92. © 1993 by The Academy of Management Executive. Reprinted by permission.

During the course of the interview, I asked Secretary Cisneros to speak about mentoring and presented him with the timeless argument, "many would say you can't make it in a career unless you have a mentor. What do you think?"

Henry Cisneros: I don't think that's true. I think we've made a good deal more of the mentoring concept in recent years. I'm a student of history and biography. History is replete with examples of people who basically were self-starters, who were internally driven, who had their own visions. It's always helpful, obviously, to have somebody look out for you in the early years and maybe pave the way a little bit. But, mentors, *per se*, where you say—this is somebody who has adopted you—I don't think that's necessary. I see a mentor as someone who actually singles out another person and sees him or her as a future leader. The mentor intentionally develops a strong work relationship and takes a personal interest in them, nurtures, sponsors, and guides them in a very intense process. I think I'm a fan in history of people who have eclectically borrowed ideas and energy and support as they went, but not really had a mentor, *per se*.

You prefer role models?

Role models, correct. And support system and family. I have been fortunate that people have broken a trail for me and probably have said, but never within my hearing, "Have you met so and so? he's an impressive guy, and maybe he has potential." I've been the beneficiary of youth development like the White House Fellows program. And there have been people that I've learned from. But mentors—a structured one-on-one long-term work relationship—I'm not sure that is as valid as borrowing, observing, and modeling after an eclectic and wide-ranging group of people over a period of time.

Tell me about your personal support system . . . other colleagues, peers, family . . .

I'm fortunate to have good friends. They're not the get-together-and-socialize kinds of friends, because in the years that I was mayor there was no time and because the job didn't lend itself to that. It's funny, but being Hispanic, in a city like San Antonio, and trying to be the bridge between cultures, I never knew who was trying to take advantage of the office, so it was difficult. I'd frequently be with friends and only as the evening wore along have them steer me toward a discussion that related to their accounting practice, or they would want to bid on a city project. And that was fine, except that there was never a relationship that was just friends—it was always somebody saying, "I can use some aspect of this relationship, this friendship, for my business." That's okay, but it puts a wall between you and what you call just sheer nonselfish, noninterest-motivated friendship—let's go camping together, let's go fishing and we're not going to talk about business. So, I have good friends who joined me in the business and good friends from my days as mayor. But, most of my personal and social time is spent trying to be with my children, because my time is scarce, and I really want to do that with what scarce time I have. I would argue that that was probably a mistake, and that one should cultivate both personal and family friendships.

As mayor, you had a tremendous public office support system. When you made the transition to the private sector, you lost parts of that system. Were there parts of it that became more important?

Obviously, it is very difficult in terms of the support system. As mayor, you're on top of the machinery of the city government which is substantial. So I had drivers for security reasons and access to multiple telephones at the tip of my fingers. I had an executive assistant who made $47,000 a year and several secretaries, typists, and so forth. By the end of my tenure it was as if "your wish is your command." If I articulated it, it would happen, and I had learned the levers of the city so it was like playing a musical instrument—you want this sound, you touch here, and you want this sound, you touch here, and the city just sort of worked. The things I went out for we won—the Dome, bond issues, police issues, whatever it was. You've got to understand that maxim about power corrupts and absolute power corrupts absolutely because after a while you live in a very artificial existence.

What are your priorities in assessing business and civic opportunities and what criteria do you use for choosing whether or not you will participate?

I think it varies. On the business side I think the question was, could we (the Cisneros Asset Management team) do it well? Could we fulfill? Could we actually produce? I have a great sense of obligation to people who engage me to do something, whether it's a television program or a business opportunity that presents itself. I'm not one who wants to exacerbate a problem of performance credibility by not being able to perform, so we assessed things very carefully. In terms of the civic opportunities that are presented to me, I've done a range of things—for example I chaired the National Civic League which puts on the All-American Cities award. I've served as a member of a Carnegie Foundation committee working to define and outline elements of American foreign policy for the next century and chaired the San Antonio Education Fund which sponsors, through scholarships, 1,000 students in San Antonio colleges and universities. I've probably been involved in too many things.

I have decided that you don't necessarily need to be in public office to make a difference. Making a difference is very important to me. I'm applying a more sincere test of what actually helps move the country, the state of the art forward. I think one needs to be pretty rational with broad perspectives to define those things. Those are really the issues that interest me. I'm not going to do a lot of peripheral things, but those that go right to the heart, right to the core of what's important. The decision to go to HUD and move back into public service is based on my deep belief that we must address pressing issues such as homelessness, jobs, and rebuilding our cities.

What is the most distasteful thing about being in public office?

I loved my days in public office. As mayor, it was the most exhilarating time in my life, I was totally fulfilled . . . one of those things where you're just pumping on all pistons, they're all working and you enjoy it. There were very few things I felt were distasteful about it other than—I don't like raising money and I don't like the sense of cynicism that enters a relationship when you have to ask someone for money. You say to the public that contributors are not going to influence you, but they're contributing because they do want to influence you. That's the distasteful part of serving in public office.

I sense that in some ways you have moved toward a more interpersonal way of dealing with people, a one-on-one basis of making a difference in a few people's lives as opposed to a broader group . . .

I think that's right—that's absolutely right. Though I would say that I'm called to macro involvements. I think we need to speak truthfully about many of the problems that face the country—about education, finance, taxes, civics and so forth. I've tried to really lay down a hard-edged truth about some of these things, which I might not have been able to do had I stayed in public life,

I loved my days in public office. As mayor, it was the most exhilarating time in my life, I was totally fulfilled . . . one of those things where you're just pumping on all pistons, they're all working and you enjoy it.

because you have to pull the punches a little bit and not lay things out in the starkest of terms. That's a positive aspect of being in the private sector.

If there were something you could change about your career now, what would it be?

Well, I guess I could make an argument that maybe I should have started my private sector work a lot earlier and perhaps flipped the order. I could have done the private sector work first and then gone to public life later, because I've worked awfully hard at a time in my life when, perhaps, I ought to be farther along in terms of building a financial base. With the investment firm, I've been working in an entrepreneurial stage at forty-five years of age.

Who was important in your life in learning the basics of leadership?

In my own life, Elliot Richardson, whom I worked for as a White House Fellow. I learned a lot from him about practical things you don't think about—like how you dress, what constitutes a good eye for the right mix in business clothing. How does a person allocate their hours? He used to come in at 8:30 and work until 8:30, generally. But he would swim at home in the morning at his pool, or worked out before that. So, I knew suddenly the kind of hours that people who are achievers, not only can, but in some sense, *must* put in and how they organize that time, how they deal with people and so forth. All that was a role model, but not a mentor in the sense that he then later saw to it that I would succeed along the way, because I had just one year's worth of exposure to him. However, it was a very important year.

Clearly, Elliot Richardson was an important leadership example. But, when I was a student at Texas A & M University, Wayne Stark, who was director of the Memorial Student Center, took me aside and said, "Your sights are set too low—you need to raise your sights." Then he made it possible for me to become a student leader in several student organizations and selected me to go to West Point. In 1966, I went to a West Point conference which was really decisive for me because it enabled me to see the way students were performing at the East Coast schools. Wayne Stark gave me a lot of time and effort in that educational setting; I became the finance director of the Student Conference on National Affairs at A & M which required that I raise funds to put on that conference—about $20,000, which was a lot of money in those days for a student to raise. As a result of that performance and being the class treasurer, he asked me to chair the Student Leadership Committee which is a committee of the leaders of the student organizations across campus. The purpose was to put on a seminar on leadership which was to be held at a camp before the school year started for all those who were going to be heading school organizations. Part of it was to talk about finance and reporting procedures, but part of it was having inspirational speakers from the campus and beyond to talk about the characteristics and traits of leadership. So that experience, matched to actual training I was getting "hands on" in the Corps of Cadets at A & M was really important. I was a battalion-level commander and there was a lot of emphasis on leadership and practice because you live in the Corps dormitory. We put together programs on leadership for the underclassmen and made them a requirement. We had academic officers who were pushing for academic performance on the part of the students in our units and athletic and drill performance. We had 300 guys and I was the commander of the unit—I was living in there and had the top room and the staff that I worked with close by, so it was quite an experience. It was as good an experience as you will find anywhere in the country, including West Point, because we were more on our own than one is in the heavily supervised environment of West Point. So, the combination of Wayne Stark and the Corps of Cadets at A & M was a tremendous leadership experience, the result of which was learning the techniques of leadership, living with them daily, and having them reinforced. And having them laid out in such a way that one would think about them and encourage them, and sort of have them pressed onto a person. So that, I think, was very important.

To be able to create scenarios, to have a vision has frequently been considered to be essential for effectively leading others. Whom did you draw on to develop a "visionary" dimension?

The vision part of it has come more from reading about figures from history and biographies. Biography, over the course of my life, has been my most frequent reading until, of late, when I have taken to reading history and chronologies of periods, nations, and times—which is my hobby for life.

What really is exciting to me and reaches my soul is that transformational dimension.

There's a distinction, clearly, between managerial skills and techniques of leadership, and leadership. It's what James McGregor Burns calls the difference between transactional leadership and transformational leadership. Transactional is where we make an arrangement that I'm the leader, you're the follower, and as long as it's in your interest to follow me you will; and I try to buy you, to incentivise you, into following—versus transformational, where we share a cause and I'm the one who's able to inspire you in the quest for that cause and together we're wedded in this transforming personal experience that is transcendental in character. I think I learned that distinction early on and I, frankly, find the narrower kind of leadership to be sterile and even boring, because it's all sort of technique-oriented. What really is exciting to me and reaches my soul is that transformational dimension—transformational in that it transforms human beings and makes them better people—touches them deeply, moves them, accomplishes greater objectives, commits itself to the common good, and has all of those dimensions.

Over my lifetime, I've read a lot of biographies, but among the visionary leaders that I have read and admired is General George Marshall, who was Chief of Staff of the Army during World War II, and later Secretary of State, who conceived the Marshall Plan as a statesman-like response to the devastation of Europe and who was soldier and statesman. I might say to you, by the way, that the code of an A & M cadet are the words on the plaque of Lawrence Sullivan Ross, who was the first president of the institution and himself a military man. And it says, the code is "soldier, statesman, and knightly gentleman." Those three themes are interwoven in my concept of leadership. And George Marshall was, in some ways, the classic southern gentleman who is warrior for his country in time of war and statesman to build the peace.

I'll never forget that at home, in his closet, my dad had Douglas McArthur's speech at West Point on the inside door of his closet, so every time you opened the door it stated: "Duty, honor, country." McArthur—I've read several books about him—was another one of those visionary leadership figures. If you read the stories of his leadership, he had a capacity, and a genius for seeing strategy and synthesis of strategy and a capacity to read people.
Reading as a high schooler, *The Day Lincoln was Shot*—and other books like that—gave me a sense that Abraham Lincoln was a person who believed in something that was always important to me—the plight of the downtrodden; the unfairness perpetrated, particularly against slaves and the blacks. Throughout my life, my mother always had a sense of righteousness and justice about her, not in that abstract sense, but in a very practical sense. One of the earliest

memories I have is riding on the bus with Mom and taking a turn on a street and having her say, "See that sign over there that says 'Colored Only' in the rest room. I can't imagine how anyone could do that to a Negro mother who has a child with her who has to use the facilities, but cannot explain to them why they cannot use the same facilities as everyone else." I was maybe eight years old and I remember that. Abraham Lincoln standing up against inhumanity always struck me as a transcendental dimension of leadership. And Martin Luther King, with people being blown down by water hoses and attacked by dogs, had it, too. I gained a respect for those qualities of leadership of these leaders who courageously paid a price.

Also, I have a master's degree in urban planning. So I developed very much a planner's future orientation. I have frequently thought that I should have gone to law school because it would have been a better preparation for politics. You manage your time, move around from firm to firm or whatever you want to do, and you're not tied down. But, as mayor, I was thankful for the two key elements of my training—a master's degree in urban and regional planning and a doctorate in public administration with a heavy emphasis in economics. Planning gave me a constant sort of sense of: where are we going? what does this mean in terms of the future? how do we get from here to there? and, what's the policy framework for that? And public administration gave me a sense of the organizations needed to pull it off. You need to be aware of the habits, behavior, distortions, characteristics of bureaucracy and organization, people in organizations, large systems, and the economic rationale that undergirds it all and makes it possible from a financial, economic standpoint. Those have been important themes for me.

A man named Joe McGraw, who was a professor of urban and regional planning at A & M, was very helpful in terms of thinking about the future. The critical experience for me, and one of the most important books that I've read that sort of integrated this was by Graham Allison who was professor at the Kennedy School of Government when I was there. He taught about the Cuban missile crisis as three levels of public decision making. One level is the substance of the matter—what was it that was actually happening here? The second was the organizational dimensions and how the organizations misunderstood each other. Communications given to the Air Force by the Army and the Chief of Staff encouraged them to do certain things that may have been misinterpreted by the Russians. It's an organizational chess game of interpretation and misinterpretation. And then, thirdly, what are the personal dimensions going on here? who's on first? who's on second? who's trying to come out the hero in this thing? who's motives are what? how does Bobby Kennedy relate to Curtis LeMay? and so forth, in the President's inner circle. It's a brilliant piece of work that is immensely useful in a public policy environment.

There are many people that I admire today for their vision: Jim Rouse, whom I have been close to; William Norris, head of Control Data whom I have also been close to; Ernie Cortes, head of Communities Organized for Public Services—a vision of a changed society; Mario Cuomo, to some degree, but mostly for his sheer strength, but there's also vision there. Those are some people that I would say are examples both in personal and other ways.

Your critics would say that your vision is overdeveloped and there wasn't a braking mechanism—the city's [San Antonio] resources couldn't keep up with your vision during your time as mayor.

I would say it's not true. The only reason the critics can say that is because I left office when I did and they got to write the final verdict instead of my really having stayed the course to prove that it could, in fact, all be done—because it could.

In your own way you have been still doing that . . . ?

Yes. I am intent, as a matter of honor, on finishing what I began and proving that it fits in the long-term vision of the city. I've not been able to integrate all the pieces because so much of it is now out of my control and all I could do is finish the individual pieces of what I started out to do and those we will see to fruition. But, I couldn't have enough control over the whole mechanism to paint the picture that I wanted, in the final analysis, to come out. And that's a very frustrating thing, but it's also part of my own personal penance and maturation—that I have to learn patience, trust other people, work within constraints, and all of those things. It was kind of murder to be in charge of it all; it was very, very hectic. We acquitted ourselves well in terms of getting it done, but it was an immense responsibility and it never quit. Yet, at the same time it was almost too easy after a point. All the pieces were working and you had this sense of power that you don't even trust yourself with.

It's one thing to have the vision, but another to know where and how to carry it out . . .

i think it's very important, in your mind, to be able to sort of parlay the present into the future and dream, at least, about one's role.

I'm impressed and pleasantly surprised that someone, including yourself, has defined a dimension of leadership that deals with being able to put yourself in it. Because I'd always had a sense that it's exceedingly important to be able to place yourself in the larger sense.

I think it's very important, in your mind, to be able to parlay the present into the future and dream, at least, about one's role. I think that helps you select routes, behavior patterns, styles, gives you motivation to keep reaching and gives you something to wake up for. It must be tempered with maturity and patience. There's a difference between a person who is overreaching because they think they have to reach for everything, every day, and they really don't have a lot of confidence in where they are going to end up, and somebody else who just sees themselves easily, that is to say, gracefully, in a leadership role. This is a person who knows, who has confidence in his or her own skills and the way that they're perceived by people so that they can gracefully move through instead of having to fight and reach and overreach.

I can't tell you that I know anyone who taught me how leaders make judgments about how to act on their vision. It's a question of judgment and understanding people. From the reading of biographical figures it's important to note their foibles, their flaws. I once read *The Parting of the Waters* about Martin Luther King, and the author was criticized for having written so much about his character flaws. They said he was doing a disservice by tearing Dr. King down. The author responded he believed he was doing Dr. King's cause a service by suggesting that these things can be accomplished, not only by saints and geniuses, but by average people with problems who overcome, who struggle, and who reach, and who achieve and therefore, young people can know that this is available to them. I thought that was a very powerful point.

So, it's just as important to know where to not have yourself as it is to know where to place yourself?

I think that's right. I think also that it's important to know that people struggle, they grow up humble, poor, that they—you know the proverbial phrase—they put on their pants one leg at a time; that they studied in certain ways; that they failed in certain ways; that they made misjudgments at certain points and therefore, one ought not be unduly discouraged by what one perceives as one's inadequate origins or whatever. Life doesn't read like a resume. It reads like a lot of pitfalls and chug holes. I think that's a really important thing to know.

But, it's also important to know how people prepared themselves so that if one feels, for example, one is taking shortcuts by getting help, then all one has to do is remember that Douglas McArthur's mother separated from her husband and moved to West Point so she could live in the hotel right off the campus to press his clothes, so that he could be more impressive from a grooming standpoint. He eventually became first cadet in the Cadet Corps. She later intervened with friends of the family to get him promoted. That's not a mentor, but it's one hell of a support system. And so, therefore, if one gets help, if one's parents want to be helpful, well that's not dishonorable. It's part of what paved the path for one of the great Americans of this century.

There are many other instances of how one can get solace in the things one might regard as somehow unmanly or dishonorable, by just reading how other people have done these things over the years. Dwight Eisenhower finished in the middle of his West Point class and maybe the latter part of his class and was not regarded by anyone as a (leader)—but he grew over a lifetime. His Kansas, midwestern traits served him well as a leader in combat. Whereas, Patton was a reacher and ambitious, maybe even carelessly bold on occasion. Eisenhower was an infantryman's leader— concerned. There are many other examples from history.

I have found over the years that it's important to read not just about those in one's own field, technical reading, or even biographies from the general area, but, for example, one of the most interesting books I read—again, a visionary figure—was about a man named Abram Sachar, who was the first president of Brandeis University. He built Brandeis in 1947 as the first Jewish university in America. But the vision of what he wanted to build is a magnificent story of how he did it: fundraising, work. He had to go to every city in the country and raise money. That's a part of things that some people don't like or feel that they're grubbing when they do it. Well, to build a great university, you've got to do it—hit the road! So, you learn that people do what they're supposed to do.

When you read about figures or you come into contact with people, what are your criteria for borrowing from them?

Obviously, if people have successfully either managed systems, structures, organizations, entities, or produced results, you've got to learn from them. But what strikes me particularly are people who seem to want to reach a societal good, help other people, and are doing it not blindly out of some innocent sense of good, although that would be valuable in and of itself. But, they have a context and see a potential for improvement. They're practical people. They deal with real people, not abstract ideas. That's the difference between Jerry Falwell and Martin Luther King, or someone else who has the capacity for humanity and understanding and is not doctrinaire. That's the screen that, for me, is the valuable screen.

....

The author wishes to thank Ray Zammuto, James Campbell Quick, Debra L. Nelson, and Jerry C. Wofford for their helpful comments on an earlier draft of this manuscript.

WHAT DO WORKERS WANT?

You aren't the first to wonder what your employees want from their jobs, nor will you be the last. . . . Here's what the surveys say

CHRISTOPHER CAGGIANO

YOU WANT TO KNOW WHAT SATISFIES YOUR WORKERS? Well, fortunately for you, a veritable industry has ballooned to tell you precisely that—what pleases them, motivates them, makes them want to never leave your company. Measuring employee satisfaction is hardly new. Social scientists have surveyed employees on the topic for decades.

We've sifted through thousands of numbers, dozens of surveys, and years of research to save you the exhausting legwork and the excruciating mind work of combing through the available quantitative research on what matters most to employees. You can rest easy. Regardless of the fact we found one survey that says white for every one that says black, the cumulative results won't startle you. It turns out your employees want the same things they've always wanted. And they're probably a lot happier with their jobs than you think. What do they want? Read on.

WHAT WORKERS REALLY WANT

HEALTH INSURANCE, BENEfits, and job security pop out as being of top importance to today's workers, which shouldn't surprise you, given an environment of mass layoffs, cost cutting, and increased health-care expenses. Since workers often must share the burden of those escalating health-care costs, it also should come as no surprise that far less than half of America's workers feel completely satisfied in terms of those three factors.

The disparity between what workers want and what they're getting may drive some employers to creative alternatives, but the gap isn't likely to close. With costs continuing to spiral upward, it's questionable just how much you can do to bridge it.

But check out how high "interesting work" ranks below. Here's a factor you *can* control far more directly and cost-effectively than benefits and, for that matter, compensation. Given the dramatic 22-point lead interesting work has over high income when it comes to importance to workers, where are *you* going to put *your* efforts?

"Yeah, right," you say. "All my employees want is more money." Well, statistically and experientially, that's just plain wrongheaded thinking. You can look it up. People will work for less (not less than a fair wage, but certainly less than the deepest pockets in town) if they enjoy their work and feel as if they're being treated fairly. If your workers are complaining about their pay, it's usually a sign that something else is missing.

Listen to C. J. Cranny, the man who wrote the book on job satisfaction, *Job Satisfaction: How People Feel About Their Jobs and How It Affects Their Performance* (Lexington Books, 1992). Ultimately, says Cranny, the chairman of Bowling Green State University's psychology department, the most important factor in creating an atmosphere that workers find satisfying is whether employees find their work "intrinsically interesting."

And it wouldn't hurt to take a hard look at how you can relieve some of that employee job stress, either.

How important is each of the following characteristics to you? How satisfied are you with it in your current job?

	% of workers who ranked it as very important	% of workers who said they were satisfied
Good health insurance and other benefits	81%	27%
Interesting work	78	41
Job security	78	35
Opportunity to learn new skills	68	31
Having a week or more of vacation	66	35
Being able to work independently	64	42
Recognition from coworkers	62	24
Regular hours (no weekends, no nights)	58	40
Having a job in which you can help others	58	34
Limiting job stress	58	17
High income	56	13
Working close to home	55	46
Work that is important to society	53	35
Chances for promotion	53	20
Contact with a lot of people	52	45
Flexible hours	49	39

Source: Gallup Poll, Princeton, N.J., 1991.

THE MORE THINGS CHANGE,
THE MORE THEY APPEAR THE SAME

THE CHANGE IN THE LEVEL OF SATISFACTION WORKERS HAVE with individual aspects of their jobs was relatively minor over the past two decades. But if anything stands out in the trend tables below and confirms some of what we observed earlier, it's that workers have grown less satisfied with benefits and pay than they have with any other characteristics of their jobs.

No surprise, argues David Abramis, an organizational psychologist at California State University at Long Beach. "When times are tight and you're worried about your job, pay becomes an important issue."

Absolutely. And when times are tight and costs are escalating, look elsewhere for a solution. It just might be found in some numbers that have hardly budged over the last 10 to 20 years, namely, the high percentage who desire "important and meaningful work" and the high level of satisfaction with "type of work." Remember how high "interesting work" ranks in importance among characteristics workers want in a job?

What do you most prefer in a job?

	1973	1980	1985	1990
	\% of workers saying aspect was the most important			
Important and meaningful work	52%	52%	48%	50%
High income	19	20	19	24
Chances for advancement	18	19	22	16
Job security	7	6	7	6
Short work hours	5	3	3	4

Source: National Opinion Research Center surveys, University of Chicago, 1973, 1980, 1985, and 1990.

How satisfied are you with these aspects of your job?

	1984	1988	1990	1992
	\% of workers saying they were satisfied			
Type of work	78%	80%	77%	79%
Coworkers	76	77	77	76
Benefits	81	77	74	71
Being treated with respect and fairness	64	62	60	58
Job security	63	64	59	58
Chances to contribute ideas	54	55	56	54
Pay	57	50	47	46
Recognition for performance	44	48	45	39
Advancement opportunities	33	36	34	27

Source: International Survey Research Corp., Employee Satisfaction Surveys, Chicago, 1984, 1988, 1990, 1992.

CAN YOU SATISFY ALL THE PEOPLE ALL THE TIME?

WHAT YOUR WORKERS WANT DEPENDS ON WHO THEY are. Forget about differences between what women and men want. Not *one* survey we found, including a recent ambitious one undertaken by Wellesley College's Center for Research on Women, suggests any difference among the desires of the sexes. "Men and women find similar aspects of the workplace rewarding and problematic," Rosalind C. Barnett, senior research associate of the center, tells us. Differences in expectations correspond more to education levels than anything else.

Employee satisfaction, says Cranny, is "a function of the difference between what employees want or think they should get, and what they're really getting." The problem is that many workers simply *don't know* what they're really getting. A study by the Wyatt Co., an international consulting firm in Boston, found that among employees who are dissatisfied with the way their benefits are communicated to them, only 13% report being satisfied with their benefits. But among those who were satisfied with communications about benefits, 75% report being satisfied. How many of your workers really know what benefits you're giving them?

Select from the following list the two factors that are most important to you in your current job.

	High school graduate or less	Some college or less	College graduate
	\% of respondents who chose each factor, by education level		
Pay	46%	42%	29%
Amount of independence	31	35	40
Pleasant working environment	30	23	17
Liking the people at work	29	24	19
Gratifying work	25	32	43
Contribution to public good	11	14	23
Important career step	10	15	19

Source: "The Chivas Regal Report on Working Americans," Research & Forecasts, New York City, 1989.

Would you say you are enjoying your work more, less, or about the same as you were five years ago?

	Overall	Professionals/ managers	Tech.	Sales/ admin.	Blue collar
More	52%	60%	55%	51%	44%
Less	19	14	18	22	24
About the same	27	24	26	26	31
Don't know/ no answer	2	2	1	1	1

Source: "The Chivas Regal Report on Working Americans," Research & Forecasts, New York City, 1989.

ALL WORK AND NO PLAY . . .

REMEMBER, WORKERS HAVE LIVES, TOO. THEY MAY spend an average of more than 25% of any given week at their jobs, but for most people, there's more to life than work—as is dramatically punctuated by the gap between "happy family life" and the first job-related answer in the chart below.

You want satisfied workers? Consider the study by the Wyatt Co. showing that employees who thought their employer's policies helped balance work and family responsibilities were far more likely to feel a commitment to their company as more than "just a place to work" than those who thought otherwise (62% versus 13%). And there's nothing like committed employees.

Which one of the following would most give you the feeling of success in your life?

	% choosing each factor
Happy family life	62%
Ability to do some good in the world	15
Earning lots of money	10
Position and prestige in your work	6
Involvement in some creative activity	4
Fame	1
Don't know/no answer	2

Source: "The Chivas Regal Report on Working Americans," Research & Forecasts, New York City, 1989.

Incentive Plan Pushes Production

The production rate at Lincoln Electric Co. is more than double that of other manufacturers in its industry. An incentive plan that pays workers for what they produce—and that promises no layoffs—is responsible.

Carolyn Wiley

Carolyn Wiley is an associate professor of management at the University of Tennessee at Chattanooga.

In 1984, an article printed in *The New York Times* praised Control Data, IBM, Hewlett-Packard, Motorola, Digital Equipment, Nissan USA, DuPont, Procter & Gamble, Exxon, Lincoln Electric, Bank of America, 3M, Upjohn and R. J. Reynolds Tobacco for maintaining extensive no-layoff policies. Today, at least one of these firms still can boast the survival of its no-layoff policy. That company is the Lincoln Electric Co., which hasn't had a layoff in 45 years.

Although the Cleveland-based manufacturer of welding machines and motors suffered a 40% decline in sales during the 1981 to 1983 recession, it didn't lay off one employee. Instead, because of an incentive plan that rewards workers based on their productivity, workers had brought Lincoln's sales back to normal by 1984—and had earned shared profits of about $15,000 each.

During the current recession, the firm lost money in its foreign operations—its first loss since it began filing consolidated annual reports. Still, it didn't lay off any

U.S. employees, and even rewarded them with a total of $48 million in year-end bonuses. In 1992, production workers received bonuses averaging between $18,000 and $22,000, which equalled approximately 75% of their salaries. Their total annual pay, including wages, profit sharing and bonuses, averaged $45,000.

These high wages are the result of a reward-and-recognition system that successfully connects the company's and the employees' goals. The comprehensive, organizationwide *Lincoln Electric Incentive Plan*, which combines pay for output, bonuses and job security, has enabled Lincoln to gain a competitive advantage in its industry. It has helped the organization increase production efficiency and lower the cost of its products.

According to Paul Beddia, VP of HR for Lincoln, the company's productivity rate is double to triple the productivity rate of any other manufacturing operation that uses steel as its raw material and that employs 1,000 or more people. (He measures the productivity rate by dividing the total sales, which is approximately $500 million for Lincoln, by the total number of employees, which at Lincoln is 2,700.)

On top of maintaining a high rate of productivity, Lincoln has been able to maintain a stable price structure as a result

of increased employee output. For several decades, Lincoln maintained 1933 prices on most of its products. These pricing policies held until the 1970s, when inflation caused a shift in pricing philosophy.

The Lincoln incentive plan links employee success to company success. The Lincoln family always has been interested in the well-being of its employees as well as the productivity of its business. When John C. Lincoln established Lincoln Electric Co. in 1895, he developed a win-win-win philosophy. The prime tenet of this philosophy is simply that all stakeholders in a business venture can win. The Lincoln Electric Incentive Plan satisfies the bottom line for:

• The stockholder, through enhanced stock values and regular dividends

• The customer, through lower-priced, quality products

• The manufacturer, through efficient operations, minimal customer problems, no strikes, increased market share and increased sales

• The employee, through job security, empowerment and good wages.

Many experts argue that, given the pressures in today's economy, compensation plans and policies quickly lose their punch. Therefore, most managers continu-

The History of Lincoln Electric Co. and Its Incentive Plan

Engineer John C. Lincoln established Cleveland-based Lincoln Electric Co. in 1895. In 1907, his son, James F. Lincoln, began working for the company for $50 a month, plus a 2% sales commission. Right away, James began developing new technologies. He saw a need for employee commitment to be able to implement his ideas. Therefore, he asked the employees to elect representatives (one representative for every 100 employees) from each department to serve on an advisory board and advise him on the company's operations.

Before World War I began, Lincoln's staple product was the battery charger. When the war caused a temporary end of the electric vehicle, however, Lincoln's battery-charger business came to an abrupt halt. In its place, the war brought to the forefront the potential of arc welding. Lincoln Electric had started experimenting with arc welding in 1902 and produced its first welding machinery in 1912. Arc welding became the company's mainstay.

The company's long-range goal was eventually to specialize in the welding process. With this vision, Lincoln saw the need to train his people in the use of welders. Therefore, in 1917, the company created the Lincoln Electric School, from which more than 70,000 welders have graduated during the last seven decades. The school continues to enroll new students on a regular basis.

In 1915, the company gave each employee a paid life-insurance policy. Four years later, the employees organized an association for health benefits and social activities. By 1923, the company also was giving employees two-week paid vacations. By this time as well, the shop was operating with a piecework plan that enabled workers to make more money for more effort. In 1929, the advisory board devised a suggestion system.

1895 John C. Lincoln founds Lincoln Electric Co.

1914 An advisory board is established to study and implement the piecework system.

1915 The company gives each employee a paid life-insurance policy.

1919 Employees organize an association for health benefits and social activities.

1923 The company adds two weeks' paid vacation to the benefit package.

1929 Advisory board devises a suggestion system.

1934 Profit-sharing bonus plan is installed. Company begins paying for pension plans and develops systems for determining base rates and bonuses using job evaluations and merit ratings.

1959 A no-layoff policy is adopted officially.

In 1928, James F. Lincoln became president of Lincoln Electric. Being in the beginning of the Great Depression, the company devised a technique that resulted in 50% price reductions. However, the Depression still took its toll, creating shorter work hours for employees and scarce sales for the company.

By 1934, work hours again increased. The company installed a bonus plan in response to employees' requests for higher wages. At the end of that year, the company distributed a cash bonus derived from profits, after taxes and dividends had been deducted. During the next 10 years (1934 to 1944), the company began paying for pension plans, developed a job-evaluation system to determine base-pay rates and instituted a merit rating to determine employee bonuses.

For several decades, Lincoln Electric maintained 1933 prices on most of its products. These pricing policies held until the 1970s, when inflation made a shift in pricing philosophy inevitable.

During the inflationary period of 1975 to 1982, the firm incorporated new technologies, and its return on investment exceeded 15%. In the late 1980s, Lincoln brought its older equipment into the 1990s to continue increasing efficiency and to do complex off-line programming. It's expected that Lincoln will continue to upgrade its machinery, its operations and the use of robotics to retain its position as a key competitor worldwide.

In 1987, Donald F. Hastings became president of Lincoln Electric. He established a Quality Committee comprising production workers who volunteered to serve and elected a leader. The committee met weekly with the factory superintendent and monthly with Hastings. His goal was to build quality into the process rather than testing it at the end of the production line. His efforts paid off—25% fewer line inspectors were needed, and 50% fewer employee-caused errors showed up during testing. This committee still is in commission today.

From 1986 to 1991, Lincoln expanded worldwide. During 1986, Chairman George E. Willis began:

- Adding plants in Brazil and Mexico
- Establishing joint ventures with companies in Venezuela
- Building a new plant in Japan
- Forming a strategic alliance with a Norwegian company to tap the potential of the unified Common Market.

This strategy will help Lincoln continue as a leader in the arc-welding industry.

—CW

ally tinker with their pay systems. This isn't the case with the Lincoln Electric Incentive Plan. It has been in its present form since 1959. Indeed, it has been enhanced, in spite of two World Wars, the Great Depression and two recessions. Although the company's biggest customers have been in highly cyclical markets, such as oil, steel and construction, Lincoln has remained solvent because of its approach to managing and rewarding people.

Lincoln Electric isn't an easy place in which to work, however. The turnover rate for employees within their probationary first two months is 20%. There's no room for the nonchalant, disengaged worker. The success of the entire enterprise depends on a high level of employee input and output, dependability and cooperation. There are no paid holidays or sick days. Workers must accept job reassignments, and overtime is mandatory. There are no reserved parking spaces, no special seats in the cafeteria and no definite or restrictive lines of promotion. The firm posts all promotional opportunities (including many senior positions), and bases promotions on merit only. There's no seniority. Workers also must compete with co-workers for bonuses based on merit. Despite all these policies, Lincoln is a desirable place in which to work. It receives nearly 1,000 unsolicited job applications a month, and the post-probationary turnover rate at Lincoln is less than 3% per year, including deaths and retirements.

The Lincoln Electric Incentive Plan combines compensation with security. Lincoln's multifaceted incentive system comprises:

- Piecework pay
- Shared profits
- Suggestion systems
- Year-end bonuses
- Stock-ownership opportunities
- Job security.

Performance-based or gainsharing programs like Lincoln's are designed to improve overall performance by allowing contributing workers to share in the proceeds. Gene Epstein, former editor and publisher of *The Managers' Consultant*, called the Lincoln Electric plan the most successful gainsharing or productivity-sharing plan at a single company. It has become a classic, focusing on employee efficiency and productivity.

The plan rewards workers for turning out high-quality products efficiently while controlling costs. Consumers throughout the industry recognize these products for their reliability. Few customers return products for repairs or replacements, so the firm makes a higher profit, and workers who produce the products enjoy larger bonuses.

The focus of the incentive program is its compensation plan. All employees receive a base annual wage. Production-support workers receive hourly wages, and production workers receive piecework pay. The piecework method encourages not only productivity but quality results as well, because the organization only pays workers for defectless products. If a customer sends a defective part back to the company, the employee who produced it must repair it on his or her own time.

The company's methods-engineering department uses past performance standards, work measurements and time studies to determine piece rates. So far, Lincoln's engineering group has established 70,000 piece rates for various production jobs. The rates don't change, except for adjustments in the cost of living or for substantial changes in manufacturing procedures. Some rates, for example, have been in effect for more than 30 years.

Because Lincoln pays its production employees on a piece-rate basis, management allows them to challenge the results of any time study or periodic piece-rate review. Workers challenge fewer than one-fifth of 1% of all rate changes. Also, if a time study results in a lower rate, the worker may request a transfer to a job that pays an equal or a higher rate.

The piece-rate concept at Lincoln Electric is a fundamental part of the capitalistic process underlying its incentive-compensation system, which allows workers to earn more for more output. The firm doesn't review the piece rate periodically to limit earnings. It also isn't a speed-up tool, but rather a tool to facilitate reward distributions that match employee output.

To reward workers further for their output, Lincoln has established a year-end bonus system that enables workers to increase their base wages to nearly double. It began in 1934 when chairman James Lincoln denied a request by employees for a 10% wage increase because Lincoln's profit picture didn't warrant such an increase. The workers responded with a request for a year-end bonus if, through increased productivity and lower costs, the annual profits increased. Lincoln agreed to their proposal, which he established as a bonus plan the same year. "We haven't missed a year since," says Beddia. This success has resulted in a distribution to employees of more than $500 million. Each year, the company allocates a percentage of U.S. sales for dividends, seed money and year-end bonuses, based on a 10-year average. Last year, 12.1% of the company's income went into bonuses and annuities.

VITALS

ORGANIZATION
Lincoln Electric Company

TYPE OF BUSINESS
Manufactures welding machines and motors

HEADQUARTERS
Cleveland

EMPLOYEES
2,700

VICE PRESIDENT OF HUMAN RESOURCES
Paul Beddia

YOU SHOULD KNOW
Lincoln Electric Co. has paid out more than $500 million in year-end bonuses to employees since it began its bonus program in 1934.

Components of Lincoln Electric's Incentive Plan

Lincoln's incentive plan combines job security with a lucrative compensation program. Below is a summary of the plan's elements.

Features	Description	Criteria
Job Security	Guaranteed 30-hour workweek.	Employees are eligible after three years of service. • Pay rates aren't guaranteed. • Job transfers may be necessary. • Overtime is required during peak demand. • Guaranteed hours may be terminated by the company with a six-month notice.
Base Wage	Standard Job Evaluation procedures are used to set the base wage. However, job evaluation and market requirements determine the actual dollar value of jobs.	Job evaluation compensable factors include skill, responsibility, mental aptitude, physical application and working conditions.
Piecework	For every job that can be standardized, normal time-study procedures are employed to establish piece rates.	Piece rates are based on the following calculation for consistency and to eliminate constant revisions: 1934 wage rates times cost of living, which fluctuates with the index (Bureau of Labor Statistics). This product is then compared with the area average skilled hourly rate to determine the adjustments to the piece rate.
Advisory Board	Employees elect representatives to an Advisory Board. All employees, except department heads and members of the engineering and time-study departments, are eligible.	The Advisory Board analyzes suggestions that lead to organizational progress. Implemented suggestions have ranged from a savings of $2,400 to over $200,000.
Merit Ratings	Twice a year, managers appraise employee performance through a merit-rating program.	This program uses four report cards. Each card rates work performance on one of the following: output, quality, dependability and personal characteristics, such as the ability to come up with ideas, and cooperation.
Profit Sharing	All business profits are split three ways: among the company, the shareholders and the employees.	The company receives seed money; the shareholders receive a dividend; and the employees receive a year-end, profit-sharing bonus.
Year-end Bonus	The annual cash bonus closely approximates the employees' annual earnings.	An employee's bonus is a function of his total annual earnings, biannual merit ratings and company profits.
Employee Stock-ownership Plan	Each employee has the opportunity to purchase a limited number of shares of company stock per year.	Employees are eligible after one year of service. On retirement or termination of employment, the company has the option to repurchase the stock. —CW

4. DIRECTING: Performance

A merit-rating system determines bonuses. Workers receive merit ratings or merit report cards twice a year as the basis of their reviews. These ratings determine the amount of bonus that they will receive at the end of the year. The company rates employees on four merit criteria:

- Output
- Quality
- Dependability
- Personal characteristics.

Output is the most measurable criterion. The production department determines this rating for each employee based on the amount of work that he or she produces.

The quality measurement involves a more complex system. "When a product comes back in from a customer as defective, the quality-assurance department traces who made each component," says Beddia. Employees in quality assurance identify which components are faulty. They identify who produced the defective product parts. This department rates each employee for the quality criteria.

An employee's department head determines his or her ratings for both the dependability and personal characteristics categories. The dependability rating is based on the number of absences, late arrivals, availability for overtime and so on. Department heads take into account how individuals work together as a team for the cooperation rating. They also evaluate such factors as:

- Attitude toward supervision, co-workers and the firm
- Efforts to share expert knowledge with others
- Cooperation in installing new methods

To determine the rating for the ideas portion of the criteria, department heads look at their employees' participation in the organization's suggestion program. An advisory board, comprising several executives and approximately 26 to 30 employees whom the employee base elects, reviews suggestions with methods engineers for implementation feasibility. The organization implements approximately 50 suggestions monthly. Implemented suggestions have saved the company from $2,000 to more than $200,000. This, in turn, affects the suggesting workers' merit ratings, which affects their year-end bonuses.

Here's how the rating system works.

How Lincoln Electric Calculates Employees' Bonuses

Under the Lincoln Electric Incentive Plan, employees at Cleveland-based Lincoln Electric Co. receive bonuses based on their productivity. The bonus is determined by a simple bonus-factor formula.

First, the board of directors sets the amount of the year's bonus pool, based on a recommendation by the chairman. The chairman looks at such factors as how much money the company has made, how much seed money is needed and how much money is needed for taxes and dividends. The average bonus pool during a recent 10-year period was 10.6% of sales revenue.

The company then divides this bonus pool amount by the total wages paid. This quotient is the bonus factor. A bonus factor of 1.00 means that the bonus pool is the same as the total companywide wages. This past year, the bonus pool was approximately 75% of wages paid.

Once the bonus factor has been determined, the company calculates bonuses by multiplying the bonus factor by individual earnings and merit ratings. Here's an example. A production worker earned $35,000. His merit rating was 100%, or 1.00. The bonus factor is .75. The formula for determining his bonus would be as follows:

$$\begin{array}{ll} \$35,000 & \text{(earnings)} \\ \underline{\times\ 1.00} & \text{(merit rating)} \\ \$35,000 & \end{array}$$

$$\begin{array}{ll} \$35,000 & \\ \underline{\times\ .75} & \text{(bonus factor)} \\ \$26,250 & \text{(bonus)} \end{array}$$

This employee's full bonus would be $26,250. However, according to Paul Beddia, VP of HR at Lincoln, employees must pay for their own hospitalization insurance, which costs approximately $3,000. The company deducts this money from employees' year-end bonuses. Thus, this production worker would receive a bonus of $23,250 (before taxes), bringing his annual salary to $58,250. —*CW*

The firm allocates each department 100 points per employee (25 points for each criterion). If a worker performs at a superior level, he or she can receive more than the allocated 25 points for any category. That means that another worker will have to receive fewer than 100 total points because there are only so many points available. Most workers in a group typically receive between 80 and 120 points.

An employee may have points deducted as well as added. A defective product shipped to a customer can reduce the merit points of its producer by as much as eight points. This could amount to as much as $1,600 in bonus money. In addition, an employee can lose points for absenteeism. "Each day of absenteeism is worth four-tenths of a point," says Beddia. "That gets deducted from the output rating." The president of the company reviews all ratings and meets with disgruntled employees to discuss perceived discrepancies.

The organization then plugs the final merit rating that an employee receives into a formula to determine that employee's bonus (see "How Lincoln Electric Determines Employees' Bonuses," right). Most bonuses nearly equal employees' base wages, almost doubling their annual salaries.

Stock ownership opportunities and job security provide employees further incentive and security.
As part of its incentive program, Lincoln also has an employee stock-ownership plan (ESOP) and an employee stock-purchase plan (ESPP). The ESPP allows only employees to buy stock and the ESOP allows them to receive stock shares annually out of profits. Approximately 80% of the employees participate in these plans and own more than 40% of the total company stock. The firm trades the stock privately. However, it does trade the stock over the counter. Employee-shareholder dividends and voting rights are the same as for stock that's owned outside the plan. Workers may buy, at book value, a certain number of shares each year, based on their base wages. Employees must pay for the shares within a 12-month period. The company has first option to repurchase shares that employees sell.

The stock opportunities provide employees with not only the incentive to produce so that they can share in the profits, but also with security for their futures. The company's guaranteed-employment plan provides employees additional security. Workers who have been at the firm for at least three years receive a guarantee of at least 30 hours of work a week. That work doesn't have to be in the job for which the company hired that employee, however. For example, Beddia says that during a slow period, a worker who was hired as an accountant may be assigned to paint fences or resurface the parking lot. That worker would receive the pay rate for the job that he or she performs, rather than the pay rate for the job for which he or she was hired.

In 1982, the company put this policy into practice and received an unexpected result. When sales fell behind production, management asked its factory workers for help in the sales department. More than 100 workers volunteered, out of which management chose 54. After a quick sales-training course, the production workers started calling on body shops across the country. Their efforts ended up bringing in $10 million in new sales and established the small arc welder as one of Lincoln's best selling items. Lincoln took a risk on its people, and the risk paid off.

This faith in and recognition of its workers continues to pay off for the firm. "We're not only surviving, we're prospering," says Beddia. "I think that this is unusual in the current business climate.

We see companies downsizing, merging, consolidating and leaving the country. We're doing just the opposite. We're still growing. Within the past five years, we've gone from five plants in four countries to something like 23 plants in 17 countries."

For people who are willing to accept the idea of individual responsibility and who are willing to commit themselves to the success of the enterprise, instituting a plan similar to the Lincoln Electric Incentive Plan can be a win-win situation. Having gone more than 54 years without losing any money in its domestic business, and more than 40 years without a layoff, Lincoln has proven that its plan survives the test of time.

Case IV: *The Indigenous Leader*

Incident

*What This Incident Is About: Employees turn to union represen-
tation when informal communication of their concerns is not
only ineffective but punished. The incident involves leadership
style in handling grievances, listening and communication skills,
problem recognition, and policy implementation.*

At 4:45 P.M. on Friday, Mike Henry, an employee in the Accounting Department, walked to the office of Herschel Jones, department head, and asked to see him privately. Henry told Jones that
he had been elected by the other 75 Accounting Department
employees to speak on their behalf about company practices
that they wished to have modified or eliminated. One practice
concerned the merit rating system, which the employees
thought was unfair and poorly administered, and utilized as a
reason for not paying higher salaries. A second practice that was
poorly accepted by the employees was the arbitrary way in
which management determined employee vacation time. Henry
said one employee told him that last year she was given two
days' notice before she received her first week of vacation in
October and five days' notice before a second week of vacation
in April.

Jones listened attentively and told Henry that since it was so
late in the day, he would consider these requests again early the
next week. During the next week, Henry noticed that Jones was
out of town, and no action was taken concerning his remarks.
However, his fellow employees treated him like a hero for
representing them in front of Jones.

Upon receiving his paycheck on Friday afternoon, Henry was
shocked to find his discharge notice and two weeks of additional
pay in his envelope. Accounting Department employees were
shaken and dismayed. They were convinced that drastic collective action was needed.

During the following week, Jones noticed an unusually high
interaction level among members of the department. On Thurs-
day, he called into his office two of the senior employees and told
them he wanted to know what was going on. They reluctantly
reported that more than 70 percent of the employees had signed
"Authorization Cards" calling for a labor election to be held in
order to unionize.

"Well, what do they hope to accomplish?" Jones exploded.
The answer was short but not sweet: (1) to reinstate Henry, (2) to
establish a formal grievance procedure, and (3) to change the
unfair and arbitrary implementation of the merit rating policy and
the vacation policy. Jones now saw the problems more clearly,
but solutions remained elusive. He felt the clear and present
danger of impending unionization as he searched for practical
decisions, policy, and action that would adequately respond to
employee grievances over personnel practices and satisfy organization requirements at the same time.

Using the Case of *The Indigenous Leader*

This case is a classic example of, at the very least, a failure to
communicate. The company is seen by the employees as being
arbitrary and unpredictable in its application of policies directly
affecting the lives of the staff. The company has further aggravated the situation by discharging the "messenger," who is the
informal group leader. They have reacted with an attempt to
unionize the accounting department, an unusual situation, to
say the least. These people are upset. They do not feel that they
count in the company, and they have decided that they are going
to do something about it.

Discussion Questions

1. How do you think Herschel Jones could have avoided this
   situation?
2. What are some of the alternatives that Mr. Jones has?

3. What do you think about Mr. Henry's position in this situation?
4. If you were Mr. Jones's supervisor, what would be your reaction?
5. If you were Mr. Henry, what would you do? Mr. Jones? The staff of the accounting department?

Exercise IV: *Listening*

Procedure

The instructor should:

1. Instruct the students to write down the numbers 1 through 10 on a sheet of paper.
2. Advise the student that the questions will be read to them twice, and their task is to record an answer to each question on the sheet of paper.
3. Emphasize to the students that they will *not* be allowed to ask for any clarification. Likewise, they may *not* discuss the question or answer with any other student.
4. Read each of the following questions (twice) aloud to the class.

Questions

1. Does England have a fourth of July?
2. Why can't a man living in Winston-Salem, North Carolina, be buried west of the Mississippi River?
3. If you had only one match and entered a room in which there was a kerosene lamp, an oil burner, and a woodburning stove, which would you light first?
4. Some months have 30 days, some have 31; how many have 28?
5. If a doctor gave you three pills and told you to take one every half hour, how long would they last?
6. I have in my hand three U.S. coins totalling 55 cents in value. One is not a nickel. What are the coins?
7. Is it legal in Louisiana for a man to marry his widow's sister?
8. How many two-cent stamps are there in a dozen?
9. How many animals of each species did Moses take aboard the Ark with him?
10. An archaeologist claimed to have discovered some gold coins dated 46 B.C. Do you believe that she did? Why, or why not?

Alternate Question A: An aircraft flying south crashes so that the wreckage is half in the United States and half in Mexico. In which country would you bury the survivors?
Alternate Question B: How many birthdates does the average woman have?
Alternate Question C: A farmer had seventeen sheep. All but nine died. How many did he have left?
Alternate Question D: How far can a dog run into the woods?

When all the questions have been answered, provide the students with the correct answers (found at the end of the Index).

Questions for Discussion

1. Think about the barriers to effective communication. Which, if any, of these barriers affected the communication process in this exercise (perceptual differences, language and meaning, noise, etc.)?
2. How did the medium of communication affect the communication process? Do you think you could have done better if the questions had been presented in written form rather than vocal form?
3. What effect did the time constraint have on your interpretation of the message?

Controlling

Managers must plan, organize, and direct the organization, but how do they know if they are doing a good job? Controlling is the function of management that evaluates their efforts. Is the plan a good one? Is the firm organized to effectively implement the plan? Is the plan being implemented so as to maximize the desired results? What changes need to be made in the plan, or the organization, or the implementation, or any combination thereof to help the firm better achieve its goals?

It is necessary to evaluate the results the firm is getting against some sort of criteria. For most firms, those criteria are often financial, defined in terms of profits. However, criteria can have other forms, as Stanley Seashore demonstrates in his classic article "Criteria of Organizational Effectiveness." Such forms include the contribution the firm is making to society, its customers, its stockholders, and its employees. History is full of effective organizations for whom profitability is not a measure of effectiveness. In fact, the entire not-for-profit sector of the economy refuses to use profitability as a measure of success. Its measures come in other ways, as exemplified by the unqualified success of the March of Dimes in winning the battle against the deadly, crippling disease of polio. The March of Dimes was a success by any standard, but profitability would not be an appropriate criterion for it or other similar ventures. The key is whether or not the organization has achieved its goals, which may or may not include profitability.

When managers talk about control in the modern corporate sense, they really are talking about two different levels of control. The first is the traditional approach to controlling the firm's operation. This control is centered around the flow of information to determine what is going on in the organization, and often information is generated on the shop floor, as may be seen in "Principles for the New or Prospective Front-Line Supervisor." The second form of control deals with the organization as a whole. In this era of hostile takeovers, mergers, and acquisitions, managers are seeking to maintain control of their firms and not lose it to someone else in some new financial arrangement. Shareholders are also awakening to this realization in terms of profitability and other issues with

which management has to deal. Management is discovering that decisions concerning the firm can no longer be made on the basis of a good financial return. Decision makers must consider what is socially and politically acceptable to the stockholders. The move by many firms to leave South Africa was just one manifestation of this new awareness of nonfinancial goals and objectives. With the recent accords between Nelson Mandela and F. W. de Klerk, some firms may decide to return to South Africa in the near future.

But this is not to say that financial control is not important. Financial control is obviously a chief concern of many firms, especially small ones, because it is usually the area where they run into trouble. Financial control is the basis of all the other types of control in the organization, since the people who own it have the final say in what the firm does. Such control makes it possible for management to protect itself from corporate raiders.

Production control is probably the area where the Japanese have made the most strides in recent years. U.S. and European firms have imported many of the ideas and techniques used in Japan over the past 20 years, and the Japanese themselves have set up their own plants in the United States, demonstrating that their techniques are transferable. Many things have happened in the area of production, including the introduction of computers and robots. These are not just developments involving machines, they include standards, policies, and, most especially, people.

Total Quality Management (TQM) is now one of the hottest topics in management. The basic idea is that everyone is responsible for quality, but most especially senior management, as may be seen in "Keys to Starting a TQM Program."

Looking Ahead: Challenge Questions

Managers are constantly evaluating how the organization is doing. What are some of the ways to evaluate organizational performance besides profits?

Industry is concerned with being more efficient and productive. How can this be accomplished?

Unit 5

Criteria of Organizational Effectiveness

Stanley E. Seashore

Summary: Most organizations have many goals, not one. These goals are of unlike importance and their relative importance changes. Problems arise because these goals are sometimes competing (i.e., have trade-off value), and sometimes incompatible (negatively correlated). A strategy of optimal realization of goals cannot be determined unless there exists some conception of the dimensions of performance, their relative importance, and their relationships with one another. These relationships may be one of causation, of simple correlation, of interaction; they may be linear and compensatory or nonlinear and noncompensatory. A framework is proposed for conceptualizing organizational performance, with distinctions among several different classes of performance dimensions and with consideration for several types of relationships among them.

MULTIPLE, CONFLICTING GOALS

The aim of the following discussion is to outline a way of viewing the relationships among the numerous criteria that might be considered in the evaluation of the performance of an organization. To understand such relationships we shall need to make some distinctions between different kinds of criterion measures. We shall need to create some encompassing conceptions that serve to aid the evaluation of performance when some desired measures are not available, or when the number of measures is inconveniently large.

The issues taken up here arise because most organizations have multiple goals rather than a single goal, and goal achievement may not be directly measurable. The formal objectives of the organization may themselves be multiple and, in any case, there are multiple short-run goals and subgoals that need to be examined. The matter would be simple if the various goals were all of similar priority and combinable in some simple additive way; but this is not the situation. The manager making decisions that rest upon multivariate assessments of the performance of his organization has to calculate the weights and the correlation values that he will apply when estimating the net outcome of a course of action.

A typical example would be the case of a manager who wishes his firm to obtain a substantial profit, and at the same time to grow in size, to insure future profit by product improvements, to avoid financial risk, to pay a substantial annual dividend to his investors, to have satisfied employees, and to have his firm respected in the community. He cannot maximize all of these simultaneously, as increasing one (e.g. dividends or risk avoidance) may imply reduced achievement on another (e.g. growth, product research). He must consider their trade-off value, their contingencies, and the presence of negative correlations among them. To

estimate an optimum course of action he has to evaluate the dependability and relevance of the various measures and then estimate the way in which they combine to provide an overall evaluation of performance or a prediction of future change in performance. This task will be easier when we have for his use a theory to describe the performance of organizations. The following suggestions are a step in that direction.

CRITERIA AND THEIR USES

To begin with we need to make some distinctions among different kinds of criteria and their uses.

1. *Ends vs. means.* Some criteria are close to the formal objectives of the organization in the sense that they represent ends or goals that are valued in themselves; others have value mainly or only because they are thought to be necessary means or conditions for achieving the main goals of the organization. Substantial profit, for example, may be a goal sought by a business organization, while employee satisfaction may be valued because it is thought to be an aid in reaching the goal of substantial profit.

2. *Time reference.* Some criterion measures refer to a past time period (profit for the past year), others to current states (net worth), and still others to anticipated future periods (projected growth). Whatever their time reference, all may be used for drawing inferences about past or future conditions or changes.

3. *Long vs. short run.* Some criterion measures refer to a relatively short period of time, others to a longer period; they may refer to performances that are relatively stable (do not change much in the short run) or relatively unstable (erratic or highly variable in the short run). The usefulness of a criterion measure is limited if the period covered is not appropriate to the usual or potential rate of change in the variable.[1]

4. *"Hard" vs. "soft."* Some criteria are measured by the characteristics of, or number or frequency of, physical objects and events, while others are measured by qualitative observation of behavior or by evaluative questions put to people. Dollar measures, for example, or tons of scrap, or number of grievances, are "hard" measures; while employee satisfaction, motivation to work, and cooperation, product quality, customer loyalty, and many others are usually "soft." *The distinction is useful, but it contains a trap,* for we commonly think of the hard variables as being in some way inherently more valid, more reliable, and more relevant to the performance evaluation problem, when this is not necessarily true. Profit rate, for example— a popular hard variable—is a rather vague concept to begin with (accountants dispute about definition and about conventions for measurement) and it is often in the short

Originally from *Michigan Business Review*, July 1965. Published by Graduate School of Business Administration, The University of Michigan.

run unreliable as a performance indicator and thus quite irrelevant to the evaluation problem, even for an organization whose long-run goals include making a profit. Similarly, a soft variable, such as one representing the intentions of key executives to stay with the organization, may be measured with high reliability in some circumstances and may be vital in the assessment of the organization's performance.

5. *Values.* Some variables appear to have a linear value scale (more is always better than less), while others have a curvilinear scale (some optimum is desired; more and less are both to be avoided). The shape of the curves determines in part the trade-off relationships among assessment variables under conditions where simultaneous optimization is not possible. Examples: profit rate is usually linear in value in the sense that more is better than less; maintenance costs, by contrast, are usually curvilinear in value in the sense that either excessively high or low costs may be judged to diminish overall firm performance.

THE HIERARCHY OF CRITERIA

A full accounting for the performance of an organization requires consideration for (1) achievement of the organization's main goals over a long span of time, (2) performance over shorter periods on each of those criteria that represent ends valued in themselves, and which, jointly, as a set, determine the net ultimate performance, and (3) performance on each of a number of subsidiary criteria that provide an immediate or current indication of the progress toward, or probability of achieving, success on end-result variables. The network of criteria of performance can be viewed as a pyramid shaped hierarchy:

1. *At the top* is the "ultimate criterion"—some conception of the net performance of the organization over a long span of time in achieving its formal objectives, whatever they may be, with optimum use of the organization's environmental resources and opportunities. The ultimate criterion is never measured (except possibly by historians); yet some concept of this kind is the basis for evaluation of lesser criteria of performance.

2. *In the middle* are the penultimate criteria. These are shorter run performance factors or dimensions comprised by the ultimate criterion. They are "output" or "results" criteria: things sought for their own value and having trade-off value[2] in relation to each other. Their sum, in some weighted mixture, determines the ultimate criterion. Typical variables of this class for business organizations are: sales volume, productive efficiency, growth rate, profit rate, and the like. There may be included some "soft" (usually behavioral) variables such as employee satisfaction or customer satisfaction. In the case of some nonbusiness organizations these penultimate criteria might be predominantly of the behavioral kind, as in the case of a school whose output is judged in terms of learning rates, proportion of students reaching some standard of personal growth or development, etc.

3. *At the bottom* of the hierarchy of assessment criteria are measures of the current organizational functioning according to some theory or some empirical system concerning the conditions associated with high achievement

on each of the penultimate criteria.[3] These variables include those descriptive of the organization as a system and also those representing subgoals or means associated with penultimate criteria. The number of criteria in this class is very large (over 200 have been used in some studies without sensing that the limits were being approached), and they are interrelated in a complex network that includes causal, interactional, and modifier types of relationships. Included are some criteria that are not valued at all except for their power to reduce the amount of uncontrolled variance in the network. Among the "hard" criteria at this level, for a business organization, might be such as: scrappage, short-run profit, productivity against standards, meeting of production schedules, machine downtime, ratio of overtime to regular time, product return rate, rate of technological innovation, and the like. Among the "soft" criteria at this level may be such as these: employee morale, credit rating, communication effectiveness, absenteeism, turnover, group cohesiveness, customer loyalty, pride in firm, level of performance motivation, and others.

CHARACTERISTICS OF BEHAVIORAL CRITERIA

Such a model locates the behavioral criteria—those descriptive of the members (in this context, customers and clients are also "members") of the organization and of their values, attitudes, relationships, and activities—mainly in the lower regions of the network of assessment criteria, distant and perhaps only indirectly related to the ultimate goals by which the organization is eventually judged.

If behavioral criteria appear near the top of the network, it is because they are valued in themselves and have trade-off value in relation to other priority goals of the organization. In general, however, the hard—nonbehavioral—criteria are the preferred ones for most business organizations for the good reason that they are more relevant to the formal objectives of the organization.

The behavioral measures are presumed to have some stable relationships to the various nonbehavioral measures; these relationships may be causal, interactional, or merely one of covariance. It is further presumed that the criteria and their relationships are not entirely unique to each organization, nor transient, but are to some degree stable and to some extent common to all or many organizations. These presumptions appear to have some partial confirmation from analyses performed so far.[4]

We come now to the question of the role of behavioral criteria in the light of this broader conception of the evaluation of organizational performance. It appears that behavioral criteria are not likely, for most business organizations, to have a prominent place in the roster of penultimate criteria although they may and do appear there. Their chief role will arise from their power to improve the prediction of future changes in the preferred "hard" criteria, i.e., their power to give advance signals of impending problems or opportunities.

A second use that they may commonly have is to complement the available hard criteria in such a way as to give the manager a more balanced and more inclusive informational basis for his decisions in the case where the hard variable measures are incomplete or not reliable for short-run evaluation.[5]

In some rare instances, the behavioral criteria have to be used exclusively instead of the preferred hard criteria of organizational performance for the reason that measurements of hard criteria are not available at all or not at reasonable cost.

There are three basic strategies that may be applied in formulating a unique version of this general scheme that may be appropriate for a particular organization.

1. There exist several partially developed general theories concerning the survival requirements of organizations. These assumed requirements may be defined in performance terms and posited as the roster of penultimate criteria or organizational goals. From this starting point, a set of subsidiary goals and performance criteria may be constructed on empirical grounds, on theoretical grounds, or on some combination of the two.

2. The existing personal values of the owners of a firm, or of the managers as representatives, may be pooled to form an agreed upon roster of penultimate criteria together with their corresponding performance indicators, and from this starting point the set of subsidiary goals and performance criteria can be constructed.

3. Comparative empirical study can be made of the performance characteristics of a set of organizations assumed to share the same ultimate criterion but clearly differing in their overall success as judged by competent observers (for example, such a study might be made of a set of insurance sales agencies, some clearly prospering and others clearly headed for business failure). Using factorial analysis methods and actual performance data to identify the sets of lower-order performance criteria, and using trend and correlational analyses to detect the relationships among these sets of criteria over time, one can, in principle, draw conclusions about the penultimate components of performance that bear upon organizational survival or failure in that particular line of business.

ALTERNATIVE THEORETICAL APPROACHES

These three approaches can and do produce strikingly different systems for describing the network of criteria to be used in evaluating organizational performance. One of the general theories, for example, proposes that there are nine basic requirements to be met, or problems to be continuously solved, for an organization to achieve its long run goals; these include such requirements as adequate input of resources, adequate normative integration, adequate means of moderation of organizational strain, adequate coordination among parts of the organization, etc. Theories of this kind are produced mainly by general organizational sociologists and stem from the view that an organization is a living system with intrinsic goals and requirements that may be unlike those of individual members. By contrast, the second mentioned approach stems from the personal values of managers. The resulting networks of criteria are different.[6]

A start has been made at the Institute for Social Research in exploring such alternative strategies. With respect to the first approach, two theoretical models have been tested against empirical data from a set of organizations in a service industry, using executive judgments of unit overall effectiveness as the ultimate criterion. Both models proved to be about equally valid, but of limited utility in explaining variance on the ultimate criterion: each "accounted for" about half of the ultimate criterion variance, with the unexplained portion arising from measurement errors and/or faulty theory. An attempt to apply the wholly empirical approach to the same set of data proved to be a failure in the sense that it was no more powerful in explaining variance on the ultimate criterion than were the simpler, theory based models, and furthermore the resulting roster of performance dimensions was not very satisfactory in common-sense terms.

A third effort is now in progress, using objective data about the performance of a set of insurance sales agencies over a span of twelve years; the early results look very promising on first examination. It appears that there will be identified a roster of about ten penultimate criteria of agency performance, each independent of the others and of varying weight in relation to ultimate performance, and each associated with a roster of subsidiary criteria of kinds that lend themselves to ready measurement and statistical combination. It remains to be seen whether these criteria are unique to this particular line of business, or have some applicability to other kinds of organizations.

NOTES AND REFERENCES

1. Many firms' current operating and financial statistics, although appropriate for control and accounting purposes, prove to be of little value for performance evaluation for the reason that they are short-period measures of unstable performances. Monthly plant maintenance costs, for example, may be extremely variable (perhaps seasonal) and may be useful as a performance criterion measure only when applied to longer periods of time. In the short run, apart from other considerations, low maintenance costs may or may not be a favorable indicator.

2. By trade-off value we mean only that an amount of one kind of performance may be substituted for an amount of another; for example, an increase in sales volume may be judged to offset a decline in profit rate per sales unit.

3. One large U.S. firm has published what appears to be a carefully considered formulation of its own roster of assessment criteria at this penultimate level. It includes one behavioral category, "employee attitudes," which is further defined in operational terms in a manner compatible with the system outlined here.

4. See "Applying Modern Management Principles to Sales Organizations," Foundation for Research on Human Behavior seminar report, 1963, for an illustration of the similarity across three sales organizations in the relevance of behavioral measures to hard penultimate criteria of organizational performance. Also, "Models of Organization Performance," an unpublished manuscript by Basil Georgopoulos, Stanley Seashore, and Bernard Indik; and "Relationships Among Criteria of Job Performance," by Stanley Seashore, Bernard Indik, and Basil Georgopoulos, *Journal of Applied Psychology*, 44 (1960), pp. 195-202.

5. As an example, a decision to raise prices is likely to rest not only upon estimates of hard performances, past and future, but also upon estimates of political and economic climate, of customer loyalty, of the feasibility of alternatives such as employee collaboration in cost reduction, etc.

6. To illustrate, take the criterion of profit: in one case, profit is likely to be treated as one of a few penultimate criteria (ends valued in their own right), while in the other case profit is relegated to a subsidiary role as one of several alternative means for insuring adequate input of resources. If this seems implausible, note that some organizations— government, educational, and religious organizations, for example— have survived and prospered without profit from their own activities.

Principles for the new or prospective front-line supervisor

Gary Bielous

Gary Beilous is a college graduate who's been associated in a supervisory capacity since 1974 with How-medica, Rutherford, N.J., an orthopedic manufacturer. He has been awarded the title "Certified Manager" from the Institute of Certified Professional Managers, Harrisonburg, VA., and has written several freelance articles.

Upon promotion to an assistant front-line supervisor, I was fortunate to work for a veteran supervisor who took me "under his wing" by explaining and demonstrating how to effectively supervise employees. This 25-year veteran defined the word effectively as "being able to consistently meet the company's goals for growth, through people." In order to supervise effectively, he believed front-line supervisors needed a set of principles. Not surprisingly, such principles assisted the supervisor in "leading by example".

He showed me that fundamental managerial concepts (planning, organizing, directing, coordinating and controlling) are *not enough* in creating a positive business environment. He believed creating and maintaining this type of environment kept the employees' attention focused on quality productivity, instead of non-productive matters (bickering, infighting, laziness and even sabotage). Once a foundation of working principles are in place, only then will those fundamental managerial concepts become truly effective. Therefore, using certain principles can enhance your work environment resulting in increased productivity. Based on what I was taught, by that veteran supervisor, whom I will respectfully refer to as "my mentor," and from what I've observed and used, I would like to share with you (5) principles that I believe will help make new or prospective supervisors effective.

As supervisor, the length of your own workday, how and what you've accomplished reflects commitment towards the company and its employees. By observing my mentor in action, I was able to choose this effective behavior pattern, which seemed advantageous towards production.

I remember him readying the employees daily tasks before they were in, then frequently, during the day, checking on the progress of those assignments (follow-up), asking job related questions and always making small talk. He would leave to go home, only after the last employee left. His actions and accomplishments helped to keep the department focused on quality productivity.

Although close to retirement, he consistently performed his duties needed in a supervisory position spurring productivity. He believed in a fair days' work for a fair days' pay from everyone, especially the supervisors. And if that was accomplished, then we did our job.

I saw the departments' employees produce for him and I wanted the same behavior. So I've made this principle first because when the supervisor shows a serious commitment towards departmental goals, the employees will reciprocate. That is good business! I've seen it happen and I've experienced it, also. It's a good feeling. Yes, it's that contagious!

(2) Control

Earlier, I mentioned how my mentor would come in early and prepare the employees daily work. Well there was a method to his madness, in performing this extra work, for he wanted to have control over what was worked on, as well as know if someone was working below standard. As time

From *Supervision,* January 1993, pp. 3-5. © 1993 by The National Research Bureau, P.O. Box 1, Burlington, IA 52601-0001. Reprinted by permission.

went on, he delegated that part of his routine to me.

During one of his vacation weeks, I continued this work distribution method, which went off without a hitch. About the fourth day, one employee suggested that I allow them to pick their own work, as a break from the routine. He had convinced me that everyone knew what to do and everything would be done, so I accepted the idea.

The following morning, as each employee entered the department, they took the work off the incoming shelf and commenced their operations. Then during the day, as things seemed to be going smoothly, I received a phone call from my mentors' boss. He asked if a particular job would be shipped out that day? Since I hadn't given out the work, I told him I would call him back. Upon checking, I found out that it was *still* sitting on the shelf, so I called him and gave the status of that job. The tone of his voice indicated he was displeased and disappointed. He issued me a directive: "Work the overtime, but get it out by tomorrow" (Saturday).

After hanging up the phone, I felt terrible, since we normally never need to work on a Saturday. But I felt worse when I went back to the shelf and noticed a bright red "rush" sticker on the box of that particular job. I turned and asked the nearby employees why no one had worked on this job, especially since it was tagged? There was only silence. When I asked that employee, the one who suggested that I try a different work distribution

---

> ## "Remember, as supervisors, we are on stage. Why do you think we are called front-line supervisors?"

method, why it hadn't been worked on, he just replied, "I'm not the only one working here!" It was then I realized the importance of this principle. I didn't have control. In effective supervision, you must maintain control. Now you needn't copy this style, but you must recognize the importance of being in control, which means working on or producing the right item, in an acceptable time period. Remember, by losing control, you place yourself in a vulnerable position with your superiors as I did. They can easily take away responsibility, feeling that you can't handle it. I was lucky, you may not be. Recognize, adopt and employ this principle.

(3) Listening

Empathetic listening should be the objective of every front-line supervisor and that means to *listen with understanding*. The only way to improve one's listening skill is to pay attention to what the speaker is saying and give feedback for clarity.

In other words, put everything aside and give that speaker your undivided attention! This isn't as easy as it sounds, considering you could be very busy. Unless you make time to pay attention first, your apt to only "hear" the words. Consequently, someone said something and you heard something else.

Years ago, I made an error on an employee timecard by omitting a vacation change that he had requested. It seems during a busy day, he came and asked me to move his vacation time up and I didn't give him the full attention he deserved. So, of course, a mistake occurred, bringing Murphy's Law into play: "Whatever can happen, will happen!"

By making the time to pay attention to the speaker, understanding the message sent, giving feedback for clarity and then taking appropriate action, you'll be on the road to fulfilling your objective as an empathetic listener. Try it!

This is defined as having integrity, being genuine and straightforward. Being anything but honest, in the presence of the department's employees will stifle any chance to gain and maintain productivity. This is what business is all about! Unless you're honest with people, you will be a marked man. This principle can be referred to as the cornerstone in supervision.

In the previous principle, I mentioned an error I made on an employee's timecard regarding his vacation, by not listening. Well, after I had found out it was my error, I was determined not to admit my mistake. I asked this employee if he would change his vacation? But when that failed, I convinced him to accept the check when he returned. All along, never being just plain honest (admitting the error and making an all out effort to correct it). Later, when it was quitting time and all the employees had left, my mentor asked me what I'd done to correct that employee's vacation? I proudly replied what I'd done and that's when his facial expression turned sour. Then, he explained how much more of a problem I'd made, by attempting to deceive someone. After his lecture, I felt bad, especially when he suggested that I meet with the employee the following day to "tell it like it happened!"

Fortunately everything turned out all right. I learned a valuable lesson that should be heeded by all new or prospective supervisors. By not being honest, I'd caused that employee to focus (concentrate) on this problem, instead of what he gets paid to do: produce. Can you imagine the rippling effect this may have caused through out the department, if it was found that I tried to deceive someone? Again, I was lucky, thanks to my mentor. You may not be. Remember, honesty is the ingredient necessary for that positive business environment.

All your department's employees will watch and see how you use this principle when the time comes. If you overlook it, you will create a problem. I learned this by observing the actions of another supervisor.

It seems he decided to cross-train a backup machine operator and asked one of his department's employees if they would be interested? Naturally, they accepted, especially when informed that every time they performed this job more pay would be received. It wasn't long before the other employees began to complain to that supervisor about being overlooked. Apparently, the supervisor's pick, although qualified, was a relatively new employee, which upset the department. They felt their seniority was ignored. Now a plan, which benefited production, had created a departmental problem, because this principle was not considered, *before* implementing the plan. Now the focus (concentration) of the employees was on the "unfairness" of the supervisor, rather than on production.

As with being honest, this principle seems to go hand in hand to maintain our positive business environment. This supervisor's only mistake was an oversight on seniority and how those employees might react. It caused him a problem, don't let it happen to you. When your planning involves the employees, don't neglect this principle.

There you have it: commitment, control, listening, honesty and fairness. Those are the (5) principles that helped me into an effective supervisor and they can help you, also. However, you must first believe in them, then make them part of your professional behavior pattern. Trust me, by using these principles, you can experience better working relations which will mean increased productivity. I know because I've seen them used (by my mentor) and experienced it (15 years in supervision)! Remember, as supervisors, we are on stage. Why do think we are called front-line supervisors? Our actions are being watched and questioned, by both the employees, as well as our superiors. This can mean the difference between increased productivity and pure laziness, by our subordinates. It's a rough road and we need all the help we can get.

THE TRICK TO MANAGING CASH? BE CREATIVE

Managing cash may sound like a mundane task, but if you do it well you can transform your cash management function into a corporate profit center.

ALEXANDER M. ANDERSON

Mr. Anderson is executive vice president of Wells Fargo Bank, Asset Management Division, in Los Angeles.

VERY FEW OF THE responsibilities you face as a financial executive are more important than corporate cash management. You must ensure that sufficient cash is available to fund all corporate requirements, ranging from working capital to acquisitions, equity buy-backs and loan repayments.

Because of the overriding importance of funding such corporate cash needs, most companies don't think of liquidity management as a profit center. But, if you can predict your spending projections reasonably accurately, you can invest cash that you don't need immediately and contribute to your bottom line.

First, examine whether you should revise your liquidity management strategies to take full advantage of today's low interest-rate environment and current market opportunities. An investment strategy predicated on Treasury bills and money-market funds may have produced high yields in the 1980s, but with current yields on these issues now so low, you may find it pays to be more creative.

THE INVESTMENT POLICY ROADBLOCK

Are your investment policies out of date? Most companies' policies are focused on minimizing risk, sometimes allowing investments in only the most conservative of money-market vehicles. If your policies are similar, you may be hindering your cash returns.

For example, some policies contain unnecessarily restrictive average maturity provisions. If you expect your firm's cash reserves to remain on the balance sheet for a period of time you can reasonably anticipate, your investment policy should be broad enough to match the maturity of investments to the date you expect to need the cash. This is especially important in today's environment, given the steep condition of the yield curve.

To illustrate, one company that hadn't reviewed its investment policy in over a decade maintained a 90-day average maturity policy restriction on a large pool of funds targeted for a facility expansion three years away. By extending the investment horizon out to match the three-year cash requirement, the firm generated incremental yield exceeding 150 basis points. Of course, enhancing returns is not always as simple as extending maturities, but this example points out how important it is that you periodically review your corporate investment policy in light of your funding needs and market conditions.

On the other hand, corporate investment policies should always remain tight enough to protect against the opposite extreme. Searching for higher yields, some financial executives have been lured by derivative securities, exotic tranches of CMOs, preferred stock or CDs of weak thrifts. Such investments typically sacrifice liquidity and safety, while offering little or no extra return.

Take, for example, that breed of collateralized mortgage obligation known as "inverse floaters." Issued by a federal agency with a short average maturity and typically a very high yield, it certainly sounds safe enough. However, nothing could be further from the truth! Inverse floaters are unusual instruments because their interest coupons float in the opposite direction of interest rates in general. They're risky because they're frequently leveraged, meaning that for every half point change in interest rates, the coupon on the inverse floater could change by a factor of two, three or even four times. Granted, if rates drop, the potential reward from these instruments is significant, but what if rates rise? A 5-percent coupon could quickly turn into a 3- or 2-percent coupon, along with a drop in principal value of as much as 20 percent to 30 percent.

THE VALUE COMPONENT

The toughest challenge for financial executives managing corporate cash is to purchase issues offering the greatest underlying value. J.P. Morgan and Citicorp, both huge banks, are rated AAA and BBB, respectively, thus standing at opposite ends of the investment-grade quality spectrum. You might decide that, based on their sizes and ratings, both are suitable investment candidates. However, if you use value as the yardstick, you might ask: Does the incremental yield offered by Citicorp

for the difference in quality? If the spread between the two debt issues is wide enough, selecting Citicorp might be appropriate. Otherwise, Morgan should be your choice.

> **Financial executives managing corporate cash can take advantage of seasonal factors in the money markets.**

While value is a criterion you should apply to all of your investment selections, remember it's not a constant. For example, government agency securities have been a good way to add yield to a portfolio in the past, but the incremental yield offered by agency securities versus Treasuries is low right now—10 basis points or less in most instances. In fact, some seasoned Treasuries occasionally provide higher yields than comparable-maturity agency issues. Under these circumstances, you should avoid agency securities since they offer little, or even negative, incremental value.

Traditional staples of the money markets include certificates of deposit and bankers acceptances. But, with lower-cost funding alternatives now available to banks, CDs and BAs are scarce, sometimes causing yields to be uncompetitive. The commercial paper market and many newer segments, like asset-backed issues, have taken the place of much bank issuance. Getting your approved list stretched to permit these newer issues can add significant value.

Certain classes of investors are legally restrained in the type, maturity and quality of securities they may own. This results in buying patterns that often drive down the yield on securities they're eligible to hold. For example, money-market mutual funds can buy only issues maturing within

one year. If your investment policies are flexible enough to allow you to buy 15-month maturities, then you aren't competing with money-market funds — and often can capture meaningful yield increases.

Financial executives managing corporate cash can also take advantage of seasonal factors in the money markets. For example, tax-exempt purchasers can usually buy more advantageously during June and July, a time of elevated supply stemming from large seasonal issuance of short-term tax and revenue anticipation notes. To a lesser degree, mid-April presents a good buying opportunity as investors liquidate short-term municipal holdings to settle tax obligations.

HOW ABOUT FLOATERS?

If your company has limited its liquidity management selections to fixed-rate income issues, you might want to consider floating-rate securities. However, you need to evaluate floaters from an appropriate maturity perspective. Many companies overlook floaters because most are issued with relatively long financial maturities. But a floater with a stated five-year maturity and an accompanying quarterly reset has price volatility characteristics more like a three- or six-month instrument than a five-year bond. As such, you should consider it a short-term, not long-term, security.

Currently, yields on floating-rate issues with quarterly or semiannual resets are 50 to 70 basis points above money-market levels, a handsome payoff indeed. Interestingly, the yield variance between a quarterly resetting floater and a 90-day money-market instrument is not so much due to greater risk but to market inefficiency caused by a smaller universe of informed buyers.

Both government agencies and the private sector have issued floaters. Most corporate issues carry an A or better rating and usually have spreads of at least 25 to 40 basis points above government paper. Government agency floaters with a 90-day reset are generally priced at the three-month Treasury bill rate plus 30 basis points, or at three-month LIBOR plus 15 basis points.

Despite their attraction, floaters aren't risk free. For instance, you should always scrutinize their interest-rate reset features in particular. There are a variety of interest-rate reset methods, with some floaters having rate ceilings or floors. Returns can be dramatically affected by these factors, should interest rates change suddenly or dramatically. So gain a thorough understanding of rate reset features before you purchase.

IF YOU HAVE TO GO OUTSIDE

If you decide to delegate responsibility for your cash management to an outside manager, here are some tips for establishing a good working relationship:

✦ Use referrals to uncover a few solid candidates. Request that each potential manager provide information about the firm's commitment to the business, its service standards and investment performance track record. Evaluate the performance of each candidate over an entire interest-rate cycle. Look for consistency in return as well as the absolute level of return.
✦ Make an effort to understand and to judge the risks that were assumed to achieve the returns. Make certain you're comfortable with the manager's investment philosophy and that it's compatible with your company's business philosophy. Also, ask how the advisor has done with accounts oper-

ating under investment constraints similar to yours. Then compare these returns with your in-house experience.
✦ Don't base your selection on historic investment returns only. Service ability is also vital. If your company needs earnings and valuation reports on a monthly or quarterly basis for financial statement purposes, make certain the advisor can issue reports that conform with your accounting standards in the time frame you require.

These reports should include descriptions of each holding, the current yield and market value, accrued earnings for the period, cash earnings for the period, and so forth. If your fiscal periods end at odd times, be

ty. There must be no self-dealing. In a properly structured custodial account, your assets will be protected from fraud, embezzlement and theft. The custodian shouldn't be able to encumber the funds in any way. Bank money managers often provide custodianship at no charge, while an extra fee is sometimes involved with investment advisors.

One way to test an investment advisor is to turn over a portion of your cash reserves and observe the service and performance. If you're satisfied after six months or a year, increase the manager's share. Many corporations decide to keep very short-term, low-risk securities under

---

A floater with a stated five-year maturity and an accompanying quarterly reset has price volatility characteristics more like a three- or six-month instrument than a five-year bond.

---

sure this too can be accommodated.

Equally important, be sure the portfolio manager is committed to communicating regularly and is accessible when needed to explain strategies and to review your company's cash management needs.
✦ Whether your outside advisor or a third party holds your assets, you must be assured of impartiality, loyalty, competence and confidentiali-

in-house management, while engaging an outside professional to handle more complicated or longer-maturity strategies.
✦ Finally, remember that a competent investment manager typically charges a fee equal to 20 to 50 basis points annually. Continually monitor whether the investment decisions the manager makes for you justifies the cost.

Competing with Crayolas®: Manufacturing as a Competitive Weapon at Binney & Smith

Joseph M. Roberts and Daniel W. Tretter

In today's competitive climate, even the most successful firms have to look for new and better ways to meet their goals. At Binney & Smith, the journey to improvement began with some careful self-assessment and it continues with a clear business objective—profitable revenue growth through continuous improvement by involvement of all employees.

Joseph M. Roberts is the director of customer service at Binney & Smith, Inc., manufacturer of Crayola® crayons. He is responsible for order processing, distribution, transportation, production planning, and operations and systems planning. He became a certified Jonah of the Goldratt Institute in January 1990. Daniel W. Tretter, CPIM, is the operations and systems planning manager at Binney & Smith, Inc. He led the implementation of Binney & Smith's High Velocity Manufacturing program and is currently the project manager responsible for upgrading the customer service and manufacturing computer systems. He became a Jonah in October 1989.

It was late in 1988 when Binney & Smith heard the wake-up call. A major retailer had consented to meet with company representatives to discuss partnership and future directions. A vice president and general manager, a sales director, a national accounts manager, and the director of customer service represented Binney & Smith and the Crayola® brand. The customer was represented by two buyers, a distribution manager, and the buyers' boss. We began to talk about the programs and products that would allow us to grow the business together as partners when, suddenly, the buyers' boss interrupted. He looked straight at me (the director of customer service) and said, "I want my orders shipped in three days. Can you do that? But before you answer, I want you to know that I will then want them shipped in two days, and then one. After that I will want to call you in the morning and have them delivered the same afternoon. What do you say?" My general manager remained silent; for the first time ever, my sales director was speechless; the national accounts manager and everyone else looked at me to answer the question. I glanced around the room for help, but there was none. I thought of a hundred different ways to answer this question and was weighing the merits of each possible answer at lightning speed the way a chess computer must examine all possible moves before picking the right one. Suddenly, I heard myself saying, "Assuming your credit is okay . . . ." The laughter that followed was a relief to us all. I think the expression on my face and the pathetic tone of my voice made it clear that I had received the message. And so we were allowed to continue the meeting but nothing that followed had the impact of that series of questions from the buyers' boss.

At that time, Binney & Smith was investigating and investing in such programs as employee involvement, just-in-time, and total quality management. There was no consensus regarding the effectiveness of any of them and there was certainly no sense of urgency for a company with our history to change. Evolution, not revolution, was our preferred pace. But, after the aforementioned meeting, we developed a sense of urgency and began spreading the word that doing things the same old way just would not be good enough anymore and would never allow us to achieve projected revenue and profit growth goals. Worse yet, we could lose what we had if we did not recognize and meet the changing and increasing demands of our customers. But what was the program or process that would make all this possible?

THE ANSWER: HIGH VELOCITY MANUFACTURING

Having been given the challenge to improve responsiveness and speed of delivery to our customers, we began to look internally at what we could do to reduce lead times, increase flexibility, and improve customer service. Since manufacturing capability was greater than that of our overall sales, theoretically the company should have been able to ship 100 percent on time, as requested by our customer. What got in the way was the lead time that it took to get something through the production pipeline, our responsiveness, and our ability to change schedules. What stopped us from being responsive? What stopped us from being able to change over quickly?

During the 1980s, new manufacturing philosophies were developed. After taking a close look at these philosophies, the direction that Binney & Smith headed in was not to replace one set of rules with another set of rules; instead, the company decided to develop a manufacturing philosophy that would allow people to use their intuition and do those things that made sense. This concept became the basis for our program for improvement—High Velocity Manufacturing (HVM)—which pulled together four manufacturing techniques: just-in-time (JIT), total quality management (TQM), theory of constraints (TOC), and employee involvement (EI) (see **Figure 1**). Are these four different philosophies or one? According to Eliyahu Goldratt in *The Haystack Syndrome* these become one thing—a new management philosophy. JIT is more than reducing inventories or kanbans, and TQM is more than just the quality of the product or statistical control. Theory of constraints is more than focusing solely on bottlenecks, and EI is more than just empowerment of people. Once we understand these philosophies, we come to understand that we are not looking at four philosophies; we are looking at one.

We pulled the techniques we needed out of each of these philosophies to be able to squeeze the most out of them. The theory of constraints was used basically as a spearhead to break the rules—not only the old rules, but some of the rules of JIT and TQM. Theory of constraints was used to teach us to do the right thing, to use our intuition to make the proper decisions, and to use the basic Socratic implementation technique.

But before individuals can pull ideas and techniques from the four different blocks of HVM, they need to understand the concepts. To accomplish this, extensive training was given throughout the company. Over three hundred individuals were trained in JIT, TQM, and TOC. Next, implementation teams were formed in each manufacturing area to create the new system. The teams consisted of management from manufacturing, accounting, engineering, management information systems, production

> ...High Velocity Manufacturing (HVM)...pulled together four manufacturing techniques: just-in-time (JIT), total quality management (TQM), theory of constraints (TOC), and employee involvement (EI)...

planning, plant materials planning, and human resources. The teams also included representatives from the manufacturing work force.

These teams met to create a vision of the future and talk about how the operation should run. To help the group create its vision, a number of questions were asked in each area:

- How do we schedule?
- How is the bill of material structured?
- How much work in process (WIP) do we hold?
- How do we size lots?
- How do we know what to manufacture?
- How do we route?
- How do we lay out equipment?
- How do we schedule work crews?
- How do we order raw materials?
- How do we cost?

In discussing these questions, the teams created a detailed vision of how these issues should be tackled in the future. Then they analyzed the present situation and asked what steps needed to be taken to get to their vision of the future. Whenever a team member would characterize a particular goal as impossible, the team would earmark that as an obstacle

Figure 1: Binney & Smith's High Velocity Manufacturing

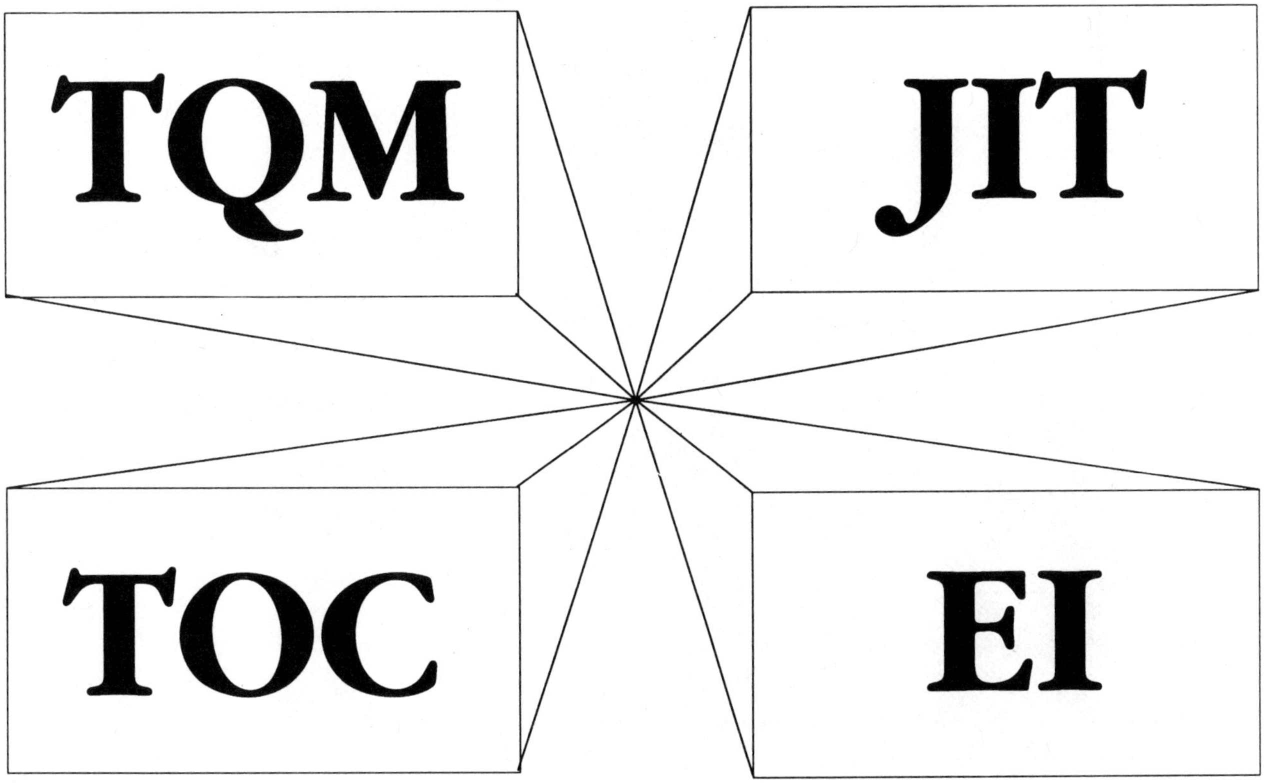

to be overcome. The group leader maintained a list of "impossibilities" so the team could go back over time and see what had been achieved.

When someone in a group says, "That's impossible, we can't do this!" the group tends to stop thinking. The members say to themselves, "I can't do it! I won't try!" But the better way to approach such situations is to say, "There's the vision, here's the obstacle. Let's figure out a way to do it. Let's find the root cause of why we can't do it. Then overcome the root problem." This is the type of breakthrough thinking used in Binney & Smith's manufacturing area.

THERE ARE RESULTS—AND THEN THERE ARE RESULTS

Within 90 to 120 days of forming its teams manufacturing realized impressive reductions in setup time, cycle time, run size, and work-in-process inventory (see **Figure 2**). With these results under its belt, the company exported its new technique to its Canadian plant and to its operations in the United Kingdom.

These results were wonderful. They illustrated that we could break the rules and get things done very quickly. The alarming and inevitable question that soon followed was, "What's next?" We had started a process

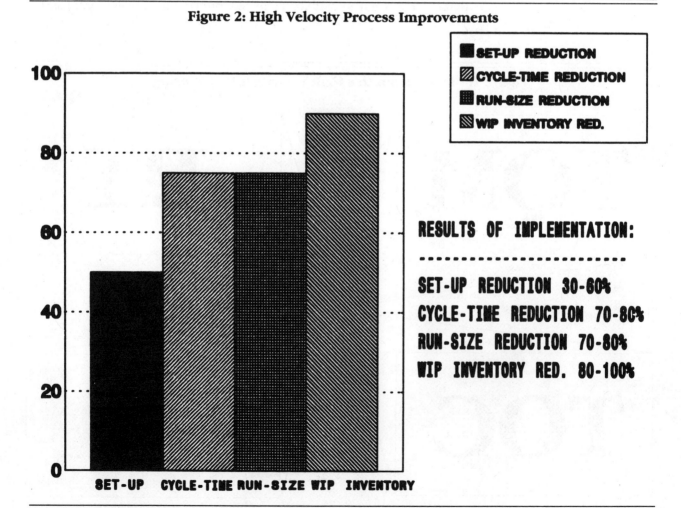

Figure 2: High Velocity Process Improvements

SET-UP REDUCTION
CYCLE-TIME REDUCTION
RUN-SIZE REDUCTION
WIP INVENTORY RED.

RESULTS OF IMPLEMENTATION:
....
SET-UP REDUCTION 30-60%
CYCLE-TIME REDUCTION 70-80%
RUN-SIZE REDUCTION 70-80%
WIP INVENTORY RED. 80-100%

SET-UP   CYCLE-TIME   RUN-SIZE   WIP   INVENTORY

and we had defined High Velocity Manufacturing as "a process of ongoing improvement that is employee-oriented and customer-focused." But to what purpose? What is improvement and what is the process?

One night after dinner with Eliyahu Goldratt we were asked to tell him of the wonderful accomplishments of our High Velocity Manufacturing process. He brushed them off as some "nice little things" and left no doubt that he was not impressed. The more we thought about it, the more upset we got. Didn't he know how hard it is to make change happen? Look at the increased productivity and reduction in space. Look at the faces of the employees who were empowered to think and make improvements. What did he mean by "nice little things"?

The next day, Goldratt gave a one-day seminar on the theory of constraints, in which he explained the different paths that improvement could take (see **Figure 3**). The "G" line (which was green) represented improvement that was quick and impressive. The "R" line (which was red) represented the results of a process of ongoing improvement. He said that it was extremely difficult to move from one line to the other and that if you tried to play both sides of the track, disaster was sure to follow.

We began reexamining our efforts in terms of our goal. Company leadership made it very easy for us, as the corporate goal had been defined as "profitable revenue growth." This is a concise and easy-to-understand goal that, from the top of the organization, is clearly measurable. However, when we look down into the layers and departments of the company, the results of specific actions and their effects on the goal of profitable revenue

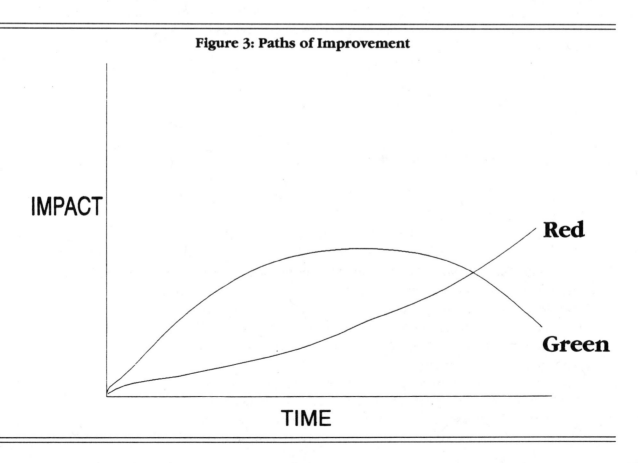

Figure 3: Paths of Improvement

growth was not only hard to define, it was not even considered. Although our company was very successful, there were things called improvements that did nothing to enhance profitable revenue growth, whereas some so-called improvements actually inhibited profitable revenue growth.

What was keeping us from making more money? What was our constraint? It wasn't the rate at which we could make our products. It wasn't the space needed to manufacture and store our products. It wasn't the amount of work in process we did or did not have. And it was not a lack of manufacturing capacity. Our constraint was not in operations; our constraint was the market. We did not sell all that we could make. The improvements that were accomplished were, indeed, very nice, but they only marginally affected our ability to increase throughput. We had to stop the alphabet soup of internally focused programs and move to a process that was focused on real, continuous improvement. Now the questions to address became:

1. What to change?
2. What to change to?
3. How to change?

These three questions are the basic foundation for the first steps of change. They define the change that is needed, how to accomplish it, and the expected outcome. Another question to ask is, "What is the purpose of moving in this direction?" Most companies today have embraced the idea of a process of ongoing improvement. This exists not only in manufacturing companies, but also in all realms of enterprise, as well as in government. What is the process of ongoing improvement? Let us break apart the words.

- What is ongoing?
- What is the process?
- What is improvement?

Improvement can be defined only in relationship to a goal. An improvement moves you toward, or gets more of, the goal.

DEFINING THE PROCESS OF ONGOING IMPROVEMENT

Improvement can be defined only in relationship to a goal. An improvement moves you toward, or gets more of, the goal. If the goal of an organization is to make more money now and in the future, then improvements will be measured relative to making more money. Reducing inventory, for example, is a nice little improvement by itself. It becomes much more important, however, when seen as it relates to the ability to make more money. Having measurements that identify progress toward the goal became such an important issue for Binney & Smith that the company changed its entire cost accounting system. Because the firm needed an accounting system that reflected its common-sense measurements and intuitive understanding of improvements, it went to an activity-based costing system. This new accounting system still has the major flaw in logic of trying to allocate unrelated and fixed costs to unrelated products. But at least we no longer use direct labor as the driver for these allocations. Instead, we absorb on the basis of production drivers that, in turn, are defined by constraints. This method of product costing still gets in the way more than it helps, but it has given the company considerably more freedom than the standard cost system based on direct labor.

Now, what is *ongoing* improvement? Some call it continuous improvement. What is this concept? Figure 3 illustrates continuous improvement as the "R" line. This is a very powerful idea with very powerful implications. For example, suppose we focus on inventory and start the journey of continuous improvement. Have we not set an endpoint for the journey? When there is no inventory, the journey is over. Outrageous decisions can be made when inventory reduction is the top priority in an operation. When an organization truly reaches zero inventory, it is considered out of business. So if we want a continuous improvement process, what should the focus be?

Sometimes we think the only improvements are those that improve cash. If we focus on cost as the number-one priority for our journey, we have once again defined a limited program—not an ongoing process. The end of this journey of cost savings or cost reduction ends when it's your salary or mine that gets reduced. A company that defines improvement primarily as cost savings is bound for disaster. Such a company will have departments fighting with other departments and managers fighting with other managers. Distrust and lack of security will be the corporate culture. The accounting department, which reduces costs by eliminating copies of reports, will be praised as a leader in the journey toward continuous improvement. But the salesperson who now has to spend time on the telephone getting information contained in that report will be spending less time with customers. Sales will then be reduced by a greater amount than the difference between the costs of producing and mailing a copy of the report and the cost of the telephone call. Operational improvements will not count until the reduction in head count is offered up for every productivity gain. The journey that focuses on cost reduction as the number-one priority will end more abruptly and more certainly than the one that focuses on inventory.

The only element that can be the primary focus for the process of ongoing improvement is throughput. Throughput is defined as all the money the system generates through sales. It does not include inventory profits. It does not include the portion of revenue that represents someone else's throughput, such as the cost of raw materials. With this definition of throughput, we can define profitability as

$NP = T - OE$ (net profit equals throughput minus operating expense).

There is no limit to how high throughput can be. By defining throughput as the primary focus for the process of ongoing improvement, we have not set the end of the journey. Of all the elements—cost, inventory, and throughput—only one is not constrained by an absolute limit. Costs can be reduced to zero, but then there is no business. Inventory can be reduced to zero with the sale of the company but then there is no business. Throughput can be increased infinitely and is the only candidate for continuous improvement.

Finally, what is the process? In his theory of constraints, Goldratt breaks the process into the following steps:

> **A company that defines improvement primarily as cost savings is bound for disaster.**

1. Identify the constraint.
2. Decide how to exploit the constraint.
3. Subordinate everything to the decision made in step 2.
4. Elevate the constraint.
5. Go back to step 1.

With a goal of profitable revenue growth, Binney & Smith began its search for the system's constraint. What was preventing us from increasing throughput? It wasn't a lack of machine capacity. It wasn't poor productivity. It wasn't unreliable suppliers with questionable quality. In fact, it wasn't a physical constraint at all. Our primary constraint was the market and the internal policies and measurements that limited our ability to compete. We had to direct our High Velocity Manufacturing techniques to the rest of the company. We began High Velocity Systems, High Velocity Management, and High Velocity everything else. The key is that the process and techniques we employ are focused on the constraints. For us, that meant that our entire company, and everyone in it, had to learn to focus on the customer. From planning to cost accounting, we had to break down the barriers of policy and inappropriate measurements and focus on the customer. We had to develop more flexible product offerings giving our customers more choices. We had to develop planning techniques to ensure that service levels would exceed those of our competitors. We had to develop flexible product display systems and began manufacturing in a "building block" concept to reduce dependence on the accuracy of sales forecasts.

> **...our entire company, and everyone in it, had to learn to focus on the customer.**

CUSTOMER FOCUS BREEDS SUCCESS

Focusing on the customer is our way of exploiting the constraint. We try to give customers every reason to buy our products. Our service must be the best and so must our quality, not for their own sake, but because that is the way to exploit the constraint. We subordinate everything else to the above decision. If we have to change computer systems, accounting systems, distribution systems, compensation systems, or any other internal system to focus on the customer's needs, then we are committed to do it.

Focusing on the customer has been the key to Binney & Smith's success for the last two years. The results have been double-digit growth during a very difficult business cycle. The real point, however, is that focus on the customer is still not an end in itself. Focus on the customer is our method of exploiting a constraint. Focusing on the customer is a step in our process of ongoing improvement. The first step was knowing the goal.

ADDITIONAL RESOURCES

Goldratt, Eliyahu M., *The Haystack Syndrome: Sifting Information Out of the Data Ocean*. Croton-on-Hudson, NY: North River Press, 1991.

Goldratt, Eliyahu M., and Jeff Cox, *The Goal*. Croton-on-Hudson, NY: North River Press, 1986.

Goldratt, Eliyahu M., and Robert E. Fox, *The Race*. Croton-on-Hudson, NY: North River Press, 1986.

Sandras, William A., Jr., *Just-In-Time: Making It Happen*. Essex Junction, VT: Oliver Wight Limited Publications, Inc., 1989.

Keys to Starting a TQM Program

Without careful analysis and planning, total quality programs are doomed to fail. The efforts have better odds if the mandate comes from the top and the programs are shaped by goals and action steps.

Shari Caudron

Shari Caudron is a free-lance writer based in Denver.

Like other major workplace initiatives, quality improvement efforts often are established for a lot of dumb reasons, according to Roland Dumas, owner of Roberts Information Services in San Mateo, California, and a judge for the Malcolm Baldrige National Quality Awards. First, everyone else is doing it. Second, the chairman wants a Baldrige Award on the credenza before retiring. Third, slick consultants have convinced managers that a prepackaged, total-quality management program (TQM) is all they need to eliminate product defects, enhance customer satisfaction, boost productivity, cut costs and propel corporate profits into the stratosphere.

Unfortunately, it isn't that easy. Last May, *The Wall Street Journal* reported that two-thirds of all quality-improvement programs ultimately fail because organizations simply don't understand what quality really means or how to attain it. "Many quality-management plans simply are too amorphous to generate better products or services," writes Gilbert Fuchsberg, author of the article.

The problem is compounded by the reality that there is no right or wrong way to achieve quality. In fact, a study conducted by the American Quality Foundation, a New York City-based think tank, revealed that the 584 companies surveyed used a total of 945 different quality-management tactics.

"How you implement a quality process that's effective is anyone's guess," Dumas points out. "I could outline several of the steps that you'd have to go through. Then you might look at it and take an approach that's absolutely backward and still do an amazing job."

Companies that have been successful at implementing TQM, however, do share these common denominators that human resources professionals can learn from:
• A view of quality as a long-term process instead of a program
• The leadership of the CEO.

CEOs must lead the way. Without a doubt, the most important contributor to the successful implementation of any quality-improvement effort is top-down leadership. Three years ago, when the Atlanta-based Ritz-Carlton Hotel Co. initiated TQM, Horst Schulze, president and CEO, told his senior management team that although the company was considered to be a leader in the luxury hotel industry, they were just lucky, because everyone else was even worse.

From then on, all quality efforts that were undertaken by the company to provide 100% guest satisfaction have been under Schulze's direction, explains Patrick Mene, corporate director of quality. For example, when a new hotel is ready to open, Schulze and other senior leaders spend a week at the new facility, modeling for new employees the correct way to interact with guests.

Having a million customer contacts each day, it's a people-intensive business. "It sends a strong message to employees when the CEO takes time to show a dishwasher how to greet and make small talk with guests," says Mene.

The involvement of Schulze and other senior leaders, including the company's VP of HR, may be one reason the Ritz-Carlton received the Baldrige Award in 1992, Mene believes, making it the first hotel company to achieve the honor. "Providing thick towels and offering customers an extensive array of luxuries is easy, compared with providing genuinely caring, highly personalized service," Mene explains. "The personal involvement of our leaders is what made this happen."

Texas Instruments' Defense Systems and Electronics Group in Dallas, a 1992 Baldrige winner in the manufacturing category, also has discovered the value of

Texas Instruments' Defense and Electronics Group credits TQM with the success of its high-speed anti-radar missile (being assembled, above). The Baldrige application prompted a review of the way it does its training and its performance appraisals.

leadership—but only after two failed attempts to achieve the coveted quality award. Hank Hayes, the company's president, had been involved in and committed to the quality effort when the Defense Systems and Electronics Group applied for the award in 1990 and 1991. According to Joe Borden, total quality manager, Hayes didn't jump in with both feet and lead the quality effort until 1992, however. Today, Hayes guides all of the strategic quality planning, beginning with the development of long-term goals and ending with final approval of each division's annual objectives.

"In a nutshell, TQM challenges leaders to accept the role of leadership," says Dumas.

Use the Baldrige as a yardstick. You must know where you are before you can chart a course for where you want to be. Therefore, before beginning a TQM process, it's important to assess the organization in terms of current quality and to define the level of quality you want to have. "Under the direction of the CEO, managers should review the company's mission, values and vision statements," suggests James F. Riley Jr., senior vice president of the Juran Institute, a quality-management consulting firm in Wilton, Connecticut. These statements provide a framework for evaluating current quality levels.

Eastman Kodak Co. in Rochester, New York, is an example. It first developed a mission statement that stated:

• Who the company was

• What the company did

• Who the customers (both internal and external) were.

According to Paul Smith, senior VP, Kodak then developed a vision statement describing the company's aspirations for the future. "This statement wasn't developed by decree," Smith says. "I worked with my direct reports in quality team meetings and they, in turn, worked with their direct reports in quality team meetings, and so on."

Once a company's vision has been identified clearly, managers can begin to assess the status of quality in the organization. Many companies, including AT&T's Transmission Systems Business Unit in Morristown, New Jersey, have found that the Baldrige Award criteria can help guide this assessment process.

The fallout of divestiture and deregulation forced AT&T's Transmission Systems Business Unit to become more competitive and customer-focused. "Before deregulation, we were our own customer," says Louis Monteforte, manager of the business unit's quality planning. "Afterward, we had to learn how to compete for and satisfy external customers."

In searching for ways to redirect the company, AT&T's Transmission Systems Business Unit used the Baldrige criteria to take a baseline measurement of the company and to provide a road map toward quality. The business unit created a cross-functional team comprising the first-level managers and engineers who were responsible for developing a mock application for the award. "We purposely got down into the company to determine what the average employee thought about our operations," says Monteforte.

Just Exactly What Is Total Quality Management?

Total quality management (TQM) has become the corporate catch-phrase of the 1990s. But like many other oft-repeated expressions, its meaning may not be entirely clear, even to those individuals involved in quality improvement programs. In seeking a definition of this expression, PERSONNEL JOURNAL went to James F. Riley Jr., senior vice president of the Juran Institute Inc., in Wilton, Connecticut. The Juran Institute is a source of training and consulting for TQM, and its consultants have worked with thousands of organizations worldwide.

Q. What's TQM?

A. TQM is a transformation in the way an organization manages. It involves focusing management's energies on the continuous improvement of all operations, functions, and above all, processes of work. Quality is really nothing more, therefore, than meeting customer needs. To do this, you must improve work processes, because it's the result of these processes that the customer cares about.

Q. Can you give me an example of a work process?

A. Take product development. New products begin in the research department with a concept. This progresses to the engineering department for the development of a prototype, which they then make ready for manufacturing. The manufacturing function designs a way to produce the product affordably, quickly and within produc-

tion schedules. The product then must become ready to enter the market-place, which involves the marketing, sales and delivery functions. To achieve quality, you have to improve work performance at each stage of this process so that you can make a product that's free of defects, meets customer needs and is manufactured in the least possible time, at the least possible cost. By necessity, TQM emphasizes teamwork because: Processes cut through an organization; and no one function, employee or manager owns the entire process.

Q. What specific issues does TQM address best?

A. Total quality addresses, among other things, customer satisfaction, revenue, market share, productivity, cost and cycle time. The way to increase customer satisfaction and reduce cost and cycle time is by removing defects. You increase revenue and market share by improving products and enhancing salability. When you re-engineer processes, you improve productivity.

Q. Why do so many quality improvement programs fail?

A. The principle reasons are: 1) Upper management support and commitment were never obtained; 2) TQM started, and instability developed in upper management, such as a key retirement or resignation; 3) The organization tried to do too much too quickly without taking the time to

learn as it went along; and 4) The organization didn't provide the effort with a full measure of support, such as educating and training employees, seeking skilled advisors, dedicating financial resources to the effort and recognizing that TQM is a continuous commitment, not a program.

Q. How should an organization implement TQM?

A. First, revisit the mission values and vision statement. Answer these questions:

• What business are we in?

• What principles guide us?

• What do we intend to become?

Next, conduct an assessment of quality in the organization. Review your standing in the marketplace and the needs, wants and expectations of your customers. Calculate the cost of poor quality to your company and assess employee attitudes toward existing quality efforts. Develop a quality action plan next. The quality action plan should define your short- and long-term goals and list individual responsibilities. Then develop support for the TQM system. This involves communicating the effort, reviewing your recognition-and-reward systems, and determining education and training needs. Finally, prioritize the issues, and determine which programs should be the first to implement. Don't try to cure world hunger all at once—take on bite-size projects that can teach you something.

—SC

The analysis of the completed application showed areas in which AT&T's Transmission Systems Business Unit was doing well in terms of satisfying customers, and areas needing improvement. For example, the application revealed that few employees understood how their responsibilities fit with the duties of their co-workers. It showed that there was little communication or teamwork. Furthermore, although most workers claimed to be committed to quality improvement, they indicated that they didn't believe that

the executives were committed to the effort. According to Monteforte, this indi-

The vision wasn't developed by decree. I worked with my direct reports in quality team meetings, and they, in turn, worked with their reports.

cated that the company needed quality training, enhanced communication and increased visibility of senior managers.

Since 1989, AT&T's Transmission Systems Business Unit has evaluated itself against the Baldrige criteria eight times. The company's senior executives serve as the business unit's Quality Council. This council personally reviews the results of these evaluations and uses them to develop annual improvement plans and guide the required actions.

Because the Baldrige criteria help develop quality goals, some companies go so far as to apply for the award, even if they don't feel they can achieve it,

Baldrige Winners Are a Good Source of Information on Quality Programs

Upon receiving the Malcolm Baldrige National Quality Award, winners are asked to share with other U.S. companies information about the development of successful quality strategies. Since the program's inception in 1988, there have been 17 winners. Listed below are the quality contacts at these organizations. Human resources professionals may find these companies a good source of information on how the HR function can support a quality effort best.

1992 Baldrige Winners

AT&T Network Systems Group Transmission Systems Business Unit (Manufacturing)
Louis Monteforte, Manager of Transmission Quality Planning
201/606-2488

AT&T Universal Card Services (Service)
Robert A. Davis, Chief Quality Officer
904/443-8875

Granite Rock Co. (Small Business)
Bruce W. Woolpert, President and Chief Executive Officer
408/761-2300

Texas Instruments Inc. Defense Systems & Electronics (Manufacturing)
Mike Cooney, Vice President of Group Quality Assurance
214/480-4800

The Ritz-Carlton Hotel Co. (Service)
Patrick Mene, Corporate Director of Quality
404/237-5500

1991 Baldrige Winners

Solectron Corp. (Manufacturing)
Margaret Smith, Mktg. Progr. Specialist
408/956-6768

Marlow Industries (Small Business)
Joy Janco, Baldrige Activities Coordinator
214/342-4293

Zytec Corp. (Manufacturing)
Karen Scheldroup
Baldrige Office: 612/941-1100

1990 Baldrige Winners

Cadillac Motor Car Co. (Mfg.)
Rosetta Riley, Director of Continuous Improvement Process
303/556-1965

Federal Express Corp. (Service)
Jean Ward-Jones, Manager of Quality Education and Administration
901/395-4539

IBM Rochester
Center for Excellence: 507/286-5000

Wallace Co.
John Wallace, CEO
713/672-5803

1989 Baldrige Winners

Xerox Corp., Business Products & Systems (Manufacturing)
John G. Lawrence, Manager of National Quality Communications Office
716/383-7502

Milliken & Co. (Manufacturing)
Patrick C. Bowle, VP of Quality
803/573-2003

1988 Baldrige Winners

Westinghouse Electric Corp. (Manufacturing)
Carl Arendt, Manager of Communications Productivity and Quality Center
412/778-5008

Motorola Inc. (Manufacturing)
Richard Buetow
Senior VP and Director of Quality
708/576-5516

Globe Metallurgical Inc. (Small Business)
Norman Jennings, Quality Director
616/984-2361

—SC

---

because the feedback from Baldrige examiners is so helpful. Texas Instruments' Defense System & Electronics Group, for example, first applied for the award in 1990 to "get objective, third-party feedback from experts who could accelerate our quality improvement efforts," says Steve Leven, VP of HR.

The Baldrige judges evaluate the applicants in seven areas:
- Leadership
- Information and analysis
- Strategic quality planning
- HR utilization

- Quality assurance of products and services
- Quality results
- Customer satisfaction.

A look at the criteria shows how easily the process of completing an application can uncover problems in an organization and help managers identify quality goals. "In terms of HR, the application helped the Defense Systems & Electronics Group find ways to align the human resources process directly with the quality objectives of the entire group, which we did by promoting teamwork and team recogni-

tion, reviewing our performance-appraisal system and revising our training curriculum to focus more on quality-improvement tools," Leven explains.

Use other methods of assessment. As useful as the Baldrige criteria are, they're by no means the only way to evaluate the status of quality in an organization. Memphis, Tennessee-based Federal Express, for example, uses statistical measures of customer satisfaction to evaluate quality. The company established quality indicators for 12 types of service problems and weighted them based on their inconvenience to customers. For instance, a missing proof-of-delivery slip rates a factor of one because it's considered a minor inconvenience, whereas a lost package rates 10 points. Federal Express tracks these service indicators every day and keeps a running total as a way of monitoring where quality improvements need to be made in the organization.

For companies that are just starting to assess quality, the Juran Institute suggests conducting:

• A marketplace review that reveals customers' needs and expectations

• A cost-of-poor-quality review

• A description of employees' attitudes toward quality efforts.

"The issues uncovered by this assessment become fodder for the development of quality goals," says Riley, "and the goals become methods for prioritizing where improvements should be made."

Tap the experience of successful firms. As HR executives review the quality needs of their own organizations, they also should learn about quality tools and techniques and about the quality experiences of other companies.

Winners of the Malcolm Baldrige Award are a good source of quality information, because they're expected to share information about their successful quality strategies with other U.S. organizations. (See "Baldrige Winners Are a Good Source of Information on Quality Programs.") Texas Instruments took full advantage of this opportunity, sending executives to quality conferences hosted by Westinghouse, Motorola, Xerox and Milliken & Co.

Benchmarking, the process whereby companies identify and learn from the best quality practices of other companies, also is helpful. When Xerox was looking for ways to boost quality of its distribution system, it turned to L.L. Bean. Federal Express became its model of billing efficiency and Cummins Engine Co. became its new standard for production.

Benchmarking is helpful only in the latter stages of TQM development, however. "There's too much industrial tourism going on. Instead of understanding their own company's processes and starting to improve them," says Dumas, "many executives get on airplanes and start visiting other organizations. This delays the important work of developing a quality infrastructure and setting some goals, and if you don't have any experience under your belt, you can't ask smart questions."

Create action plans and set goals. Once an organization has a sense of how and where quality improvement should be implemented in the company, it should develop some strategic goals and action plans. At this stage, Riley recommends appointing a staff support person who can serve as the internal quality expert. This person can help define the company's short- and long-term goals and coordinate responsibilities. By no means should this person become the quality expert, Riley says. "His or her role should be one of facilitation."

At AT&T, the group that prepared the mock Baldrige application that uncovered quality problems devised a quality-action plan listing 18 objectives. "We didn't want the employees simply to present problems. We wanted them to present solutions based on what they had learned," says Monteforte.

A similar process was undertaken by Ritz-Carlton, which established teams to review the criteria and establish goals in each of the seven examination categories of the Baldrige Award.

At the goal-setting stage, companies may find it helpful to conduct a pilot program to see if employees will be responsive to a major quality initiative. At Fort Sander Health System in Knoxville, Tennessee, an 11-week team alliance program was established to "test the water with employees," explains John Milner, senior VP of HR. "We established voluntary teams throughout the organization and defined a procedure for the teams to follow when they create and submit ideas

to improve patient care, increase savings and increase revenue," he says. If a suggested idea was implemented, team members received points to cash in for awards. A full 90% of the company's 2,800 employees participated in the program, generating $3.2 million worth of ideas.

Through the pilot program, Fort Sanders learned that workers wanted to share their ideas. It theorized that a TQM process that rewarded them for participation probably would work well. The pilot also uncovered key areas for training and indicated which managers weren't as supportive of the quality effort. "We spent 10 months after the pilot working with these reluctant managers and devising a training program that supported our quality goals," Milner says.

HR plays a role in a quality start-up. In the early stages of TQM, HR professionals should be part of the company's effort to evaluate quality needs and establish goals and objectives. Ideally, HR should be represented on the senior management team that reports to the CEO.

HR professionals must share their understanding of corporate culture with company leaders, who may think a certain program will work just because it worked at Florida Power & Light or Federal Express. If the program won't work, the HR person must point out why. This is critical, because the longer you're in senior management, the more out-of-touch you become with the company."

Leven has another bit of advice for HR people. "In the current atmosphere of layoffs and recession, you'll hear a lot of reasons against implementing quality improvement—because quality eliminates jobs, for example. I recommend that you remain tone-deaf to such suggestions. There always are reasons the time isn't right, no matter what the program."

Just as there's no right or wrong way to pursue quality, it appears there's no absolutely right or wrong time to start. For every dumb reason you have for wanting to start a program, there's a smart reason just waiting to reveal itself to you.

Case V: *Evaluation of Organizational Effectiveness*

The American Corporation, a $2.4 billion diversified conglomerate, acquired the $130 million Cordle Manufacturing Company. At a private luncheon with Sam Priest, American's chief executive officer, Carla Judson, a strategic planner with American's Division of Strategic Planning, learned that she was one of several persons being considered to replace, on an acting basis, Cordle Manufacturing Company's president, whose resignation was part of the acquisition agreement. Priest informed Judson that if the acting president could function effectively, the position would be permanent. He indicated, however, that one troublesome problem would have to be eliminated within six months. The problem had been revealed through a confidential survey conducted among 25 members of Cordle's middle management group. Judson was told that the survey results would be available to her and that a meeting of all officers would be held in two weeks to select the acting president. At that time, all candidates would be required to make a presentation outlining how problems revealed by the survey could best be handled.

In studying the survey results, Judson learned that each of the middle managers had been asked to evaluate other departments. The survey was designed to determine, if possible, the respect, cooperation, and goodwill generated between departments. Of the departments evaluated, all were rated satisfactory in efficiency, organization, work relationships, and cooperativeness, except for the sales department. From the 25 questionnaires returned, 18 participants said the sales department needed reorganizing. They said department members were difficult to work with and rarely cooperated with other departments.

As a strategic planner, Judson knew there were a number of feasible strategies she could present to American's officers. She knew that the survey results might be challenged as unreliable and invalid. On the other hand, she was aware that the distinct nature of the objectives, activities, and responsibilities associated with various departments often led to conflict between individuals in various areas. If she acknowledged the survey's validity, she would have to outline a plan for achieving efficient integration and coordination among departments and functional areas. Judson realized her future at American would be decided in the next few days by how her strategies would be perceived by American's officers and then by how effectively she could implement her strategies. What to decide on was her major task.

Using the Case on *Evaluation of Organizational Effectiveness*

Carl Judson is faced with the problem of trying to propose an organization for the new Cordle Manufacturing division of the American Corporation based upon the results of a study that was recently completed at the newly acquired business. The study indicates that most of the departments work well together with one major exception—sales. Ms. Judson's task is to develop a strategy to address and rectify this condition.

Discussion Questions

1. Should Ms. Judson challenge the validity and reliability of the study?
2. If Ms. Judson accepts the study, what are some of the possible strategies she could use to address this situation?

Exercise V: Win As Much As You Can!

1. Divide the group into groups of eight and have each group (cluster) divide into teams of two (dyads).
2. The goal of this exercise is to win as much money as you can.
3. Using the chart at the top of the tally sheet, each dyad is to decide whether it will choose an "X" or a "Y" (with the hope of winning money). The dyads then write their choices on their tally sheets for round 1 while not letting any other dyads see their choices. No conversation among dyads should occur, except when provided for in rounds 5, 8, and 10.
4. After the allotted time for round 1 (2 minutes) has passed, each dyad will show its choice to the other dyads in the cluster. Using the chart on the tally sheet, each dyad should determine how much money it won or lost in round 1, and record this amount on the tally sheet. No comments among dyads are allowed. Proceed immediately to round 2, then 3, and so forth, as outlined on the tally sheet. Note that in rounds 5, 8, and 10, dyads can confer with each other at the beginning of the round. Note also that the amounts won or lost in these rounds are multiplied by three, five, and ten.
5. At the end of the exercise, determine which dyad won the most and which ended up furthest behind. Then compare clusters.

4 X's:	Lose $1.00 each
3 X's: 1 Y:	Win $1.00 each Lose $3.00
2 X's: 2 Y's:	Win $2.00 each Lose $2.00 each
1 X: 3 Y's:	Win $3.00 Lose $1.00 each
4 Y's:	Win $1.00 each

Strategy: You are to confer with your partner(s) on each round and make a joint decision. Before rounds 5, 8, and 10, you confer with the others in your cluster.

Questions for Discussion

1. How was the goal defined? What conflict did it create? (Do I win for my dyad or my cluster?)
2. Do people react differently in games than they do in real life? Do goals in life create conflict?
3. How does trust relate to influence? How many times can one person betray another and still retain his/her confidence? Did anyone stick to her/his word throughout?
4. What effect did communication have on the influence process?
5. What strategies were used to win? What conflict did these strategies create? What strategies were used to manage the conflict?
   • The win/lose approach = self-oriented. (I win at your expense.)
   • The lose/win approach = martyrdom. (You win at my expense.)
   • The lose/lose approach = pride and revenge. (I may lose, but you do, too.)
   • The win/win approach = trust. (We both win.)
6. Why is the win/win approach the most effective strategy in life?

Round	Time Allowed	Confer With	Your Choice Circle	Clusters Patterns of Choices	Payoff	Balance	
1	2 mins.	partner					
2	1 min.	partner					
3	1 min.	partner					
4	1 min.	partner					
5	3 mins. 1 min.	cluster partner					Bonus round payoff × 3
6	1 min.	partner					
7	1 min.	partner					
8	3 mins. 1 min.	cluster partner					Bonus round payoff × 5
9	1 min.	partner					
10	3 mins. 1 min.	cluster partner					Bonus round payoff × 10

Staffing and Human Resources

- **Management Classic (Article 28)**
- **Developing Human Resources (Articles 29 and 30)**
- **Organized Labor (Article 31)**
- **Maintaining an Effective Workforce (Article 32)**
- **Case VI: The "Homes" Is Where the Union Is**
- **Exercise VI: Assumptions about People at Work**

Managers of organizations get things done through people. Managers can plan, organize, direct, and control, but the central focus of all their efforts is people. People determine whether or not an organization is going to succeed, and the way people perceive their treatment by management is often the key to that success. Douglas McGregor demonstrated this principle in "The Human Side of Enterprise," with his Theory X and Theory Y. These two approaches represent opposite ends of the same continuum. Theory X states that people have to be watched, that they cannot be trusted, and that management needs to be supervising them constantly. Theory Y, on the other hand, states that people need to enjoy their work, that they want to do a good job, and that they can be trusted to perform. Most people tend to be in between these two extremes. Situations vary, and the managerial approach that favors Theory Y may or may not be appropriate. The same can be said for Theory X. Neither approach is good or bad; it is a question of appropriateness to the situation.

Since human resources are a key to the success of any organization, firms need to hire the very best people they can find, because it is human beings who make the plans, organize the operation, direct the process to accomplish the organizational goals, and evaluate the results. But while people contribute directly to a firm's success, they also represent a significant cost to the organization. Not only salaries, but the costs for benefits are rising at an alarming rate. Benefits cost more today than just a few years ago, and workers not only want to keep the benefits they have, but seek to add others. Some of their demands include dental plans, eye care plans, child care, and senior care for their relatives. Managers have had to respond in part by "Rethinking Diversity" in new and creative ways, because the reason demands are changing is that the workforce is changing. There are more

minorities, women, and other groups with different needs, and if a corporation wants to hire these people, many of whom are outstanding, then they are going to have to meet their needs. Otherwise, these potential employees will go elsewhere, frequently to the competition, and put their skills, expertise, and ambition into driving the recalcitrant firm out of business. No organization can afford to turn its back on such a large pool of potential talent.

Human resources often involve labor unions. While unions in North America have suffered in recent years with declining membership and plant closings, they have nevertheless served an important historical role as well as providing a balance for the potential excesses of management. Today, American labor unions need to define their roles in American industry, and their leaders must implement these changes. Unions, as discussed in "The Future of Labor-Management Relations," will have to change the way they conduct business if they plan to survive in the future.

Because of the increasing demand for qualified employees, organizations will have to do everything possible to retain good workers. Firms are responding to changes in the workforce in a variety of ways, including "Leasing Workers." To meet the needs of the future, management must recognize that people, organizations, and the environment will continue to evolve.

Looking Ahead: Challenge Questions

People are the keys to the success of any organization. What are some of the approaches that managers can use to direct individuals?

Labor unions are in transition. How do unions need to change to meet the changes in the environment?

The workforce is changing. What are some things managers of firms need to do to meet the changes?

Unit 6

The Human Side of Enterprise

Douglas M. McGregor

*Douglas M. McGregor was born in 1906. He was graduated
A.B. from City College of Detroit (later Wayne University) in
1932 and was graduated A.M. from Oberlin College in 1933.
He earned a Ph.D. from Harvard University in 1935. He is
best known for his book,* The Human Side of Enterprise, *published in 1960. McGregor died in 1964.*

It has become trite to say that industry has the fundamental know-how to utilize physical science and technology for the material benefit of mankind, and that we must now learn how to utilize the social sciences to make our human organizations truly effective.

To a degree, the social sciences today are in a position like that of the physical sciences with respect to atomic energy in the thirties. We know that past conceptions of the nature of man are inadequate and, in many ways, incorrect. We are becoming quite certain that, under proper conditions, unimagined resources of creative human energy could become available within the organizational setting.

We cannot tell industrial management how to apply this new knowledge in simple, economic ways. We know it will require years of exploration, much costly development research, and a substantial amount of creative imagination on the part of management to discover how to apply this growing knowledge to the organization of human effort in industry.

MANAGEMENT'S TASK:
THE CONVENTIONAL VIEW

The conventional conception of management's task in harnessing human energy to organizational requirements can be stated broadly in terms of three propositions. In order to avoid the complications introduced by a label, let us call this set of propositions "Theory X":

1. Management is responsible for organizing the elements of productive enterprise—money, materials, equipment, people—in the interest of economic ends.

2. With respect to people, this is a process of directing their efforts, motivating them, controlling their actions, modifying their behavior to fit the needs of the organization.

3. Without this active intervention by management, people would be passive—even resistant—to organizational needs. They must therefore be persuaded, rewarded, punished, controlled—their activities must be directed. This is management's task. We often sum it up by saying that management consists of getting things done through other people.

Behind this conventional theory there are several additional beliefs—less explicit, but widespread:

4. The average man is by nature indolent—he works as little as possible.

5. He lacks ambition, dislikes responsibility, prefers to be led.

6. He is inherently self-centered, indifferent to organizational needs.

7. He is by nature resistant to change.

8. He is gullible, not very bright, the ready dupe of the charlatan and the demagogue.

The human side of economic enterprise today is fashioned from propositions and beliefs such as these. Conventional organization structures and managerial policies, practices, and programs reflect these assumptions.

In accomplishing its task—with these assumptions as guides—management has conceived of a range of possibilities.

At one extreme, management can be "hard" or "strong." The methods for directing behavior involve coercion and threat (usually disguised), close supervision, tight controls over behavior. At the other extreme, management can be "soft" or "weak." The methods for directing behavior involve being permissive, satisfying people's demands, achieving harmony. Then they will be tractable, accept direction.

This range has been fairly completely explored during the past half century, and management has learned some things from the exploration. There are difficulties in the "hard" approach. Force breeds counterforces: restriction of output, antagonism, militant unionism, subtle but effective sabotage of management objectives. This "hard" approach is especially difficult during times of full employment.

There are also difficulties in the "soft" approach. It leads frequently to the abdication of management—to harmony, perhaps, but to indifferent performance. People take advantage of the soft approach. They continually expect more, but they give less and less.

Currently, the popular theme is "firm but fair." This is an attempt to gain the advantages of both the hard and the soft approaches. It is reminiscent of Teddy Roosevelt's "speak softly and carry a big stick."

IS THE CONVENTIONAL VIEW CORRECT?

The findings which are beginning to emerge from the social sciences challenge this whole set of beliefs about man and human nature and about the task of management. The evidence is far from conclusive, certainly, but it is suggestive. It comes from the laboratory, the clinic, the schoolroom, the home, and even to a limited extent from industry itself.

The social scientist does not deny that human behavior in industrial organization today is approximately what management perceives it to be. He has, in fact, observed it and studied it fairly extensively. But he is pretty sure that this behavior is *not* a consequence of man's inherent nature. It is a consequence rather of the nature of industrial organizations, of management philosophy, policy, and practice. The conventional approach of Theory X is based on mistaken notions of what is cause and what is effect.

Perhaps the best way to indicate why the conventional approach of management is inadequate is to consider the subject of motivation.

PHYSIOLOGICAL NEEDS

Man is a wanting animal—as soon as one of his needs is satisfied, another appears in its place. This process is unending. It continues from birth to death.

Man's needs are organized in a series of levels—a hierarchy of importance. At the lowest level, but preeminent in importance when they are thwarted, are his *physiological needs*. Man lives for bread alone, when there is no bread. Unless the circumstances are unusual, his needs for love, for status, for recognition are inoperative when his stomach has been empty for a while. But when he eats regularly and adequately, hunger ceases to be an important motivation. The same is true of the other physiological needs of man—for rest, exercise, shelter, protection from the elements.

A satisfied need is not a motivator of behavior! This is a fact of profound significance that is regularly ignored in the conventional approach to the management of people. Consider your own need for air: Except as you are deprived of it, it has no appreciable motivating effect upon your behavior.

SAFETY NEEDS

When the physiological needs are reasonably satisfied, needs at the next higher level begin to dominate man's behavior—to motivate him. These are called *safety needs*. They are needs for protection against danger, threat, deprivation. Some people mistakenly refer to these as needs for security. However, unless man is in a dependent relationship where he fears arbitrary deprivation, he does not demand security. The need is for the "fairest possible break." When he is confident of this, he is more than willing to take risks. But when he feels threatened or dependent, his greatest need is for guarantees, for protection, for security.

The fact needs little emphasis that, since every industrial employee is in a dependent relationship, safety needs may assume considerable importance. Arbitrary management actions, behavior which arouses uncertainty with respect to continued employment or which reflects favoritism or discrimination, unpredictable administration of policy—these can be powerful motivators of the safety needs in the employment relationship *at every level,* from worker to vice-president.

SOCIAL NEEDS

When man's physiological needs are satisfied and he is no longer fearful about his physical welfare, his *social needs* become important motivators of his behavior—needs for belonging, for association, for acceptance by his fellows, for giving and receiving friendship and love.

Management knows today of the existence of these needs, but it often assumes quite wrongly that they represent a threat to the organization. Many studies have demonstrated that the tightly knit, cohesive work group may, under proper conditions, be far more effective than an equal number of separate individuals in achieving organizational goals.

Yet management, fearing group hostility to its own objectives, often goes to considerable lengths to control and direct human efforts in ways that are inimical to the natural "groupiness" of human beings. When man's social needs—and perhaps his safety needs, too—are thus thwarted, he behaves in ways which tend to defeat organizational objectives. He becomes resistant, antagonistic, uncooperative. But this behavior is a consequence, not a cause.

EGO NEEDS

Above the social needs—in the sense that they do not become motivators until lower needs are reasonably satisfied—are the needs of greatest significance to management and to man himself. They are the *egoistic needs,* and they are of two kinds:

1. Those needs that relate to one's self-esteem—needs for self-confidence, for independence, for achievement, for competence, for knowledge.

2. Those needs that relate to one's reputation—needs for status, for recognition, for appreciation, for the deserved respect of one's fellows.

Unlike the lower needs, these are rarely satisfied; man seeks indefinitely for more satisfaction of these needs once they have become important to him. But they do not appear in any significant way until physiological, safety, and social needs are all reasonably satisfied.

The typical industrial organization offers few opportunities for the satisfaction of these egoistic needs to people at lower levels in the hierarchy. The conventional methods of organizing work, particularly in mass production industries, give little heed to these aspects of human motivation. If the practices of scientific management were deliberately calculated to thwart these needs, they could hardly accomplish this purpose better than they do.

SELF-FULFILLMENT NEEDS

Finally—a capstone, as it were, on the hierarchy of man's needs—there are what we may call the *needs for self-fulfillment*. These are the needs for realizing one's own potentialities, for continued self-development, for being creative in the broadest sense of that term.

It is clear that the conditions of modern life give only limited opportunity for these relatively weak needs to obtain expression. The deprivation most people experience with respect to other lower level needs diverts their energies into the struggle to satisfy *those* needs, and the needs for self-fulfillment remain dormant.

MANAGEMENT AND MOTIVATION

We recognize readily enough that a man suffering from a severe dietary deficiency is sick. The deprivation of physiological needs has behavioral consequences. The same is true—although less well recognized—of deprivation of higher level needs. The man whose needs for safety, association, independence, or status are thwarted is sick just as surely as the man who has rickets. And his sickness will have behavioral consequences. We will be mistaken if we attribute his resultant passivity, his hostility, his refusal to accept responsibility to his inherent "human nature." These forms of behavior are *symptoms* of illness—of deprivation of his social and egoistic needs.

The man whose lower level needs are satisfied is not motivated to satisfy those needs any longer. For practical purposes they exist no longer. Management often asks, "Why aren't people more productive? We pay good wages, provide good working conditions, have excellent fringe benefits and steady employment. Yet people do not seem to be willing to put forth more than minimum effort."

The fact that management has provided for these physiological and safety needs has shifted the motivational emphasis to the social and perhaps to the egoistic needs. Unless there are opportunities *at work* to satisfy these higher level needs, people will be deprived; and their behavior will reflect this deprivation. Under such conditions, if management continues to focus its attention on physiological needs, its efforts are bound to be ineffective.

People *will* make insistent demands for more money under these conditions. It becomes more important than ever to buy the material goods and services which can provide limited satisfaction of the thwarted needs. Although money has only limited value in satisfying many higher level needs, it can become the focus of interest if it is the *only* means available.

THE CARROT-AND-STICK APPROACH

The carrot-and-stick theory of motivation (like Newtonian physical theory) works reasonably well under certain circumstances. The *means* for satisfying man's physiological and (within limits) his safety needs can be provided or withheld by management. Employment itself is such a means, and so are wages, working conditions, and benefits. By these means the individual can be controlled so long as he is struggling for subsistence.

But the carrot-and-stick theory does not work at all once man has reached an adequate subsistence level and is motivated primarily by higher needs. Management cannot provide a man with self-respect, or with the respect of his fellows, or with the satisfaction of needs for self-fulfillment. It can create such conditions that he is encouraged and enabled to seek such satisfactions for *himself*, or it can thwart him by failing to create those conditions.

But this creation of conditions is not "control." It is not a good device for directing behavior. And so management finds itself in an odd position. The high standard of living created by our modern technological know-how provides quite adequately for the satisfaction of physiological and safety needs. The only significant exception is where management practices have not created confidence in a "fair break"—and thus where safety needs are thwarted. But by making possible the satisfaction of low level needs, management has deprived itself of the ability to use as motivators the devices on which conventional theory has taught it to rely—rewards, promises, incentives, or threats and other coercive devices.

The philosophy of management by direction and control—*regardless of whether it is hard or soft*—is inadequate to motivate because the human needs on which this approach relies are today unimportant motivators of behavior. Direction and control are essentially useless in motivating people whose important needs are social and egoistic. Both the hard and the soft approach fail today because they are simply irrelevant to the situation.

People, deprived of opportunities to satisfy at work the needs which are now important to them, behave exactly as we might predict—with indolence, passivity, resistance to change, lack of responsibility, willingness to follow the demagogue, unreasonable demands for economic benefits. It would seem that we are caught in a web of our own weaving.

A NEW THEORY OF MANAGEMENT

For these and many other reasons, we require a different theory of the task of managing people based on more adequate assumptions about human nature and human motivation. I am going to be so bold as to suggest the broad dimensions of such a theory. Call it "Theory Y," if you will.

1. Management is responsible for organizing the elements of productive enterprise—money, materials, equipment, people—in the interest of economic ends.
2. People are *not* by nature passive or resistant to organizational needs. They have become so as a result of experience in organizations.
3. The motivation, the potential for development, the capacity for assuming responsibility, the readiness to direct behavior toward organizational goals are all present in people. Management does not put them there. It is a responsibility of management to make it possible for people to recognize and develop these human characteristics for themselves.
4. The essential task of management is to arrange organizational conditions and methods of operation so that people can achieve their own goals *best* by directing *their own* efforts toward organizational objectives.

This is a process primarily of creating opportunities, releasing potential, removing obstacles, encouraging growth, providing guidance. It is what Peter Drucker has called "management by objectives" in contrast to "management by control." It does *not* involve the abdication of management, the absence of leadership, the lowering of standards, or the other characteristics usually associated with the "soft" approach under Theory X.

SOME DIFFICULTIES

It is no more possible to create an organization today which will be a full, effective application of this theory than it was to build an atomic power plant in 1945. There are many formidable obstacles to overcome.

The conditions imposed by conventional organization theory and by the approach of scientific management for the past half century have tied men to limited jobs which do not utilize their capabilities, have discouraged the acceptance of responsibility, have encouraged passivity, have eliminated meaning from work. Man's habits, attitudes, expectations—his whole conception of membership in an industrial organization—have been conditioned by his experience under these circumstances.

People today are accustomed to being directed, manipulated, controlled in industrial organizations and to finding satisfaction for their social, egoistic, and self-fulfillment needs away from the job. This is true of much of management as well as of workers. Genuine "industrial citizenship"—to borrow again a term from Drucker—is a remote and unrealistic idea, the meaning of which has not even been considered by most members of industrial organizations.

Another way of saying this is that Theory X places exclusive reliance upon external control of human behavior, while Theory Y relies heavily on self-control and self-direction. It is worth noting that this difference is the difference between treating people as children and treating them as mature adults. After generations of the former, we cannot expect to shift to the latter overnight.

STEPS IN THE RIGHT DIRECTION

Before we are overwhelmed by the obstacles, let us remember that the application of theory is always slow. Progress is usually achieved in small steps. Some innovative ideas which are entirely consistent with Theory Y are today being applied with some success.

Decentralization and Delegation
These are ways of freeing people from the too-close control of conventional organization, giving them a degree of freedom to direct their own activities, to assume responsibility, and, importantly, to satisfy their egoistic needs. In this connection, the flat organization of Sears, Roebuck and Company provides an interesting example. It forces "management by objectives," since it enlarges the number of people reporting to a manager until he cannot direct and control them in the conventional manner.

Job Enlargement
This concept, pioneered by IBM and Detroit Edison, is quite consistent with Theory Y. It encourages the acceptance of responsibility at the bottom of the organization; it provides opportunities for satisfying social and egoistic needs. In fact, the reorganization of work at the factory level offers one of the more challenging opportunities for innovation consistent with Theory Y.

Participation and Consultative Management
Under proper conditions, participation and consultative management provide encouragement to people to direct their creative energies toward organizational objectives, give them some voice in decisions that affect them, provide significant opportunities for the satisfaction of social and egoistic needs. The Scanlon Plan is the outstanding embodiment of these ideas in practice.

Performance Appraisal
Even a cursory examination of conventional programs of performance appraisal within the ranks of management will reveal how completely consistent they are with Theory X. In fact, most such programs tend to treat the individual as though he were a product under inspection on the assembly line.

A few companies—among them General Mills, Ansul Chemical, and General Electric—have been experimenting with approaches which involve the individual in setting "targets" or objectives *for himself* and in a *self*-evaluation of performance semiannually or annually. Of course, the superior plays an important leadership role in this process—one, in fact, which demands substantially more competence than the conventional approach. The role is, however, considerably more congenial to many managers than the role of "judge" or "inspector" which is usually forced upon them. Above all, the individual is encouraged to take a greater responsibility for planning and appraising his own contribution to organizational objectives; and the accompanying effects on egoistic and self-fulfillment needs are substantial.

APPLYING THE IDEAS

The not infrequent failure of such ideas as these to work as well as expected is often attributable to the fact that a management has "bought the idea" but applied it within the framework of Theory X and its assumptions.

Delegation is not an effective way of exercising management by control. Participation becomes a farce when it is applied as a sales gimmick or a device for kidding people into thinking they are important. Only the management that has confidence in human capacities and is itself directed toward organizational objectives rather than toward the preservation of personal power can grasp the implications of this emerging theory. Such management will find and apply successfully other innovative ideas as we move slowly toward the full implementation of a theory like Y.

THE HUMAN SIDE OF ENTERPRISE

It is quite possible for us to realize substantial improvements in the effectiveness of industrial organizations during the next decade or two. The social sciences can contribute much to such developments; we are only beginning to grasp the implications of the growing body of knowledge in these fields. But if this conviction is to become a reality instead of a pious hope, we will need to view the process much as we view the process of releasing the energy of the atom for constructive human ends—as a slow, costly, sometimes discouraging approach toward a goal which would seem to many to be quite unrealistic.

The ingenuity and the perseverance of industrial management in the pursuit of economic ends have changed many scientific and technological dreams into commonplace realities. It is now becoming clear that the application of these same talents to the human side of enterprise will not only enhance substantially these materialistic achievements, but will bring us one step closer to "the good society."

RETHINKING DIVERSITY

JACK GORDON

Jack Gordon *is editor of TRAINING Magazine.*

The new gospel [of multiculturalism] condemns [the traditional American] vision of individuals of all nations melted into a new race in favor of an opposite vision: a nation of groups, differentiated in their ancestries, inviolable in their diverse identities. The contemporary ideal is shifting from assimilation to ethnicity, from integration to separatism....

Instead of a nation composed of individuals making their own free choices, America increasingly sees itself as composed of groups more or less indelible in their ethnic character. The national ideal had once been e pluribus unum. Are we now to belittle unum *and glorify* pluribus? *Will the center hold? Or will the melting pot yield to the Tower of Babel?*—Arthur M. Schlesinger Jr., *The Disuniting of America*, 1991.

Managing diversity is about coping with "unassimilated differences," says R. Roosevelt Thomas Jr., president of the American Institute for Managing Diversity at Morehouse College in Atlanta. "It's about managing people who aren't like you and who don't necessarily aspire to be like you."

Thomas and Schlesinger, then, are philosophical enemies? Not necessarily. Schlesinger is right, Thomas says, to worry about the prospect of "Balkanization," the fragmentation of society by race, culture and even gender under the banner of multiculturalism. "But what he's calling multiculturalism is not what we're calling managing diversity," Thomas adds. As applied in a business or government organization, "managing diversity means: How do we build systems and a culture that unite different people in a common pursuit without undermining their diversity? It's taking differences into account while developing a cohesive whole."

Can we achieve *unum* without asking the *pluribus* in the melting pot to do quite so much melting? If that was ever the plan on college campuses, it doesn't appear to be working out. From Schlesinger's book: "The cult of ethnicity exaggerates differences, intensifies resentments and antagonisms, drives ever deeper the awful wedges between races and nationalities.... Campuses today, according to one University of Pennsylvania professor, have 'the cultural diversity of Beirut. They are

separate armed camps. The black kids don't mix with the white kids. The Asians are off by themselves. Oppression is the great status symbol.'"

Suppose, however, that we could go at this *pluribus* business without losing sight of the fact that *unum* is, indeed, our goal—a broader, more inclusive *unum*, to be sure. Might there not be payoffs for everybody?

"Some corporations are finding," Thomas says, "that their biggest 'diversity' problem lies in the differences between junior white male managers and senior white male managers. Young whites are not intending to play the success game by the same rules."

Managing diversity is not a synonym for equal employment opportunity (EEO), Thomas told a group of personnel specialists at a conference last year. Neither is it a code word for affirmative action, although he insists that affirmative action programs must continue for the next 20 years or so. Managing diversity isn't even the same thing as "valuing differences."

"You can learn to respect each other, you can like each other, you can minimize racism and sexism, you can have better interpersonal relations. You can do all that and still not know how to manage diversity—because people don't know what management *is*," Thomas says.

Until recently, he argues, "assimilation has made it unneccesssary to learn to manage." The corporation dictated a mold for up-and-comers to fit: Always arrive early and work late, never turn down a transfer to another city, dress like so, talk like so, express the right opinions. "Managing" was largely a matter of enforcing the mold and rewarding those who fit it best.

"Unassimilated differences" have to do only partly with blacks who don't want to lose their "blackness" and women who don't want to give up their "femininity"—but who do want the same shot at promotions, pay hikes and authority as is given to white male Republicans with the right school ties and low golf handicaps. The problem of diversity, Thomas says, is not limited to questions of race, gender, ethnicity, disabilities and sexual orientation. The differences that sap energy and undermine productivity and performance in an organization extend to things like personality styles; your Myers-Briggs type can blind you to the abilities of people with different types. Diversity issues rear their heads whenever different professional mind-sets clash: the accountants vs. the marketers vs. the engineers.

Managing diversity is not primarily about ethics or social responsibility or "doing the right thing," Thomas says. It's about human performance. It's about making a profit. It's about remaining competi-tive. "The 'managing' is more important than the 'diversity,'" he insists, "because if managers are really managing, diversity will take care of itself."

The widely publicized demographic changes commonly referred to under the heading "Work-force 2000" make it inevitable that more minorities, women and immigrants will be hired, he says. And what about retaining and promoting the ones we hire? If we assume that the current clustering of

GETTING STARTED ON 'DIVERSITY WORK'

The problem cannot be that white folks in Louisiana haven't heard the news that racism is bad.

Suppose you want to launch a diversity training effort in your organization. Suppose further that you subscribe to the broadened definition of diversity—the one in which the "differences" being managed and valued belong to everybody, rather than just to groups covered by anti-discrimination laws. How do you get things off on the right foot?

Here is an outline for the introductory portion of a training campaign. It comes from Robert Hayles, newly appointed vice president of cultural diversity for Grand Metropolitan Food Sector in Minneapolis (formerly Pillsbury Co.). Before moving to Grand Met last summer, Hayles was "manager of valuing differences" for Digital Equipment Corp., widely regarded as a leading light in the diversity area. He has acted as a consultant on diversity to organizations including Exxon, the World Bank and the Internal Revenue Service.

Grand Met is not yet one of the "model" diversity companies, Hayles says; the organization is a relative newcomer to what he calls "diversity work." But he is confident about where to take the work and how to take it there. Any organization that wants to start a diversity campaign, he says, must start by answering three questions.

1. What is diversity?

More specifically, whom does diversity include? The answer must be explained, Hayles says, "in words, in writing and experientially." And the answer is, it's about everybody: "This work is about me, whoever I am."

To convey the message on an experiential level, the trainer might ask the group to recall and discuss two types of experiences. First, remember a situation in which you were with a group of people very similar to yourself. It may have been at work, at school, in church, wherever. How did you feel? What did you accomplish?

Almost always, Hayles says, the memories people dredge up are happy ones. They felt good. They were productive. They did something interesting. They did something skillfully. They suc-ceeded.

Next, describe a situation in which you were "the only one"—the only young person, the only engineer, the only male, the only white. Almost al-ways, the experiences people describe are nega-tive. They felt bad. They felt resentful. They fel clumsy. They did something awkwardly.

"I use that to define diversity," Hayles says. "I means all the ways we differ that affect our perfor-mance." If your coworkers are serious fisherme and you aren't, you'll be an outsider. And being a outsider affects the way you do your job.

2. Why do the work?

The answer comes in four "pieces."

The personal piece. "I can tell about 30 stories," says Hayles, "of people who've come to me [afte two or three years of diversity work] and said, 'M friends and family tell me I'm a better person.' That is, a better listener, a better communicator, more understanding friend. Hayles cites decade of research by Stuart W. Cook, professor emeritu of the University of Colorado, focusing on the e fects of desegregation on public schools. Cook' studies confirm, according to Hayles, that peopl who have learned to function in desegregated situ ations develop superior communication skills They tend to be better leaders, better coaches, bet ter at influencing others, better at giving and re ceiving feedback.

The social piece. Bring in the demographics Give people some of the widely available "Work force 2000" data about the changing complexion o the American labor force: It will contain more fe males, more minorities, more immigrants, mor older people, more disabled people, and so on Also, discuss the "global economy" in which th organization now must survive, and the foreig markets in which it may be competing for custo mers and employees. The message: Love it or hat it, we're all going to be forced to deal gracefully with more and more people who are not "like" us.

The legal piece. This one is quick, simple an brutal. In case anyone has somehow missed th news that discrimination lawsuits are expensive Hayles suggests you cite a few noteworthy cases State Farm Insurance settles a class-action suit fo $300 million. General Motors gets hit for mor than $40 million, again in a class-action case. US Corp. is hammered for $42 million. Judgments o that size can affect the stock price of *Fortune 50(*

women and minorities at the bottom of the organizational pyramid is due to a corporate environment that is somehow unfriendly to them—that the "glass ceiling" reflects bias and not any lack of hard work or intelligence or merit—then what we're talking about is "the underutilization of human resources," Thomas says. "It's a managerial issue as opposed to a legal, social or moral issue."

Quite so, agrees the director of management training at a major insurance company, who asked not to be identified because her company is about to launch a new diversity effort on a worldwide scale. "To a large extent," she declares, "it's what we've been saying about management all along—people are individuals and they have to be managed as individuals. Now we're just saying, 'Hey, we were right. So let's get with it.'" If her company can learn to "manage diversity" well, she says, "That means

companies. On a smaller but still impressive scale, Northwest Airlines settled a racial discrimination case last year for $1.2 million. A sexual harassment suit cost K Mart almost triple that. As a matter of fact, the cultural diversity effort that Hayles now directs was born as part of a class-action settlement by Pillsbury—$1.76 million, according to *Business Week*. The average discrimination case brought against a company by an individual now costs the company about $75,000, Hayles says.

The profit piece. "The bottom line is a powerful reason" to do diversity work, Hayles maintains. Differences get in our way. They cost us time, effort and money. But if we deal with them skillfully, differences can be turned into a powerful advantage. "I begin with the egg and the sperm," he says. "When the sperm tries to fertilize an egg and the genetic material is too similar, the egg rejects it." Similarly, he contends, heterogeneous groups of people, when well managed, can outperform homogeneous groups "in both quality and quantity. Research supports that statement." (See main story.) A good demonstration is to split a class into several small groups, some homogeneous (all white females, for instance) and some heterogeneous (blacks, whites, males, females, gays, straights, etc.). Assign the groups a task, such as developing a budget for how to spend X dollars. Then have the entire class evaluate the various solutions on the basis of feasibility and creativity. Almost invariably, Hayles says, the ratings will be higher for the heterogeneous groups.

Plenty of examples can be cited of business blunders caused by too much homogeneity at top management levels. This is especially true of businesses that want to operate in international markets. A single Spanish speaker in the decision-making loop could have saved General Motors the expense of trying to market the Chevy Nova in Mexico ("No va" means "won't go."). With a little more intercultural savvy, the Gerber baby food folks would have known that marketing their products in Africa would not be a simple matter of changing the white baby on the labels to a black baby. In one African country, Hayles says, it is customary for a label to picture the product, not the intended customer. In addition to recalling and re-labeling a lot of jars, Gerber had to apologize to its customers for suggesting that they were cannibals.

3. How do we do the work?

Again, there are four pieces.

Cognitive. This is the informational component of diversity work—"the head piece," as Hayles calls it. Everyone needs to understand the laws and regulations governing employment discrimination, how affirmative action and Equal Employment Opportunity programs work, the demographics of the labor pool, the demographics of the company's customer base, and so on.

Behavioral. Give people specific guidance about unacceptable behavior. "Don't call women girls, don't call black men boys, don't tell sexist jokes—all of that stuff," says Hayles.

Complete those two tasks, he says, and you can make your company an acceptable place to work. To be outstanding, however, you'll need to tackle two other pieces—and doing so will involve much more than an introductory workshop or two.

Emotional. Be careful here, Hayles warns. "I'm talking about safe, professionally facilitated, non-mandatory emotional work. This is where organizations get into trouble with unqualified facilitators." Under the "emotional" heading Hayles places all the exercises and quasi-therapeutic techniques that encourage people to dredge up and examine their own deep-seated prejudices and those of others in the group.

Organizational. This is the "systems" component, and it's a big one. A company that wants to encourage, appreciate and capitalize on diversity instead of just tolerating it will probably need to change some policies and practices. Performance appraisal systems, pay and benefits systems, coaching practices, mentoring schemes, management development programs, flex-time arrangements, job sharing, day care, affirmative action plans—all these things and more need to be examined.

What's the goal of all this? To build an organization that can recognize and capitalize on the strengths of everybody in it, and turn "synergy" from a buzzword into a reality.—**J.G.**

'We can't do it the way we've been trying to do it.'

we'll have created a climate where everyone can contribute to the best of their ability." And "everyone" includes white males.

If this sort of talk about "diversity" doesn't catch practically everybody by surprise today, it would have just a few years ago, says Robert Hayles, vice president of cultural diversity for Grand Metropolitan Food Sector (formerly Pillsbury Co.) of Minneapolis.

With a handful of exceptions—Digital Equipment Corp., US West and a few other companies—" 'diversity,' five years ago, meant protected groups," Hayles says. That is, "diverse people" were members of groups covered by anti-discrimination laws, period. Diversity was, indeed, a code word for affirmative action. Over the past year or two, however, a wider definition has gained much greater currency. Hayles, who, like Thomas, is black, subscribes to the broad view himself.

According to this view, "diversity work" addresses the biases of the male manager who is reluctant to send a female to New York on business because it's too dangerous, thus denying her a fast-track career opportunity. But it also addresses the female—or male—who really *doesn't* want to make business trips to New York. Is there some other way, equally valid or even more so, to give this person the experience and seasoning needed for a promotion?

This broader view of diversity is by no means universal—and by no means universally welcomed. Most of the time, "diversity program" is still used as a synonym for EEO or affirmative action. And in some circles, a view of "diversity" that includes white males is looked upon as blasphemous. Hayles says he catches plenty of heat for his approach: "African-Americans say, 'Hey, our ancestors were brought here by force, we've suffered from racism for hundreds of years, and statistics say it'll be somewhere between the years 2100 and 3000 before we achieve parity [with whites] in jobs, income and home ownership. If you dilute diversity work, we won't see parity until the year 5000.'"

Along with dismay at the prospect of white males edging in beneath the diversity umbrella comes suspicion. "I know a professor at a university in New York who thinks it's a George Bush plot to do away with progress by women and minorities," says Sivasailam Thiagarajan, adjunct professor in the School of Education at Indiana University in Bloomington. "At universities, it is still politically incorrect to say, 'Let's use a bigger yardstick to measure differences.' It's seen as another sneaky way to get around affirmative action."

To be sure, affirmative action supporters needn't be paranoid these days to figure that someone is out to get them. Many whites see affirmative action as reverse discrimination, plain and simple. "Quota" has become a dirty word on the national scene. George Bush leads a long list of politicians who have made hay with voters by denouncing racial hiring targets. One of the few things we do know about the Senate-probe-resistant legal views of new Supreme Court Justice Clarence Thomas is that he thinks affirmative action programs are bad news. Other nonwhite writers and professionals have also stepped forward to assert that affirmative action stigmatizes its minority beneficiaries in more ways than it helps them.

There is, however, another way to look at the broadening definition of diversity.

In light of the societal backlash against "political correctness" and the police-state atmosphere said to be enveloping many college campuses, "diversity" may have been on the road to joining "quotas" as a word to be spat out in public with distaste. Something had to change.

'**D**iversity' no longer refers to a range of views on a disputed question but rather entails enlisting in a whole set of ideological causes that are identified as being "for diversity"....

[In 1989], when the University of Pennsylvania was planning to require all freshmen in campus residences to participate in consciousness-raising sessions dealing with racism, sexism, and heterosexism, one undergraduate on the "diversity education" planning committee sent a note to the administration noting her reservations about the program. She expressed her "deep regard for the individual and my desire to protect the freedoms of all members of society." A university administrator sent her note back, with the word "individual" underlined and the comment, "This is a RED FLAG phrase today, which is considered by many to be RACIST. Arguments that champion the individual over the group ultimately privilege the 'individuals' belonging to the largest or dominant group."—Dinesh D'Souza in "Illiberal Education," The Atlantic Monthly, March 1991.

Today's radicalism-from-above uses administrative power to impose an improved "consciousness" on [college] students. It uses various instruments of indoctrination, from mandatory instruction in officially approved thinking (about race, gender, sexual preference) to codes of permissible speech. This is done in the name of "sensitivity" to the needs of "diversity."— George Will in Newsweek, May 6, 1991.

Observations like Will's are sometimes waved aside as part of a "predictable backlash" by a "white-male power structure" terrified at the prospect of having to share any power whatsoever with minorities and women. But for those who do favor advances by minorities and women, there is a nonideological issue at work here also, a straightforward problem of strategy and tactics.

Unless I have some sort of gun to hold to your head, I can only exercise a moral claim on you to the degree that you are willing to accept my claim as valid. As a society, our tolerance for the moral claims of others is running low. A lot of people are now saying openly what they've been thinking for some time. In 1991, it was almost as if a dam burst. To wit:

The politics of penance may be most fruitless of all. You can only harangue people and tell them what bad guys and oppressors they are and that they have a debt and better make good on it for so long before they tell you to get lost.—Meg Greenfield in Newsweek, Aug. 5, 1991.

As the list of victims and rights expands, and as the special-interest groups that promote them grow increasingly numerous, militant and shrill, the people who constitute what remains of the social mainstream are feeling ever more beleaguered and unsympathetic.

Their well of guilt is running dry, a phenomenon that is known as "compassion fatigue"... —John Taylor in "Don't Blame Me! The New Culture of Victimization," *New York* magazine, June 3, 1991.

What is odd about the PC [politically correct] people... is their dopey belief that people can be bullied into being kind, good and sensitive to each other, never speaking thoughtlessly to, or thinking unkindly of, people whatever their race, religion, country of national origin, sex or sexual habits.

Mostly the bullying is done by wielding brutish language.... [A]busive epithets are used mercilessly on people whose words or ideas defy the dogma of goodness.... Standard PC epithets include 'racist,' 'elitist,' 'sexist,' 'anti-Semite' and 'homophobe,' each carrying its own built-in exclamation mark. It's a language for people who talk at the top of their lungs. —Russell Baker in a *New York Times* piece syndicated nationally in August 1991.

Those epithets are losing their sting; they don't shut the other guy up as quickly today as they did yesterday. The pointed finger of guilt is less useful as a lever. Blame it on the excesses of PC. Blame it on George Bush cynically fanning racial tensions with Willy Horton in 1988 and with "quotas" ever since.

Or, better, blame it on an economy in which "mainstream people" have increasing reason to fear for their own futures, never mind anybody else's. Corporate "downsizings" have thrown millions out of work and left millions more clinging fearfully to their jobs. Adjusted for inflation, average weekly earnings have fallen 12 percent over the past 20 years. Confidence in the American Dream is fading. Perhaps for the first time in the nation's history, there is serious, widespread doubt that our children will live better than we do.

In the past few years, ugly white-racist incidents have made headlines in some pretty odd places—not in the Old South but at Stanford and the University of Massachusetts. Between July and November 1991, police recorded 12 separate cases of cross burnings in the yards of black citizens in Dubuque, IA.

As this is written, a badly shaken nation heaved a sigh of uneasy relief as voters in Louisiana decided that they would not, after all, choose as their governor David Duke, erstwhile neo-Nazi and ex-grand wizard of the Ku Klux Klan.

We can blame all of this on just about anything we like. But unless we assume for some reason that the people of Louisiana have not seen a national news magazine or watched a network television broadcast for the past 30 years, we can't blame it on a lack of sermons. The problem simply cannot be that white folks in Louisiana haven't heard the news that racism is bad. It makes no sense any longer to pretend that the answer to the Duke problem—or the

sexism problem or the homophobia problem—is to tell white males one more time, or 1,000 more times, that they are "bad guys and oppressors and that they have a debt and better make good on it."

They've all heard the message. If anything, the message now seems to be exacerbating the very problems it's supposed to solve. The blame game even shows signs of coming full circle and collapsing into comic absurdity. The San Jose *Mercury News* reports that a small group of white Californians has formed to protest stereotypes of whites as oppressors. They will badger people to use the term European-American instead of Anglo or white. One member is quoted as saying, "If someone uses the term 'lily white,' we'll contact them and explain that that shows insensitivity to European ethnic diversity."

Apparently this is earnestness, not social satire.

If we want to build a society with equal opportunity and justice for all—and businesses that function effectively with the diverse employees and customers thrust upon them by demographic changes and the global economy—the road of guilt and blame looks increasingly like a dead end.

"We can't do it the way we've been trying to do it," says Lewis Griggs of Copeland Griggs Productions in San Francisco, producer of the "Valuing Diversity" series of training films. "We've got to go back and come in through a different door."

The risk of expanding the definition of diversity, says Grand Met's Hayles, is that you may contribute to a "state of denial" about the special problems of protected groups. This must be guarded against. The advantage of starting with the premise that *everybody* is diverse, however, is that "you don't make white males the subject of the work rather than part of it."

The idea behind managing diversity is to learn to look at people as individuals, and to see individual strengths and weaknesses instead of merely registering bothersome variances from arbitrary corporate norms. The goal, says Thomas, is an organization that is able to function as productively with heterogeneous workers as it once did with homogeneous ones.

Hayles takes issue with Thomas on that point. He insists that research has established beyond any reasonable doubt that well-managed heterogeneous groups are more productive than homogeneous ones. Managing diversity, therefore, is about improving corporate performance, not just holding the line as the work force becomes less Anglo. To back his claim, Hayles cites research and writings by authorities such as Stuart W. Cook, professor emeritus at the University of Colorado, and Harvard's Rosabeth Moss Kanter. In her 1983 book *The Change Masters*, for instance, Kanter describes a study showing that companies with "progressive human resource practices" such as affirmative action and participative management showed unusually high profitability and financial growth over a 25-year period.

Thomas doesn't argue about what such studies have proved or failed to prove. If heterogeneous

WARNING: ANY BIAS YOU CONFRONT MAY BE HELD AGAINST YOU...

These are porcupines, bristling with hyperacute sensitivities, circling one another warily and on tiptoe.

If you decide you need special training workshops to teach your managers not to discriminate against minorities or women, have you just admitted you have reason to believe your managers discriminate against minorities and women? And couldn't that admission come back to haunt you in a lawsuit?

It's a chilling thought, and no longer a hypothetical one. As this issue of TRAINING went to press, organizations around the country were nervously awaiting a court decision that will address the question.

The case in San Francisco federal court involves Lucky Stores Inc., a subsidiary of American Stores Co. of Salt Lake City.

In 1988 Lucky put its supervisors through a series of workshops that featured some common diversity-training exercises. In one, participants closed their eyes and imagined a "successful manager." Most of them envisioned a white male. In another exercise they discussed racial and gender stereotypes.

When a group of female and minority employees later sued Lucky for discrimination, they obtained some notes taken during the workshop. The notes recorded comments from the supervisors. Sample comments, according to *The Wall Street Journal*: "Black females are aggressive." "Women cry more." "Women want to stay home."

Lucky's lawyers protested that the supervisors were not stating their actual opinions, but were citing examples of stereotypical views as part of the workshop. This is, in fact, one of the most common exercises in diversity training.

The plaintiffs' lawyer, however, described the notes as "direct evidence of discriminatory attitudes" and "the proverbial smoking gun," according to the *WSJ*.

As of mid-November, attorneys for both sides had presented their closing briefs and the case was in the judge's hands.

The consensus in the diversity-training community seems to be that the Lucky affair will prove merely a cautionary tale about the value of due diligence and professionalism in the conduct of workshops. Adriana Arzac, executive director of the International Society for Intercultural Education, Training and Research, says it points out the need for confidentiality contracts in sessions where employees are urged to confront their own unconscious biases about people of other races, religions, cultures or genders.

It also points out the need to destroy the evidence. After the session, say experienced trainers, get rid of flip-chart pages and other written records of things people said while being encouraged to identify stereotypes—or to bare their own souls.

The stereotype-listing exercise that apparently got Lucky into trouble "is one that everybody uses," says Robert Hayles, vice president of cultural diversity for Grand Metropolitan Food Sector in Minneapolis. He predicts the judge will agree that the supervisors were not describing attitudes that routinely guided their own conduct. "If Lucky did the exercises right," he says, "they'll come out OK in court."

If the judge decides otherwise, however, "chilling effect" might be far too mild a word to describe the impact on diversity programs nationwide.

J.G.

groups can indeed become more productive than homogeneous ones, he says, "that's icing on the cake. But the first challenge is to get the same level of productivity. We need to learn how to bake the cake before we worry about putting on the icing. And we don't know how to bake the cake yet."

Whether the goal is equal performance or superior performance, both men agree that the way to get there is to stop treating diversity as a moral issue and start treating it as a business issue. This focus helps explain the emphasis in diversity training on teaching lessons that often sound embarrassingly simplistic. Why would anyone over the age of eight need workshops and games and exercises to inform him that everybody is "different" in some way? Where's the blinding revelation in the news that we have all been culturally inculcated with unconscious biases? "The revelation," says Hayles, "is that our problems with differences cost money. They cost productivity."

"The attempt of diversity training is precisely to get out of the guilt cycle," says Adriana Arzac, executive director of the International Society for Intercultural Education, Training and Research (SIETAR). "The point is not to say, 'OK, you white guys, clean up your act and shame on you'....The same stereotypes the white male has of minorities and women are also working in reverse."

The guilt-free diversity trolley may still jump the track, however, unless we find a better way to conduct discussions about stereotypes and sensitivities. Merely adding white male gripes to the ever-expanding pile of behavioral do's and don'ts is pointless. If the idea behind all this is to help people work together more productively, then learning to respect or "value" differences cannot be a matter of everyone exchanging and memorizing lists of peeves: Joe learns that he must never forget himself and use a term like "salesman" or "chairman" around Betty, and he must always refer to Maya as a "woman of color," to Diana as "black," and to Sam as a "Chinese American" rather than an "Asian American." Betty, Maya, Diana and Sam learn to call Joe a European American but never to call Bob one because Bob thinks the term is extraordinarily silly, although he must never say so or laugh at it because that would transgress against Joe's diversity....

These are not people who will like one another, trust one another, be comfortable with one another or do any creative work together. These are porcupines, bristling with hyperacute sensitivities, circling one another warily and on tiptoe.

Thiagarajan quotes George Bernard Shaw: "A friend is somebody in whose presence I can do as I damn please." We might expand that sentiment and suggest that a coworker with whom I can accomplish great things is one to whom I can say what I damn well think.

Confronting bigotry is one thing, Hayles declares. But what about all the well-meaning people who are struggling as best they can to work together effectively? Surely there must be something better to offer them than checklists of booby-trapped words and forbidden opinions.

*T*he spirit of the age favors the moralist and the busybody, and the instinct to censor and suppress shows itself not only in the protests for and against abortion or multiculturalism but also in the prohibitions against tobacco and pet birds. It seems that everybody is forever looking out for everybody else's spiritual or physical salvation.... The preferred modes of address number only three—the sermon, the eu-phemism, and the threat—and whether I look to the political left or the political right I'm constantly being told to think the right thoughts and confess the right sins....

A society in which everybody distrusts everybody else classifies humor as a dangerous substance and entertains itself with cautionary tales.... I see so many citizens armed with the bright shields of intolerance that I wonder how they would agree on anything other than a need to do something repressive and authoritarian.—Lewis H. Lapham in *Harper's*, October 1991.

It is in that spirit of humorless, sermonistic distrust that we have grown used to carrying on the national conversation about stereotypes and biases and who has been thinking the wrong thoughts about whom. Thiagarajan notes ruefully that a national training association has recently begun warning speakers at its conferences that it will not tolerate any attempts at humor that might prove offensive to any individual or group—this in the name of respecting diversity. "So I can't make fun of Hindus?" asks Thiagarajan, who is Hindu. "I can't make fun of stupid people?"

If the goal of diversity work is a high-performance organization rather than just a climate in which nobody's feathers are ever ruffled, we need a different way to talk about the problem of differences.

"We've got to be *more* willing to accidentally offend each other," says Griggs. "Let's know that we're going to make mistakes and try to patch them up instead of trying to ward off all possible mistakes. That's the wrong tack. If we develop the right attitude of 'standing in neutral' with respect to the likelihood that somebody has a different attitude about something, we won't need lists of wrong words to avoid."

The Plight of the Seasoned Worker

There's a limitless pool of young talent out there and industry is largely practicing its own form of euthanasia.

Joseph F. McKenna and Brian S. Moskal

They've been battered by downsizing like everyone else, maybe worse. They know how intense the competition for each promotion has become and have seen younger, more inexperienced co-workers get the promotions they themselves feel they have earned. And they understand the dystrophy of talents that don't get enough use. They are the mid-to-late-career whitecollar professionals in the 45-to-65-year age group. Increasingly they're being asked to retire early, whether or not they are pension-eligible. Many of them are accepting what they know will be their last promotion at a time when, in fact, they are still vibrant and vigorous and ready for more growth in authority and responsibility. Some of them, fearful of the push of younger colleagues, simply opt to bail out. Consider the story of this manager, who finally walked away from his job at a major corporation's aerospace division.

"People who have seniority need to be reinforced about being valued," he tells INDUSTRY-WEEK. "Nothing works more as a demotivator than feeling you have been shoved aside and that your ideas don't count. That's what made me leave the company at the age of 44. As the company was making cuts, I was hearing guys 39 and 42 saying 'We've got to get rid of old Sam in HR because he's no good anymore.'

"It occurred to me that I could be one of those guys," he adds. "Maybe not fired, but just set over on the side and not paid attention to. That scared the hell out of me."

He searched for a company "with a CEO who was at least a year older" than himself. In a short time, another major corporation latched on to him, recognizing his abilities as a motivator of employees and a disciple of worker empowerment. Ironically, his former company, itself having grown older and wiser in the interim, ultimately tried to lure him back—but to no avail.

And so go the winners and losers who function and malfunction respectively amid the myths and the realities about seasoned workers—a vulnerable but competent human-resource component of business organizations.

One myth is that these "older" workers are set in their ways, that they can't adapt to new work situations, and that they rely on stale information to make business decisions. Yet, even if they carry a knowledge base with some outdated parts, that doesn't mean they can't accept new information and apply it.

MATURE WORKERS HAVE "MORE PATIENCE TO ROLL WITH THE PUNCHES THAN DO THEIR YOUNGER COUNTERPARTS."

"The workplace expectations of our management seem to decrease as we mature workers age. Our assignments start to get stale and less challenging and it almost ensures that management will perceive our job-performance skills as being on the decline. This can become a deadly self-fulfilling prophecy," says a member of the 45-plus age group, who adds, "If you want to stay vital during the aging process you have to take charge of yourself and your work life. You can't become a victim of the system."

Another myth: Only the younger workers need developmental programs to help them grow on the job. The truth is that mature professionals need job- and skill-growth programs to keep them fired up and to bolster their self-esteem on the job—and most welcome such growth opportunities.

"It's a sad commentary when so many companies are in a downsizing mode. There is a myth that the 45-plus-year-old workers don't contribute and can't wait to get out the door—and that only young people are full of energy. People in their prime are put in this category," asserts Robert L. Faulkner, superintendent, Reliability Dept., Packard Electric Div. of General Motors Corp., Warren, Ohio. Echoing that sentiment are Drs. Denise Tanguay Hoyer and Barbara Hirshorn, researchers who have extensively studied how retirees in particular fit into the contemporary American economy. Mature workers bring a much more quality-oriented work ethic to the job as compared with their younger counterparts, reports Dr. Tanguay Hoyer, professor of management at Eastern Michigan University's College of Business, Yipsilanti.

Moreover, she says, "they tend to have job experience that exceeds the level of the current job." Dr. Hirshorn, an associate professor for research at Wayne State University's Institute of Gerontology, Detroit, adds that some companies are particularly interested in seasoned workers' ability to transfer their workplace knowledge to younger workers. "We've found this in workplaces of all sizes," she says. "*Nobody knows this area like Charlie.*"

Mature professionals are "the backbone of American commerce and industry. As a group, they are more sensitive to superiors who might think their workplace skills are on the decline. Sometimes senior management makes cuts to save dollars and, as a result, workers in this age group feel more threatened or endangered [than their younger co-workers]," says Dr. Jack Thompson, president and CEO, RHR International Co., Wood Dale, Ill., a consulting firm that applies the behavioral sciences to business management issues.

"Eventually you get past the demons of wanting to get ahead and making more and more money. You start taking a broader view of what is important to yourself and to society as a whole. You ask yourself how you can contribute to society as a whole," says James A. Lenarz, at age 69 a partner in Exploration Inventories, Eden Prairie, Minn. His firm creates assessment tools that help managers explore their strengths and weaknesses in order to develop a road map for future job growth and development.

Despite such realities, though, myths continue. One concerns whether the 45-plus whitecollar worker should be or deserves to be promoted, say mature professionals. "Companies are reluctant to 'waste' promotions on people in the 40-to-45-plus age group. Nowadays, companies start encouraging people to leave at age 50 to 55 or so, and management feels it is wasting a promotion on someone with only seven to 10 years left," says one professional middle manager who is 45-plus and thinks he'll be lucky to get another promotion with his current employer.

"My boss actually *told* me I would not receive another promotion and informed me who my 'replacement' is when he promoted him," says another manager, 48. "Am I supposed to care anymore?"

"I know what will and won't work," says Mr. Lenarz who retired from Honeywell Inc. in 1982 at age 58 after 30 years as a line manager in engineering, quality, and professional development of scientists and engineers. Well before his retirement, he says his work life was "getting a little dull. Even the crises were getting predictable. I felt stymied and I didn't have much energy to go to work every day." Mr. Lenarz then took more control of his work life and reinvigored himself with a succession of new positions, including quality manager at Honeywell's Golden Valley plant and manager of development for technical and engineering professionals. As a result of working as corporate manager of professional development of engineers, scientists, and technicians in the late '70s and early '80s, his workplace philosophy now says the ideal mixture in business is the older worker teamed with younger workers. It can be a mutual admiration society. "These days I don't think the wisdom of the elders is revered in our society. There is a lot of information and experience that older people have to share but it usually doesn't dawn on people to ask us for it," he adds.

"YOU START TAKING A BROADER VIEW OF WHAT IS IMPORTANT TO YOURSELF AND TO SOCIETY AS A WHOLE."

Consider David L. Schiska, who accepted early retirement at 55 from his position as manager in the regulatory department of Ohio Bell, a unit of Ameritech. "I've managed up to 100 people at one time and it's hard for early career people to have these work-related skills," says Mr. Schiska of Lakewood, Ohio. He now wants to embark on a second career because "55 is too young to stop working and because I have a lot of productivity left in me."

A slightly different perspective comes from Mr. Faulkner, who just completed his college degree requirements on weekends while working full-time for Packard Electric. He not only offers 20 years of experience after starting at the bottom as a first-line supervisor at Packard Electric but also an education that is as up-to-date as those received by recent college graduates. Mr. Faulkner completed his final 2.5 years of college courses in business management and sociology during four years of weekend classroom instruction.

"Professionally, I offer the experience of having a number of assignments in manufacturing, quality control, and engineering. I haven't just focused on one area and I can put together all the experiences from various jobs that a younger professional would find hard to match," says Mr. Faulkner, who studied weekends at Hiram College, Hiram, Ohio, in a program tailor-made to retool seasoned workers for today's marketplace challenges. "Because of my experience, I can get to people and cut through the red tape in order to get done quickly a job that a younger professional wouldn't be able to do. It takes time to acquire that kind of knowledge and expertise," says the 47-year-old Mr. Faulkner, who is also president of the local school board in Warren—7,000 students in grades one through 12—and serves as the local president of the United Negro College Fund.

"I interface with adults and young people, get a chance to talk to them about careers, I'm a mentor in the community and a very positive reflection on Packard Electric. Not many younger professionals can say the same," stresses Mr. Faulkner.

In addition to experience, mature workers also have "more patience to roll with the punches than do their younger counterparts," thinks Dr. Thompson of RHR International.

The advantages offered by seasoned workers are becoming more obvious. The question is, will management better use the inherent wisdom, savvy, knowledge, and experience of the 45-plus professional?

If the answer ultimately is yes, management must change its level of expectations for the group. "One of the most deadly things is if top management has a low level of expectation for the 45-plus whitecollar professional. If managements want to tap into the power of older professionals they need to reinvest in the training of these workers. They should help create a learning organization for all, including mature and late-career professionals," says Exploration Inventories' Mr. Lenarz.

"THERE IS A MYTH THAT THE 45-PLUS-YEAR-OLD WORKERS DON'T CONTRIBUTE AND CAN'T WAIT TO GET OUT THE DOOR. . . ."

Eastern Michigan's Dr. Tanguay Hoyer and her colleague found that workplace experience helps flatten the learning curve for employees who were never trained in a particular skill. "Because of their other work characteristics," she says, "they were given training and were successful at responding to that training."

Organizations should, in addition, apply continuous quality-improvement techniques to workers and the workplace. "Otherwise you send a silent message to people over 40 that they should stop improving. When management doesn't ask members of this age group to improve their workplace skills, it sends a message that top management believes their productivity will fall off, regardless," says Mr. Lenarz.

If there is concern that being in a position too long will cripple performance, argues Wayne State's Dr. Hirshorn, companies should consider intentional reassignment—matching certain experience-related characteristics to positions. That, she says, shows an unquestionable interest in retaining seasoned workers.

But, at the very core of managing people, there's no real difference between a young union worker on the production line and a senior accounting manager who's been around the company for ages, says Paul J. Giddens, corporate director of organizational effectiveness at Georgia-Pacific Corp., Atlanta. "I had expected major differences between the young, the middle-aged, and the older person," he says, "but I've found that everybody is just working out of their own comfort zone."

The real managerial skill, then, lies in navigating through those zones. As Mr. Giddens sees it, "the comfort zone for young folks is 'There's more to life than work.' The middle-aged employees are concerned about their jobs and being able to send their kids to school. And the older employees are reluctant to change because they're comfortable. They don't want to give up what they perceive to be their power, and they're afraid of having to relearn anything."

For Mr. Giddens, a former HR "wizard" at General Electric Go., managing the most seasoned of workers translates into "having their managers create an empowering environment where they discover the needs of both the team and the individual employees and then serve as a positive resource to getting them what they need to do their jobs, rather than getting them to leap out of their comfort zones." (See "Workforce Wizardry: How Empowerment Transforms Scarecrows," IW, July 16, 1990, page 8.)

One case in point is the reworking of accounting processes at Georgia-Pacific. This makeover is more than a new way of bean-counting; it requires the use of a team, a contemporary business term that still raises eyebrows among veterans. "Older employees are less into teams than younger ones—unless you do it right," notes Mr. Giddens. "If people don't like the word team, don't call it a team. Call it a banana. Let's say we have 150 accountants across the board and we're saying, 'Your role is changing. The green eyeshade is gone. You all are going to be business partners. You're going to have to access data, work with your partners, extract appropriate data, and then turn that data into some type of meaningful information for others.' Now strangely enough, the older employees are looking at

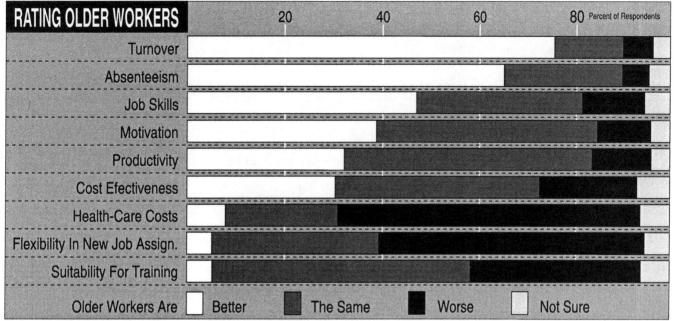

RATING OLDER WORKERS	20	40	60	80 Percent of Respondents
Turnover				
Absenteeism				
Job Skills				
Motivation				
Productivity				
Cost Efectiveness				
Health-Care Costs				
Flexibility In New Job Assign.				
Suitability For Training				

Older Workers Are □ Better ▨ The Same ■ Worse ▢ Not Sure

SOURCE: THE CONFERENCE BOARD. BASED ON INTERVIEWS WITH 406 HUMAN-RESOURCE EXECUTIVES: OLDER WORKERS IN THIS CASE ARE 55 AND OLDER.

this as an opportunity to do something they always thought they were doing and not getting recognized for." So, insists Mr. Giddens, managing older workers isn't really much different from managing their younger counterparts. "It's the way you color the banana," he says.

Ah, but what if the banana, be it bright green or golden yellow, gets sliced? Downsizing is quickly becoming a constant in the economy of the '90s. But if companies want to wipe out older workers and go only with younger employees, they will be losing experience and knowledge gained over decades. A better solution is to blend old and new ideas together.

In its 1992 report "The Availability of a Quality Work Force," The Conference Board notes that "the current focus on downsizing and cost reductions may be obscuring the potential for skills loss represented by the growing number of early retirees. The aging of the labor force, combined with the trend toward early retirement, represents a potentially large loss of experienced workers from the labor force. Employers are faced with the ironic possibility that they will be remediating large numbers of unqualified job entrants while simultaneously encouraging the early exit of many highly trained employees."

Adds Mr. Schiska, "If you wipe the slate clean and end up with only younger workers without much experience, you run a risk. It's much better to have a blend of age groups and ideas." On the bright side, he sees a natural, though still largely untapped, landing pad for mid- and late-career professionals: small business.

"It would be very productive for small businesses to use those people who have been removed from the payrolls due to downsizing. Their experience could be vital to such companies. But I don't even know if small businesses are thinking about hiring the displaced of corporate America."

He cites himself as an example: "I could come in and train people two to three days a week and I wouldn't mind working for less money and having my weekends free after having worked long hours for most of my career. Small companies and mature workers can complement each other with a very mature working relationship but I don't know if small companies recognize the potential yet."

Meanwhile, other pre-baby boom professionals think they need to be shown more patience and tolerance. They should be given the chance to do the next-level-up job. Eastern Michigan's Dr. Tanguay Hoyer advises, fit them into positions where their current characteristics—both physical and experiential—fit. And if they need mentoring, mentor them.

Otherwise, the productivity of this age group will live up to the expectations of management—it will decline significantly.

An "attitude adjustment" on the part of top management should be threefold: training, investment, and mentoring.

"The real message I would like people to take home is that the leader in business has the obligation to value the unique contributions of their employees," says Georgia-Pacific's Mr. Giddens. "This is the real meaning of diversity. Diversity is not just some government number to meet in terms of race, sex, etc. It's more than a competitive edge. It is the key to innovative survival in the years to come.

"Diversity means creating a business culture that encourages and reinforces honest and candid input from a wide variety of people, ages, and races. Diversity means a greater source of ideas."

There is, says Mr. Giddens, no difference in the basic approach of managing the seasoned employee and the rest of the workforce. However, "it takes a gutsy leader to actually know his people well enough to uncover individual 'hot buttons,' and to be a unique resource to the team members," he says.

Mr. Giddens reaches back some 20 odd years for a lesson he learned from his Army Master Sergeant—"all I'll ever need to know about leadership, or young, middle-aged, and older people," he says. "Addressing me in private, he said, 'Sir, do you want to be some kind of cowboy hero, or do you want to live? It ain't complicated. You don't need anyone's permission to be a good leader—not your mommy's, not your daddy's, not your Colonel's, not even mine.

" 'Just be a resource to your team. All you have to do is 1. Know your people. 2. Look out for their welfare. 3. Keep them informed. 4. Let them take part in the decisions that affect them. You don't need to be a hero. Wear your medals on *their* chests.'

"If," says Mr. Giddens, "we in management would simply lead and follow this simple, yet profound, advice, we would see that people are people regardless of age.

"We all have unique differences in perception, apprehension, and approach. But we are more alike than we are different in how we approach our work: We want to be valued, respected, and listened to."

THE FUTURE
OF LABOR-MANAGEMENT
RELATIONS

Scott Seegert
and Brian H. Kleiner

Brian H. Kleiner, Ph.D., is a professor of management at California State University–Fullerton.

We have all heard how out-dated and inefficient our production system is in the United States. The Japanese, as well as other countries, have moved far ahead of us in terms of both quality of product and productivity of the worker. We tend to blame a great deal of this on the fact that Japan has newer and thus technologically advanced tooling available to their production system. Perhaps an even greater reason for the obvious separation in production, however, is in the treatment of the worker and the mutual definition of what productivity is and should be.

The United States, being a capitalistic society, has always thought of productivity in terms of production rates and their corresponding effects on the profits of an organization. The worker is fitted to a task (often machine-oriented) and his job is made as simple and repetitive as possible in order to increase the efficiency in which the task is completed. What is suggested here, however, is that productivity involves more than just the needs of the organization. For a society as a whole to be productive, it must do more to satisfy the needs of the individual people in it. For this to occur, the relationship between management and labor (and labor unions) must head in new directions.

Irving Bluestone, in the book *Work in America - the Decade Ahead*, suggests collective bargaining between labor and unions and management to help fill certain needs

and rights that our society should but does not provide adequately to its members. Included among these rights are health care, life insurance, retirement benefits and no loss in pay for holidays, vacations and absence due to illness. These are areas of present concern in labor-management negotiations and fall into the area of hard-line controversial issues as discussed by Bluestone. He cites two other general areas of

> *Cooperation between management and labor/ unions in instituting and/or continuing these programs is a must if the labor force is to be trustful and thus receptive to them.*

concern, namely issues for joint cooperative programs between labor and management and worker participation in decision making.

Hard-line controversial issues

This constitutes the real emphasis of present day labor/union negotiations. Included in these issues are basic needs as far as pay, security and fringe benefits are concerned; and negotiations in this area are strongly adversarial in nature. If our ultimate goal is, as it should be, societal productivity rather than simply higher profits for an organization, then job security must involve not only keeping the present workforce employed but also employing those who are out

of work. For a society to be productive and efficient as a whole, each member of that society must be a contributor. Our country has a history of high unemployment, and not much is being done by the legislative body to alter the situation. As was mentioned earlier, collective bargaining has been filling the void created by society's lack of action to provide for basic needs and rights, such as the right to earn a living. This is the problem that must be addressed in hard-line negotiations in the future.

Steps have already been made in the reduction of nationwide unemployment through mandatory retirement ages (with compensation) and reduced length of work weeks, which provides more jobs to obtain a specific level of production.

A push is currently in effect to reduce the standard work week from five to four days. Management's fear is that a four day work week will underutilize its capital investment in production equipment. By staggering days off, however, a plant may operate its normal forty hour week and also provide more jobs to the unemployed. If workers' income is not to decrease while working fewer hours, however, total wages

Reprinted with permission from *Industrial Management*, Vol. 35, No. 3, March/April 1993, pp. 15-16. © 1993 by The Institute of Industrial Engineers, 25 Technology Park, Norcross, GA 30092.

will increase as a result of the increased number of employees while production should remain constant. It should be suspected, on the other hand, that individual hourly productivity will increase due to the shorter work week, absenteeism will decrease and more employed consumers in the market will create a higher demand. This, in turn, will trigger more production within an organization. These factors should, to a large extent, tend to offset the increase in total wages within an organization, especially as the shorter work week gains popularity throughout industry.

Issues for joint cooperative programs

Another area of major concern in the management-labor relationship involves issues that require the involvement and cooperation of both labor/unions and management. These programs are designed to improve the quality of working life within an organization. When organized and conducted effectively, such programs will benefit both the worker and his management. Included here are programs in new employee orientation, health and safety and, more recently, drug and alcohol rehabilitation.

Again, the recurring theme of societal welfare is the driving force here. Of specific interest is the drug and alcohol rehabilitation issue. For years management has dealt with substance abusers with escalating levels of disciplinary action, usually resulting in termination. This scenario benefits neither the laborer nor the company's management. The worker loses his source of income and suffers possible loss of family and friends as well. Management loses an employee on which training time and money has already been spent and must suffer the expense of hiring and training a new employee.

Rehabilitation programs are in use in many industries and organizations and are increasing in acceptance throughout the country. Other programs have been designed to offer psychiatric counseling as well.

Cooperation between management and labor/unions in instituting and/or continuing these programs is a must if the labor force is to be trustful and thus receptive to them. The presence of the union as an active member is also an invaluable aid in communicating the intent and composition of such programs.

Worker participation in decision making

The Japanese are rapidly altering the way in which this country views the management-labor relationship. Management in the United States as a rule has a very authoritarian approach to how workers should be treated. They should be given orders, shown

how to carry them out and then do so. Tasks are simplified in an attempt to reduce human error as much as possible. It is felt that this will result in peak productivity and performance. What really comes out of this type of relationship is a feeling that management does not trust its labor force. It certainly does not regard it as the human resource it is.

As was mentioned earlier, improved technology is not the only, or even the main,

> *Management in the United States as a rule has a very authoritarian approach to how workers should be treated.*

reason the Japanese are leaving this country's production system behind. More importantly, it is the way in which they treat their workforce that separates our societies. Many would argue that this separation is due to cultural differences and in some instances this is valid. It is not, however, a viable excuse to ignore necessary changes, which need to be made in the treatment of the workforce of this country.

Many current labor-related problems with which management must contend are not the result of a technically inefficient production system. Problems such as increased absenteeism, high labor turnover and decreased quality of output are more people-related and need to be dealt with in a less scientific manner. Management has long stated that the worker is the most important step in the production process. Despite this prevalent opinion, management has done little to make use of the creativity that abounds among the labor force. Improving the quality of worklife through increased worker involvement in the decision making process will allow some of this latent creativity to surface. As a democratic society, we trust and even encourage individuals to make their own decisions in everyday life. Increasing an employee's direct bearing on the production process will lead to a greater sense of pride within that employee in regard to his or her job. This will most naturally lead to a decrease in labor turnover and

absenteeism and a marked increase in product quality.

If the Japanese really appear to dominate an aspect of production right now, it is the quality aspect. In Japan many large production organizations operate with complete quality control. Each worker is responsible for the quality of the product as it leaves the individual's work station. If upon inspection by the worker the part is found to be defective, that worker triggers a shut down of the line until the problem is found and eliminated. In this manner every part coming off the end of the line is of acceptable quality. The worker is trusted, given the responsibility of quality. The results are dramatic.

The aforementioned lack of trust pervades American industry and is easily seen in the quality control process. Typically a network of inspectors and other quality control measures are set up at the end of an assembly process. A worker will operate an assigned machine and repetitively mass produce a product or process relating to the product. As quality control finds defects, the problem must be pinpointed within the entire assembly process. This takes time, time during which more defective products are being turned out, increasing scrap. This is an example of how increased worker participation in decision making benefits the production system. It also enhances the total societal welfare by increasing the quality of worklife within the organization.

It would be useful at this point to discuss how this increased worker participation may be attained. First and foremost, a sense of trust must be developed between management and labor/labor unions. The two forces must develop a history of cooperation on the hard-line issues before anything may be accomplished in the more humanistic areas.

Through past trials and experimentation, basic criteria has been established that is essential to the success of any such program. First, the program should be voluntary. If workers are forced into such changes, the feeling that they are being treated in an authoritarian way will remain. Second, the workers must be convinced that any progress resulting from such a program will not also result in a loss of job security as more trivial jobs are eliminated. Third, and perhaps most important, management must design the jobs to fit the workers rather than making the worker fit the job. Individual creativity is only of value when it is unconstrained in its environment. A final necessity to successful implementation of an increased worker involvement in a decision making program is that the worker must be able to foresee how this program will benefit him. A framework of promotion and increased income corresponding to an increase in responsibilities must be developed and communicated to the labor force effectively. This is far from an exhaustive list of essential program features, but they all seem extremely important from past experience in various industries.

Being that an increased worker involvement program is far from a scientific endeavor, the program must be flexible to compensate for various human needs and emotions. Being a fairly new concept to all parties involved, a rigid framework would only serve to create hostility and excuses when problems occur.

Labor unions may be an invaluable tool if the future of such programs is to be successful. The unions could be of great importance in the development of the initial trust that must coexist between labor and management. A communication tool between the two groups, the union will serve as a buffer, helping each side to understand the other's point of view. Perhaps most importantly, unions give the labor force the unified power to alter today's authoritative system.

In summary, if we as a country are to reverse our current trend of falling productivity relative to many other countries, we must take the societal productivity approach. An overall improvement in the quality of worklife among the labor force should be the prime objective, thereby creating more of a team-oriented atmosphere in which the creative talents of the workers in our society could flourish. We as individuals are America's greatest resource and should be used to maximum capabilities.

For further reading

Buffa, Elwood S. *Meeting the Competitive Challenge.* Homewood, Illinois: Dow Jones-Irwin, 1984.

Chase, Richard B. and Nicholas J. Aquilano. *Production and Operations Management.* Homewood, Illinois: Irwin, 1985.

Hughes, Charles L. *Making Unions Unnecessary.* New York: Executive Enterprises Publications Co., Inc., 1976.

Kerr, Clark and Jerome M. Rosow. *Work in America: The Decade Ahead.* New York: Van Nostrand Reinhold Company.

Ouchi, William G. *Theory Z.* Reading, Massachusetts: Addison-Wesley Publishing Co., Inc., 1981.

Sandras, Bill. "JIT/TQC Changes in Thinking, Materials: Multiple Source vs. Single Source." *P&IM Review,* Jan. 1987, pp. 26,57.

Leasing Workers

Rosalind Resnick

Rosalind Resnick is a free-lance writer in Hollywood, Fla.

Three years ago, David Hinds' small business was hit with an increase of nearly 100 percent in workers' compensation costs on top of annual health-insurance price hikes averaging 20 percent. Whether Hinds' firm, Van Tone Co., a Dallas producer of flavoring extracts, could survive was uncertain.

Hinds' efforts to find a new insurance carrier failed. "We were a 24-employee group, and nobody wanted us," the president of Van Tone recalls. In desperation, on the advice of a friend who was also a business owner, he turned to employee leasing, which offers smaller firms a way to cut benefit costs and get out from under mountains of payroll and administrative paperwork.

The prospect of saving money and time has great appeal to small-business owners and managers, who tend to be chronically short of both. Because it can deliver convenience and savings, employee leasing is expanding rapidly.

There are now more than 1,300 employee-leasing companies and roughly 1 million leased employees nationwide, according to the Aegis Group, a San Bernardino, Calif., consulting firm that specializes in employee leasing. Most of these workers are located in the Sunbelt states. And Aegis forecasts that the industry will expand by about 20 percent a year throughout the decade.

"Small-business owners are facing a mounting tide of regulation and rising health-care costs, and they don't know which way to turn," says T. Joe Willey, president of Aegis and the author of several books on leasing. "Increasingly, they're turning to employee leasing."

Hinds is among the satisfied clients of this growing industry. If it weren't for employee leasing, he says, "we'd probably be out of business." He attributed 70 percent of Van Tone's 1991 profits to savings derived from employee leasing.

But the experiences of some other business owners show there can also be pitfalls in leasing. In recent years, a

Leasing your workers can cut benefit costs and reduce piles of paperwork. But it can be risky unless you sidestep the pitfalls.

half-dozen large leasing companies covering about 36,000 workers have collapsed, leaving hundreds of small employers and their workers responsible for millions of dollars in health-care and workers' compensation claims.

For example, CAP Staffing, a North Carolina leasing firm, closed its doors in August 1989 after less than a year in operation, leaving workers with $2.2 million in unpaid health claims in eight states. According to testimony at a Senate subcommittee hearing, company officials drained money from company accounts to pay personal debts. CAP Staffing's president ultimately pleaded guilty to multiple counts of fraud and received a federal prison term of up to six years.

While employees get stuck with unpaid health-insurance claims, employers are left with the tab when something goes wrong with workers' compensation insurance. Paragon Industries, Inc., a Sapulpa, Okla., oil-field-pipe manufacturer that employs 125 workers, was hit with $350,000 in unpaid disability and medical claims after its leasing company, Alliance Temporary Services Inc., failed to purchase workers' compensation coverage. Alliance is now defunct.

Russell A. Weidner, Paragon's vice president, says that his company remained liable despite a signed agreement from the leasing company that the claims would be covered. "The state goes after the next guy up the ladder," he says.

Given the differing experiences of firms like Van Tone and Paragon, companies considering leasing should do so with caution. Begin by understanding what is involved. Basically, here's how leasing works:

You "fire" your workers, who are immediately hired by a leasing company. You then lease them back from that company. Typically, you continue to make all personnel and operating decisions as you did previously, although you may contract with the leasing company to assist with employee recruitment, screening, and performance reviews. "How much of that happens depends on the leasing company the business selects," says Gregory Hammond, an Akron, Ohio,

From *Nation's Business*, August 1993, pp. 34-35.

lawyer whose law firm—Hammond and Cunningham—represents more than 100 leasing companies nationwide.

As the employer of record, the leasing organization takes over payroll and benefits administration for your "former" employees. You cover these costs, just as before, and pay the leasing company a service fee.

Although leasing once was used as a union-busting technique, Hammond says that employers and unions increasingly are working together to craft leasing arrangements for their mutual benefit.

For employees, the switch to leasing doesn't necessarily mean the end of long-standing pension plans or the disappearance of seniority benefits such as added vacation days, says Hammond. Employers often leave pension plans and vacation policies unchanged.

For very small firms, the switch to leasing means giving up their exemption from certain state and federal regulations that apply only to firms with 20, 25, or more employees. Companies with fewer than 25 workers, for example, currently are exempt from the employment requirements of the new Americans with Disabilities Act. After entering a leasing arrangement, the law would apply because the small company's work force is considered to be part of the leasing company's larger group.

Once he decided to pursue the leasing option, Hinds settled on Employers Resource Management Co., an employee-leasing company based in Boise, Idaho. The leasing company lowered his health premiums because it has access to cheaper, pooled rates not available to small employers. And it cut Hinds' workers' compensation costs because the leasing company's pool of workers had a better safety record—and therefore lower rates—than Hinds' own firm.

Even as he cut costs, the leasing arrangement made it possible for Hinds to expand the benefits offered to his workers. The leasing company's health plan added dental and vision care as well as yearly physicals, and it offered a lower deductible and out-of-pocket annual maximum. In addition, Hinds' workers now have access to a credit union through the leasing firm.

Edward Semlitz, owner of Sunstate Courier Inc., in Tampa, Fla., wasn't so lucky, however. Four years ago, he signed up with Action Staffing, Inc., a nationwide leasing firm also based in Tampa. Action Staffing not only agreed to process the payroll for Sunstate's 30 employees but also promised him a 50 percent reduction in health-care costs. But Sunstate's arrangement began to crumble late last year when Action Staffing ran into financial trouble. Hospital and doctor bills that normally were paid within three weeks started taking as long as two months to be paid, Semlitz says. Other claims were never paid.

Then, under pressure from the Florida Department of Insurance, which declared the leasing company to be insolvent, Action Staffing pulled out of the employee-leasing business—leaving Sunstate and hundreds of other companies on the hook for a total of $4.4 million in unpaid claims.

Semlitz, 63, says that he and his employees now face about $60,000 in unpaid health-care bills—and they are being dunned by local hospitals and their collection agencies. Meanwhile, the new employee-leasing company he has signed up with won't insure his wife, who suffers from multiple sclerosis. "It was the only deal we could get," Semlitz says. "I didn't have a choice."

The problems caused by a relatively few leasing companies generally stem from the ease with which large sums of money can be improperly used. A leasing company doesn't need a huge client base before it is dealing with millions of dollars. "In this business, we handle a lot of money," says Rex Eley, president of the Sunmark Cos., an employee-leasing company in Little Rock, Ark. "That's why the people in this business need to be financially responsible."

According to the U.S. Senate Permanent Subcommittee on Investigations, abuses developed because the leasing industry operates in a near vacuum of regulation, with neither state nor federal agencies having clear authority. The subcommittee found that many leasing companies claim they are exempt from state insurance regulation under provisions of the federal Employee Retirement Income Security Act (ERISA). However, the subcommittee concluded that this claim was largely an excuse to avoid state regulation. But the states argue that ERISA is too complex, creating opportunities for leasing companies to escape regulation.

In the wake of leasing-company failures, industry leaders have now taken the lead in promoting federal and state laws to protect employer-clients. Proposals include requirements for licensing and registration with state agencies that supervise insurance. The National Association of Insurance Commissioners has incorporated some of these ideas into model laws it now recommends for state adoption.

Over the past year, four states—Florida, Arkansas, Maine, and Utah— have passed laws to regulate the nascent industry, and at least seven more are considering such action.

Under the new Florida rules, for example, leasing companies must now be licensed by a state board and show a tangible net worth of $50,000 each year and positive working capital. The Arkansas statute calls for licensing fees of up to

Growth Of Employee Leasing Companies

Number Of Companies

98 (1984), 113 (1985), 207 (1986), 292 (1987), 528 (1988), 891 (1989), 1,184 (1990), 1,264 (1991)

Source: The Aegis Group

$5,000 a year plus a $50,000 bond, or equivalent securities, or a financial statement showing a net worth of $100,000.

"It's in our best interests" to support the reform efforts, says Carlos Saladrigas, president of the Washington-based National Staff Leasing Association, the largest industry trade group. "This is an industry that still is in the entrepreneurial stage. You have a lot of cash flowing through, and that's a recipe for unscrupulous operators to come in."

In addition, the industry is asking Congress to give state and federal regulators greater enforcement powers and to clear up current confusion about who is responsible for regulating leasing companies—the states or the federal government. Congress this year considered four separate bills that would toughen regulations affecting leasing companies, but failed to act.

Although employee leasing has gained much of its momentum over the past several years, the practice actually dates back to the 1970s, when a loophole in federal tax law made staff leasing advantageous for high-income professionals who wanted to exclude their lower-paid workers from company pension plans.

When Congress closed that loophole with the Tax Reform Act of 1986, the leasing industry sought other markets. The timing was right. The economic boom of the 1980s had produced a massive increase in the number of small businesses whose owners were open to prospects of paperwork reduction, lower administrative costs, and discounted insurance plans.

The fast-expanding industry was able to convince more and more employers that achieving those goals would leave them better off financially after covering the cost of the leasing arrangement itself. In most cases, leasing arrangements do save the client businesses money.

George Gersema, chief executive of Employers Resource Management, in Boise, says that leasing companies charge 1 to 5 percent of the client company's payroll—typically $30 to $75 per employee per month—for administrative services such as payroll processing. That doesn't include the monthly premiums for health and workers' compensation benefits.

As a rule, Gersema says, businesses that buy their benefits through employee-leasing companies can expect to save 15 to 30 percent on their health premiums, depending on the size of the company, the age of its employees, and the state where the firm is located.

Leasing companies can typically deliver lower costs and better benefits because they purchase health plans for thousands of employees. Size gives leasing companies far more purchasing power than a typical small employer could obtain in shopping alone for a health plan.

Savings on workers' comp can also be substantial, says Gersema. Unlike health insurance, workers' comp does not involve a volume discount. Premiums are tied to each company's accident record. In general, the higher the accident rate, the higher the workers' comp premium.

Nonetheless, leasing can cut a company's workers' comp costs both in the short run and in the long run. Here's how:

Many small companies—even though they have low accident rates—must purchase their workers' comp insurance from state high-risk pools, in most instances because these firms simply cannot find an insurer interested in their business. Risk pools typically charge higher rates than the so-called voluntary market, and many impose surcharges. "It's not uncommon for us to pick small businesses out of the residual market [high-risk pools] and cut their costs in half," says Gersema.

Even companies with poor accident records can cut their workers' comp costs over time through leasing, Gersema says. The key is to improve safety through a program supervised by the leasing firm. His company, for example, conducts safety inspections of client companies and requires each. one to appoint a safety manager.

Once an accident occurs, Gersema's company provides clients with the names of doctors who are skilled in treating workplace injuries and who will treat leasing-company clients for discounted fees.

Before signing up for any leasing company, it's important to understand how its health and workers' comp plans work. Find out if the company's health plan is insured or self-insured. Leasing firms that purchase a policy from an insurance company offer insured health plans. Those that pay claims out of a pool of premiums collected from companies serviced by the leasing firm are self-insured plans.

"Probably about one-third of all leasing companies self-insure," says Akron lawyer Hammond. He adds that self-insurance "is declining because of regulatory pressure."

If the health plan is backed by an insurer, ask about the insurance company's financial condition, turnaround time on claims processing, and approach to rate increases once someone becomes ill or develops a chronic medical condition.

Leasing companies that self-insure do so for the same reason most large companies self-insure—to save money on premiums by eliminating insurance company overhead. Self-insured plans work well when managed properly. But the premium dollars pouring into these plans can also be mismanaged or even siphoned off by unscrupulous operators.

When a leasing company self-insures, it hires a third-party administrator to handle the claims paperwork and pay bills. In some instances, these administrators also are major insurance companies. But just because a big-name insurance company serves as the claims processor doesn't mean that the insurer is backing the leasing company plan with an insurance policy. Some leasing companies have misled clients about the role of major insurers whose only responsibility is to process claims, not underwrite the health plan.

It's also important to know how the leasing company manages workers' comp premiums and claims. A good leasing company will help employers contain costs through screening of job applicants, workplace safety programs, and case management once a worker is injured, says Saladrigas. In addition to being president of the National Staff Leasing Association, he is chief executive of Vincam Human Resources, Inc., an employee-leasing firm in Miami.

Beware of new leasing companies that manipulate the system to slash premiums, Saladrigas warns. "This is the biggest source of abuse," he says. Here's what can happen:

A new leasing company starts with a clean accident slate and low workers' comp premium rate, making it attractive for companies with poor safety records and high rates to switch to the leasing company for a big discount. But without an effective safety program, the big discounts won't last because adverse claims experience from client companies will eventually drive up the leasing company's workers' comp rates. "It won't take long for the leasing company's experience rating to go through workers' comp meltdown," says Saladrigas. "Once the rates go up 300 percent, the leasing company closes down and starts a new company, beginning the cycle again."

The National Council on Compensation Insurance (NCCI), an insurance industry trade group based in Boca Raton, Fla., has been hot on the trail of leasing scams in the workers' compensation arena. In May, a Texas judge approved a settlement requiring a Louisiana leasing company to pay a group of workers' compensation insurers $18 million plus interest.

The insurers, in a suit filed by NCCI, alleged that the leasing company was formed by a Louisiana trucking firm to avoid paying its appropriate level of workers' comp insurance premiums.

NCCI is cooperating with a group of workers' compensation insurers to crack down on premium fraud from all sources. Sally Narey, NCCI's general counsel, notes that the battle against leasing fraud is far from over. "We think that [workers' compensation] fraud is still a very important area and that we need to continue our efforts," says Narey.

Nonetheless, small businesses that exercise caution and do sufficient research can avoid such problems and find leasing an attractive proposition, the industry says.

These examples, provided by Employers Resource Management Co., the employee-leasing firm based in Boise, show how the savings can add up:

■ By signing up with an employee-leasing company, an Ohio manufacturer with 48 employees pays biweekly premiums of $651 for workers' compensation coverage (a savings of $496.50 over the company's existing coverage). And it pays $3,820.50 monthly for health- and life-insurance benefits (a savings of $783).

Although health costs were cut, benefits improved. For example, the annual medical deductible dropped to $100 from $250. And the new health plan offered dental coverage and free generic drugs. The old plan did not cover dental work, and it required individuals to pay 20 percent of prescription drug costs. On the downside, the new plan gave everyone $15,000 in life insurance; the old plan gave everyone a policy equal to annual salary.

■ A California plumbing company with 12 employees pays a biweekly premium of $348 (a $98 savings) to buy its workers' compensation coverage through a leasing company and $494 (a $464 savings) for health and life insurance.

Again, benefits improved. The annual per-person deductible fell to $250 from $500, and employees now pay 10 percent toward the purchase of generic drugs, compared with a flat charge of $15 per prescription under the old plan. Everyone received $15,000 in life insurance, up from $10,000 each under the old plan.

Signing up with a leasing company doesn't always mean paying less, however. For some businesses, it means paying out more money to gain benefits that were unavailable before. A five-employee Texas medical clinic, for example, saves $13 biweekly (paying $42) on its workers' compensation premiums through an employee-leasing plan. The same company, which was not able to afford health- or life-insurance benefits before, now pays $375 biweekly for a health plan that includes the same benefits as the plan covering the 48-employee Ohio manufacturer.

But dollar considerations aren't always the determining factors in deciding whether to go with or continue with

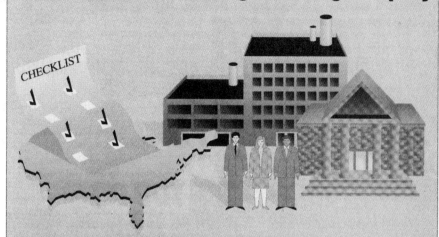

A Checklist For Screening A Leasing Company

Before making a commitment to a leasing company, make sure that it is honest, well-managed, and financially stable. To help you decide if it meets the criteria, ask the company these questions:

How long has your company been in business?

The longer the company has been around, the more likely it will continue to exist. Don't accept rapid growth as a substitute for longevity. Such growth could mean that the leasing firm has been low-balling its insurance rates to gain market share or putting too much of its revenue into slick marketing campaigns.

What are the names of clients I can contact for references?

It's important to talk to clients who can attest to the leasing company's accuracy and timeliness in meeting payroll as well as to the responsiveness of its insurance carriers or third-party administrators in paying claims.

If the company won't give you client references, take your business elsewhere. Even if you receive a listing, it might be a sanitized one. Use your business contacts to get names of clients not on the company's list. Also, make sure you can cancel the contract with 30 days' notice if the arrangement doesn't work out.

What are the names of your bank, insurance broker, and insurance carrier?

To find out about a leasing company's financial health, it's vital to ask for credit references from its bank. The leasing company can authorize its bank to give out references. The leasing company's insurance broker can provide details on the company's workers' compensation and health-insurance plans, and the duration of the company's relationship with its insurance carriers.

Ask the insurance broker for the A.M.

Best financial rating of the insurance companies used by the leasing firm. A Best rating of A or higher means the insurer is in solid financial shape.

Also check to see what kind of reinsurance the leasing company has—that's your guarantee against catastrophe if the company's claims exceed a certain level.

Is your company or your third-party administrator licensed to sell insurance in my state?

Many employee-leasing companies are self-insured, which means they use an independent company known as a third-party administrator to handle claims paperwork and pay bills. Call your state insurance commissioner to check on the status of the administrator's license.

Have you been audited by an independent third party?

If the answer is yes, ask to see an audit report. A negative response is a warning signal. It's important to get proof that all tax deposits, insurance premiums, and employee-benefits payments have been made on time. If the leasing company doesn't pay, you could get stuck holding the bag.

In addition, check to see if the leasing company can furnish an opinion letter from a law firm stating that the company is in compliance with the applicable state and federal labor and pension laws.

Are you licensed to do business in my state?

Most of the time, the answer will be no. To date, only Florida, Arkansas, Maine, and Utah have set up boards to regulate employee-leasing companies.

For companies outside those states, check on whether they belong to the National Staff Leasing Association, which represents most of the industry's major players and maintains a database of information on leasing companies.

leasing. "Price is the reason why most companies switch to leasing, but convenience is why they stay," Gersema says. "It's just a better way to do business."

David Kibby, owner of Kibby Labs, Inc., a 42-employee commercial photographic printing lab in Madison Heights, Mich., switched to leasing nearly two years ago after a dispute with his insurance company over a medical bill. Back then, Kibby recalls, he was spending so much time dealing with paperwork that he didn't even have time to call on customers.

Last year, with a leasing company handling everything from payroll and withholding taxes to federal workplace-safety requirements and the company's 401(k) savings plan, Kibby was back making sales calls—and single-handedly ringing up a whopping $500,000 in orders.

Although Kibby hasn't calculated how much the leasing arrangement has saved his firm, he knows it has saved him a lot of headaches. "All I know is that now I go home with a lot fewer problems," he says.

Brenda Counsell also finds leasing convenient. Counsell, corporate secretary of Community Medical Equipment Corp., a Fort Lauderdale, Fla., company with six employees, says her firm has shaved 40 percent off its health-care bills since signing on with Payroll Transfers, Inc., a Tampa leasing company, in October 1991. Previously, she says, her company was paying $140 to $150 per employee per month for health insurance; now it's paying about $100. Payday is also a snap. "All I do is fax my hours to them, and they put the payroll on my desk," Counsell says. "I've never had a problem."

Convenience was also a selling point for Bruce Forge, president of CityWide Mortgage, Inc., a nine-employee mortgage broker in Tustin, Calif. Forge, who switched to employee leasing in 1987, says

he used to handle the payroll himself. He also tried to keep current on every new government regulation. These days, his leasing company, Your Staff, Inc., of Woodland Hills, Calif., takes care of all of his personnel matters, right down to placing the "Help Wanted" ads in the newspaper and screening would-be employees.

"Before, it was very labor-intensive" Forge says. "Even with one employee, you have the burden" of keeping up with rules and regulations. Payroll, which once took him hours, is now wrapped up in about five minutes, Forge says.

Despite the spate of reform efforts and the many positive experiences that small employers report with employee leasing, business owners still must tread cautiously—even when dealing with a legitimate leasing company. One potential pitfall is employer liability. Just because a leasing company becomes the employer of record does not mean that the client company—often the one that hired the workers in the first place and continues to supervise their day-to-day activities—no longer has legal liability for workers' actions.

Hammond, the Akron lawyer, says that a contract between a leasing company and a client may be considered, in the eyes of the law, a "shared employment" arrangement. This means that the small-business owner is partly responsible for sexual-harassment claims, discrimination suits, and the like. The degree of employer liability rests with the circumstances of each case, he says.

"A good leasing company is in the business of nightmare reduction," Hammond says, "but a leasing company cannot take the liability away from you."

Although there are risks inherent in employee leasing, they are outweighed by the numerous benefits of such an arrange-

ment, say many small-business owners. Even Paragon Industries' painful experience with employee leasing hasn't soured the firm on the concept. "If it were a bona fide company, we'd consider it again," says Weidner, Paragon's vice president.

The key to making the most of employee leasing, experts say, is picking the right leasing company.

Saladrigas, who also is chairman of Florida's newly created Board of Employee Leasing Companies, suggests that employers check with their state employee-leasing board to see if the company they are considering is licensed and, if there is no board, to check on whether the company is a member of the National Staff Leasing Association.

It's also a good idea to call a few of the leasing company's clients and ask them about the company's reputation and track record in paying claims, Saladrigas says.

Overall, says Saladrigas, small businesses exploring leasing should remember that the same principle applies here as in any other business transaction: "You don't get something for nothing. If, all of a sudden, somebody offers you a dollar for 50 cents, beware."

For More Information

For a free fact sheet on employee leasing and a list of key questions to ask before leasing, or for assistance in picking a leasing company, write or call the National Staff Leasing Association, 1735 North Lynn St., Suite 950, Arlington, Va. 22209; (703) 524-3636.

To obtain a copy of T. Joe Willey's book *The Business of Employee Leasing*, which sells for $37.50, write to the Aegis Group, 1911 Commercenter East, Suite 300, San Bernardino, Calif. 92408-3318, or call 1-800-262-3447.

Case VI: *The "Homes" Is Where the Union Is*

Recently 700 employees of a city nursing home and the city home for the aged (two facilities located on the same plot of land) voted overwhelmingly to be represented by a union. The bargaining unit includes a great variety of employees, from custodial and maintenance to social workers and professional nurses. When interviewed after the union had won bargaining rights, the employees claimed that arbitrary and inconsistent treatment by management, and the supervisors in particular, comprised the main reasons for their voting for the union. They charged discriminatory treatment and flagrant favoritism. They also charged that the supervisors made it a practice to discharge employees for trivial reasons or without adequate prior warnings. Employees were subjected to frequent criticism by their supervisors with regard to their job performance. Although many of the supervisors had been promoted from the "ranks," many of them seemed to abuse their authority in dealing with their subordinates.

Top managers in both locations were genuinely surprised when they first learned during negotiations about this serious and widespread employee discontent.

Using the Case on *The "Homes" Is Where The Union Is*

For this case you should consider yourself an arbitrator who has been presented with this case. After reading the case, what decision would you give, knowing that other people had had time off and that memos were only requested at varying intervals?

Go over the review questions at the end. How does the class feel about this as a group? Why?

Exercise VI: *Assumptions About People at Work*

Instructions

The purpose of this exercise is to help you better understand the assumptions you make about people and their work behaviors. On the following questionnaire, you will find 10 sets of questions. Assign a rank from 0 to 10 to each item in each pair. (0 indicates that you completely disagree with the statement, and 10 means that you completely agree with the statement.) Answer each question as honestly as you can. There are *no correct answers,* so don't give a response to a question that will sound good to others or that you think is the way you are supposed to answer.

Questions

1. It's only human nature for people to do as little work as they can get away with. _____ (a)
   When people avoid work, it's usually because their work has been deprived of its meaning. _____ (b)
2. If employees have access to any information they want, they tend to have better attitudes and behave more responsibly. _____ (c)
   If employees have access to more information than they need to do their immediate tasks, they will usually misuse it. _____ (d)

3. One problem in asking for the ideas of employees is that their perspective is too limited for their suggestions to be of much practical value. _____ (e)
   Asking employees for their ideas broadens their perspective and results in the development of useful suggestions. _____ (f)
4. If people don't use much imagination and ingenuity on the job, it's probably because relatively few people have much of either. _____ (g)
   Most people are imaginative and creative but may not show it because of limitations imposed by supervision and the job. _____ (h)
5. People tend to raise their standards if they are accountable for their own behavior and for correcting their own mistakes. _____ (i)
   People tend to lower their standards if they are not punished for their misbehavior and mistakes. _____ (j)
6. It's better to give people both good and bad news because most employees want the whole story, no matter how painful. _____ (k)
   It's better to withhold unfavorable news about business because most employees really want to hear only the good news. _____ (l)
7. Because supervisors are entitled to more respect than those below them in the organization, it weakens their prestige to admit that a subordinate was right and they were wrong. _____ (m)
   Because people at all levels are entitled to equal respect, a supervisor's prestige is increased when s/he supports this principle by admitting that a subordinate was right and s/he was wrong. _____ (n)
8. If you give people enough money, they are less likely to be concerned with such intangibles as responsibility and recognition. _____ (o)
   If you give people interesting and challenging work, they are less likely to complain about such things as pay and supplemental benefits. _____ (p)
9. If people are allowed to set their own goals and standards of performance, they tend to set them higher than the boss would. _____ (q)
   If people are allowed to set their own goals and standards of performance, they tend to set them lower than the boss would. _____ (r)
10. The more knowledge and freedom a person has regarding his job, the more controls are needed to keep him/her in line. _____ (s)
    The more knowledge and freedom a person has regarding his/her job, the fewer controls are needed to ensure satisfactory job performance. _____ (t)

After Completing the Questionnaire

When you have completed all of the questions, you may score the questionnaire in the following manner. Add together the scores of items: (a), (d), (e), (g), (j), (l), (m), (o), (r), and (s). The sum of these scores will provide you with your "Theory X" score. Then add together the remaining scores: (b), (c), (f), (h), (i), (k), (n), (p), (q), and (t). The sum of these scores will give you your "Theory Y" score.

In a group, discuss the relative strength of each of your scores. Is there a significant difference in the two scores? What might this mean? How do you believe your assumptions might affect your actions as a manager? Do your past experiences support the self-profile that has emerged from your discussion? Discuss with other members of your group how your scores may be related to the concepts of "espoused theory" and "theory-in-use."

Perspectives and Trends

Managers are facing new challenges. While it is never possible to determine exactly what the future will hold, there are certain trends and movements that can be perceived by an aware and thoughtful manager. Derek Bok, former president of Harvard University, offered some interesting insights into possible future trends for prospective managers in his June 1982 baccalaureate address, which has been adapted in the article "Social Responsibility in Future Worlds." Bok speaks from two perspectives in this article, for not only was he an academic trying to look into the future, but he was also the manager of a very old and reasonably large and diverse organization, Harvard University.

Most people recognize the movement toward the internationalization of the economy. The North American continent no longer stands alone, as it did at the end of World War II, as the main source of manufactured goods. As the world enters a new millennium, Japan and Europe are making their economic muscle felt. Japan is not alone in the Far East in the manufacture of goods. Taiwan, Korea, and Singapore, not to mention the awesome untouched potential of China, are also factors. This is not, however, a huge, monolithic block. It is a collection of similar countries and societies, but each one is unique and does business in its own way. Koreans and Japanese do have somewhat similar countries, roughly comparable to Great Britain, France, and Germany. But each establishes and maintains business relationships in its own individual way.

While most of the world was focusing on the occurrences in Eastern Europe and the republics of the former Soviet Union, important things were already in progress in Western Europe prior to the opening of the Berlin Wall. In 1992 the European Economic Community became, for the first time since the days of the Roman Empire, a truly integrated economy. This, of course, represents a significant change and presents American firms with both challenges and opportunities. Now Europe will change in more ways than even the planners of the Common Market can foresee, and the multinational corporation will continue to play an increasing role, as discussed in "Multinationals: Back in Fashion."

Another development in American society has been the rise of the small businessperson. Over the past decade, the number of people employed by *Fortune* 500 companies has declined, while the size of the workforce has increased. Many of these new workers entered small firms. Small businesses tend to be family businesses, and it is often difficult to determine where the business ends and the family begins. In addition, these businesses are entrepreneurial in nature. Entrepreneurs serve the highly creative function of creating new jobs and new businesses. They develop and market new products and services and are often on the cutting edge of the new technology of tomorrow, both technical and managerial.

Managers and their organizations have been criticized in the past several years for a lack of ethics and morality. A small, and, when they are caught, highly publicized minority have indeed played fast and loose with the law and ethics. This has caused all managers to look more closely at their behavior, and the courts are starting to take a dimmer view of white-collar crime, to the point of sending some executives, such as Charles Keating and Michael Milkin, to prison.

While the study of management tends to focus on profit-making organizations, not-for-profits also need to be managed effectively. This sector of the economy is very large and includes all levels and functions of government, churches, associations, schools, charities, and many health care facilities. It is a very large piece of American industry.

Finally, managers are starting to examine their careers in light of the new developments in the marketplace. In earlier generations, managers would work for the same firm for their entire lives. That is no longer the case. Managers in today's environment must be flexible. They have to be responsible for their own careers, because the firm they join could go out of business or be purchased, and they could be left without a job. Managers must look after themselves and make career moves independently if they hope to succeed.

Looking Ahead: Challenge Questions

There are many new developments facing managers in the near future. What are some of the areas of controversy you expect to see soon?

As a prospective manager, what do you expect to be doing in the next five years? Ten years?

Social Responsibility in Future Worlds

Derek C. Bok

Derek C. Bok, President, Harvard University, Cambridge, Mass.

PROFESSIONAL STUDY

If the past is any guide, more than 90 percent of you will eventually find yourselves studying law, business, or medicine or enrolling in some other kind of graduate or professional school. The training you receive will open the door to a vocation of your choice. But what sort of experience will you find there? What will it do for you? And what kinds of dangers should you be on guard to avoid?

Many people have a slightly distorted view of what a good professional training can achieve. Some feel that it stocks the mind with a vast supply of specialized knowledge—about legal rules and procedures, about corporate organization and behavior, or about the human body and how it functions. Others think that professional training gives students a set of special tools and advanced techniques with which to pry open problems impervious to the lay mind. Both these notions are partly true, but both are incomplete. A good professional education does convey a lot of special knowledge and a grasp of sophisticated technique but it incorporates them into something greater and more important—an instinctive ability to recognize the characteristic problems of the profession and to break them down into manageable parts that can be thought through systematically. The normal way to develop this ability is to subject students to a period of total immersion in which almost all their time is spent in studying, going to class and living and talking and arguing about the problems of the profession with other students like themselves.

Such training brings great benefits to those who pursue it diligently. Not only can you receive the proper credentials of your calling; you gain a power of analysis not available to people outside your profession. That power in turn opens up opportunities to render great service to others, to achieve the satisfactions of good craftsmanship, to find an identity to define your role in life, not to mention gaining your economic security and material rewards.

Along with all these benefits, however, come certain dangers. As Richard Wilbur once remarked, the genie is powerful because we have pressed him into a bottle. The pressures imposed by a good professional education can be a transforming experience. But few transformations occur without the risk of losing something of value along the way. In graduate education, the risk you run is of acquiring a somewhat distorted perspective, a set of values that seem slightly askew, a cast of mind that evidences what the French describe as "deformation professionelle."

THE DEFORMATION OF PROFESSIONALISM

And what, precisely, are these deformations? One of them surely is a tendency to grow less concerned about society's problems and more preoccupied with the special predicament of your client. It is the client, after all, to whom you will owe your loyalty and it is the client who pays the fee. Most of all, it is the client's problem that has immediacy and concreteness. What are the distant issues of national health insurance or neighborhood clinics compared with the urgent details of a swelling tumor, a baby's cleft palate, or a damaged heart? How long can you be distracted by the injustices of our penal system or the wasteful delays of our trial courts in the presence of a corporate client facing a union election, a company take-over, or an antitrust decree?

TENDENCY TO WITHDRAW FROM SUFFERING

As you address the problems of your clients, it is also tempting to conceive of their predicament in terms that are more and more intellectual and less and less human. All professional schools tend to turn human situations into problems that can be picked apart and analyzed rationally. Professional life often supports this view of the world. Most of you who enter law or business will offer your services to banks, manufacturing companies, or retail stores—and it is easy to perceive these organizations as hollow abstractions rather than communities of living people. In medicine, the process of abstraction is even more understandable and compelling. As every study of medical education reveals, few students have feelings tough enough to cope with the terrifying immediacy of death and disease. Many tend to withdraw from the suffering and abnormalities of their patients and begin to conceive of them less as frightened, vulnerable human beings and more as a puzzling deficiency in red blood cells, an unusual kidney malfunction, an odd lesion in the lower intestine. Reinforcing these pressures is the image of

Based on the Baccalaureate Speech by [then-] President Derek C. Bok at the Commencement Ceremony of Harvard University, Cambridge, Mass., June 1982.

success that society has imposed on all of our professions, the image of the emotionless practitioner—cool, detached, objective, and totally in control.

Still another tendency in graduate or professional school is to become so steeped in its special methods of analysis that one ignores other ways of apprehending human experience. Each of these schools arouses an immediate insecurity in its students and a corresponding desire to prove themselves by mastering the technical apparatus of the profession. As you grow more and more adept in these techniques, it is only natural that you be tempted to press these methods on problems where they do not fit. Business school students may cease to wonder about how to work with other human beings and begin to think about the efficient management of human resources. Law students may seize their yellow pads and jot down all the arguments for and against marrying their high school sweethearts. Psychiatrists often see every conceivable human situation as a product of repressed sexual desires.

The quirks I have described may strike you as quaint, but they can have serious effects, not only on your personal and family life, but on your careers as well.

HUMAN DIMENSIONS

I mentioned that most professional schools tend to emphasize the intellectual aspects of practice and to set aside the personal, the emotional, the deeply human dimensions of their calling. The bias is understandable, since formal learning is much more suited to dealing with intellectual and analytic problems than with the more intuitive and psychological aspects of experience. And yet, if you begin to accept this view of the world, you may lose many of the greatest rewards of professional life by failing to perceive much of the human interest and drama that arise in every professional practice. Not only can your work grow colorless and dull; you may accomplish less as well. After all, solutions to most legal disputes and most corporate problems cannot be found through analysis alone but depend on being aware of the feelings, the motives, the needs and aspirations of all the human beings involved. The same is even true in more

technical fields such as medicine. How can anyone expect to cope effectively with human health by scientific methods alone when one-third of all patients fail to take the drugs their doctors have prescribed, when half of all illness results from drinking, smoking, and other personal habits; when one-third to a half of all cases in general medicine practice have a strong psychosomatic base.

GREAT SOCIAL CONTRIBUTIONS

Apart from the effects on your careers, the deformations I have described can also have consequences for the professions themselves. For example, if you come to regard the problems of your clients as an intellectual challenge and not as an intensely human predicament, you are likely to move toward certain kinds of careers where the intellectual demands seem greatest—toward the sophisticated specialties in medicine; toward corporate legal practice; toward finance, planning, or consulting in business. While there is nothing inherently wrong with these lines of work, they are not necessarily the fields in which the greatest social contributions lie. For the next generation at least, our health care system will probably need able practitioners in primary care and family medicine more than specialists in cardiology or neurosurgery. As attorneys, you may serve society better as public interest lawyers and neighborhood practitioners, or dare I say it—by not becoming lawyers at all, than you will by being fresh recruits for corporate tax, securities regulation, and antitrust litigation. The economy, with its lagging productivity, may benefit more from production managers than from investment analysts, corporate planners, or roving consultants.

ETHICAL DILEMMAS

Another byproduct of professional training is that the constant emphasis on solving problems through conventional modes of analysis may cause young professionals to ignore the ethical dilemmas of their practice. Alas, you are not likely to detect much serious attention to ethics in the professional school you enter. And that is a serious deficiency at a time when every profession bristles with moral di-

lemmas and the public trust in professionals has everywhere declined. As a "New York Times" article recently concluded: "If medical education does not come to grips with the ethical as well as the technical problems of the field, society may soon discover that modern medicine has given a relatively small number of men and women enormous power—which they have not been adequately trained to wield." Exactly the same could be said of all the other major professions as well.

There is a final danger to consider that may be even more important. I have already observed that students in professional schools grow more and more preoccupied with the needs and problems of the clients they serve and less and less concerned with the impact of their profession on the larger society. That would be a problem in any era. It is a particularly serious problem today.

SOCIETY'S CONCERNS

I cannot remember a time when society's concerns about the professions have seemed more distant from the daily preoccupations of our professional schools and the body of practitioners they serve. In medicine, for example, the public is not greatly troubled by the technical quality of service that doctors offer their patients. What does concern the public is how medical services can be organized to extend adequate care to all segments of society; how to contain medical costs so that they cease to rise at much faster rates than those of other goods and services; and how to address the great moral dilemmas of euthanasia, abortion, and artificial insemination. What troubles thinking people most about our legal system is not that lawyers are poorly trained but that we rely too much on law and litigation in most of our institutions while failing to insure that poor people have proper access to basic legal services at prices they can afford. In business, our principal concern is how our corporations can work more effectively with government to increase productivity and address social problems and how business can be kept accountable to the public interest in an age when markets do not provide a perfect discipline and government regulation is often inefficient and ineffective.

FAILURE OF GOVERNMENT REGULATION

These are not problems that receive much attention in our professional schools today despite their high priority in the public mind. And that is a serious matter, for there is one thing that we have surely learned from the failures of government regulation over the years. If we wish our professions to serve the public better, we must enlist the active cooperation of professionals themselves. Without their help, little of lasting value can occur.

The problems I have described are not your problems now, but they will be your problems very soon. I hope that you will address them boldly and never regard yourselves as human clay to be molded and shaped by your professional school experience. There was a time when I could not have brought myself to utter this last remark: it would have seemed too obvious and banal. But I was startled to find in my last years as a faculty member that many students had managed to persuade themselves that the Law School was "programming them" for lucrative corporate practice and co-opting them from careers fighting for noble causes or serving the needy. Such attitudes are not merely far-fetched; they are extremely dangerous, for they offer easy rationalizations to avoid responsibility for what you make of your lives. Pro-

fessional schools graduate every kind of practitioner serving every conceivable segment of society. They give you tools with which to work. But the ends and values to which you direct your talents are yours and yours alone to decide, and professional maturity begins with that realization.

FRESH FIELDS AND PASTURES NEW

In making these decisions, you begin with a strong defense against narrowing tendencies of professional training, for you would not have been admitted to Harvard College had you not been interested in a broad range of human and social questions, and four years here should have helped to cement that foundation. In one respect, however, I fear that your Harvard experience may not have served you well. By gaining admission here you prevailed in a remarkably stiff competition. By working hard to win acceptance by a professional school, you have continued to run in a demanding race. Fresh opportunities lie before you to compete for the best residencies, the best law firms, the best positions in the best corporations. These competitions are excellent motivation devices that call on powerful human instincts.

A LIFE THAT ENGAGES ALL OF YOUR INTERESTS

But it is a characteristic that one must

play by other people's rules and compete for prizes that other people have chosen. And that is a poor preparation for life, especially if you mean to live an independent existence and resist the deformations I have tried to describe.

To guard against these dangers, I hope that you will pause now and then to free your minds from your immediate problems and ambitions and imagine how your lives will seem to you at the end of your careers. If you can somehow manage the feat of looking back upon your future lives, I suspect that you will begin to feel less concerned with whether you succeed by narrow professional standards. Instead, I suspect that you will hope more and more for a life that continuously engages all of your interests and absorbs all of your energies. And as you think further, I suspect you will come to realize that no life can engage you fully unless it is open to the feelings of everyone around you and that no career can absorb your energies for very long unless it allows you to contribute generously to the welfare of others. If these be your sentiments, I hope that you will guard them well so that you can make a life that is worthy of your talents and equal to this brave beginning. Congratulations you to all. You deserve the very best. I feel sure that you will find it.

MULTINATIONALS

Back in fashion

Multinational firms and their foreign investments are again attracting admiring looks. Yet neither investment growth nor the political welcome should be taken for granted, writes Bill Emmott

LENIN wrote that foreign investment was a distinctive feature of the final stage of capitalism. It is a nice irony, therefore, that the world's greatest boom in corporate investment across borders took place in the dying years of Lenin's communism. From 1983 to 1990 such investment grew four times faster than world output and three times faster than world trade. Now, although the boom has faded in the recession-hit industrial countries, foreign investment is rushing enthusiastically to those countries that for decades were blighted by communism, by forms of state socialism and by authoritarian, isolationist government: to China, India, other parts of Asia, Latin America and even Eastern Europe. Not for the first time, Lenin's analysis missed the mark.

He is not alone, however, in having misunderstood and mispredicted the future of cross-border business. It is marching on, but not in the ways that were widely expected. A quarter of a century ago, when multinational firms suddenly loomed large on the radar screens of pundits and politicians, they aroused a mixture of awe and fear. The thought of the global enterprise, placing itself wherever costs and resources dictated, made business thinkers gasp with excitement. Such firms, fuelled by economies of scale and scope, would grow faster and bigger than whole countries and would soon dominate the world economy with their unbeatable efficiency. Echoing Marx and Lenin, many assumed this would entail the concentration of industries in fewer and fewer hands.

Similar ideas, also influenced by Marx and Lenin, led others to be terrified of multinationals: huge, ruthless and stateless, these firms would exploit the poor, manipulate governments and flout popular opinion. Raymond Vernon, a Harvard professor and one of the leading (and most sober) students of this phenomenon, observed in a 1977 book called "Storm over the Multinationals" that "the multinational enterprise has come to be seen as the embodiment of almost anything disconcerting about modern industrial society."

Yet now it is only a slight exaggeration to say that it is seen as the reverse, as the embodiment of modernity and the prospect of wealth: full of technology, rich in capital, replete with skilled jobs. Governments all around the world, especially in the developing countries, are queuing up to attract multinationals. The United Nations, which spent decades tut-tutting about these firms and drawing up codes of conduct to control them, now spends much of its time advising countries on how best to seduce them.

This change of view is so extreme that it brings with it the risk of a backlash. This survey will ask whether and where a backlash is likely, after mapping the present and future shape of the multinational firm. Over the past decade or more, the trend towards a more integrated world economy, in which businesses stride across borders with minimal effort, has felt so remorseless that it is easy both to take it for granted and to assume that it is leading towards a pure, seamless economic system. This survey will question those assumptions.

Big, but not that big

Before pondering the future, however, it is best to understand the past and the present. Why have attitudes to multinationals changed? One answer could be that governments have shrugged their shoulders and accepted the inevitable. But that is not what has happened. Rather, experience has refuted expectation.

Global enterprises have not taken over the world, even though the pace of cross-border corporate investment has accelerated strongly. In the early 1970s Howard Perlmutter, a professor at the Wharton School of Management in Philadelphia, predicted that by 1985 around 80% of the non-communist world's productive assets would be controlled by just 200-300 companies. Researchers at the United Nations reckon there are now at least 35,000 multinationals, controlling some 170,000 foreign affiliates. Within that number, power is indeed concentrated: the UN thinks that the largest 100 multinationals, excluding those in banking and finance, accounted for $3.1 trillion of worldwide assets in 1990, of which $1.2 trillion was outside firms' respective home countries (see table 1 for the top 50).

The top 100 multinationals probably account for about 40-50% of all cross-border assets. Yet this does not bring the sort of dominance that Mr Perlmutter was predicting. These estimates of the top 100's assets need to be compared with a worldwide total. There are no reliable figures for this, but a reasonable guide must be America, which accounts for a quarter of world output. The commerce department reckons the gross stock of fixed private non-residential capital in America was around $8.5 trillion in 1990. On the back of an envelope, it might be reasonable to raise that to $20 trillion for the world, on the assumption that most other economies are less capital-intensive. That would give the top 100 roughly a 16% share of the world's productive assets, or perhaps 25% for the top 300. This is not domination.

Simple extrapolations of multinational power were probably always going to be wrong. But they also made the error of assuming that all forces in the world economy were working in the same direction. Cross-border business has been driven forward by three main things: falling regulatory barriers to overseas investment; tumbling telecommunications and transport costs; and freer domestic and international capital markets in which companies can be bought, and currency and other risks can be controlled.

All these have made it easier for companies to invest where they choose to, to do so more cheaply and with less risk. Yet such factors favour small firms as well as big ones, new boys as well as old. A freshman in the computer business, such as Dell Computer of Austin, Texas, which was born in 1984 and now has annual sales of almost $2 billion, can build international networks quickly and cheaply to catch up with its elders. Small and medium-sized firms in many industries have proved nimbler and more innovative than the old corporate giants. They have also been quick to become international, fragmenting the markets the giants might otherwise monopolise.

International firms are now also more international in origin. In 1970, of the 7,000 multinationals identified by the UN, more than half were from two countries: America and Britain. But now just under half of the UN's 35,000 firms are from four countries: America, Japan, Germany and Switzerland. Britain comes seventh. Currency movements, capital surpluses, faster growth rates: all these have helped multinationals from other countries join the cross-border fray. And although most are small, there is also an increasing amount of foreign investment by firms from the third world and the industrialising Asian dragons such as Taiwan and South Korea.

Sovereignty as sideshow

Another reason for the change of heart is that multinationals are no longer considered synonymous with the loss of sovereignty by nation-states. Mr Vernon's most famous book on the subject was called "Sovereignty at Bay" and was published in 1971, when the world was abuzz with the threat posed by itinerant, stateless firms to national independence. The buzz about sovereignty has not gone away—if anything, it has grown louder—but it has changed.

It is now realised that the multinational company is merely a part of a much wider force that has eroded sovereignty while integrating the world economy and even, to an extent, world politics. To be sure, international firms do pose all sorts of challenges to national governments. But today's books about the subject, such as "Twilight of Sovereignty", published in late 1992 and written by Walter Wriston, a former boss of Citicorp, America's biggest bank, devote only a chapter or so to multinationals. They are a sideshow to the main issue.

Flows of short-term investment capital in and out of currencies and securities markets are many times bigger than those of direct corporate investment. Currency and other money markets transmit economic forces more rapidly, and less resistably, than corporations do. For example, the limits to Britain's economic sovereignty were revealed far more powerfully by sterling's turmoil before and after leaving Europe's exchange-rate mechanism in September 1992 than could have been the case with an investment by a Japanese car firm, or a takeover by a Swiss food multinational. And in the political domain the power of satellite telecommunications to transmit text and pictures cheaply has done more to weaken the grip of governments than any

The top 25...   1

Largest non-financial multinationals 1990, ranked by foreign assets*

Rank		Industry	Country	Foreign assets $bn	Total assets $bn	Foreign sales $bn	% of total sales
1	Royal Dutch/Shell	Oil	Britain/Holland	n.a.	106.3	56.0†	49
2	Ford Motor	Cars and trucks	United States	55.2	173.7	47.3	48
3	General Motors	Cars and trucks	United States	52.6	180.2	37.3	31
4	Exxon	Oil	United States	51.6	87.7	90.5	86
5	IBM	Computers	United States	45.7	87.6	41.9	61
6	British Petroleum	Oil	Britain	39.7	59.3	46.6	79
7	Nestlé	Food	Switzerland	n.a.	27.9	33.0	98
8	Unilever	Food	Britain/Holland	n.a.	24.8	16.7†	42
9	Asea Brown Boveri	Electrical	Switzerland/Sweden	n.a.	30.2	22.7‡	85
10	Philips Electronics	Electronics	Holland	n.a.	30.6	28.6‡	93
11	Alcatel Alsthom	Telecoms	France	n.a.	38.2	17.7	67
12	Mobil	Oil	United States	22.3	41.7	44.3	77
13	Fiat	Cars and trucks	Italy	19.5	66.3	15.8	33
14	Siemens	Electrical	Germany	n.a.	50.1	15.1†	40
15	Hanson	Diversified	Britain	n.a.	27.7	5.6	46
16	Volkswagen	Cars and trucks	Germany	n.a.	41.9	27.5‡	65
17	Elf Aquitaine	Oil	France	17.0	42.6	12.2	38
18	Mitsubishi	Trading	Japan	16.7	73.8	41.2	32
19	General Electric	Diversified	United States	16.5	153.9	8.3	14
20	Mitsui	Trading	Japan	15.0	60.8	43.6	32
21	Matsushita Electric Industrial	Electronics	Japan		59.1	16.6	40
22	News Corp.	Publishing	Australia	14.6	20.7	5.3	78
23	Ferruzzi/Montedison	Diversified	Italy	13.5	30.8	9.1	59
24	Bayer	Chemicals	Germany	n.a.	25.4	21.8	84
25	Roche Holding	Drugs	Switzerland	n.a.	17.9	6.8‡	96

Source: United Nations   *where not available, foreign assets have been estimated for ranking   †outside Europe   ‡including export sales

scheming capitalist giant. Put another way, CNN matters more than ITT.

A village, but how global?

The world economy has become more integrated. But to travel is not the same as to arrive. Full integration will be reached only when there is free movement of goods, services, capital and labour, and when governments treat firms equally, regardless of their nationality.

The reason why Lenin bothered to comment on foreign investment (which he saw as imperialism) was that trade and cross-border investment also boomed in 1870-1913, a period he found convenient to label as capitalism's final stage and during which the world economy approached integration at an even faster pace than has been seen in the past 40 years. Investment from slow-growing Europe rushed to the newly industrialising countries of the time: the United States, Canada, Argentina and Australia. Most of the world took part in a monetary union called the gold standard. World trade grew 25-fold in the century before 1913, and there was a huge migration of people from Europe to these new worlds. In other words, the labour market became more integrated. Yet this did not lead to a global Utopia. It was brought to an end by a set of non-tariff barriers and regulatory obstacles called the first world war, which were followed by tariff barriers in the 1920s and 1930s.

So far, the current boom in cross-border investment has been interrupted merely by something as mundane as a recession. Even while the boom was under way, however, it did not bring the world anywhere near to full integration.

One measure, the growth of world trade, suggests integration is slowing rather than accelerating. Although trade grew rapidly in 1950-73 as successive GATT rounds lowered tariffs, and fixed exchange rates helped businesses plan ahead, its growth slowed after 1973 as currencies became more volatile and, in the 1980s, as non-tariff barriers rose to inhibit trade in both goods and services between the industrial countries. Trade is no longer leading integration—which is why the GATT's Uruguay round of liberalisation is needed, in order to dismantle new barriers, to extend freedom into new areas such as agriculture and services, and to give trade a new lease of life.

The world labour market is far from free. Although immigration into America has averaged 600,000 people a year in the past five years and Germany has received an average of 440,000 immigrants from Eastern Europe in each of the past five years, these exceptions confirm the rule: labour does not move. Even in the European Community, where any citizen is entitled to live and work in any member country, migration has been minimal despite wide disparities in standards of living.

That leaves capital, which is indeed where the most rapid progress has been made since 1980. Chart 2 on the next page shows how flows of corporate investment grew in the 1980s and how those flows became more and more concentrated on the richest parts of the world. Where in the 1970s around 25% of foreign direct investment flowed to developing countries, in the 1980s the proportion dropped below 20%. Many developing countries

became cut off from international capital markets because of debt problems; beginning in the 1970s, many had banned or severely restricted foreign direct and portfolio investments.

In North America, the EC and Japan, by contrast, barriers to the free flow of capital were falling. Exchange controls were abolished in Japan and Britain in 1979-80. The European monetary system was established in 1979 and capital controls inside the EC were then gradually dismantled. Financial-market regulations were relaxed, especially in Japan, Britain and the United States. Meanwhile, macroeconomic conditions led to gigantic surpluses of capital in Japan and Germany, and a large appetite for foreign capital in the United States.

Although other forces doubtless helped push business across borders, these stand above the rest: capital was available to move, and a number of governments allowed it to. Cyclical factors in the rich countries also helped, even though cause and effect were mingled: strong growth rates in America, the EC and Japan encouraged investment, as did rising prices for financial assets such as shares and property. But the distribution of cross-border investment within the rich countries confirms that open capital markets were the main driver. America and Britain, which had the most liberal markets for shares and hence companies, received the biggest flows. Japan and Germany, where it is hard to make

...and the next 25

Largest non-financial multinationals 1990, ranked by foreign assets*

Rank	Industry	Country	Foreign assets $ bn	Total assets $ bn	Foreign sales $ bn	% of total sales
26 Toyota Motor	Cars and trucks	Japan	n.a.	55.5	26.3	42
27 Daimler-Benz	Cars and trucks	Germany	n.a.	48.8	32.7‡	61
28 Pechiney	Metals	France	n.a.	14.3	9.2	65
29 Philip Morris	Food	United States	12.5	46.6	15.2	3
30 Rhône-Poulenc	Chemicals	France	12.2	21.4	10.4	72
31 E.I. Du Pont de Nemours	Chemicals	United States	11.9	38.1	17.4	43
32 Hoechst	Chemicals	Germany	n.a.	23.8	14.1‡	50
33 Michelin	Tyres	France	n.a.	14.9	9.1	79
34 Dow Chemical	Chemicals	United States	10.9	24.0	10.3	52
35 Total	Oil	France	n.a.	20.8	18.2	77
36 Thomson	Electronics	France	n.a.	20.7	10.4‡	75
37 Amoco	Oil	United States	10.6	32.2	8.5	30
38 Saint-Gobain	Construction	France	9.9	17.6	8.3	65
39 ENI	Chemicals	Italy	n.a.	60.5	7.9	19
40 Electrolux	Electrical	Sweden	n.a.	11.7	12.5‡	89
41 Petrofina	Oil	Belgium	n.a.	12.3	5.7	33
42 Générale des Eaux	Miscellaneous	France	n.a.	27.9	5.9	29
43 Hitachi	Electronics	Japan	n.a.	49.3	10.5‡	21
44 Chevron	Oil	United States	8.4	35.1	9.8	25
45 Sandoz	Chemicals	Switzerland	n.a.	10.1	6.3‡	70
46 C. Itoh	Trading	Japan	n.a.	47.8	19.1	13
47 Toshiba	Electronics	Japan	n.a.	32.7	8.5†	29
48 Xerox	Office machinery	United States	8.0	31.5	7.5	42
49 Stora	Paper	Sweden	n.a.	15.0	8.9‡	84
50 Texaco	Oil	United States	7.8	26.0	18.0	44

Source: United Nations   *where not available, foreign assets have been estimated for ranking   †outside Europe   ‡including export sales

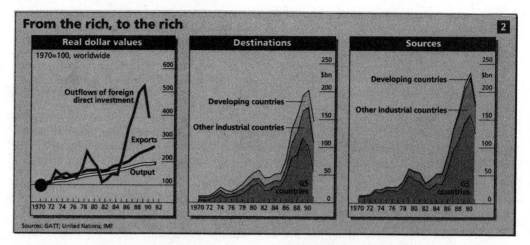

From the rich, to the rich

Real dollar values — Destinations — Sources

Sources: GATT; United Nations, IMF

takeovers, received fewer investments.

The removal of other barriers also played a big part. In theory, utilities and other service industries are natural candidates for foreign investment: they are hard to trade across borders, so the only way to profit from your skills abroad is to invest there. But such industries were off-limits. Electricity, water, air travel, telecoms, banking, even insurance: these and others were either state monopolies in most countries or were restricted to domestically owned firms. That changed in the 1980s, thanks to privatisation and deregulation—which is a big reason why by the late 1980s more than half the annual investment flows were heading for service businesses.

Two conclusions suggest themselves. One is that if the lowering of barriers to capital movements played such a big part, then the surge in investment seen in the 1980s could have been merely a once-off adjustment rather than a continuing trend. Once investors have adapted themselves to the new rules, capital will no longer flow across borders in such quantity; multinational business may still grow, but at a slower rate.

The second conclusion, however, is that there are still further once-off adjustments to be made. The future size and distribution of foreign investment will depend most critically on where barriers are likely to fall next—and whether they fall at all. Labour markets are unlikely to become markedly more integrated, because of political worries about migration. The trend of trade barriers remains uncertain as long as the Uruguay round remains incomplete; although many developing countries are liberalising, the rich ones are either stalling or are imposing new controls. Again, integration looks like depending mostly on capital flows.

Proper global economic integration is a distant prospect, and even continued progress towards it cannot be taken for granted. This harsh reality also offers a clue about how multinational firms are developing. "Globalisation" sounds like a movement towards perfect, seamless markets; it is therefore often assumed to involve convergence on some sort of a model, globe-spanning firm. But there is no such process. And if there were, there would be fewer multinationals, not more of them.

Entrepreneurial Start-up and Growth: A Classification of Problems

David E. Terpstra and Philip D. Olson

David E. Terpstra is Hearin-Hess Professor of Management at the University of Mississippi.

Philip D. Olson is Professor of Management at the University of Idaho.

The purpose of this study was to develop a classification scheme for the types of problems encountered by emerging organizations using an open-ended approach to generating the initial response data. The CEOs of 121 *Inc.* 500 firms were asked to state the most significant problem during their firms' first year and during a later growth stage. The open-ended responses were systematically sorted into classes of problems, and the resulting classification schemes appeared to be more comprehensive and exhaustive than some previously developed schemes that relied on closed-ended response categories to develop their problem classes. Once developed, the classification schemes were used to examine the relative frequencies of types of problems at both the start-up and later growth stage. The findings indicated mixed support for previous research linking types of dominant problems to different stages of organizational development.

The development of a comprehensive, systematically derived classification scheme for the types of problems encountered by emerging entrepreneurial companies would be of both theoretical and practical utility. Such a classification scheme might serve as a starting point for the conceptualization and systematic study of distinct problem types. The development of a comprehensive classification scheme for the types of problems encountered by new organizations may also provide a basis for linking these problem types to problem-solving activities,

and ultimately to organizational performance (Cowan, 1988). For example, the classes could provide a focus for future research studying the relationship between certain problem types and problem formulation and subsequent information-processing activities. The initial classification framework may have implications for resolution methods, as it may influence the perceived problem solutions by directing and controlling attention and diagnostic activity (March & Simon, 1958; Volkema, 1986).

Several classification frameworks have been proposed for the categorization of organizational problem types. For example, over 30 years ago, Dearborn and Simon (1958) classified organizational problems into three general types: (1) sales, marketing, or distribution; (2) clarifying the organization; and (3) human relations, employee relations, or teamwork. More recently, Walsh (1988) proposed that organizational problems can be grouped into five general categories: (1) accounting-finance; (2) human relations; (3) marketing; (4) internal management; and (5) external management. Both of the above studies, however, were narrowly focused on the role of selective perception, or the extent to which affiliation with a specific department in an organization influences the types of problems identified. In Dearborn and Simon's (1958) and Walsh's (1988) studies, managers were given only one hypothetical company case and were asked to identify the problem(s) facing that company. Thus, the research methodology employed in these studies quite likely limited the number and range of problems initially identified. The relatively small sample of managers (23) employed in the Dearborn and Simon study may also have limited the range of problems identified. The study by Walsh employed a larger sample that consisted of 121 middle- and upper-level managers that had been selected by their organizations to attend a master's degree program at a large university. But again, the range of problems initially identified may have been limited by the one hypothetical case presented to the participants (the case

From *Entrepreneurship Theory and Practice*, Vol. 17, No. 3, Spring 1993, pp. 5-20. © 1993 by Baylor University. All rights reserved. Reprinted by permission.

portrayed a company with a mature product line that was specifically challenged by the advent of private-label and generic competition). One might also question whether the fact that all of the managers in Walsh's study were enrolled in the same executive master's program (and hence, subject to the same specialized training) may have limited the range of their problem responses.

A recent study by Cowan (1990) found some partial support for the frameworks proposed by both Dearborn and Simon (1958) and Walsh (1988). In this study, 59 middle- and upper-level managers who were all enrolled in a two-year MBA program at a private midwestern university were asked to write down an example of an organizational problem they had experienced recently. Thus, Cowan's study did not limit managers to identifying problems associated with a single case or company. There may have been some bias due to the fact that all of the managers were exposed to similar training in the MBA program, however. Additionally, the demand characteristics associated with a university classroom setting may be cause for concern in the above studies by Dearborn and Simon (1958), Walsh (1988), and Cowan (1990). Asking CEOs in the field to nominate significant organizational problems may result in a different set of initial problem types from those nominated by functional managers attending an MBA class. Additionally, the above problem classification studies were not focused on the types of problems encountered by new or rapidly growing entrepreneurial entities.

Some information regarding the types of problems encountered by emerging organizations can be drawn from studies of business failures and studies of problems facing rapidly growing firms. For example, Dun and Bradstreet (1987) collected data on new business ventures that failed, and listed the following as major reasons for failure: (1) inadequate market knowledge; (2) poor product performance; (3) ineffective marketing and sales efforts; (4) inadequate awareness of competitive pressures; (5) rapid product obsolescence; (6) poor timing for the start of a business venture; and (7) financial difficulties. The method employed to arrive at these classes of reasons, however, was not specified. In another study of business failures, Bruno, Leidecker, and Harder (1987) contacted the founders of 10 failed high-technology firms and concluded that there were three major reasons for failure: (1) product/market problems; (2) financial difficulties; and (3) managerial problems. The sample size of the above study was rather small, however; and the authors simply stated that the founders' responses were grouped into three classes. The studies by Dun and Bradstreet (1987) and Bruno et al. (1987) yield some insights into the types of problems encountered by firms in the start-up stage, but they may provide limited information about the types of problems encountered by firms in the later growth stage.

Regarding studies of the types of problems facing rapidly growing firms, Anderson and Dunkleberg (1987)

surveyed the CEOs of the 100 fastest-growing public firms in the United States. These firms had the largest percentage increase in revenues over a five-year period (the average five-year growth was 1,086 percent). The average annual sales for these firms was $54.8 million (the revenue of these firms for the first year of the five-year period ranged from $100,000 to $25 million). The 35 CEOs that responded to the survey indicated that management and employee development were the greatest challenges to maintaining growth. The 35 CEOs were also asked what they thought would present the greatest challenge to their firms in the next five years. The resulting classes of responses, in order of frequency, were: (1) maintaining/controlling growth; (2) the rapidly changing market; (3) training and motivation; and (4) developing career paths. Anderson and Dunkleberg (1987) made no mention of the method or basis for arriving at their classes of problems. The studies of business failures and studies of rapidly growing firms mentioned above provide some valuable insights into the types of problems that new entrepreneurial firms may encounter. However, the nature and size of the samples employed and the likelihood that the classes of problem types were not systematically or empirically developed may limit their contribution somewhat.

Theories and models of organizational life-cycles and stages of development may also shed some light on the types of problems encountered by organizations over time. Several models have been advanced that attempt to label and explain the various stages of development that organizations may pass through (Adizes, 1979; Chandler, 1962; Churchill & Lewis, 1983; Cooper, 1979; Flamholtz, 1986; Greiner, 1972; Hannah & Freeman, 1984; Hosmer, Cooper, & Vesper, 1977; Kazanjian, 1988; Kimberly & Miles, 1980; Kuratko & Hodgetts, 1989; McKelvey & Aldrich, 1983; Miller & Friesen, 1984; Olson, 1987; Quinn & Cameron, 1983; Scott, 1970; Smith, Mitchell, & Summer, 1985; Van de Ven, Hudson, & Schroeder, 1984). Generally speaking, these models suggest that organizations may progress sequentially through major stages of development (e.g., birth or start-up, growth, maturity, etc.). Additionally, some of these models suggest that each stage of development is associated with a unique set of problems. Kuratko and Hodgetts (1989), for example, suggest that marketing and financial problems characterize the start-up stage, while strategic, administrative, and managerial problems characterize the growth stage. Olson (1987) has suggested that the start-up stage is more apt to be associated with problems related to the creation and development of products and services, while the growth stage is more apt to be associated with problems related to management and organization design. Kazanjian (1988) has provided some partial empirical support for a link between types of dominant problems and organizational stages of development. Kazanjian (1988) reviewed the theoretical literature on stages of development, and identified 18 types of problems on the basis of his review. He then conducted a cross-sectional study of approximately 100 firms in stages of development ranging from start-up through stability. The CEOs of these firms were asked to rate each of the 18 problems on a 7-point scale in terms of its dominance to the firm. Thus, a closed-ended response format was employed to assess the types of problems facing the organizations. The CEOs' ratings of the 18 problems were then subjected to a factor analysis, and the following six problem types or factors emerged: (1) organizational systems (developing management information systems, controlling costs, financial systems and controls, defining organizational roles and responsibilities, and administrative burdens and red tape); (2) sales/marketing problems; (3) people problems (attracting capable personnel and finding talent, and achieving management depth); (4) production problems (meeting demand, and developing reliable vendors and suppliers); (5) strategic positioning; and (6) external relations (securing financial resources and backing, and acquiring key outside advisers and board members). In relating these types of problems to stages of organizational development, Kazanjian (1988) found that some types of problems, such as sales/marketing and strategic positioning, were more dominant than other problems in all stages of development. However, he found that external relations problems (securing financial resources and backing) were more dominant in the start-up stage than in the later growth stage of development. On the other hand, sales/marketing and organizational systems problems were more dominant in the growth stage than in the start-up stage.

Research investigating the concept of stages of development and the relationship of those discrete stages to the types of dominant problems encountered is important because it may help us understand the types of problems that firms need to solve to continue to grow and perform effectively. However, research investigating the relationship between stages of development and the relative frequency of occurrence of various problem types would seem to benefit from a more open-ended initial effort to develop the classes or types of possible problems.

RESEARCH OBJECTIVES

The primary objective of the current research was to attempt to systematically develop a comprehensive and exhaustive classification scheme for the types of problems encountered by emerging entrepreneurial firms. Previous research that has sought to systematically or empirically develop classification schemes for the types of problems faced by new or rapidly growing firms has employed closed-ended response categories developed from a priori theoretical speculations as to possible problem types. The danger in such an approach is that important problem types may be overlooked. As Babbie (1973) has noted with respect to closed-ended categories, even when an "other" category is provided, respondents will still attempt to force their answers into one of the

categories provided. An open-ended approach for generating response data allows the investigator to "capture the points of view of other people without predetermining those points of view through prior selection of questionnaire categories" (Patton, 1990, p. 24). Thus, an open-ended response format was employed in this study in an attempt to capture a wider range of initial problem types, and develop a classification scheme based upon those problems. The sample of organizational problems was generated by asking CEOs to describe their firms' most significant problems at two points in time—during the start-up stage and during a later growth stage of development. Few of the existing classification schemes of organizational problem types have been focused on emerging entrepreneurial firms. The current study sought to provide some new insights regarding the types of problems faced by these organizations. More specifically, the following research question was advanced:

Research Question 1: Will the open-ended approach used in the current study yield a more comprehensive and exhaustive classification scheme for the types of problems encountered in emerging entrepreneurial organizations than previous studies that have relied upon closed-ended response categories to develop problem classification schemes?

A secondary objective of the current research was to explore possible changes in the patterns of problems that firms experience as they move from the start-up stage to a later growth stage. The classification scheme(s), once developed, will be applied and examined with regard to the relative frequency of mention of problem types at both the start-up and later growth stage. The study by Kazanjian (1988) represents, perhaps, one of the better empirical investigations that addressed the relationship between types of dominant problems and stages of development. Kazanjian's (1988) study found that some types of problems were more dominant than all other problems in all stages of development; however, the relative importance of some other types of problems did appear to vary by stage. It is difficult to generate specific hypotheses related to Kazanjian's earlier findings for two reasons. First, the classes of problems that emerge from the current study may not be directly comparable to those used by Kazanjian. Second, the conceptualization and measurement of organizational stages employed in his study differed somewhat from that of the current study. Thus, the following general research question was tentatively advanced:

Research Question 2: Will the types and frequencies of significant problems experienced at the start-up stage differ from the types and frequencies of significant problems experienced at the later growth stage?

METHOD

Sample

The sample was drawn from the 500 firms listed in the December, 1987, issue of *Inc.* magazine. These firms represented the fastest-growing privately held companies in the U.S. based on percentage of sales increases over the 1982–1986 five-year period. Twenty-six of the firms were deleted from the sample due to an inability to obtain mailing addresses. Thirty-two additional firms were dropped because their founding date was over 15 years ago (firms starting before 1973 were dropped because recalling facts about a firm's early years becomes increasingly difficult the older the firm is). Questionnaires were mailed to the CEOs of the remaining 442 firms in November of 1988. One hundred twenty-one questionnaires were returned for a response rate of 27 percent. Six of the CEOs who responded had not been the CEO during the first year of operation of their organization; thus, their questionnaires were deleted from the study. The final sample consisted of 115 firms.

The median 1988 age of the responding firms was 9 years, and the mean 1988 age was 9.4 years. The earliest year that firms could have started and been included in the *Inc.* 500 list was 1973, and the latest year was 1982. Firms starting up in different years within this ten-year period quite likely encountered varying environmental and economic conditions. For example, there were differences in the health of the economy, the supply of money, the rate of inflation, and the price of oil over this time period (Branson, 1989). On the one hand, these differences in external conditions contribute to the primary objective of the current study. Varying external conditions would seem to further increase the likelihood of capturing the entire range of possible problem types experienced in the start-up stage, thus contributing to the development of a more complete and exhaustive classification scheme. On the other hand, however, the fact that the firms in the current sample started in different years makes it more difficult to address the secondary research objective. The different years that organizations started up, and the different environmental conditions associated with those years, may have influenced the types and frequencies of problems experienced both at start-up and in 1988 (our growth stage). Analyses designed to assess the impact of age on both start-up problems and 1988 problems were conducted and are reported later in this paper.

The distribution of firms by industry type was as follows: computer-related—21.7%; business service—22.6%; medical and pharmaceutical—3.5%; telecommunications—1.7%; publication and media—2.6%; industrial equipment—6.1%; construction and engineering—10.4%; consumer goods—11.3%; and other—20.0%. Chi-square analyses indicated that the observed percentages of industry representation in the obtained sample did not differ significantly from the percentages listed in *Inc.* 500.

The median percentage of sales increases for the firms over the five years (1982–1986) was 906 percent with a range of from 529 percent to 9,160 percent. Analyses were also conducted to test for possible differences in sample representation by percentage of sales increase levels. The

Inc. 500 firms were subdivided into the following five classes based on their percentage of sales increases: the top 100, the second 100, the third 100, the fourth 100, and the fifth 100. Thus, each class contained 100 firms, or 20 percent of the 500. For the firms that responded, the following frequencies and percentages were observed: 13 (11.3%) from the top 100, 24 (20.9%) from the second 100, 26 (22.6%) from the third 100, 30 (26.1%) from the fourth 100, and 22 (19.1%) from the fifth 100. A chi-square analysis indicated that the observed class percentages did not differ significantly from the hypothesized 20 percent levels.

The median and mean number of employees of the firms during the first year of operation were 3 and 9.6, respectively. The median and mean number of employees of the firms during 1988 were 60 and 234, respectively. Comparisons of the firms that responded to those listed in the *Inc.* 500 list again indicated no significant differences.

It might also be noted that all of the CEOs in this study had been the CEO since the first year of operation of their organization.

Questionnaire and Measures

The questionnaire that served as the primary data-gathering device was developed by one of the authors and was pretested by three business professors and three practicing entrepreneurs. In one section of the questionnaire, the respondents were asked to state their firms' most significant problem during the first year of operation. The CEOs were also asked to state their firms' most significant problem in 1988. The open-ended response format for these questions was in line with the primary objective of the study, and did not limit the CEOs' responses to predetermined closed-ended response categories. The open-ended response format was employed in order to capture a potentially wider range of distinct problem types.

Information on the age, sales increase percentages, and industry classifications of the responding firms was obtained archivally from *Inc.* magazine. The questionnaire also asked the respondents to indicate the industry classification of their firms (computer-related, business service, medical and pharmaceutical, telecommunication, publishing and media, industrial equipment, construction and engineering, consumer goods, and other). Additionally, the questionnaire asked the CEOs to write down the number of employees in their firms during the first year of operation, and the number of employees during 1988.

The use of retrospective measures to obtain data regarding the CEOs' perceptions of significant problems during the first year of operation of their organizations was not thought to pose a major threat to the primary purpose of this study. The primary objective was to generate a large sample of distinct types of organizational problems. Furthermore, all of the respondents were also the CEOs during their firms' first year of operation, and it is likely that those early years are quite salient.

Currently, no consensus exists as to specific operational definitions that should be employed in demarcating different organizational stages of development. Frequently, however, such factors as changes in number of employees, changes in sales growth rates, or firm age are employed to define various stages. Kazanjian (1988), for example, used employee size, firm age, and sales growth to characterize an organization's stage of development. Smith et al. (1985) have stated that firms in their start-up stage tend to be small in size (number of employees) and young in age, while firms in their growth stage are larger in employee size and older. Miller and Friesen (1984) have characterized organizations with annual sales growth rates greater than 15 percent as being in the growth stage. In the current study, the first year of operation was used to represent the start-up stage, while 1988 was used to represent the growth stage. Employee size may be one of the more important defining factors of organizational stage, as it would seem to have more direct implications for structural and managerial changes and challenges. In the current sample, the average number of first-year employees was 9.6, and this number increased dramatically to 234 in 1988. To check whether the sampled organizations were still in a growth stage in 1988 (*Inc.* classified these firms as rapidly growing based on figures over the 1982 to 1986 time period), changes in employee size from the 1982 to 1986 time period were compared to changes from 1986 to 1988. The mean number of employees increased from 17 in 1982 to 94.5 in 1986 for an average annualized growth rate of 133.5 percent. From 1986 to 1988 the mean number of employees increased from 94.5 to 234, for an average annualized growth rate of 260.5 percent. The average percentage change in employee growth for the two-year period (from 1986 to 1988) was 520.9 percent. Thus, the sampled organizations still appeared to be in a definite growth stage in 1988. Employee size may be the most significant factor in defining an organization's stage of development (because of its impact on structural and management challenges), but age and sales growth are also sometimes employed to assess organizational stage. The sampled organizations can be classified as being in the growth stage in 1988 based on age; however, 1988 sales figures were not collected. (The *Inc.* firms were privately held; thus, sales data could not be obtained from such sources as 10-K disclosures, CRSP, or Compustat.) The five-year growth rates of the responding organizations from 1982 to 1986 were phenomenal—they ranged from 529 percent to 9,160 percent, with a median value of 906 percent. The lack of 1988 sales data precludes the calculation of sales growth figures from 1986 to 1988, but the previously mentioned increase in employee growth figures from 1986 to 1988 suggests that the sampled organizations may have had similar growth rates for sales. It is possible that a few of the firms originally listed in the 1987 issue of *Inc.* magazine subsequently experienced problems and would no longer be classified as successful or rapidly growing; however, it seems quite likely that these few firms would not have responded to this study's survey instrument. The cover letter attached to the survey opened by congratulating the CEO for presiding over a successful, rapidly growing firm. The cover letter then identified the purpose of the study as being to specifically gather information about effective management practices of "very successful, rapidly growing firms."

Development of the Classification Schemes

The initial generation of the distinct organizational problems was accomplished by asking the CEOs to state their firms' most significant problem during the first year of operation, and also their firms' most significant problem in 1988.

Each of the written responses to the two above-mentioned questions was edited for spelling and typed on a 4 × 8 1/2 inch sheet of paper. Three management faculty (from different disciplines) and three MBA students participated in the classification of the responses to these two questions. Each individual was given two packets of responses (first-year problems, and 1988 problems). The order in which the two unlabeled packets were given to the six individuals was systematically varied, and no reference to stage of development was made within each packet, in an attempt to minimize the potential problem of priming or contamination in the development of the classes of problems for the two stages. For each packet, the individuals were asked to independently read through the sheets of papers, sort the sheets into as many piles as they felt necessary for the adequate classification of the responses, and label the classes. Additionally, both of the current authors read through the packets and sorted the material into classes. In the case of multiple-stated responses, the sorters were instructed to consider the most drastic or serious stated response. If a judgment could not be made regarding the degree of seriousness, the sorters were instructed to consider the response that was stated first. Thus, each of the six individuals (plus the two current authors) generated two classification schemes.

To arrive at the final classification schemes for the CEOs' responses, the authors examined the classes developed by the six sorters and made a judgment based upon two considerations: distinctness and comprehensiveness. The first consideration involved the degree to which the classes consisted of distinctly different and mutually exclusive forms of responses. The second consideration involved the degree to which the classes were exhaustive and capable of capturing the entire range of the observed responses. There was a high degree of overlap among the sorters' classification schemes. Most of the classes identified by the sorters included the same types of problems, but were simply given slightly different class labels. The only real disagreements among the sorters were instances where some sorters had collapsed classes to a greater extent than had other sorters. For example, two of the sorters had collapsed "obtaining external financing" and "internal financial management" into one general class of "financial problems." Similarly, another sorter had collapsed "economic environment" and "regulatory environment" classes into one general "environment" class. Based upon the previously mentioned criteria (distinctness and comprehensiveness), the final judgment always favored the schemes that had not been collapsed.

To assess the reliability and validity of the classification schemes, two more MBA students were given the final classification schemes along with class definitions, and were asked to code all of the responses using the new classification schemes. The percentage of paired item agreement between the two individuals' classifications across all sets of responses was computed to be 88.64 percent. The instances of disagreement between the two raters were identified and discussed, and a final classification for each was settled upon.

The two coders were also asked, in classifying the responses, to note any responses that could not be suitably slotted into the existing classes, and which might require the creation of a new class. Neither of the coders nominated any responses that constituted classification problems, thus indicating the apparent comprehensiveness of the schemes.

RESULTS AND DISCUSSION

Problem Classification

The classification schemes for the types of organizational problems for both the first year and 1988 are presented below in Table 1. (Appendices A and B provide more detail as to the specific problems included within each class.) The relative frequency of occurrence of the classes of problems is also presented in Table 1; however, this data will be discussed in a later section.

The classes that emerged from the first-year problems and those that emerged from the 1988 problems were identical, with the exception of one new class (organization structure/design) in the 1988 classification scheme.

A comparison of the classes of problems that emerged from this open-ended approach to existing classification frameworks and problems identified in previous research suggests that the current study may have yielded a more comprehensive and exhaustive classification scheme for the types of problems encountered by emerging entrepreneurial organizations. Dearborn and Simon's (1958) classification framework included only three classes of problems. Walsh (1988) proposed five classes of problems in his framework. The current study identified nine distinctly different classes of problems for the start-up stage and 10 for the later growth stage. The greater

number of classes were a function of both finer distinctions and the identification of new problem types. The problem classes identified in earlier studies of business failure (Bruno et al., 1987; Dun & Bradstreet, 1987) and studies of rapidly growing firms (Anderson & Dunkleberg, 1987) also seem somewhat limited in comparison to the classes developed in the current study. For example, Bruno et al. (1987) identified only three general classes of problems leading to failure. Similarly, Anderson and Dunkleberg (1987) collapsed the types of problems or challenges confronting rapidly growing organizations into only two classes. The current classification scheme compares more favorably to the classification structure developed by Kazanjian (1988). Kazanjian identified six problem classes on the basis of a factor analysis of 100 CEOs' responses to predetermined categories of problems. The sales/marketing problems, production/operations management problems, and human resource management problems identified in this study are somewhat comparable to Kazanjian's (1988) sales/marketing problems, production problems, and people problems, respectively. But some of Kazanjian's other classes seem to lump distinctly different types of problems together. For example, his organizational systems class includes such diverse problem types as controlling costs/financial controls, defining organizational roles and responsibilities, and administrative burdens and red tape. In comparison, the current classification scheme includes at least four distinctly different problem classes (internal financial management, organization structure/design, general management, and the regulatory environment) that could be collapsed under the above one problem class of organizational systems under Kazanjian's scheme. Similarly, Kazanjian's external relations class lumps securing financial resources and backing (which is similar to the current obtaining external financing class) and obtaining key outside advisers together under one rubric. Some seemingly diverse problem types are included within one class in Kazanjian's framework in part because of the factor analytic approach employed; this can easily be justified on statistical grounds. The current classification scheme, however, might be more logically appealing to entrepreneurs and managers because of its greater degree of face validity. If, in fact, the initial classification by problem type influences problem solutions by controlling attention and diagnostic activity (March & Simon, 1958; Volkema, 1986), then the new classification scheme may possess more practical utility than Kazanjian's scheme.

In general, the new classification scheme appears to be more complete than some previously developed schemes. The open-ended approach to gathering the initial response data seems necessary for studying the diverse happenings in emerging entrepreneurial organizations. Some of the new classes that were identified may be practically and theoretically important. The more comprehensive classification scheme might provide a better basis for the study of the types of problems encountered

Classes of Organizational Problems

TABLE 1

First-Year Classes	Frequency	Percentage
1. Obtaining external financing	17	17
2. Internal financial management	16	16
3. Sales/Marketing	38	38
4. Product development	5	5
5. Production/Operations management	4	4
6. General management	11	11
7. Human resource management	5	5
8. Economic environment	3	3
9. Regulatory environment	1	1

1988 Classes	Frequency	Percentage
1. Obtaining external financing	1	1
2. Internal financial management	22	21
3. Sales/Marketing	23	22
4. Product development	2	2
5. Production/Operations management	8	8
6. Organization structure/design	6	6
7. General management	14	14
8. Human resource management	17	17
9. Economic environment	2	2
10. Regulatory environment	8	8

by emerging firms. Additionally, if entrepreneurs are better able to anticipate the possible problems that might be encountered at the start-up and later growth stage, they should stand a better chance of dealing effectively with those problems and guiding their firms through the difficult early stages.

Start-Up and Growth Problems

A secondary objective of this study involved exploring possible changes in the patterns of problems experienced by organizations as they move from the start-up to the later growth stage. Table 1, presented earlier, shows the relative frequency of occurrence of the types of problems encountered at the start-up stage and at the growth stage. The dominant problems at start-up were sales/marketing (38%), obtaining external financing (17%), and internal financial management problems (16%). General management problems were also frequently cited in the start-up stage (11%). In the later growth stage, sales/marketing remained as the most dominant problem (22%), but it was relatively less important than in the start-up stage. Internal financial management (21%) also continued to be a dominant problem in the growth stage. Human resource management problems (17%) and general management problems (14%) were also frequently mentioned problems in the growth stage. Additionally, there were relatively more regulatory environment problems in the growth stage (8%) than were mentioned in the earlier

start-up stage (1%). Finally, organization structure/design (6%) emerged as a newly cited problem in the growth stage.

The most dramatic changes from the start-up to the growth stage were as follows: the percentage of organizations citing obtaining external financing as the most significant problem decreased from 17 percent in the start-up stage to 1 percent in the later growth stage; no firms mentioned organization structure/design as the most significant problem in the start-up stage, whereas 6 percent did in the later growth stage; the percentage of firms mentioning human resource management as the most significant problem increased from 5 percent in the start-up stage to 17 percent in the later growth stage; the percentage of organizations citing sales/marketing as the most significant problem decreased from 38 percent in the start-up stage to 22 percent in the later growth stage; and the percentage of firms mentioning the regulatory environment as the most significant problem increased from 1 percent in the start-up stage to 8 percent in the later growth stage.

As was mentioned earlier in this paper, the start-up year for the firms varied from 1973 to 1982. Firms starting up in different years encountered varying environmental and economic conditions, and this may have influenced the types and frequencies of problems experienced and reported in both their start-up and later growth period. To examine this possibility, the sample was subdivided by the median 1988 age (9 years). Thus, those firms starting up between 1973 and 1978 were compared to those start-

213

ing up between 1979 and 1982. Chi-square analyses indicated that there were no significant differences between these two groups of organizations in terms of either the observed frequencies of first-year problems ($x^2 = 4.01$, $p > .05$), or in terms of the observed frequencies of 1988 problems ($x^2 = 3.46$, $p > .05$). The lack of significant differences suggests that the year of start-up had little influence on the pattern of problems experienced at the start-up or later growth stage of development.

The current findings seem to loosely support some of the existing literature regarding organizational life-cycles and stages of development. For example, Kuratko and Hodgetts (1989) suggested that marketing and financial problems characterize the start-up stage, while administrative, managerial, and strategic problems characterize the growth stage. Olson (1987) also suggested that the growth stage is more likely to be associated with problems related to management and organization design. These characterizations are generally in line with this study's findings. Kazanjian's (1988) study found that external relations problems (securing financial resources and backing) were more dominant in the start-up stage than the later growth stage, while sales/marketing and organizational systems problems were more dominant in the growth stage than in the start-up stage. Kazanjian also found that sales/marketing and strategic positioning were relatively more dominant than other problems in both stages. The current findings support Kazanjian's results regarding the significance of problems related to securing financial resources in the start-up stage, as 17 percent of the respondents cited obtaining external financing as the most significant problem in the start-up year as opposed to only 1 percent in the later growth stage. The current findings did not support Kazanjian's contention that sales/marketing problems were relatively more dominant in the growth than the start-up stage. Additionally, limited support was found for Kazanjian's finding that organizational systems problems were relatively more dominant in the growth than the start-up stage. For example, there was little change in the relative importance of internal financial management problems (similar to "controlling costs," and "financial systems and controls") from the start-up to the growth stage. The current study did, however, find that the relative importance of organization structure/design and regulatory environment problems increased somewhat from the start-up to the growth stage, and these problem classes may be somewhat similar to Kazanjian's "defining organizational roles and responsibilities," and "administrative burdens and red tape." (These results seem to further emphasize the potential problems with Kazanjian's statistically derived factor structure.) This study did support Kazanjian's finding that sales/marketing problems were more dominant than other problems in both stages, as this problem was found to be the most frequently mentioned significant problem in both the start-up stage (38%) and the later growth stage (22%).

The differences observed between the current findings and some of the existing literature regarding the types of dominant problems associated with different stages of development might be due, in part, to the nature of the present sample or to the way in which the two stages were operationalized. For example, 1988 sales data were not obtained to verify that the responding organizations in the current study were still in a growth stage in 1988, although 1988 employee size figures would seem to indicate that these firms were still in a definite growth stage. But some of the observed differences may also be a function of the different ways that problem types were initially identified and classified. This underscores the need for and importance of a valid and comprehensive problem classification scheme for studying the changes in patterns of problems across different organizational life-cycle stages or stages of development. This study, in general, supports the existence of differing patterns and frequencies of problem types across differing stages of development of emerging entrepreneurial organizations. There is currently a shortage of empirical information as to how well existing theories and models of organizational development apply to new ventures. If more information were available regarding the types and patterns of problems that accompany the early stages of development of new ventures, it may also be possible to more effectively manage those problems. It is hoped that the current study has provided some information that will be of use to both theorists and practicing entrepreneurs.

Limitations and Suggestions for Future Research

In the future, more research of an open-ended nature might be conducted in emerging organizations to test the validity, reliability, and comprehensiveness of the current classification schemes. For example, steps were taken in the current study to minimize the likelihood that the sorting of classes for one stage would influence the sorting of classes for the other stage. However, future studies might be designed to more definitively rule out the potential problem of priming or contamination in the development of classification schemes for the start-up and growth stage. Another suggestion for future research would be to employ confirmatory factor analysis, and use multi-item scales on a number of samples to see if the classes that emerged in the current study continue to hold. Additionally, future research could compare the reliability and comprehensiveness of the current schemes with that of previously reported classification schemes. For example, the reliability of various schemes could be assessed by having independent samples of individuals sort a set of problems into the schemes' classes, and then comparing the interrater reliability figures associated with the different classification schemes. The relative degree of comprehensiveness of different classification frameworks (or the degree to which the classes are capable of capturing the entire range of possible problem types) could be assessed by comparing the relative number of problem types that cannot be suitably slotted into the existing classes of the different schemes, and which would require the creation of new classes. A bias may also exist in the current study because the sampled organizations were all quite successful. Perhaps similar research could be conducted with different populations of organizations, such as failures or those that are not as successful as the organizations in the current sample. It could be argued that the systematic study of the problems of unsuccessful firms is, in a sense, more important than the study of the problems encountered by successful, rapidly growing firms. It might also be noted that the current study analyzed only one problem at the start-up stage and one problem during the growth stage (the most significant problem at each stage). It is possible that this set of problems may not adequately represent the content domain of interest. More research of a true longitudinal nature would also be beneficial for investigating the types and patterns of problems encountered by organizations at different stages of development.

CONCLUSION

Few of the existing problem frameworks or classification schemes found in the literature are focused on the types of problems encountered by emerging entrepreneurial firms. Additionally, few problem classification schemes have been developed that have been based upon an open-ended response format to generate the initial problems. In the current study, a classification scheme for the types of problems encountered by emerging organizations was developed utilizing an open-ended approach to generate the initial problem response data. The classification scheme that emerged appeared to be more comprehensive and exhaustive than previously developed schemes. The new scheme was characterized by both finer class distinctions and new problem types. Thus, the classification scheme developed in the current study may be theoretically and practically useful. The classes might provide a better basis for theory and research related to the types of problems associated specifically with new and rapidly growing firms. The classification scheme might provide a better focus for research investigating the relationship between specific problem types and problem formulation and subsequent information-processing activities. The scheme may also have some implications for resolution methods, as it may influence the range of perceived problem solutions by directing and controlling attention and diagnostic activity. In summary, it is hoped that the results of the current study will provide some new insights into the types of problems faced by emerging firms, and aid future research directed toward the study and resolution of those problems.

REFERENCES

Adizes, I. (1979). Organizational passages—Diagnosing and treating lifecycle problems of organizations. *Organizational Dynamics, 8*(1), 3–25.

Anderson, R. L., & Dunkelberg, J. S. (1987). *Managing growing firms*. Englewood Cliffs, NJ: Prentice Hall.

Babbie, E. R. (1973). *Survey research methods*. Belmont, CA: Wadsworth.

Blau, P. M., & Schoenherr, R. A. (1971). *The structure of organizations*. New York: Dryden Press.

Branson, W. H. (1989). *Macroeconomic theory and policy*. New York: Harper & Row.

Bruno, A. V., Leidecker, J. K., & Harder, J. W. (1987). Why firms fail. *Business Horizons*, March/April, 50–58.

Chandler, A. D., Jr. (1962). *Strategy and structure*. Cambridge, MA: M.I.T. Press.

Child, J. (1973). Predicting and understanding organization structure. *Administrative Science Quarterly, 18*, 168–185.

Churchill, N., & Lewis, V. L. (1983). The five stages of small business growth. *Harvard Business Review, 61*(3), 30–50.

Cooper, A. (1979). Strategic management: New ventures and small business. In D. Schendel & C. Hofer (Eds.), *Strategic management: A new view of business policy and planning*, pp. 316–327. Boston: Little, Brown & Co.

Cowan, D. A. (1988). Executives' knowledge of organizational problem types: Applying a contingency perspective. *Journal of Management, 14*, 513–527.

Cowan, D. A. (1990). Developing a classification structure of organizational problems: An empirical investigation. *Academy of Management Journal, 33*, 366–390.

Daft, R. L., & Bradshaw, P. J. (1980). The process of horizontal differentiation: Two models. *Administrative Science Quarterly, 25*, 441–445.

Dearborn, D. C., & Simon, H. A. (1958). Selective perception: A note on the departmental identification of executives. *Sociometry, 21*, 140–144.

Dewar, R., & Hage, J. (1978). Size, technology, complexity, and structural differentiation: Toward a theoretical synthesis. *Administrative Science Quarterly, 23*, 111–136.

Dun & Bradstreet. (1987). *The business failure record: 1987*. New York: Dun & Bradstreet.

Flamholtz, E. G. (1986). *How to make the transition from an entrepreneurship to a professionally managed firm*. San Francisco: Jossey-Bass.

Greiner, L. E. (1972). Evolution and revolution as organizations grow. *Harvard Business Review, 50*(4), 37–46.

Hage, J., & Aiken, M. (1967). Relationship of centralization to other structural properties. *Administrative Science Quarterly, 12*, 72–91.

Hannan, M., & Freeman, J. (1984). Structural inertia and organizational change. *American Sociological Review, 49*, 149–164.

Hoad, W. M., & Rosko, P. (1964). *Management factors contributing to the success and failure of new small manufacturers*. Ann Arbor, MI: Bureau of Business Research, University of Michigan.

Hosmer, L. T., Cooper, A., & Vesper, K. (1977). *The entrepreneurial function*. Englewood Cliffs, NJ: Prentice Hall.

Kazanjian, R. K. (1988). Relation of dominant problems to stages of growth in technology-based new ventures. *Academy of Management Journal, 31*(2), 257–279.

Kimberly, J. R., & Miles, R. H. (1980). *The organizational life cycle*. San Francisco: Jossey-Bass.

Kuratko, D. F., & Hodgetts, R. M. (1989). *Entrepreneurship: A contemporary approach*. Chicago: Dryden Press.

Lawyer, K. (1963). *Small business success: Operating executive characteristics*. Cleveland, OH: Bureau of Business Research, Case-Western Reserve University.

Mansfield, R. (1973). Bureaucracy and centralization: An examination of organizational structure. *Administrative Science Quarterly, 18*, 477–488.

March, J. O., & Simon, H. A. (1958). *Organizations*. New York: Wiley.

McKelvey, B., & Aldrich, H. (1983). Populations, natural selection, and applied organizational science. *Administrative Science Quarterly, 28,* 101–128.

Meyer, M. W. (1972). Size and the structure of organizations: A causal analysis. *American Sociological Review, 37,* 434–440.

Miller, D., & Friesen, P. H. (1984). A longitudinal study of the corporate life cycle. *Management Science, 30,* 1161–1183.

Olson, P. D. (1987). Entrepreneurship and management. *Journal of Small Business Management, 25*(3), 7–13.

Patton, M. Q. (1990). *Qualitative evaluation and research methods.* Newbury Park, CA: Sage.

Pugh, D. S., Hickson, D. J., Hinings, C. R., & Turner, C. (1969). The context of organization structure. *Administrative Science Quarterly, 14,* 91–114.

Quinn, R. E., & Cameron, K. (1983). Organizational life cycles and shifting criteria of effectiveness: Some preliminary evidence. *Management Science, 29*(1), 33–51.

Reimann, B. (1973). On the dimensions of bureaucratic structure: An empirical reappraisal. *Administrative Science Quarterly, 18,* 462–476.

Scott, B. (1970). *Stages of corporate development* (Parts 1 & 2). Working paper, Harvard Business School, Boston.

Siegel, S. (1956). *Nonparametric statistics.* New York: McGraw-Hill.

Smith, K. G., Mitchell, T. R., & Summer, C. E. (1985). Top-level management priorities in different stages of the organizational life cycle. *Academy of Management Journal, 28,* 799–820.

Van de Ven, A. H., Hudson, R., & Schroeder, D. (1984). Designing new business start-ups: Entrepreneurial, organizational, and ecological considerations. *Journal of Management, 10*(1), 87–108.

Volkema, R. J. (1986). Problem formulation as a purposive activity. *Strategic Management Journal, 7,* 267–279.

Walsh, J. P. (1988). Selectivity and selective perception: An investigation of managers' belief structures and information processing. *Academy of Management Journal, 31,* 873–896.

APPENDIX A

Types and Classes of First-Year Problems

1. *Obtaining external financing*
   Obtaining financing for growth
   Other or general financing problems

2. *Internal financial management*
   Inadequate working capital
   Cash flow problems
   Other or general financial management problems

3. *Sales/Marketing*
   Low sales
   Dependence on one or few clients/customers
   Marketing or distribution channels
   Promotion/public relations/advertising
   Other or general marketing problems

4. *Product development*
   Developing products/services
   Other or general product development problems

5. *Production/Operations management*
   Establishing or maintaining quality control
   Raw materials/resources/supplies
   Other or general production/operations management problems

6. *General management*
   Lack of management experience
   Only one person/no time
   Managing/controlling growth
   Administrative problems
   Other or general general management problems

7. *Human resource management*
   Recruitment/selection
   Turnover/retention
   Satisfaction/morale
   Employee development
   Other or general human resource management problems

8. *Economic environment*
   Poor economy/recession
   Other or general economic environment problems

9. *Regulatory environment*
   Insurance

APPENDIX B

Types and Classes of 1988 Problems

1. *Obtaining external financing*
   Obtaining financing for growth

2. *Internal financial management*
   Inadequate working capital
   Cash flow problems
   Controlling margins/profits/expenses
   Collection of accounts receivable
   Other or general financial management problems

3. *Sales/Marketing*
   Low sales
   Dependence on one or few clients/customers
   Marketing or distribution channels
   Promotion/public relations/advertising
   Changes in markets
   Increased competition
   Other or general marketing problems

4. *Product development*
   Product development
   Product line changes

5. *Production/Operations management*
   Quality control (product or service)
   Suppliers/supplies/raw materials
   Production capacity problems
   Becoming computerized
   Other or general production/operations management problems

6. *Organization structure/design*
   New division
   Changing from custom programming to product
   Other or general organization structure/design problems

7. *General management*
   Lack of management experience
   CEO overworked/overwhelmed
   Managing growth
   Planning
   Leading
   Other or general general management problems

8. *Human resource management*
   Recruitment/selection
   Turnover/retention
   Training/development
   Other or general human resource management problems

9. *Economic environment*
   Poor economy/recession
   Stock market problems

10. *Regulatory environment*
    Insurance
    Licensing/bonding
    Changes in federal/state regulations
    Other or general regulatory environment problems

Human Rights: The Social Investing Issue of the 1990s

SIMON BILLENNESS

Simon Billenness is a researcher at Franklin Research & Development Corporation, 711 Atlantic Ave., Boston, MA 02111. Phone 617/423-6655.

W HEN *DATELINE NBC* recently aired a segment showing children working at a Bangladesh factory that manufactured Wal-Mart shirts, company CEO David Glass appeared dumbfounded. So were social investors, who had been attracted to the company by its green marketing and enlightened employee relations. Now they began to wonder whether they should dump the stock.

As companies expand globally and face problems similar to those of Wal-Mart, many investors are finding that the social issue of the 1990s is human rights. And as these issues have begun to take on a new urgency, the concept itself has broadened. Concerns about workplace safety, environmental protection, and discrimination based on gender, disability, and sexual orientation are fast becoming mainstream human rights issues. Also, activists joining these crusades are no longer willing to accept that infringements of these basic rights might have a cultural justification.

Why have human rights issues moved so rapidly to the top of the social investing agenda? Part of the reason lies in the global trend toward privatization and looser government regulation of business. In countries as far removed as Hungary, Chile, and China, governments have relinquished their tight economic control. Filling this vacuum have been multinational corporations seeking access to new markets and cheap labor. Never before have multinational corporations had such a major impact on people's lives. However, in the wake of this new corporate clout come demands that corporations exercise their power responsibly.

As the growing power of multinational corporations collides with demands that they respect a broader definition of human rights,

ILLUSTRATION BY CAROLINE PRICE.

Social investors are in a unique position to insist that multinational corporations support human rights.

social investors find themselves taking a crucial role. As both activists and shareholders, they are in a unique position to insist that multinational corporations support human rights.

Investors can address human rights issues in two ways: They can hold their shares and lobby corporations by proposing shareholder resolutions that address human rights concerns, or they can publicly divest their holdings of firms that abuse human rights. Whatever course they choose, investors require relevant and timely information.

Obtaining such information, however, is not always easy. Many countries, particularly developing countries, lack even minimal standards of corporate disclosure. In addition, repressive governments invariably have a keen interest in restricting information about their abuse of human rights.

Traditional social investment sources cover certain issues well. For instance, the Investor Responsibility Research Center (IRRC) covers corporate involvement in South Africa and religious discrimination in North-

When in Rome...

Multinational corporations often claim that, because of their respect for "local culture," they should relax standards of corporate responsibility commonly accepted in their home country. How can concerned investors demand social responsibility standards when faced with such an argument?

In the absence of a clear definition of human rights, social investors may wish to develop criteria that reflect their own values. To draft such standards, though, requires a review of human rights literature. A good place to start is the United Nations International Bill of Human Rights. This document is the world's most widely accepted statement of human rights. Moreover, it is designed as a yardstick by which to measure the degree of compliance with international human rights standards. It includes not only the Universal Declaration of Human Rights but also international covenants covering economic, social, cultural, civil, and political rights.

As a baseline, investors may also use the Tripartite Declaration of Principle Concerning Multinational Enterprises and Social Policy. This is a voluntary code of conduct that sets out principles in the field of employee relations. The code was devised by the International Labor Organization (ILO), a United Nations agency representing employers and employees from more than 150 countries. The ILO also has drafted numerous conventions that address issues such as child labor, forced labor, workplace safety, and discrimination. These conventions are voluntarily ratified by countries all over the world and, in conjunction with these countries' own laws and regulations, establish minimum workplace standards that corporations should be required to respect.

ern Ireland. Religious shareholders and labor activists are good sources of information on such emerging issues as poor working conditions in the Mexican *maquiladoras* plants and the use of forced labor in Chinese government factories. The IRRC tracks shareholder resolutions on these and other issues, while the Interfaith Center for Corporate Responsibility coordinates those efforts.

Issues with no history of shareholder activism require more diligent research. My firm Franklin Research & Development Corporation, is currently engaged in a dialogue with several corporations doing business in Burma, where a brutal dictatorship has refused to respect the results of free elections and continues to abuse human rights. Amnesty International, Asia Watch, and the Lawyers Committee for Human Rights have provided us with excellent information and helped us contact Burmese dissidents who monitor foreign companies operating there. We are now talking with PepsiCo and Amoco, both of which have agreed to provide a report on their Burmese operations and address concerns about their impact on human rights in that country.

HOW SOCIAL INVESTMENT FIRMS ADDRESS THE ISSUES

At Franklin Research & Development Corporation we look at a company's non-U.S. ventures separately from their domestic operations. Non-U.S. operations are evaluated against internationally accepted human rights standards. We then award the company a human rights rating that is distinct from other categories, such as employee or community relations. For instance, in a recent report on Ford Motor Company, we felt the company's domestic workplace programs had earned Ford an above-average employee relations rating, but we gave Ford our worst human rights rating because of abuses at its plants in Mexico and Northern Ireland.

We pay particular attention to companies

operating in repressive countries such as Burma and China, or areas of the world noted for poor working conditions such as Indonesia, Bangladesh, and the *maquiladoras* of Central America. We are currently lobbying U.S. companies to adopt human rights standards, with strict compliance procedures, for their foreign suppliers and contractors.

The Calvert Social Investment Fund approaches this issue in a slightly different way. Instead of formulating separate human rights standards, the fund's advisor, United States Trust Company of Boston, has added an international dimension to its existing social guidelines. U.S. Trust has recently refined its human rights standards for international operations and criteria for boycotting countries. The firm plans to review multinational corporate practices in such countries as China and Mexico as well as prohibit investment in any company with economic ties to boycotted countries. (At present, only South Africa qualifies for a total country boycott.)

Working Assets, which produces the Citizens Funds, considers human rights issues to be inherent in its existing labor, economic justice, and environmental standards. According to Ina McGuinness, vice president of social research, Working Assets uses the International Bill of Human Rights as a guide and relies on information published by Amnesty International, *Multinational Monitor,* and *Franklin's Insight,* an investment newsletter affiliated with Franklin Research. Working Assets attributes their divestment of Wal-Mart stock to allegations that the company purchased products made by forced labor in China.

George Gay, the new manager of the Schield Progressive Environmental Fund, says he plans to expand the fund's original environmental focus. Aiming to avoid companies operating in countries whose governments fail to respect human rights, Gay says he intends to avoid all companies with operations in South Africa and China.

Human rights also is an important is-

sue for the Calvert World Values Fund, the first socially responsible global fund. The fund will not invest in companies that provide strategic goods to "repressive governments." In screening for human rights, Calvert considers both the direct role of the company under review and the country's political climate. "Our human rights criteria are constantly being updated by our board of trustees," says Jon Lickerman, the fund's social research director. Trustees include Muhammed Yunus, Bangladeshi founder of the Grameen Bank, and British social investing pioneer Tessa Tennant. Recently, the Calvert board adopted a policy to avoid investing in bonds issued by the World Bank after determining that the institution failed the fund's environmental and human rights criteria.

MAKING A DIFFERENCE

Social investors are already proving they can make a difference on human rights issues. After seeing the *Dateline NBC* story, Franklin Research & Development filed a shareholder resolution at Wal-Mart asking the company to adopt social responsibility standards for its vendors. After three months of negotiations, Wal-Mart drafted a set of standards that ruled out any use of child, prison, or forced labor by its vendors. The new standards also address issues such as fair wages, work hours, health and safety, the environment, and discrimination. Satisfied with the standards and Wal-Mart's commitment to enforcing them through on-site inspections, Franklin Research withdrew its resolution.

As more and more corporations go global, so will socially responsible investing. Although this requires that concerned investors tackle tricky questions and find new sources of information, the potential for social activism is substantial. It is time corporations realize that the new global "borderless economy" requires a borderless respect for human rights, as well.

Decisions, Decisions

How I Made — And Agonized Over — My Choices At NBC

Brandon Tartikoff

Brandon Tartikoff was the head of NBC Entertainment for 10 years. This article is adapted from his book, "The Last Great Ride." Reprinted with permission. All rights reserved.

I'm the last person to tell you that ratings aren't vital to a network's health. Network executives have a fiduciary responsibility to deliver the largest possible audience. But every network executive worth his programming tiles knows he has another responsibility as well—a moral and ethical duty to regard the public airwaves with care and thoughtfulness. The airwaves do not belong to you or your networks, they belong to the public.

I had some moments that I was especially proud of at NBC, moments when the Nielsen numbers mattered not. There were times, though, that I wish I'd been tougher on myself. Times I did have the Nielsen numbers foremost in my mind — and shouldn't have. But when you're deeply involved in a project you can lose perspective. I know now that there are two words that serve as a signal that you're operating in an area of questionable taste. Those words are "Geraldo Rivera."

Before I tell you the story of the Satanism special Geraldo did for NBC in 1988, let me first say that the whole thing was my idea. Sort of. Actually, the part that was my idea was to hire Geraldo. His syndicated specials — digging into Al Capone's vaults, exploring the wreck of the Titanic — played on a consortium of affiliates and local stations and they cleaned our clock. The shows themselves hardly qualified as Great Moments in Broadcasting; the Capone excavation, as you may remember, consumed ninety minutes and turned up one old whiskey bottle. (An inspection of Dana Andrews' old dressing room could have turned up the same.) But the fact is, they achieved great ratings, and in many cases it was our own NBC affiliates who were preempting their regular network programming to broadcast them. It was a case of "If you can't beat 'em, join 'em." I told Rick Ludwin, NBC's vice president of specials and late-night programming, that I'd rather have Geraldo on my team than

continue to compete against him in a depleted lineup of stations. In addition, a writers strike hit the industry that summer and as a result, the premieres of NBC's new fall dramatic series would be delayed until after the World Series. ABC's "Roseanne," however, was the most touted new series of the season, and I didn't want to give the show a bye in its opening two months on the air. Geraldo would be a great blunting weapon to counter "Roseanne" on its first regular episode after the pilot.

After the deal was worked out, we had a meeting with Geraldo, and he presented us with several ideas. The one we chose, "Satan's Underground," dealt with devil worship and the sudden increase in satanic cults across the United States. Yes, from the start it did have a kind of "carny" feel to it, but this was hardly the first time the subject had been covered on national TV. One reason we settled on Satanism, in fact, was that we knew that every time it came up on a news show or a drama the result was always a high rating. For whatever reason — maybe because they were worried about their kids getting involved, or merely because of the cheap sideshow thrill it provided — a lot of viewers seemed inextricably drawn to this weird topic.

What we didn't count on was that Geraldo was actually going to turn up a lot of shocking stuff. In the back of our minds, I think we assumed he'd give us an hour of somewhat titillating but ultimately unprovocative superficial television.

But Geraldo and his investigative team actually went out and found startling evidence of heavy-duty devil worship and satanic acts in the Midwest and Southwest — I'm talking about really disturbing footage. When the Broadcast Standards people saw the show in its original state, they went from initially being speechless to being very vocal indeed. They asked Geraldo to tone it down — a lot — and to diffuse the picture in certain places so the graphic images would be tolerable. I have to admit, Geraldo was a good soldier about it all. He cooperated with the editing by creating wraparounds (commentary sections that ran before and after each

From *Ethics: Easier Said Than Done*, Issue 21, 1993, pp. 54-56. Adapted from *The Last Great Ride* by Brandon Tartikoff. ©

segment of the special) in which he gave Satanism a context, tried to prepare the viewers for what they were about to see. The end result was a show that had been dialed back drastically—but which, in truth, still struck me as too powerful for prime time.

The day before the special was set to air, I called Bob Wright and told him that I was having serious thoughts about the Geraldo show. "I don't know if we should go through with it," I said. Bob had been equally disturbed by the program cut he'd seen, plus he was back in New York, where he had to quell the uprising of irate sales and financial executives, apoplectic over not being able to sell one commercial to any willing advertiser in this two-hour program.

"Well, check out the situation," Bob said. "And see what our options are."

As it turned out, our options weren't that great. The NBC legal department told me that if we canceled the special at the eleventh hour, Geraldo could say we hadn't lived up to our part of the agreement and had impugned his credentials as a journalist, and he would have a good case if he wanted to sue us. There was another problem, too. Our affiliates, while not being all that excited about getting a questionable Geraldo show nevertheless would not be pleased if we told them we'd changed our minds and were scrapping the broadcast. Remember the old saying "Stuck between a rock and a hard place"? Remember the other one, "The Devil made me do it"?

Finally, the day of judgment came. The special was an attempt to get ratings, pure and simple; it was never an attempt to do great TV. Still, I was damned if I did and damned if I didn't, and I knew it. "Let's put this thing on the air," I rationalized. I figured it would all be behind us the next day.

Let me say I've made better decisions in my life. The next morning I came in and found that Exposing Satan's Underground had drawn a huge audience. (To this day, it is the highest-rated non-news documentary special in network history.) Normally, I would have celebrated a 35 share, but instead I was just glad the whole thing was over. Then, an hour or so later, I found out it wasn't.

Disturbing reports began to trickle in about people inspired by the broadcast to copycat incidents contained in the special. I was appalled. The press focused on those stories and really ripped NBC for putting on such a depraved show. The other side of the coin was the calls

and letters our affiliates got thanking NBC for exposing this very real problem that was in their midst, infecting their communities.

If I had to do it all over again, I wouldn't. There aren't thousands of ways to get to 35 share, but there isn't just one, either.

The moral of this story is that it's tough to be your own censor. That's why networks do have a system of checks and balances in which the Broadcast Standards department never reports to programming. This does set up a naturally adversarial relationship, but that's not to say it has to be that way.

I've always been amazed at the things that get by—and don't get by—Broadcast Standards. When I worked at ABC, the "BS people," as they're unfortunately known, were extremely strict about eliminating "damn" and "hell." It didn't matter that Rhett Butler had broken certain barriers forty years before; you just couldn't get those words through. The ABC censors also seemed to have absolutely no sense of humor, but the writers didn't mind so much because they could use that to their own advantage. Among the first shows that came under my supervision at ABC was a series called "Dog and Cat," which was notable only for being the television debut of a young model from Georgia named Kim Basinger. Watching dailies of an episode of the show one afternoon, I saw a take of a scene in which Basinger walks into a police station wearing a slinky, low-cut evening dress through which you could clearly see the outline of her (you should excuse the expression) nipples. Kim's series costar, Lou Antonio, ad-libs a line that fits the situation perfectly. "Hey, is it cold in here?" he says to her, "or are you just glad to see me?" I braced myself for the BS people sitting next to me, but it never came. Because the script hadn't tripped any alarms by using "bad words," and the Mae West allusion was totally lost on the censor types, the line went out over the airwaves.

I got into a lot more hassles later on at NBC, thanks to Steven Bochco. He demanded autonomy on "Hill Street [Blues]" and "L.A. Law," but because he was always layering his scripts with double entendres, sexual situations, bare skin, and his trademark scatological humor, he, in effect, gave me another job to do—that of liaison with Broadcast Standards.

Whenever something risque was slipped into an

> *I know now that there are two words that serve as a signal that you're operating in an area of questionable taste. Those words are "Geraldo Rivera."*

episode, the BS people would go over each frame in the rough cut like Jim Garrison scrutinizing the Zapruder film. Sometimes they'd miss rather obvious things—like Furillo telling Davenport that she "gives good succor"—and insist that a scene calling for Furillo and Davenport to take a bath together not be shot unless it was clear they were both wearing clothes in the tub. The occasional absurd scenes Hill Street became famous for pale when compared to these kinds of directives. So Bochco began to put in provocative language and scenes that he didn't care about—on purpose. That way, when Broadcast Standards objected to something he thought was important, he could say, "Look, I'll take out these other four things if you give me this, okay?" I don't mean to imply that Bochco invented this ploy, or was the only producer who worked it, but as a tactician he was the best.

His longest fight lasted several weeks. It involved a Hill Street story line in which Hill and Renko discover a dead man in a hotel room. Shortly thereafter, they hear a bleating sound from the bathroom. When they open the door, they discover a sheep tethered to an overhead pipe. The sheep has a bow on its head. The fight wasn't about the sheep being there; it was about whether the bow stayed or not. Go figure.

No program tested my skill with the censors more than "Saturday Night Live." The show constantly skirts the danger zone each and every week. Often, I'd be dealing with Broadcast Standards about problems in the upcoming show while taking phone calls from affiliates and sponsors about what had been on the week before. Let's face it, this comes with the territory of doing the only live show of its kind left on television. Besides, what else can you expect when you're dealing with a cast that is primarily an all-star team of irreverent comics? The funny thing is, for all their griping and moaning, I always got the feeling that the affiliates and the sponsors accepted Saturday Night Live. They may not have understood it, but they accepted it. And for a very compelling reason: The show gushed money for them and for NBC. Still, some limits had to be observed.

One night I was sitting at home watching SNL when Charlie Rocket, one of the regular cast members at the time, said the f-word in the middle of a sketch, right over the airwaves into millions of homes. Rocket had to go. TV is like private school. In private school, there are rules about drinking, and if you break those rules, you get expelled.

Sometimes I'd spend a week arguing about a single word in a script. I remember once when there was an SNL sketch containing the word "schmuck," and Broadcast Standards said it had to be cut.

"Why can't they say 'schmuck'?" I said to the head censor. "Johnny Carson says 'schmuck' all the time."

"I know what Johnny Carson says," he replied. "But Johnny Carson has a certain stature at NBC. He's been here more than twenty-five years. He can say 'schmuck.' When these people have been here that long, they can say 'schmuck,' too."

The SNL sketch that gave me the most grief, however, was the "Jew/Not-a-Jew" game show. Tom Hanks played the host. A slide of a famous personality would appear on the screen, and the panelists had to decide whether the person was Jewish. "Our first famous personality," Hanks said, affecting in his best game-show-host voice, "is Penny Marshall, the affable star of television's Laverne & Shirley! Okay, panelists, Jew or Not a Jew?" After the panelists locked in their answers, the sketch cut to a fake commercial, a parody of those

> **The SNL sketch that gave me the most grief was the "Jew/Not-a-Jew" game show.**

"IBM invites you to make the call" spots: "Sandy Koufax is on the mound for the Los Angeles Dodgers, Game Seven of the World Series against the Minnesota Twins. The stylish lefthander is involved in a tense battle with the score locked at two to two. Okay, IBM invites you to make the call. Sandy Koufax—Jew, Not a Jew?" Then they cut back to Hanks, who announced that Penny Marshall was really Italian, and gave the winners their rewards. It was funny, I thought—but was it anti-Semitic? All week long, I agonized over that question, not just with Broadcast Standards but with myself. Since I'm Jewish, I wondered if I was being too sensitive or maybe too blase. If this was about Italians, would I think it was awful? Should I think it was awful? Finally, a few hours before airtime, I took a deep breath and conferred with the Standards people, and we decided to go with it. The morning after controversial material is aired on television is usually taken up with a flood of phone calls—most of them negative (when was the last time you made a phone call when you liked something?). In this case, it was Sunday morning, I was home, and still my phone rang off the hook. Of the many calls I received, the one I remember best was from my mother. "I cannot believe it," she said. "I'm embarrassed to call you my son. This was the most anti-Semitic thing I've ever seen." Then she paused. "Besides, I always thought Penny Marshall was Jewish!"

Organizing the Voluntary Association

William B. Gartner

William B. Gartner is an Associate Professor in the School of Business Administration at Georgetown University.

This article offers a cursory overview of academic and practitioner-based approaches to understanding the process of creating voluntary associations (e.g., direct action community organizations, unions, and social movements). A model outlining the actions involved in forming a direct action community association is offered.

Parallel to the entrepreneurship literature on the formation of "for-profit" organizations is a significant body of literature on the development of "not-for-profit," or voluntary associations. Knoke and Wood (1991) define voluntary associations as "formally organized, named collectivities in which the majority of participants do not derive their livelihood from their activities in the group (p. 8)." The literature on voluntary associations can be segmented into two types: (1) the academic literature, in which voluntary associations are "objectively" studied and modelled by university researchers, and (2) the practitioner literature, in which individuals involved in the day-to-day development and maintenance of voluntary associations offer anecdotal stories, advice, and "how-to" prescriptions.

The academic literature on voluntary organizations is very broad in scope, covering such topic areas as: political organizations (Wilson, 1973), religious organizations (Wilken, 1971), social movements (McCarthy & Zald, 1973; Zald & McCarthy, 1987), sociable organizations (Aldrich, 1971), labor unions (Burgess & Conway, 1973) and farmer's cooperatives (Warner & Heffernan, 1967). For an overview of the voluntary organization literature see Smith et al., 1972.

A recent rigorous attempt to understand the factors that influence the development and growth of voluntary associations is Knoke and Wood's book *Organized for Action* (1991). This book offers a model of voluntary

association behavior and an empirical test of specific factors using data collected on 32 voluntary social influence organizations in the Indianapolis area. Their findings suggest that voluntary associations that provided purposive incentives to their members, offered opportunities for members to influence the association's decisions, and had leaders who are perceived to have power in the environment, showed a significant positive growth in membership and resources. In addition, voluntary associations with a professionalized formal structure (e.g., paid staff) were more likely to generate more resources as well as exercise power in their environment. Since this research is theory-based, insightful, comprehensive and detailed, this article will not reiterate the model. Readers are advised to seek this book out.

This article offers a model of organization formation based on the literature that describes practitioner efforts at organizing voluntary associations. This practitioner literature is grounded in such books as *Reveille for Radicals* written by Saul Alinsky in 1946 and the subsequent outgrowth of systematic attempts to train organizers (Bobo, Kendall, & Max, 1991). A number of different "how-to" manuals for organizers exist (e.g., Alinsky, 1989a; Alinsky, 1989b; Boyte, 1989; Delgado, 1985; Hedemann, 1981; Kahn, 1981; & Staples, 1984). Table 1 offers a model of the sequence of events that occurs in creating a "direct action" association.

A direct action association is an organization composed of members who are willing to take action against a particular individual (labelled a target) in the expectation that the target will undertake changes that will benefit the membership. For example, a direct action association might be started in a local neighborhood to take action against the owner of a local trash hauling company so that this person will not convert a nearby wetland into a toxic waste dump. A fundamental tenet of direct action organizing is that associations are based on issues that will result in real, immediate and concrete improvements in the lives of its members. Rather than creating the types of direct economic benefits that accrue to individuals starting for-profit firms in the business environment (e.g., cash income or capital gains to the owners), the direct action association accrues economic and social benefits to

The author wishes to thank Jennifer A. Starr for her efforts in identifying information on this topic.

Table 1

Steps in Organizing a Direct Action Association[1]

I. The Universe of Human Problems
II. Choose an Issue
   A. Action on an issue must result in real, immediate, and concrete improvements in people's lives
   B. Action on an issue must give people a sense of their own power
   C. Action on an issue must alter the relations of power in the community
III. Develop the Issue Strategy
   A. Identify goals
   B. Consider resources required to achieve goals
   C. Identify constituents, allies and opponents
   D. Identify Targets (individuals with power who will give you what you want)
   E. Choose Tactics (e.g., media events, actions, public hearing, accountability sessions, elections, negotiations
      1. A tactic must never go outside the experience of the association's membership
      2. A tactic must attempt to go outside the experience of the target
      3. A good tactic is one that members will enjoy
IV. Announce the Campaign
V. Begin Outreach Activities
   A. Appeal to people's self-interest
   B. Be visible in the community
   C. Recruit to an activity, not a business meeting
VI. Stage Direct Encounters with Targets (see tactics)
VII. Plan for Building the Organization
VIII. Win or Regroup

[1]Adapted from Bobo, Kendall & Max, 1991.

its members and to the community at large through changes in the political, judicial, legislative, and consumer environments (e.g., more jobs in the community, cleaner air, less traffic). In other words, the benefits generated through the association's actions are intended to be both specific to its members as well as of value to the community.

In many respects, the types of activities necessary to form an association that are listed in Table 1 (e.g., identify goals, consider resources, identify allies) are similar to the types of actions specified in many "how-to" business manuals such as Schilit (1990), Bangs (1989) and Timmons (1990). Yet, what appears to differentiate the voluntary association organizing process from the for-profit organizing process is a heightened emphasis on the "other." Voluntary associations are, by definition, membership based. The voluntary association organizer must consciously appeal to the interests and needs of other individuals in order for an association to grow in members. Through increases in the number and commitment of members comes power for the voluntary organization to effect change. Rather than focussing on the needs and motivations of the entrepreneur as the primary impetus for organization creation, the voluntary association literature focuses on the needs and motivations of the community from which members are recruited.

I believe the entrepreneurship network literature has not yet answered the question of how an entrepreneur's contacts with other individuals eventually results in their involvement in the entrepreneurial process. Entrepreneurship scholars should find the strategies for involving individuals in the membership of an association useful for reconceptualizing the process of networking in new venture development. Rather than assuming that individuals involve themselves in organizations solely for direct economic benefits (e.g., salary, investment income and capital gains), we need to consider other types of benefits that accrue to individuals through membership. Some entrepreneurship researchers have uncovered these non-economic motivations for involvement. For example, Freear and Wetzel's (1992) review of research on informal venture capital markets found that a majority of informal investors considered non-financial factors as a part of the investment process. Yet, additional research needs to explore the variety of ways that entrepreneurs discover the needs of other individuals and how entrepreneurs use this knowledge to involve others in the venture formation process.

One idea that is central to understanding voluntary association organizing is the value-added aspects of organizing; that is, an organization as a goal-directed collective of individuals provides benefits that cannot be generated through individual actions alone. The voluntary association organizer believes that organizations are the best vehicle for solving social and community problems: Individual action has less potency than the combined and coordinated efforts of many individuals working together. What the entrepreneurship scholar might appreciate is the importance of organization. Organizations, by definition, require the involvement of many individuals. Entrepreneurship needs to be reconsidered in the context of community, rather than as an outcome of individuality. Rather than celebrating the achievements of the individual entrepreneur, the entrepreneurship field might seek more recognition for those individuals who play a critical role in supporting the context of organizing: the first buyers of a product, investors, the first employees hired, silent partners, and the entrepreneur's spouse and family.

REFERENCES

Aldrich, H. E. (1971). The sociable organization: A case study of Mensa and some propositions. *Sociology and Social Research*, 55 (July), 429–441.

Alinsky, S. D. (1989a). *Reveille for radicals*. New York: Vintage Books.

Alinsky, S. D. (1989b). *Rules for radicals*. New York: Vintage Books.

Bangs, D. H. (1989). *The start up guide*. Dover, NH: Upstart Publishing Company.

Bobo, K., Kendall, J., & Max, S. (1991). *Organizing for social change*. Cabin John, MD: Seven Locks Press.

Boyte, H. C. (1989). *Commonwealth: A return to citizen action*. New York: The Free Press.

Burgess, P. M., & Conway, R. (1973). *Public goods and voluntary associations: A multi-state investigation of collective action in labor union locals*. Beverly Hills, CA: Sage.

Delgado, G. (1985). *Organizing in the movement: The roots and growth of ACORN*. Philadelphia: Temple University Press.

7. PERSPECTIVES AND TRENDS: Not-for-Profits

Freear, J., & Wetzel, W. E., Jr. (1992). The informal venture capital market in the 1990s. In D. L. Sexton & J. D. Kasarda (Eds.), *The state of the art of entrepreneurship*, pp. 462–486. Boston: PWS-Kent.

Hedemann, E. (1981). *War resisters league organizer's manual*. New York: War Resisters League.

Kahn, S. (1981). *Organizing: A guide for grassroots leaders*. New York: McGraw-Hill.

McCarthy, J. D., & Zald, M. N. (1973). *The trend of social movements in America: Professionalization and resource mobilization*. Morristown, NJ: General Learning Press.

Schilit, W. K. (1990). *The entrepreneur's guide to preparing a winning business plan and raising venture capital*. Englewood Cliffs, NJ: Prentice Hall.

Smith, D. H., Reddy, R. D., & Baldwin, B. R. (1972). Types of voluntary action: A definitional essay. In D. H. Smith (Ed.), *Voluntary action research*, pp. 449–468. Lexington, MA: D. C. Heath.

Staples, L. (1984). *Roots to power: A manual for grassroots organizing*. New York: Praeger Press.

Timmons, J. A. (1990). *New venture creation*, 3rd edition. Homewood, IL: Irwin.

Warner, W. K., & Heffernan, W. D. (1967). The benefit-participation contingency in voluntary farm organizations. *Rural Sociology, 29*, 139–153.

Wilken, P. (1971). Size of organizations and member participation in church congregations. *Administrative Science Quarterly, 16*, 173–179.

Wilson, J. Q. (1973). *Political organizations*. New York: Basic Books.

Zald, M. N., & McCarthy, J. D. (1987). *Social movements in an organizational society*. New Brunswick, NJ: Transaction Books.

WHITE COLLAR WASTELAND

*A hostile economy has cut short careers
for many of America's best and brightest*

Few Americans were so groomed for success as Jim Bennett of New Canaan, Conn. His diplomas read Princeton University and Stanford University Law School. His honors include Phi Beta Kappa. And his résumé boasts such gold-plated employers as General Electric. Yet when a budget cut wiped out his job as corporate counsel with Conair Corp. in February 1992, Jim Bennett was as helpless as any working stiff. Bennett, 55, hasn't held a steady job since.

So it goes for the men and women who were once the mandarins of American commerce. Their influential positions, their princely paychecks, their corner offices and their job security all crumpled under the weight of the 1990–91 recession. For the first time on record, white-collar workers have surpassed blue-collar workers in the nation's unemployment lines, and many of the casualties are still reeling. "Your foundation turns out to be sand," says Bennett. "There's no recovery for people like me."

Jim Bennett is right. The recession officially ended more than two years ago. But

white-collar unemployment kept on climbing: from 2.8 million in March 1991, past the 3 million mark, to 3.4 million late last year. And though it has ebbed slightly in recent months, it still stands at 3.1 million today—higher than at the recession's trough. Even in May, when the labor market seemed to shake off its doldrums and created a respectable 209,000 jobs, an additional 15,000 managers and professionals were thrown out of work. "We don't have an answer for these people," says Columbia University Prof. Katherine Newman, who explores the crisis in a new book called "Declining Fortunes." "If credentials, skills and education can't protect you, then there is no recipe for security in the American market."

In past recessions, a growing demand for professionals, managers and technicians actually cushioned the economy. During the 1981–82 downturn, for example, employers kept right on creating office positions, so that the nation's white-collar payrolls rose by a stunning 838,000 jobs *before* the 1983 recovery began. In the 1990–91 recession, on the other hand, white-collar

payrolls shrank by 354,000 jobs. And today, the white-collar job machine is generating jobs at only half the pace of past recoveries because industries such as banking, real estate and aerospace have been hit by financial crises of their own. Last month, banks shed 1,300 jobs, pharmaceutical makers 1,500 and aerospace manufacturers 1,638. Since its 1991 merger with Manufacturers Hanover, for example, Chemical Bank alone has eliminated 5,700 white-collar jobs.

Sadly, the economic recovery can't move into high gear if white-collar workers aren't on board. True, blue-collar workers bear the brunt of most recessions because they are idled and recalled with the ebb and flow of factory orders. Even today, their unemployment rate is 9.1 percent, more than twice the rate for white-collar workers. The crucial difference, however, is that blue-collar layoffs often are temporary. In fact, blue-collar unemployment has declined since the recession's trough. But a white-collar worker who loses a job is very likely never to get it back. As a result, permanent separations accounted for 85 percent of job losses in the last recession, compared with 56 percent in four previous downturns. Moreover, blue-collar workers today are a minority in the American labor force. The white-collar work force, which reaches from the executive suite to the back office, represents more than 6 in 10 workers and dominates the labor market.

Harvard University economist James Medoff, in a paper called "The New Unemployment," has documented these trends and their crippling impact on prosperity. Medoff notes, for example, that as employers shed high-pay, high-perk positions, the share of new jobs that offer pensions and health insurance has dropped by as much as 35 percent since the late 1970s. And because white-collar cuts represent a permanent downsizing of a corporation, the number of new jobs advertised by employers has dropped almost 40 percent, relative to the size of the labor force, since the mid-1980s. The result has been devastating to consumer confidence and spending power. In a *U.S. News* poll, nearly 4 out of 10 white-collar workers said their family income has fallen behind the cost of living since 1992. Says Medoff, "People who were primary breadwinners are getting creamed."

Ironically, many white-collar workers may have become victims of their own success. By piling up 10 or 15 years of annual promotions and salary increases, they became targets when budget-cutting time rolled around. Though many corporations insist they grant raises on merit alone, a study of corporate pay practices by Medoff and colleague Katharine Abraham found that longevity, not performance, explains some 40 percent of the pay gap between senior and junior workers in the same jobs. "When push comes to shove, the company looks for employees whose pay exceeds the value of their marginal product," says Medoff. "These people are vulnerable."

Pay cuts. Consider the typical unemployed senior executive, as profiled by Drake Beam Morin, a New York-based outplacement firm. He is 45 years old and held his previous job for nearly 12 years. He was earning $91,000. He had highly specialized skills, perhaps in insurance underwriting or computer design. No wonder, then, that he is having enormous trouble matching his previous salary. Fully 52 percent of white-collar workers in a recent survey by the Conference Board, a New York business research group, took pay cuts before finding new jobs, even after six months of intensive job hunting. Repeated thousands of times, this trend has taken a toll on the incomes of affluent Americans and on the economy in general. Inflation-adjusted wages for executives and managers have

fallen 4 percent since the recovery began, according to the Economic Policy Institute, a Washington, D.C., think tank. Since these college-educated workers were the only group to enjoy rising wages in the 1980s, their hard times spell trouble for the economy, according to Lawrence Mishel, EPI's research director. Says Mishel, "The few sources of income growth in the 1980s are fading fast."

Sooner or later, America's white-collar industries will stanch their losses. But a hiring frenzy is unlikely. The American Management Association—reporting that 1 in 4 employers plans layoffs this year, often on the heels of cutbacks—says that downsizing has become "an addiction" as corporations strive for ever greater efficiency. Until that trend fades, even 24-karat résumés like Jim Bennett's will tarnish, no matter how much polish is applied.

BYTING THE DUST

IBM lays off a legion of executives, and a community copes with the pain

Striding through grassy fields on the 13-acre farm where he rents a homestead outside Kingston, N.Y., former International Business Machines accountant David Shahbazian still reacts to the lightning-bolt shock of a year ago, when his supervisors told him he was a "surplus" employee, IBM's curious jargon for workers who will be cut from the payroll. "I felt insulted, betrayed, very bitter," says the 30-year-old Shahbazian, who was earning about $40,000 at the time. "I never missed a day; I believed in the white shirt. I placed on IBM a higher trust."

WHITE-COLLAR WORKERS WHO FEAR THAT A FAMILY MEMBER MAY LOSE A JOB

62%

WHITE-COLLAR WORKERS WHO SAY THEY HAVE FALLEN BEHIND SINCE 1992

38%

Because IBM had located its burgeoning mainframe operations in the scenic Hudson Valley cities of Poughkeepsie, Kingston and East Fishkill, about 80 miles north of New York City, the company's presence had grown to envelop the region. Even though the company has been scaling back over the past five years, by the end of 1992 IBM still accounted for 1 out of every 5 jobs in the area. The Shahbazian clan, like most local families, sent more than one son and daughter to the plants. David Shahbazian's father, brother, sister, uncle and cousin—a total of 91 years' experience—were all proud bearers of the IBM ID that was a ticket to the good life. Around them the company spun a cocoon of security: lifetime employment, ever rising income, bountiful benefits. Along with most IBM kids, Shahbazian attended day camp at the lush IBM Country Club—complete with a golf course, swimming pool, tennis courts, bowling lanes, baseball diamonds and more. For its annual Family Day, IBM rented the Dutchess County Fairgrounds for a carnival. "IBM was our big brother," recalls Shahbazian. "The company's philosophy spilled over into our upbringing, like putting in a hard, honest day's work and committing to excellence."

But the IBM fount gradually stopped gushing in recent years. Though mainframe computer orders kept rising, revenues dropped as innovative competitors turned out lower-priced machines powered by off-the-shelf systems. The company had no choice but to slash the highly skilled work force that once crafted every IBM system. Some employees chose lucrative early retirement packages, and the unlucky ones who were selected for cuts were offered alternatives. In Shahbazian's case, the choice was between an entry-level manufacturing position on the second shift of an Austin, Texas, plant or a buyout that offered two weeks of pay for every year's service with the company. Last July, Shahbazian joined the 2,900 IBMers who walked away from their once cloistered corporate sinecures in 1992.

By choosing the buyout, Shahbazian united with the swelling legion of white-collar workers across the country who are perched on the slippery slope of downward mobility. Squeezed by cost cuts and replaced by computers, these midlevel managers may never again see the generous salary and benefit packages that seemed their birthright only a few years ago.

Shahbazian lucked out by finding work immediately as an accountant at a real-estate-development firm. But like many displaced white-collar professionals, his income is only slightly more than half his previous take. Shortly after he left IBM, it became clear that the 1992 buyouts would not be sufficient to keep pace with the falloff in mainframe revenue. By last winter, the company announced it might be forced to embrace a previously unimaginable alternative: the first layoffs in its proud 79-year history. On three drizzly, gray days at the end of March, the covenant of mutual loyalty that had bound IBM and its Hudson Valley workers for 52 years was sundered. Nervous IBM executives, under surveillance by a beefed-up security force, took only minutes with each of 6,000 individuals to break the news: They were surplus and they had to go. Of the 6,000, 2,700 were laid off and 3,300 opted for a buyout.

The mid-Hudson Valley region, which had always been cushioned by IBM—even during recessions—today is devastated by the loss of those 8,900 jobs. Marist College economist Ann Davis calculates that for each eliminated IBM job, an additional 1 1/2 to two will disappear in an economic ripple effect. Along rural Route 52 through East Fishkill, "For Sale" signs line up like sentries guarding well-tended lawns. And the list of foreclosure notices is lengthening. Poughkeepsie real-estate executive William Lavery took the extraordinary step of hiring a psychologist to work with his emotionally shaken agents, some of whom have had to break the agonizing news to sellers that their homes are worth less than their mortgages. Says Lavery: "The same security that every individual IBMer felt, this community shared. IBM was our bulwark. Whatever happened in other parts of the country wasn't supposed to happen here."

Messy divorce. Hudson Valley social-service organizations have mobilized to reach out to distressed families. Counselors have fanned out to schools to help children deal with their fears (box, next page). Psychiatrists and psychologists in private practice have offered free counseling. Churches, synagogues and county mental-health organizations are sponsoring support groups to encourage the displaced employees to work through feelings of anger, panic and betrayal. Says Lawrence E. Dresdale, clinical psychologist and director at Kingston Psychological Services: "This [situation] is like a marriage. People who have been loyal and given the best years of their lives to the company are now being asked to divorce."

Stress also continues to reverberate among the survivors at IBM's three Hudson Valley locations. Rumors of further cuts or possible plant closings constantly circulate, keeping employees on a very thin edge. Dresdale says those who have held on to their jobs "try to work like crazy [so they won't be laid off], which creates stress and burnout, but on another level, their anxiety and uncertainty interfere with job performance."

Perilous journey. The heightened tensions make last summer's job victims almost glad they have navigated their first year outside IBM's previously sheltered halls—even though their journeys have been perilous. Jim Turner, who lost his $60,000 computer-sales job last summer, for example, recently declared bankruptcy. He, his wife and three children are living in a rented home in Newburgh, N.Y., while they try to make a go of a year-old interior-decorating and venetian-blind-cleaning business. Looking back at his 12 years with IBM, the 35-year-old Turner recalls with pain a Christmas vacation at Disney World when he missed most of the family fun by spending six hours a day on his cellular phone discussing business. "I breathed IBM, ate IBM," he says. "I went for it hook, line and sinker."

Brimming with confidence at the apex of his IBM career, Turner borrowed to the hilt and invested in six houses, five of which he rented out. Once the wicked recession of 1990-91 struck, however, this highly leveraged strategy swiftly unraveled. Reliable tenants began to miss payments. Turner's IBM commissions, which made up 35 percent of earnings, dwindled as the company's orders lost momentum. In 1991, for the first time, he missed a quota. By April of last year, Turner's supervisors gave him three options: produce more sales, find another job in the company or leave. Today, his former office has shrunk from 16 sales representatives to four.

Turner now says he has only "one nostril above water" financially and that his IBM health insurance has run out. But he doesn't receive much sympathy when interviewing for a new job. "People say IBMers were highly overpaid, babies, given everything. They say, 'Now you have to face reality and take half of what you used to be paid,'" explains Turner. "I don't know if I'll ever get to the point of making $60,000 again."

Half an hour east of Newburgh, in a pretty little town with the soap opera name of Pleasant Valley, Jim Reed, 56, is also scrambling to patch together a new life. Reed used to earn more than $40,000 as a financial analyst for IBM, where he spent 30 years. Today, the wiry, energetic native of the Hudson Valley is adjusting to an early retirement urged on him last year by supervisors who said he would have trouble keeping up with future changes. To supplement his $18,000 pension, Reed earns $10 an hour collecting tolls at the Newburgh-

DAVID S. MERRILL—USN&WR

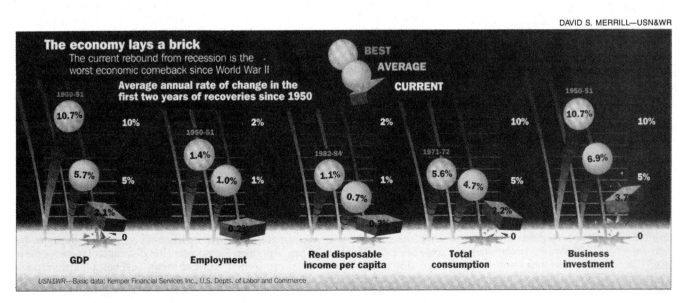

The economy lays a brick
The current rebound from recession is the worst economic comeback since World War II

BEST AVERAGE CURRENT

Average annual rate of change in the first two years of recoveries since 1950

	GDP	Employment	Real disposable income per capita	Total consumption	Business investment
1950-51	10.7%				10.7%
Best	10%	1.4%	2%	10%	10%
	5.7%	1.0%	1.1%	5.6%	6.9%
Average	5%	1%	0.7%	4.7%	5%
Current	2.1%	0.2%	0.3%	2.2%	
	2%	1%	1%	5%	

USN&WR—Basic data: Kemper Financial Services Inc., U.S. Depts. of Labor and Commerce

Beacon Bridge that spans the majestic Hudson north of West Point, N.Y. Reed had a powerful motive to join IBM back in 1962. "My wife said there would be no children until I joined [the company]," he recalls. Today, the youngest of Reed's three children, 22-year-old J. J., can't afford to return to Berklee College of Music in Boston for his senior year. To save money, J. J. is living at home, working as a landscaper.

While Reed, Turner and Shahbazian struggle to make peace with feelings of rejection, they are also casting about for extra work. Reed hustles with three part-time jobs plus his bridge duties. Turner runs a tire wholesaling business out of his house. And Shahbazian has a side enterprise clearing land and performing light demolition.

Still, cutting fields, taking tolls and cleaning blinds are a world apart from the prestige, perks and pay of a secure white-collar job. And like their unemployed counterparts across the country, IBM's former brethren are deeply wounded. It's clear that their financial sores and emotional scar tissue may never heal.

BLOWN AWAY

White-collar defense workers are cut loose in the prime of their careers

In the Hollywood version of the brutal downsizing of corporate America, Michael Douglas loses his wife, his job—and his mind. The recent movie "Falling Down" opens with Douglas, a laid-off missile worker identified by his vanity license plate "D-FENS," stuck in a traffic jam. Something snaps. The jobless Douglas soon goes from being a victim of the relentless cutbacks taking place in California's huge defense industry to a victimizer. He stalks Los Angeles, the City of Angels, with knives, a bazooka, you name it. Just before he is shot by a cop at the end of the film, a puzzled Douglas asks: "I'm the bad guy?"

Ed Dillard used to have a vanity license plate—but he got tired of paying the $25 fee for it. Dillard hasn't seen "Falling Down," but he is familiar with the plot. Very familiar. On April 8, not long after the film came out, Dillard's supervisor at Hughes Corp.'s recently acquired missile plant in San Diego called him into his office and asked him to close the door. What followed shouldn't have come as much of a surprise—the post-cold-war "peace dividend" has crashed into San Diego like a terrorist car bomb—but Dillard, 38, couldn't help but feel stunned. He had

FAMILIES IN CRISIS

Finding hope after losing a job

In the Broadway hit "The Sisters Rosensweig," actress Madeline Kahn, portraying an indulged talk-show hostess named Gorgeous Teitelbaum, bursts into tears and confesses that she has been supporting her family for two years while her out-of-work husband writes mysteries.

Teitelbaum's plight—and her humiliation—are shared by formerly affluent couples across the country. Despite the fact that wives have been toiling in offices and factories for decades, some now shoulder an unfamiliar burden: sole breadwinner for the family. Many are embarrassed that the jobs they once took to supplement their husbands' wages today provide essentials such as mortgage payments and medical insurance. These feelings are part of the shock as a job loss ripples through a family. At the deepest level, mental-health experts say, the issues are those of survival: Will we lose our house and possessions? Where will we live? What will we do to pay bills?

Getting along. In Westchester County, north of New York City, Ruth Speier, whose husband, Mel, lost his job as vice president at the U.S. headquarters of the Austrian steel producer Voest-Alpine, says she is tiding their family over as a real-estate agent. "We're getting along," says the mother of two teenagers. "I do the best I can. We know this isn't forever." The Speiers' 15-year-old daughter, Nicole, finds the situation "a little scary." Her 17-year-old brother, Jonathan, says: "I think now that only the strong will survive, and I will have to work that much harder." Fortunately, Jonathan and Nicole's parents established education funds for the children. As a result, Jona-

than will enter the School of Engineering and Applied Science at Columbia University this fall. "I want to have a skill where I have some control [over my work]," says Jonathan.

Dorothea Braginsky, a social psychologist at Fairfield University in Connecticut, has studied college students whose parents have lost their jobs. Her research suggests that, unlike Jonathan Speier, they are more cynical about social institutions and less inclined to work hard than others. She also concludes that children from once affluent families fare worse than those from working-class families. Says Braginsky: "The cynicism that comes from having it all and then losing it is worse than not having it at all." Joseph Perl, a psychologist in Poughkeepsie, N.Y., adds that in his practice, he sees "spouses who get scared, sometimes resentful, blaming, even openly hostile and rejecting. Children can end up insecure, needy, dependent and eventually angry."

To avoid destructive reactions, Perl advises, family members—especially children—should express feelings. And though the kids' contribution is more symbolic than practical, they should pitch in. Four-year-olds can turn off lights to save money or collect bottles for deposits. Teenagers can cut lawns or sell lemonade.

While some families fracture under the stress, with both adults unable to cope, the opposite is often true. Says Perl: "I have seen time after time situations loaded in the beginning with anxiety, fear and bad feelings that are transformed into a sense of togetherness and mutual support."

BY LINDA GRANT

been with the company for 14 years, won two extraordinary achievement awards and found his job as a material cost estimator for the cruise missile program both challenging and rewarding. His jaw dropped and he turned white as he received his layoff notice. "I can relate to a person snapping," he says, "because it's just so frustrating sometimes." Dillard leaves Hughes next month.

In sun-drenched San Diego, there are enough people like Dillard to fill Jack

Murphy Stadium. An estimated 28,000 defense jobs will have vanished in the area between 1990 and the end of 1993, probably for good. And the biggest hits are taking place right now. As part of the ongoing consolidation of the nation's fast-shrinking defense industry, Hughes purchased General Dynamics' San Diego-based missile business late last year. To cut costs, Hughes is moving the missile programs to its renovated facilities in Tucson, Ariz. The result: Fewer than 1,400 of the 4,500 engineers, line workers and support staff remain at the sprawling plant where Dillard works in Kearny Mesa, about 10 miles from downtown San Diego—and that number will fall to just several hundred by next winter. Other local defense contractors, such as Rohr Inc., also plan big payroll reductions.

The military is to San Diego what aerospace is to Seattle and cars are to Detroit. With more than 80 U.S. Navy and Marine shore commands in the region, San Diego County boasts the largest military complex in the nation. One in 5 residents depends on the military directly for his or her livelihood, and the defense industry accounts for a hefty 16 percent of the area's nearly $62 billion economy. As a result, the end of the cold war has had a positively chilling effect: Defense sector layoffs alone are expected to drain more than $630 million in wages from the economy by the end of 1993. And as those paychecks disappear, the sting is being felt all the way down the economic food chain—at dry cleaners, office supply shops and grocery stores. Just a few minutes from Dillard's office is a popular hamburger joint called Boll Weevil. "Before [Hughes] reduced the work force, we used to have a waiting list at lunch," grumbles franchise owner Rick Hackley as he surveys a half-empty dining room. Across the street from Boll Weevil is another grim monument to San Diego's defense cutbacks: an out-of-business Church's Fried Chicken.

For Dillard, who was born and raised in east San Diego, General Dynamics was a natural place to turn after graduating from San Diego State University in 1979 with a degree in accounting. With the Reagan administration's massive defense buildup, Pentagon dollars soon poured into the region—and Dillard, his co-workers and San Diego as a whole rode the wave like the best surfers at nearby Solana Beach. "When it was cranking, we stayed until 1 or 2 in the morning," recalls Dillard. "I thought it would never end." During the Persian Gulf war, he and his colleagues took particular pride as they watched their cruise missiles share top billing on CNN. It was about then that Dillard purchased his $134,000 home in Chula Vista, Calif., 6 miles from the Mexican border.

Unanswered résumés. Today, in the depressed San Diego real-estate market, Dillard's home is worth about $12,000 less than he paid for it. Dillard has just a few weeks to go before he will have to clear out his desk at Hughes, but he still hasn't sent out a single résumé. With its jobless rate averaging 7.6 percent so far this year—0.6 of a percentage point above the national unemployment figure for the same period—San Diego is hardly a job hunter's paradise today. And Dillard has heard countless tales from discouraged peers of résumés that simply go unanswered. What's more, a new study by the University of California at Los Angeles found that more than half of the aerospace workers who lost their jobs in San Diego County in 1991 were still out of work or had left the state since that time.

After receiving his layoff notice, Dillard began cutting back on spending and has managed to save $7,000—perhaps enough to help him start his own small business someday. Twice divorced at 38, he is hopeful that he can eventually land on his feet. Stewart Cochran, who works with Dillard in Hughes's contracts and estimating department, is less optimistic. The 54-year-old General Dynamics veteran hasn't received a pink slip yet, but he knows it's just around the corner.

Several hundred of Hughes's San Diego-based workers have been offered transfers to Arizona, but unfortunately Cochran isn't one of them. Translation: He's as good as gone.

Second start. Cochran, who makes $38,500, may soon find himself in a white-collar purgatory that seems to be expanding. He's too young to retire and too old, he fears, for another company to hire him. A few weeks ago, Cochran retrieved and updated his résumé for the first time in years. But like Dillard, he hasn't bothered sending it around. "I haven't tried looking for a job in 34 years," Cochran explains. "To go out now and try to sell yourself at this stage in the game is frightening. I'm just flat scared." He hasn't lost his sense of humor, however. To prepare for his pending unemployment, Cochran had new business cards printed with his name, home address, phone number and the words: "A Second Start."

In Training Room No. 3 at the San Diego Career Center, about two dozen laid-off workers—including six former General Dynamics employees—are also seeking a second start. An instructor is drilling them in the fine art of the job interview. The mood is surprisingly upbeat, but when a visitor asks how many of the jobless workers are confident about finding new positions, only about one third of them raise their hands. Like Dillard and Cochran, they, too, seem to recognize that second starts are not something that America's growing legion of unemployed white-collar workers can take for granted these days.

BY DAVID HAGE, LINDA GRANT AND JIM IMPOCO

CORPORATE IMAGE, RECRUITMENT IMAGE, AND INITIAL JOB CHOICE DECISIONS

Robert D. Gatewood, University of Georgia, Mary A. Gowan, University of Texas at El Paso, and Gary J. Lautenschlager, University of Georgia

Robert D. Gatewood (Ph.D., Purdue University) is the chairman of the Department of Management at the University of Georgia. His research interests include recruitment, selection, and job loss.

Mary A. Gowan (Ph.D., University of Georgia) is an assistant professor in the Department of Marketing and Management at the University of Texas at El Paso. Her research interests include job search and choice, recruitment, and job loss.

Gary J. Lautenschlager (Ph.D., University of Illinois at Chicago) is an associate professor in the Department of Psychology at the University of Georgia. His research interests include personnel decision making, ethical judgment, and the effects of using computers to collect test and questionnaire responses.

Aspects of corporate image, or the image associated with the name of an organization, and recruitment image—the image associated with its recruitment message—were studied. Data collected from five student groups indicate that the image of an organization is related to the information available about it. Additional results are that different external groups only moderately agree on ratings of corporate image, potential applicants have different corporate and recruitment images of the same organizations, and corporate image and recruitment image are significant predictors of initial decisions about pursuing contact with organizations.

We wish to thank the two reviewers for this journal for comments that significantly changed and improved the content of this article.

The job choice process can be characterized as a series of decisions made by an applicant as to which jobs and organizations to pursue for possible employment. Following Schwab, Rynes, and Aldag's (1987) model, we excluded labor force participation decisions and career decisions from this process. Instead, we considered the job choice process to begin with an individual's evaluation of information obtained from recruitment sources, including printed advertisements, media messages, and friends. Logically, the individual uses the information obtained from a recruitment source to decide whether or not to pursue possible employment with an organization. These decisions are the initial ones in the individual's job search process and affect all subsequent decision alternatives and the outcomes of the search process.

However, almost all studies of the job choice process have focused on decisions made after the initial decisions (Rynes, 1991); therefore, little is known about variables that influence those initial decisions. Herriot and Rothwell (1981), in the only study we found that explicitly examined recruitment sources and initial decisions, concluded that recruitment brochures did influence potential applicants' intentions to apply to organizations. They could not, however, determine specific characteristics of the brochures that were related to those intentions.

Rynes (1991) suggested that, given the small amount of information applicants have early in the job choice process, initial application decisions are heavily based on general impressions of organizational attractiveness. She labeled those general impressions "organiza-

From *Academy of Management Journal*, Vol. 36, No. 2, April 1993, pp. 414-427. © 1993 by The Academy of Management Journal. Reprinted by permission.

tional image" and stated that "one useful direction of future research would be to determine the major components of organizational image, and whether any of them can be cost-effectively modified or communicated to improve applicant attraction" (Rynes, 1991: 435–36). Fombrun and Shanley (1990) also indicated that image is a major component of early job choice decisions.

A search of the literature yielded only one empirical study that examined organizational image and applicant responses. Belt and Paolillo (1982) determined the favorableness of the image of each of 20 fast-food establishments and selected one very highly rated and one very poorly rated restaurant. Recruitment advertisements were written that manipulated the names of the two organizations and a second variable, the specificity of required applicant qualifications. In this study's results, image was a main effect: applicant response to the organization with the better image was significantly higher.

Fombrun and Shanley (1990) reported an important study of corporate reputation, which we view as another term for image, but did not directly address the job choice process. The study's purpose was to identify the components of reputation. The authors' measures of reputation were the ratings gathered by *Fortune* in its 1985 survey of corporate executives. Data gathered from 292 firms supported Fombrun and Shanley's hypotheses that reputations are based on a firm's position relative to competitors. Specifically, the most important variables were "market and accounting signals indicating economic performance, institutional signals indicating conformity to social norms, and strategy signals indicating strategic postures" (Fombrun & Shanley, 1990: 233).

RESEARCH QUESTIONS

There is some preliminary evidence, therefore, that the image of an organization affects the initial job choice decisions of potential applicants. What is not understood, however, is how image affects those decisions, or what constitutes the components of image. To better understand the role of image in initial job choice decisions, we addressed four research questions. The first was, Is general corporate image consistent across various external groups, or does image vary according to a group's relationship to an organization?

This research question is directly related to one Fombrun and Shanley (1990) posed as to whether different groups held different corporate images. By corporate image we mean the construct studied by Fombrun and Shanley (1990) and Belt and Paolillo (1982)–the image associated with the name of an organization. Our interest was in the consistency of the image perceptions of potential applicants and executives who were similar to those in Fombrun and Shanley's study. Consistent perceptions would suggest that image is a universal construct. Inconsistent perceptions would suggest that image is associated with different correlates for different groups.

The second research question addressed was, Do potential applicants hold a corporate image that is different from the general corporate image? Whether or not applicants hold the same general corporate image as others, they may develop a specific recruitment image of a firm. We assumed that potential applicants use the information presented in the recruitment messages of firms in making their initial decisions to pursue employment or not. This information specifically addresses employment topics and need not be correlated with the economic, marketing, and social variables Fombrun and Shanley (1990) found to be related to corporate image.

Our third research question was, If potential applicants hold a specific recruitment image, what are the dimensions and correlates of this image? This question reflects Rynes's (1991) statement of the importance of determining the major components of image and of assessing if any of those components can be modified in a cost-effective manner to increase applicant response rate. The recruitment image of a firm applicants hold may be largely a function of the recruitment message with which they are presented. If that is the case, a firm could easily change the characteristics of its recruitment message to affect response rate. Another possibility is that the recruitment image is a function of potential applicants' previous knowledge of or contact with a firm as well as of the recruitment message. If that is true, modification of the components of image would be more complex, time-consuming, and costly.

Finally, we asked, If general corporate image and recruitment image differ, are both related to applicants' intentions to pursue further contact with an organization? This question focuses on the importance of both concepts of image–corporate and recruitment– in the initial decisions made by potential applicants. We could logically argue that recruitment image is strongly correlated with an applicant's decision to pursue employment with a company. The relationship of the general corporate image to the pursue-not-pursue decision is less clear.

METHODS

Overview

Data collection involved four sets of measures, five groups of respondents, and two groups of organizations. Table 1 summarizes information on data collection. The four types of measures included (1) three forms of corporate image, used to test agreement among various external groups in perceptions of image

TABLE 1
Summary of Measures, Organizations, and Respondents Used in Data Collection

Measures	Organizations	Respondents[a]
General corporate image		
Reputation ratings, Fortune[b]	Fortune	
Applicant reputation ratings, Fortune	Fortune	Group one
Overall corporate image	Fortune	Group one
	CPC Annual	Group two
Recruitment image		
Overall recruitment image	CPC Annual	Group three
Similarity of recruitment image	CPC Annual	Group three
Correlates of image		
Familiarity with companies	CPC Annual	Group two
	CPC Annual	Group four
Economic performance, marketing, social benefit[c]	Fortune	
Dependent measures		
Probability of responding, names	CPC Annual	Group four
Probability of responding, advertisement	CPC Annual	Group five

[a] Groups one–five contained 88, 177, 62, 77, and 66 individuals, respectively.

[b] Data came from the 1990 Fortune 500 survey.

[c] Data came from COMPUSTAT, O'Neill Datagraphs, the Taft Foundation Reporter, the Directory of Corporate Philanthropy, and various business periodicals. These are the same sources Fombrum and Shanley (1990) used.

and also to measure relationships among corporate and recruitment images; (2) one form of recruitment image, used to test agreement between corporate and recruitment images of organizations; (3) two sets of correlates of image to assist in understanding the basis for perceptions of image; and (4) two forms of the probability of responding (continuing the application process), which were the dependent measures of the study and were correlated with various image measures. The five groups of respondents were juniors and seniors at the University of Georgia. Essentially, the juniors provided information about image of the organization, and the seniors, all of whom were in the job search process, supplied information about the probability of continuing the application process. A sample of 26 Fortune 500 companies and another sample of 13 firms that placed recruitment advertisements in the College Placement Council Annual were used. The former allowed for testing agreement in perceptions of corporate image among external groups. The latter, because of the recruitment advertisements, allowed for examining the relationships among corporate image, recruitment image, and probability of continuing the application process.

Organizations

Fortune 500 organizations. Corporate reputation ratings were obtained for a group of Fortune 500 companies selected from the ninth annual Fortune magazine Corporate Reputation Survey, published in 1990. Fombrun and Shanley (1990) used the 1985 edition of the survey for their study. We selected every 12th company for study, obtaining a total of 26 companies for inclusion in this study.

College Placement Council (CPC) Annual organizations. We also used 13 companies advertising in the 33rd annual edition of the College Placement Council Annual, published in 1990, for the study. This publication is geared toward recruiting graduating college students. We chose companies whose advertisements in the CPC Annual identified similar jobs requiring educational backgrounds that matched those of the respondents for this study.

Measures

General corporate image. Measures of general corporate image included the following: Reputation ratings, Fortune 500, were the ratings for each of the studied organizations listed in the 1990 Fortune survey. To obtain applicant reputation ratings, Fortune 500, we asked the students to first indicate their familiarity with each of the 26 Fortune 500 organizations and then asked students familiar with a company to rate it on the same eight attributes used in the Fortune study. For overall corporate image, respondents indicated familiarity with a list of company names that included both companies from the Fortune 500 organizations and the CPC Annual organizations; students indicating familiarity with a company then rated the image of that company on a five-point scale.

Recruitment image. Overall recruitment image was a five-point rating of the image of each CPC Annual organization respondents made after reviewing recruitment advertisements for each company. For *similarity of recruitment image,* respondents indicated how similar their responses to pairs of recruitment advertisements from the *CPC Annual* would be.

Correlates of image. To provide information for interpreting the image measures, we gathered the following data thought to be correlated with various image measures: For *familiarity with companies,* respondents indicated whether or not they were familiar with each company in the *CPC Annual* organizations and indicated how familiar they were with a company by responding to a set of six questions; examples are "Have you ever worked for [company name]?" and "Have you ever studied about [company name] in any of your classes?" *Economic performance, marketing, and social benefit indicators* were the correlates of the reputation ratings of *Fortune* 500 organizations used by Fombrun and Shanley (1990), such as total sales, advertising intensity, and charitable contributions.

Dependent measures. We gathered data for two forms of the dependent measure, the probability of students' responding to a company's recruitment efforts. For *probability of responding, advertisement,* respondents reviewed actual recruitment advertisements for the *CPC Annual* organizations; for *probability of responding, names,* they reviewed a list of names of companies from the *CPC Annual.* For both forms, respondents indicated the probability of their responding by writing the exact probability estimate, which could vary from .00 for no probability to 1.00 for 100 percent probability.

Respondents

Five groups of respondents were used to eliminate same-source bias in the subsequent correlational analyses. In only two of the sets of correlations reported in the Results section was the information about the variables obtained from the same group of respondents. This process eliminated spurious correlations due to source so that results could be appropriately generalized. Table 1 includes information on the data provided by each group. Each group consisted of from 62 to 177 college students in general business courses required of all business majors at the University of Georgia.

RESULTS

The first three analyses used only data about the *Fortune* 500 firms and addressed the first research question of whether general corporate image is consistent across various external groups. The first analysis involved correlating, for the 26 *Fortune* 500 firms, the reputation ratings reported in the 1990 *Fortune* survey with the applicant reputation ratings, *Fortune* 500. This correlation was nonsignificant ($r = .25$), indi-

cating that the two groups, executives and potential job applicants, did not agree in their overall corporate image ratings.

Fombrun and Shanley (1990) found that the *Fortune* reputation ratings correlated significantly with several market and accounting performance measures. In our second analysis, we correlated the applicant reputation ratings, *Fortune* 500, with the 11 measures from Fombrun and Shanley's study. None of these correlations were significant; their range was from $-.38$ to .32, indicating that the applicant reputation ratings were not related to these market and accounting performance signals.

The third analysis examined the overall corporate image ratings respondents provided for the *Fortune* 500 firms. This measure was correlated significantly with the *Fortune* reputation ratings ($r = .39, p < .01$) but not with any of the Fombrun and Shanley performance indicators.

The remaining analyses used only data that we had gathered about the *CPC Annual* organizations. Table 2 presents descriptive statistics for all the variables in the analyses related to those firms. The reported correlations are based on averages calculated across all responses for a given variable and organization.

To learn about variables related to overall corporate image ratings, we examined the correlations between the variables measuring overall corporate image and familiarity with the company. Overall image for the *CPC Annual* organizations was correlated significantly with five of the six variables: (1) overall familiarity with the company ($r = .95, p < .01$), (2) knowing someone who works for the company ($r = .91, p < .01$), (3) using the products or services of the company ($r = .91, p < .01$), (4) having studied the company in class ($r = .90, p < .01$), and (5) frequency of contact with company advertisements ($r = .88, p < .01$). We concluded that the overall corporate image ratings made by potential applicants, although moderately related to the image ratings made by executives, were most strongly related to the potential applicants' amount of exposure to a company. Overall corporate image was the measure used in subsequent analyses involving questions about the general image of organizations.

The second research question asked if, for potential applicants, the overall corporate image and the recruitment image of an organization were the same. We collected these measures for the 13 firms with advertisements in the *CPC Annual.* Overall corporate image ratings were provided by respondents with exposure to only the names of the organizations. Overall recruitment image ratings were provided by another group of respondents after they had been exposed to the organizations' advertisements in the *CPC Annual.* This correlation was nonsignificant, indicating that the two images may be independent.

The third research question concerned the dimensions and correlates of overall recruitment image. Two

TABLE 2
Descriptive Statistics and Correlations for *CPC Annual* Firms

Variables	Means	s.d.	1	2	3	4	5	6	7
1. Total information in advertisement	0.00	1.42							
2. Emphasis on telecommunications and technology	0.00	0.86	.01						
3. Information about company	0.00	0.71	−.05	.00					
4. Company description	7.00	3.78	−.47	.11	.70**				
5. Types of positions	7.00	3.69	−.70**	.47	−.07	.14			
6. Desirable qualifications	7.00	3.69	−.02	−.05	.30	.41	.04		
7. Training and development	6.08	3.56	−.39	−.22	.38	.53	.29	.60*	
8. Benefits	7.00	3.82	−.73**	.19	−.09	.32	.64*	.01	.18
9. Response probability, advertisement	3.12	0.77	.95**	−.01	.15	−.21	−.69**	.22	−.17
10. Overall recruitment image	3.74	0.65	.96**	−.10	−.07	−.45	−.66*	.14	−.18
11. Response probability, name	3.17	0.66	.51	.50	.23	.25	−.22	.38	−.08
12. Overall corporate image	3.44	0.42	.37	.37	.31	.36	−.11	.49	.22
13. Are you familiar with X?	0.51	0.35	.07	.24	.35	.36	.18	.60*	.43
14. Know someone who works for X?	0.07	0.10	.38	.33	.45	.45	−.26	.37	.19
15. Ever worked for X?	0.01	0.00	.83**	.48	−.11	−.41	−.28	−.06	−.45
16. Used products or services?	0.24	0.31	.32	.21	.51	.45	−.12	.51	.40
17. Ever studied X in a class?	0.06	0.08	.35	.22	.48	.51	−.24	.48	.40
18. Frequency of contact with X	1.84	0.94	.29	.25	.55	.50	−.08	.53	.42
19. Overall familiarity with X	0.00	0.86	.43	.33	.43	.36	−.16	.47	.27
20. Attribute average rank	6.82	2.49	−.69**	.15	.36	.72**	.63*	.61*	.76**

* $p < .05$
** $p < .01$

analyses were conducted. In the first, we correlated overall recruitment image with the six items measuring familiarity with the company. Only one item, having worked for the company, was significantly related to overall recruitment image ($r = .78$, $p < .01$). This was the one item of the six that was not correlated with overall corporate image.

The second analysis involved multidimensional scaling (MDS),[1] (Hair, Anderson, & Tatham, 1987). The input data for this analysis were the paired-comparison ratings for similarity of recruitment image. Solutions ranging from one to three dimensions were obtained. We used two fit indexes, Kruskal's stress formula 1 and R^2 of data by distances, to assess fit.[2] On the basis of these two indicants, we judged the three-dimension model to be appropriate.

The second part of this analysis was interpretation of the dimensions. Two types of information were used for this interpretation. First, we computed average ranks for each of the 13 advertisements on each of five common content topics. The five common topics were descriptions of (1) the company, (2) the types of positions for which recruitment was occurring, (3) the desirable employee qualifications, (4) the training and career development opportunities, and (5) the benefits offered. Each of us independently ranked each advertisement on each content topic, using as a criterion the amount of information the advertisement provided in each content area. There were no ties in these rank-

ings. The average rank-order correlation was .87 for all pairs of raters across the five content areas, and the range was from .73 to .98.

Second, the advertisements were carefully read and the stimulus plots[3] studied. We also used visual interpretation of the dimensional stimulus plots, in relation to the 13 recruitment advertisements, to interpret the dimensions of the MDS analysis. The three dimensions for corporate recruiting image were *total information in the advertisement*, *emphasis on telecommunications and technology*, and *information about company*. The first dimension was based on the significant correlation ($r = .69$, $p < .01$) between the rankings of the 13 advertisements on the amount of total information across all content areas and their weights on the first dimension of the MDS analysis. None of the correlations between the rankings of the organizations on the amount of information in the five content areas and the second MDS dimension were significant. Therefore, we named this dimension after visual inspection of the advertisements relative to the dimension plot. The dimension weights for the second dimension, *emphasis on telecommunications-technology*, appeared to correspond to the location in the advertisement of statements indicating that the organization was prominent in the telecommunications industry or a high-technology communications field. The advertisements with positive dimension weights presented these statements very early in the printed material, usually in the first three

TABLE 2 (continued)

8	9	10	11	12	13	14	15	16	17	18	19
−.73**											
−.72**	.94**										
−.15	.66*	.51									
−.06	.57*	.44	.90**								
.09	.27	.24	.65*	.81**							
−.18	.59*	.39	.81**	.91**	.59*						
−.46	.78**	.78**	.72**	.54	.30	.46					
−.19	.57*	.42	.80**	.91**	.83**	.87**	.45				
−.14	.58*	.42	.82**	.90**	.71**	.89**	.41	.93**			
−.09	.53	.37	.81**	.88**	.81**	.83**	.43	.98**	.95**		
−.19	.64*	.51	.89**	.95**	.82**	.90**	.59*	.97**	.94**	.96*	
.65*	−.48	−.57*	.05	.26	.49	.17	−.50	.31	.30	.37	.22

sentences. The advertisements with negative dimension weights either emphasized a single industry not in telecommunications−for instance, the L.A. Times emphasized journalism, and R. R. Donnelly & Sons, Inc., printing−or a diversity of industries: U.S. West noted its involvement in communications, data solutions, financial services, and marketing services.

The third dimension, *information about company,* reflected the correlation ($r = .70$, $p < .01$) between the rank order of the advertisements on the amount of information provided in the content area of the general description of the company and their weights on the third dimension.

The final analysis for this research question was correlation of the weights of each organization on each of these three recruitment image dimensions with the organizations' mean overall recruitment image ratings. These were the averages of the ratings of overall corporate image for each advertisement across all respondents. Mean overall recruitment image was significantly correlated with only the first dimension, *total information in the advertisement* ($r = .96$, $p < .01$).

The fourth research question focused on the relationships between the potential applicants' perceptions of both corporate image and recruitment image and their intentions to pursue further contact with an organization. Two analyses were conducted to investigate this question. First, we determined correlations between each of the image ratings and the dependent measures, probability of responding, name, and probability of responding, advertisement. Second, we regressed probability of responding, advertisement, on both image ratings.

Overall corporate image was significantly correlated with both probability of responding, name ($r = .90$, $p < .01$), and probability of responding, advertisement ($r = .57$, $p < .05$). Overall recruitment image rating was significantly correlated with probability of responding, advertisement ($r = .94$, $p < .01$), but not with probability of responding, name. These correlations indicate that both images are related to response probability and that corporate image may have a carryover effect on response probability even after people are exposed to recruitment advertisements.

We regressed probability of responding, advertisement, on both the general corporate and the overall recruitment images to further address the issue of that carryover relationship. Overall corporate image explains 32.3 percent of the variance in the probability of responding, advertisement, variable. However, overall recruitment image explains an additional 59.7 percent of this variance. Together, the two image variables almost fully explain the total variance ($R^2 = .92$).

DISCUSSION

Our findings contribute to the understanding of initial job choice decisions. First, there is empirical support for Rynes's (1991) suggestion that image is highly related to potential job applicants' intentions to pursue further contact with a firm. Perceptions of both overall corporate image and recruitment image were significantly correlated with those intentions, the latter more strongly than the former.

Second, we have some information about what constitutes image. It appears that the perception of image is a function of the information that is available to an individual at a given time. Overall corporate image was positively related to potential applicants' personal interaction with a company in the form of exposure to advertisements, use of products or services, studying the organization in class, and so forth. Recruitment image was strongly related to the amount of information presented in the recruitment advertisement of an organization and to applicants' having worked for the organization.

A major point of interest is that these findings indicate that mere exposure to information is central to an individual's perception of image. This idea is antithetical to the assumption that people will use the information presented in a company's recruitment advertisement to analyze the match between their employment interests and the firm's characteristics. If our respondents had carried out such matching activity, the pattern of correlations we found would have been different. We would expect some respondents to have used the additional information in the advertisement to decide that the match between their interests and the characteristics of an organization was not good. We would also assume that those respondents would, as a result of this low match, indicate a low probability of pursuing further contact. Therefore, the correlations among amount of information in an advertisement, recruitment image, and probability of pursuit would be lower than those found in this study.

However, the magnitudes of the correlations among those variables clearly indicate that exposure to a greater amount of information enhances image and is also positively correlated with intentions of pursuing employment. Other work has identified a similar positive function of exposure to information. Rynes and Miller (1983) manipulated the amount of information provided by a recruiter to applicants about specific job characteristics, including salary, career paths, geographical assignment, and fringe benefits. The actual attractiveness of the job features was held constant across experimental "conditions." Increased information positively affected several variables, including an applicant's perception of the attractiveness of an organization and willingness to follow up on an interview. Similarly, Zajonc (1968) found that repeated exposure to an object resulted in an increase in the positive evaluation of the object. This effect occurred even when subjects were not instructed to evaluate the objects to which they were exposed. The enhancement

occurred with stimuli that were initially viewed as neutral or positive. Judd and Brauer (in press) reviewed studies of the mere exposure effect and presented a theory describing increased positive evaluation of an object as a result of increased exposure. They even concluded that repeated exposure to an initially disliked object can result in slightly more positive evaluations because of the mere exposure effect.

Perhaps the positive relationship between the length of an advertisement and image and intention is also partially a function of the type of information that is presented. All the advertisements consisted of positive descriptions of the characteristics of the firms. Therefore, more information meant more positive information, especially in the content areas of description of a company, benefits, and career development. The only statements we considered potentially restrictive to applicants concerned specific degree and course requirements, information contained in the content area of applicant qualifications. However, in our judgment, nearly all our respondents would have met the stated requirements as a consequence of obtaining bachelor of business administration degrees.

The results of this study lead to tentative statements regarding Rynes's (1991) question as to whether organizations can cost-effectively manipulate elements of image. Potential applicants appear to react positively to long recruitment messages that can be considered to be attractive statements about organizations. Recruitment advertisements can easily be manipulated. The cost-benefit advantages depend on the additional number and quality of applicants attracted by such advertisements. This conclusion supports a basic assumption of the traditional method of recruitment: advertising that portrays an organization in a positive manner increases applicants' interest in it.

Other findings of this research that bear on Rynes's question are that different groups have different images of organizations and that an applicant group may have multiple images that are not necessarily highly related. The implication of these findings is that an organization can successfully influence its recruitment image for applicants, independent of its general corporate image. This implies that organizations that do not have high-profile corporate images may successfully compete in the initial stages of job choice in the applicant pool through the use of recruitment messages.

A limitation of this study is the small number of companies studied—26 in the *Fortune* group and 13 in the *CPC* group. The internal consistency of the results and their compatibility with findings from studies in other areas support their credibility. However, it is necessary to be aware of the smallness of the groups in the interpretation of results. Of particular concern is the interpretation of correlations as nonsignificant as a result of low statistical power. In some cases, the magnitude of the correlations was high, but they were not statistically significant in the context of the small amount of data. These nonsignificant correlations could more clearly be interpreted if they were based on larger groups. It is obvious that further studies with larger samples are necessary.

Another logically related study would be one in which the content areas of recruitment advertisements would be systematically manipulated. After measuring the applicants' responses to the various advertisements, researchers could draw feasible conclusions about the cause-effect relationships between the amount of information about specific topics and applicants' intentions to pursue further contact. Such conclusions would be useful in further discussion of Rynes's question about cost-effective methods of increasing applicant pools.

A third avenue of research would be to examine recruitment sources other than advertisements in terms of their relationship to recruitment image and applicants' intentions to pursue contact. Advertisements were an appropriate source of data for this study because they are commonly used by organizations for recruitment, they can easily be reproduced for controlled exposure to respondents, and they have features that can be measured and related to measures of applicant intention. Potential applicants, however, have many other sources of recruitment information, such as media messages and family and social contacts. The previously mentioned similarity between the findings in this study and those of Rynes and Miller (1983) implies some generalizable applicant reactions to various recruitment sources.

In summary, this study presents some preliminary data indicating that initial job choice decisions are highly related to the image of an organization held by potential applicants. This image is, in turn, highly related to the information available to the applicant pool. In many ways, these findings support the commonly held assumption of traditional recruitment advertising, which is that the presentation of favorable information will positively influence potential applicants.

NOTES

1. Multidimensional scaling (MDS) is a method that allows researchers to study relations among objects when the underlying dimensions on which those objects vary are unknown. Starting with pairwise judgments about the perceived similarities, or dissimilarities, among all possible pairs of objects in the set, MDS programs construct plots that best reflect the variability present in those judgments. Objects that are perceived as most similar to one another should appear closest together in an obtained space. This method involves the use of multiple solutions, each with a different number of dimensions, to determine which configuration best charac-terizes the initial judgments of similarity among pairs of objects. The MDS configurations obtained may reflect quantitative and qualitative aspects of the objects.

2. The data were analyzed using the classic nonmetric multidimensional scaling method available in the ALSCAL program (SPSS, Inc., 1986). The program provides two goodness of fit indexes, namely Kruskal's stress formula 1 and R^2 of data by distances. One can then plot the value of stress against the number of dimensions, much like a scree plot in factor analysis, and inspect this plot to aid in the choice of an appropriate number of dimensions to retain. The R^2 index is based on the proportion of variance in the original similarity judgments that can be explained by corresponding variability in the distances obtained in a solution of a given number of dimensions. As the number of dimensions increases, the value of R^2 also increases. Technical details of the computation of these fit indexes can be found in Young and Lewyckyj (1979).

3. A stimulus plot represents a derived graphical configuration of the advertisements in the multiple dimensional space resulting from the MDS analysis.

REFERENCES

Belt, J. A., & Paolillo, J. G. P. 1982. The influence of corporate image and specificity of candidate qualifications on response to recruitment advertisements. *Journal of Management,* 8: 105–112.

Fombrun, C., & Shanley, M. 1990. What's in a name? Reputation building and corporate strategy. *Academy of Management Journal,* 33: 233–258.

Hair, J. F., Jr., Anderson, R. E., & Tatham, R. L. 1987. *Multivariate data analysis with readings* (2d ed.). New York: Macmillan.

Herriot, P., & Rothwell, C. 1981. Organizational choice and decision theory: Effects of employers' literature and selection interview. *Journal of Occupational Psychology,* 54: 17–31.

Judd, C. M., & Brauer, M. In press. Repetition and evaluative extremity. In R. E. Petty & J. A. Krosnick (Eds.), *Attitude strength: Antecedents and consequences:* Hillsdale, NJ: Erlbaum.

Rynes, S. L. 1991. Recruitment, job choice, and post-hire consequences: A call for new research directions. In M. D. Dunnette & L. M. Hough (Eds.), *Handbook of industrial and organizational psychology,* vol. 2 (2d ed.): 399–444. Palo Alto, CA: Consulting Psychologists.

Rynes, S. L., & Miller, H. E. 1983. Recruiter and job influences on candidates for employment. *Journal of Applied Psychology,* 68: 147–154.

Schwab, D. P., Rynes, S. L., & Aldag, R. J. 1987. Theories and research on job search and choice. In K. Rowland & G. Ferris (Eds.), *Research in personnel and human resources management,* vol. 5: 129–166. Greenwich, CT: JAI Press.

SPSS, Inc. 1986. *SPSSX user's guide* (2d ed.). New York: McGraw-Hill.

Young, F. W., & Lewyckyj, R. 1979. *ALSCAL-4 user's guide* (2d ed.). Chapel Hill, NC: Data Analysis and Theory Associates.

Zajonc, R. B. 1968. The attitudinal effects of mere exposure. *Journal of Personality and Social Psychology,* 9: 1–27.

Case VII: *What to Do?*

You are the administrator, chief operating officer of a large medical school. You have been informed by your board chair that he has been able to gain major funding from a single giver, a major distiller and brewer, for a center to study and treat alcohol and drug abuse. This would enable the medical school to become far and away the leader for such issues in your geographical region.

- What do you do?
- What are your reasons for doing that?
- What values do those reasons reflect?

Using the Case of *What to Do?*

This is obviously the Faustian bargain, the chance to do good with the powers of evil. This case would be particularly interesting after a discussion of ethics and morality in industry. Try to get a discussion going on the merits of each position. It will be hard to tell where it may lead, but it could be very interesting.

Exercise VII: *Career Strategy*

What is your career goal?
Have you developed a plan to achieve your goal?

The concepts of business strategy can be adapted to help you formulate, implement, and fulfill your own "mission" in life. Your personal strategy should be designed to assess and utilize strengths (and overcome weaknesses), to accurately assess the opportunities and threats in the external environment, to develop, assess, and select from available alternatives, and to establish objectives for implementing your career plan. Finally, you will set milestones to provide evaluative feedback on your strategies for a successful and fulfilling career. Remember, strategic planning is a *process*—you can use this plan as a beginning point to review, renew, or adapt your career strategy during your entire work life. Think of this as a beginning rather than an end product.

Although the specific steps in developing a career strategy may vary, the process usually involves these steps: (1) prepare a personal profile, (2) develop professional goals in the form of a mission statement, (3) analyze the external and internal environment, (4) develop strategic career alternatives based on your analyses, (5) evaluate alternatives; select and defend the one most attractive to you now, (6) develop specific short-range career objectives and action plans, and (7) prepare a set of guidelines and milestones for evaluating your strategic plan as you set it into action.

Use these seven steps as major headings for your written career plan; follow directions and suggestions provided under each heading to follow.

1. Prepare a Professional Profile

The personal profile includes two steps, and the first is the most difficult because it asks you to examine yourself. This self-examination is an essential first step in developing a career strategy. Use the "Personal Goals/Values" to establish a set of priorities for yourself; begin by understanding what you value and what you hope to achieve with your life.

Second, examine those constituencies that shape your values and contribute to your life. What effect will home, church, or friends have on your career plans? For example, if you do not wish to move away from your geographic home, this represents a constraint that will be reflected both in your mission and the alternatives available to you.

2. Develop Professional Goals in the Form of a Mission Statement

Mission statements for organizations usually answer these questions: what business(es) are we in, and what business(es) do we want to be in for the future? Analogous individual questions may be: how am I positioned now, and where do I want these skills/interests to lead me? Answer these questions by focusing on the three aspects of mission development: what service/product do we offer the marketplace? who is our constituency? what is our distinctive competence in the marketplace? In other words, what do you have to offer or hope to offer that distinguishes you from all others? Your mission statement should be broad enough to encompass the activities you anticipate for your life and work, but not so broad as to be applicable to every other person. Begin to focus your interests on products, markets, and competencies you have.

3. Environmental Analysis

External Environment Many factors are beyond organizational control; these same factors are outside your control, but they nevertheless affect your career opportunities. Assess each aspect of the external environment as follows: competition (see *Occupational Outlook Handbook* or similar sources to assess the labor market; see *Industry Surveys* to assess a particular industry of *U.S. Industrial Outlook* for future prospects); economy; geography; technology; demographics (see *American Demographics* or similar sources for information); government rules and regulations.

Analyze these external factors to identify the threats and opportunities for achievement of your mission. If your mission statement focuses on a particular industry, then evaluate the external factors for the industry in this section. Otherwise, evaluate general conditions as they can apply to the general environment for business. Consider how situational conditions may shape opportunities. For example, joining an expanding company usually provides more career opportunities than working for a mature company that is not expected to grow. Similarly, working for a mobile manager means an increased probability that the position of the superior will become vacant; or one might progress along with a competent mobile manager.

While these external factors are listed separately here, we know that they have interactive effects on businesses and they will interact with one another in shaping your career opportunities. Thorough career plans will acknowledge these links. Successful career planning requires a systematic scanning of the environment for opportunities and threats. One has to be concerned about the present as well as forecast the future. Since there are a great many factors that need to be analyzed, planning one's career necessitates being selective and concentrating on those factors critical to personal success.

Internal Environment What are your strengths and weaknesses, given the external environment you face? If the market is competitive, what will make you most attractive? What weaknesses must you address to compete well in a compact market? Assess these strengths and weaknesses on internal dimensions of the firm as follows: marketing; management (including values); production; accounting and finance. Make a list of your strengths and weaknesses in each functional area. The relative importance of these skills differs for the various positions in the organizational hierarchy, with technical skills being very important on the supervisory level and conceptual skills being critical for top managers.

By assessing your weaknesses and strengths, now you are preparing to address them in the objectives and implementation phases of your career plan.

Conclude this section by making an overall assessment of your competencies. Do they match the market you face, and if not, what must you do to fill those gaps?

4. Develop Strategic Alternatives for Your Career

In developing career strategies, several alternatives are available. The most successful strategy would be to build on one's strengths to take advantage of opportunities. For example, if you have an excellent knowledge of computers and many companies are looking for computer programmers, you should find many opportunities for a satisfying career. On the other hand, if you are interested in programming but lack the necessary skills, the proper approach would be a developmental strategy to overcome the weakness and develop these skills in order to take advantage of the opportunities.

Your strategic plan thus far indicates that the market offers specific opportunities and presents threats. In addition, you bring identifiable strengths and weaknesses to that market. A person may have excellent managerial and technical skills but work in a declining company or industry. If this individual wishes to advance, he or she should find employment in an expanding firm or in a growing industry.

Use your environmental analyses to develop two or three viable alternatives for your career. State these alternatives in sentence form, then follow each with a list of the strengths and weaknesses for each alternative. In other words, what makes each attractive or problematic? Be sure that all are viable alternatives, given the market forecast as well as your goals, strengths, and weaknesses.

5. Select an Alternative

This is the part of career planning that most people like least—now you have to decide! Many people do not like making this commitment, fearing that it may limit them. That is true to some extent because every choice eliminates competing alternatives. Moreover, by setting goals we provide a measure by which success or failure can be judged. Sometimes we would rather have things "happen" than acknowledge failure to achieve objectives.

Factors that inhibit goal setting can be used to your advantage. First, as occurs in organizations, performance goals become a part of your personal appraisal process. If you know where you are going and how to get there, then you will be able to recognize and evaluate new opportunities that arise. Second, strategic planning for your career is a process just as it is for organizations. One does not set career goals all at once. Rather, goal setting is a continuing process that allows flexibility; professional goals can be revised in the light of changing circumstances. Another factor that reduces resistance to goal setting is the integration of long-term aims with the more immediate requirement for action. For example, the aim of becoming a doctor makes it easier to study difficult subjects that are necessary for the medical degree.

Strategic choices require tradeoffs. Some alternatives involve high risks, others low risks. Some choices demand action now; other choices can wait. Careers that were glamorous in the past may have an uncertain future. Rational and systematic analysis is just one step in the career-planning process, for a choice also involves personal preferences, personal ambitions, and personal values.

Do your alternatives all pass a consistency test? Are they in line with your preferences, ambitions, and values? Why or why not? Adapt strategies that do not meet the consistency tests.

6. Set Objectives; Action Plan for Implementation

How far in advance should you plan? The answer depends on your goals. Planning should cover a period of time necessary to fulfill the commitments involved in the decision made. Thus, the time frame of your career plan will differ with the circumstances. For instance, if you want to become a university professor, it is necessary to plan for university studies and preparation of seven to nine years. Regardless of your career, your long-term aim has to be translated into short-term objectives.

What are your long-range professional goals? Where do you want to be next year? In five years? In ten years? At retirement, what do you want to have accomplished? How far do you want to advance? How do you want to be remembered? (see Five-Year Projection below for direction).

So far your concern has been with the career direction. But the strategy has to be supported by short-term objectives and action plans that can be a part of the performance appraisal process. Thus, if the aim is to achieve a certain management position that requires a master of business administration degree, the short-term objective may be to complete a number of courses. Here is an example of a short-term verifiable objective: to complete the Business Policy course this semester with a grade of A. This objective is measurable, as it states what will be done, by what time, and the quality of performance (the grade).

How will you implement your career plan? What steps must you take? How much time will it take to implement your career plan? What are your short-term objectives? What detailed action plans will help you reach these objectives? Objectives must be supported by action plans. Continuing with our example, the completion of the management course may require a schedule for attending classes, doing the homework, and obtaining the support of friends and family, whose time with you is interrupted by university responsibilities. As you can see, the long-term strategic career plan needs to be supported by short-term objectives and action plans.

Develop Contingency Plans

Career plans are developed in an environment of uncertainty, and the future cannot be predicted with great accuracy. Therefore, contingency plans based on alternative assumptions should be prepared. While one may enjoy working for a small, fast-growing venture company, it may be wise to prepare an alternative career plan based on the assumption that the venture may not succeed.

If your top career choice is not attainable, what are your other options (given your education, preferences, etc.)? What other career plans do you have?

7. Evaluation of the Career Plan

Once you have articulated career goals, then you can monitor and evaluate your progress toward reaching them. Assuming that you work for a company that has formal evaluation, an opportune time for assessing yearly objectives is at the performance appraisal. This is the time not only to review performance against objectives in the operating area, but also to review the achievement of milestones in the career plan. In addition, progress should be monitored at other times, such as the completion of an important task or project.

Moreover, a career is more than the work you do, but includes other goals important to you. You need to supplement annual performance appraisals with your own schedule of evaluation. How will you monitor your career progress? What factors will you examine? What standards will you use to measure your own performance? How will you know if you are successful? If your interests or other opportunities take you in new directions, when will you revise your career goals?

A career plan doesn't guarantee that you will achieve your goals, any more than a strategic plan guarantees organizational success. What it does provide is a clear set of goals and objectives against which you can assess new opportunities, new challenges, and new directions for fulfilling your mission in life.

CASE VII; EXERCISE VII

Five-Year Projection

Project yourself into the future five (or ten) years. How old will you be in five years? What will your life be like then? How will your personal, family, and career circumstances have changed by that date? Of course, this is a highly imaginative projection, but attempt to be as realistic and objective as possible.

In completing this projection, you will be bothered by two questions repeatedly: (1) Should I describe my future the way I want it to be? or (2) Should I describe my future the way I really think it is going to be?

You will probably allow both factors to enter into your answers. Such a solution is both natural and desirable. This projection is for your benefit.

1. In five (ten) years my age is _____.
2. My occupation is (be as specific as possible) _____.
3. My specific responsibilities are _____.
4. My approximate annual income (or my family's is) _____.
5. My most important personal possessions are _____.
6. My family responsibilities are _____.
7. Of my experiences in the last few years, the most pleasant were _____.
8. Of my experiences in the last few years, the ones that gave me the greatest sense of accomplishment were _____.
9. In the last few years, several dramatic things have happened in my business and/or community that have interested me. Below is a summary of the highlights, including a description of how I was involved in these events _____.
10. In reviewing my "Five-Year Projection," the most important observations I made were _____.

Index

Answers to Exercise Questions on Page 86:

15 - Box of matches; 4 - Food concentrate; 6 - 50 feet of nylon rope; 8 - Parachute silk; 13 - Portable heating unit; 11 - Two .45 caliber pistols; 12 - One case dehydrated Pet milk; 1 - Two 100 lb. tanks of oxygen; 3 - Stellar map of the moon's constellation; 9 - Rubber life raft; 14 - Magnetic compass; 2 - Five gallons of water; 10 - Signal flares; 7 - First-Aid kit containing injection needles; 5 - Solar-powered FM receiver-transmitter

---

Answers to Exercise Questions on Page 143:

1. Yes, it follows July 3rd; 2. The man is not dead so he cannot be buried; 3. Light the match first; 4. All months have 28 days; 5. One hour. Take one immediately, followed by a second a half-hour later, and the third one hour after the first; 6. Two quarters and a nickel (the question says *one* is not a nickel); 7. No, the man is dead; 8. Twelve; 9. None—Noah was aboard the Ark, not Moses; 10. No, since at the time the coin was made, there was no way for someone to know it was 46 years before Christ was born; Alternate Question A: You don't bury survivors; Alternate Question B: One birthdate; Alternate Question C: Nine; Alternate Question D: Half way (because then it is on the way out).

Credits/ Acknowledgments

Cover design by Charles Vitelli

1. Managers, Performance, and the Environment

Facing overview—New York Stock Exchange photo.

2. Planning

Facing overview—United Nations photo.

3. Organizing

Facing overview—Apple Computer photo.

4. Directing

Facing overview—Sony Corporation of America photo.

5. Controlling

Facing overview—Ford Motor Company photo. 164—Photo by Texas Instruments.

6. Staffing and Human Resources

Facing overview—Chrysler Corporation photo.

7. Perspectives and Trends

Facing overview—United Nations/WHO/Almasy photo.

ANNUAL EDITIONS ARTICLE REVIEW FORM

■ NAME: _____ DATE: _____

■ TITLE AND NUMBER OF ARTICLE: _____

■ BRIEFLY STATE THE MAIN IDEA OF THIS ARTICLE: _____

_____

_____

_____

_____

■ LIST THREE IMPORTANT FACTS THAT THE AUTHOR USES TO SUPPORT THE MAIN IDEA:

_____

_____

_____

_____

_____

_____

■ WHAT INFORMATION OR IDEAS DISCUSSED IN THIS ARTICLE ARE ALSO DISCUSSED IN YOUR
TEXTBOOK OR OTHER READING YOU HAVE DONE? LIST THE TEXTBOOK CHAPTERS AND PAGE
NUMBERS:

_____

_____

_____

_____

_____

_____

_____

■ LIST ANY EXAMPLES OF BIAS OR FAULTY REASONING THAT YOU FOUND IN THE ARTICLE:

_____

_____

_____

_____

■ LIST ANY NEW TERMS/CONCEPTS THAT WERE DISCUSSED IN THE ARTICLE AND WRITE A
SHORT DEFINITION:

_____

_____

_____

_____

_____

*Your instructor may require you to use this Annual Editions Article Review Form in any number of ways:
for articles that are assigned, for extra credit, as a tool to assist in developing assigned papers, or simply
for your own reference. Even if it is not required, we encourage you to photocopy and use this page;
you'll find that reflecting on the articles will greatly enhance the information from your text.

We Want Your Advice

ANNUAL EDITIONS: MANAGEMENT, Third Edition
Article Rating Form

Here is an opportunity for you to have direct input into the next revision of this volume. We would like you to rate each of the 40 articles listed below, using the following scale:

1. **Excellent: should definitely be retained**
2. **Above average: should probably be retained**
3. **Below average: should probably be deleted**
4. **Poor: should definitely be deleted**

Your ratings will play a vital part in the next revision. So please mail this prepaid form to us just as soon as you complete it.
Thanks for your help!

Annual Editions revisions depend on two major opinion sources: one is our Advisory Board, listed in the front of this volume, which works with us in scanning the thousands of articles published in the public press each year; the other is you—the person actually using the book. Please help us and the users of the next edition by completing the prepaid article rating form on this page and returning it to us. Thank you.

Rating	Article	Rating	Article
	1. The Manager's Job: Folklore and Fact		21. What Do Workers Want?
	2. Management's New Gurus		22. Incentive Plan Pushes Production
	3. How to Spot Unsuccessful Executives		23. Criteria of Organizational Effectiveness
	4. Managing in the Midst of Chaos		24. Principles for the New or Prospective Front-Line Supervisor
	5. Can You Manage in the New Economy?		25. The Trick to Managing Cash? Be Creative
	6. Business in the 21st Century		26. Competing with Crayolas®: Manufacturing as a Competitive Weapon at Binney & Smith
	7. How We Will Work in the Year 2000		
	8. A New Look at Managerial Decision Making		27. Keys to Starting a TQM Program
	9. Implement Entrepreneurial Thinking in Established Organizations		28. The Human Side of Enterprise
			29. Rethinking Diversity
	10. A Bible for Benchmarking, by Xerox		30. The Plight of the Seasoned Worker
	11. Planning Deming Management for Service Organizations		31. The Future of Labor-Management Relations
	12. How Corporate Culture Drives Strategy		32. Leasing Workers
	13. The Coming of the New Organization		33. Social Responsibility in Future Worlds
	14. Can GM Remodel Itself?		34. Multinationals: Back in Fashion
	15. High Skills under the Hood		35. Entrepreneurial Start-up and Growth: A Classification of Problems
	16. Golden Employees—In Their Golden Years		36. Human Rights: The Social Investing Issue of the 1990s
	17. A Decisive Response to Crisis Brought Ford Enhanced Productivity		37. How I Made—and Agonized Over—My Choices at NBC
	18. A Theory of Human Motivation		38. Organizing the Voluntary Association
	19. A 21st Century Communication Tool		39. White Collar Wasteland
	20. Developing Effective Leadership: An Interview with Henry Cisneros, Secretary, U.S. Department of Housing and Urban Development		40. Corporate Image, Recruitment Image, and Initial Job Choice Decisions

(Continued on next page)

ABOUT YOU

Name_____ Date_____

Are you a teacher? ☐ Or student? ☐

Your School Name _____

Department _____

Address _____

City _____ State _____ Zip _____

School Telephone # _____

YOUR COMMENTS ARE IMPORTANT TO US!

Please fill in the following information:

For which course did you use this book? _____

Did you use a text with this Annual Edition? ☐ yes ☐ no

The title of the text? _____

What are your general reactions to the Annual Editions concept?

Have you read any particular articles recently that you think should be included in the next edition?

Are there any articles you feel should be replaced in the next edition? Why?

Are there other areas that you feel would utilize an Annual Edition?

May we contact you for editorial input?

May we quote you from above?